COMPREHENDING TECHNICAL JAPANESE

COMPREHENDING
TECHNICAL JAPANESE

EDWARD E. DAUB

College of Engineering
University of Wisconsin, Madison, Wisconsin

R. BYRON BIRD

College of Engineering
University of Wisconsin, Madison, Wisconsin

NOBUO INOUE

Faculty of Engineering
Science University of Tokyo

THE UNIVERSITY OF WISCONSIN PRESS
UNIVERSITY OF TOKYO PRESS

Published 1975 by
The University of Wisconsin Press
Box 1379, Madison, Wisconsin 53701
The University of Wisconsin Press Ltd.
70 Great Russell Street, London
Second printing 1982
Printed in Japan
ISBN 0-299-06680-0, LC 74-5900

TABLE OF CONTENTS

PREFACE

Japan is one of the leading technological nations in the world. Although its scientific and engineering achievements have been most impressive, few scientists and engineers have developed the ability to read the literature of their Japanese counterparts. There are several reasons for this: (a) the extensive efforts of the Japanese to learn Western languages and their willingness to share their research results in those tongues; (b) the complexity of the Japanese language for foreigners; and (c) the absence of appropriate instructional materials for scientists and engineers. These points are discussed here briefly.

Although much of Japan's scholarly research has been published in English and other languages, there remains a vast literature of patents, handbooks, engineering journals, government reports, and transactions of technical meetings which is not normally translated. Furthermore there is substantial interest in graduate and postdoctoral study in Japan, joint US-Japan research projects, and multinational industrial ventures. All these activities serve to emphasize the need for providing more people with the opportunity to learn that part of the Japanese language which is vital to them, namely the technical part.

The Japanese used in modern technical writing is not nearly as difficult as that encountered in the literary or the spoken language. Written technical Japanese is considerably more direct in grammar and style than the literary language with its delightful nuances and tantalizing ambiguities. Large segments of Japanese grammar, such as humble and honorific verbs, irregular "counters", words for family relationships, the verbs for giving and receiving, the formulas for polite requests, and the whole hierarchy of greetings and apologies are entirely absent. Moreover, surprisingly, causatives, desideratives, alternatives, the -*masu* conjugation, and other verb forms do not occur frequently. The basic grammar needed to read scientific texts is remarkably limited and can be easily mastered. The big hurdle—and this cannot be minimized—is the development of a recognitional knowledge of the Chinese characters, the *kanji*.

Until the publication of this book there has been no reader designed specifically to meet the needs of the scientist or engineer. Concerned with the efficient use of his time, the technical man may wonder which of the approximately 2000 *kanji* he should learn first in order to gain access to Japanese technical literature. In the preparation of this book, therefore, we have stressed the mastery of the five-hundred most important *kanji*, and the scientific vocabulary which can be constructed from them.

The organization of lessons is such that the reader will learn these characters as a result of relentless repetition. To insure that we are introducing the most important *kanji*, we have made use of frequency counts which have been made

on physics, [1] chemistry, [2] and biology texts. [2] We believe that the mastery of the five-hundred *kanji* emphasized in this book will provide a very sound basis for technical reading.

Assuming that the student has had a one-year course in beginning Japanese (basic grammar, the two *kana* systems, and the use of a *kanji* dictionary), we have structured the lessons in the following way:

1. At the beginning of each lesson a tabulation of the 20 new REQUIRED *KANJI* with *ON* and *kun* reading which are of importance for scientists and engineers is presented. These required *kanji* should be learned thoroughly; the reader is expected to recognize them in all subsequent lessons.

Next to each *kanji* two numbers are given. The upper one refers to the *kanji* designation in F. Sakade, *A Guide to Reading and Writing Japanese*, Tuttle, Rutland, Vt. (1959). The lower one refers to the number of the character in A. N. Nelson, *The Modern Reader's Japanese-English Character Dictionary*, Tuttle, Rutland, Vt. (1962). The Sakade book gives the stroke order and the most important readings; the Nelson reference gives a complete listing of the readings as well as a number of compounds.

2. Next the READING SELECTION, using the twenty new *kanji*, is given. Many of these texts are taken from high school books, which are less difficult and less formal in style than research journals or reference works. The subject material is rather elementary and hopefully the topics selected will also be of general interest. A vocabulary list, *romaji* version of the text, a complete translation, and explanatory notes accompany the reading selection. For this part of the lesson no effort is spared to help the reader.

Note that the vocabulary introduced in the reading selection will not be repeated in later parts of the lesson or in subsequent lessons. *Furigana* will always be appended to *kanji* not previously included as required *kanji* so that the reader need not master these *kanji* and may concentrate on the required twenty in each lesson.

3. In each reading selection several constructions appear which recur frequently in technical reading. We single these out and give several examples further illustrating their use. These CONSTRUCTION EXAMPLES should be studied with great care, and any new vocabulary words introduced here should be learned thoroughly, for they will not be repeated subsequently.

4. Next several SUPPLEMENTARY READINGS are included. For these additional vocabulary is given but no other assistance. The new words introduced here need not be memorized. Many of these readings are taken from college

---

1. R.B. Bird, *Scientific Japanese*, Univ. of Wis., Engr. Expt. Sta. Report # 33, Part I (Jan.1967), and part II (Aug. 1967).
2. N. Inoue, unpublished compilation.

level textbooks, reference works, and technical journals. Their purpose is to provide additional experience in *kanji* recognition and comprehension.

5. The final essay is a TRANSLATION TEST. Here *furigana* are added to non-required *kanji*, but otherwise no help is given. The reader is on his own here—he may have to use a dictionary or grammar book to perform the translation. In this translation test each of the twenty required *kanji* for the lesson will appear at least once.

Thus each lesson progresses from elementary texts with considerable assistance, to more difficult readings with some vocabulary aids, and then on to a fairly realistic translation task with no help at all. The final essay should serve as a guide to the student in judging his mastery of the lesson and in deciding whether to move on to the next.

Although written primarily to assist the engineer and scientist in learning to read technical literature, the book may be useful to some technical people who are interested only in acquiring vocabulary for conversation purposes. Such people can take a "short course" by using just the romanized readings and the vocabulary lists. In addition several other groups of people might find this book helpful: technical librarians, who wish to translate titles and tables of contents; language majors, who want to train themselves to do technical translation; and students from non-English-speaking countries who plan to study technical subjects at Japanese universities.

Our primary purpose, however, is to provide the means for courageous scientists or engineers to learn to read technical Japanese by hard work. We trust this book will guide them through those first critical stages of learning to comprehend written technical texts and hope that the riches of Japanese scientific thought will be their reward.

E. E. D.

R. B. B.

N. I.

井の上に　　舞いおりし鳥　　雪の鳩

Madison, Wisconsin

ACKNOWLEDGMENTS

The authors wish to acknowledge financial support and encouragement provided by the Office of International Studies and Programs, the Engineering Experiment Station, and the Graduate School of the University of Wisconsin. In addition some financial aid was made possible to one of us (RBB) through the William F. Vilas Trust Estate. We are greatly indebted to Mr. and Mrs. Eiichi Hamanishi for preparation of the manuscript, to her for the calligraphy and typing, and to him for advice and proofreading.

EXPLANATORY NOTES

1. ROMANIZATION
The following system is used

a (ア)	i (イ)	u (ウ)	e (エ)	o (オ)
ka (カ)	ki (キ)	ku (ク)	ke (ケ)	ko (コ)
sa (サ)	shi (シ)	su (ス)	se (セ)	so (ソ)
ta (タ)	chi (チ)	tsu (ツ)	te (テ)	to (ト)
na (ナ)	ni (ニ)	nu (ヌ)	ne (ネ)	no (ノ)
ha (ハ)	hi (ヒ)	fu (フ)	he (ヘ)	ho (ホ)
ma (マ)	mi (ミ)	mu (ム)	me (メ)	mo (モ)
ya (ヤ)		yu (ユ)		yo (ヨ)
ra (ラ)	ri (リ)	ru (ル)	re (レ)	ro (ロ)
wa (ワ)				o (ヲ)
ga (ガ)	gi (ギ)	gu (グ)	ge (ゲ)	go (ゴ)
za (ザ)	ji (ジ)	zu (ズ)	ze (ゼ)	zo (ゾ)
da (ダ)	ji (ヂ)	zu (ヅ)	de (デ)	do (ド)
ba (バ)	bi (ビ)	bu (ブ)	be (ベ)	bo (ボ)
pa (パ)	pi (ピ)	pu (プ)	pe (ペ)	po (ポ)
kya (キャ)		kyu (キュ)		kyo (キョ)
sha (シャ)		shu (シュ)		sho (ショ)
cha (チャ)		chu (チュ)		cho (チョ)
nya (ニャ)		nyu (ニュ)		nyo (ニョ)
hya (ヒャ)		hyu (ヒュ)		hyo (ヒョ)
mya (ミャ)		myu (ミュ)		myo (ミョ)
rya (リャ)		ryu (リュ)		ryo (リョ)
gya (ギャ)		gyu (ギュ)		gyo (ギョ)
ja (ジャ)		ju (ジュ)		jo (ジョ)
bya (ビャ)		byu (ビュ)		byo (ビョ)
pya (ピャ)		pyu (ピュ)		pyo (ピョ)
-n (ン)				

Long vowels are written with a macron (ā,ō,ū) except for *ii*. The terminal ん is always transcribed as *-n* although it is pronounced as *-m* before *b*, *m*, and *p*; if it is followed by a vowel sound, then an apostrophe is used, as in *sen'i* (せん い). Doubled consonants are written as *tt*, *pp*, *kk* etc., except for the doubled *sh* and *ch* sounds, which are written *ssh* and *tch*. The particles は, へ, and を are written as *wa*, *e*, and *o*, (and never as *ha*, *he*, and *wo*) to correspond to their pronunciation. The Romanization used here is that found in the leading Japanese-English dictionaries.

We make liberal use of hyphens in transcribing words which are compounds of three or more characters in order to facilitate reading. For example:

shūki-teki	周期的	periodic
en-undō	円運動	circular motion
enshin-ryoku	遠心力	centrifugal force

We also use a hyphen to separate the two parts of a double verb:

kuri-kaesu	くり返す	to repeat
tori-atsukau	取りあつかう	to deal with

Note that verbs are given in their plain present form, but the English "equivalent" is always given as the infinitive.

2. OKURIGANA

We have followed the *Monbushō* (Japan Ministry of Education) rules for *tōyō kanji* and *okurigana* throughout. In the *kanji* lists at the beginning of each lesson the official *okurigana* are given in parentheses.

3. SOURCES FOR READINGS

The majority of the Reading Selections and Supplementary Readings were taken from Japanese technical books and have been adapted for instructional purposes in one or more of the following ways: 1) the *okurigana* have been changed to conform with modern standard usage; 2) older forms of *kanji* have been replaced with modern standard ones; 3) *furigana* have been appended to those *kanji* which do not appear in the *kanji* lists at the beginning of the lessons; 4) particularly difficult passages have been rewritten and passages not germane to the immediate topic have been eliminated.

The selections were taken from the following books:

B   *Kōtō-gakkō Butsuri B*, Seishi Kaya (ed.) Kōgakusha, Tōkyō, 1963.

BK   *Butsuri-kagaku*, Haruhiko Noda, Asakura Shoten, Tōkyō, 1971.

BKJ *Butsuri-kagaku Jikken-hō*, Akira Kotera (ed.), Asakura Shoten, Tōkyō, 1955.

BN   *Butsuri-gaku Nyūmon*, Nobuo Hori (ed.), Maki Shoten, Tōkyō, 1959.

FK   *Fu-kanzen Kitai*, Tarō Kihara, Asakura Shoten, Tōkyō, 1950.

I   *Idō-sokudo-ron*, Daizō Kunii et al., Iwanami Shoten, Tōkyō, 1968.

IG   *Iden-gaku*, Yoshito Shinotō and Kaichirō Yanagisawa, Iwanami Shoten, Tōkyō, 1971.

1K   *Kagaku B*, lst edition, Yūji Shibata, Sakae Tsuda, Osamu Shimamura, Dai-Nihon Tosho, Tōkyō, 1961.

K   *Kagaku B*, new revised edition, Yūji Shibata, Sakae Tsuda, and Osamu Shimamura Dai-Nihon Tosho, Tōkyō, 1966.

KB   *Kō-bunshi no Butsuri*, 3rd edition, The Japan Physical Society (Ed.) Asakura Shoten, Tōkyō, 1966.

KJE *Kōjien*, Izuru Shimamura (ed.), Iwanami Shoten, Tōkyō, 1955.

KK   *Kagaku Kikai no Riron Keisan*, Saburō Kamei (ed.), Sangyō Tosho, Tōkyō 1959.

KKT *Kagaku Kōgaku Tsūron*, 3rd edition, Kōichi Iinoya, Asakura Shoten, Tōkyō, 1959.

KS   *Kagaku Sen'i*, revised edition, Minoru Iinoto, Iwanami Shoten, Tōkyō, 1972.

N   *Netsu-rikigaku*, Masahiro Yorizane, Kagaku Gijutsu-sha, Tōkyō, 1957.

2RJ *Rika-gaku Jiten*, revised 2nd edition, Iwanami Shoten, Tōkyō, 1958.

3RJ *Rika-gaku Jiten*, 3rd edition, Iwanami Shoten, Tōkyō, 1971.

S   *Seibutsu*, Tomo-o Miwa and Midemichi Oka, Sanseidō, Tōkyō, 1972.

SJ   *Seibutsu-gaku Jiten*, Iwanami Shoten, Tōkyō, 1960.

SK   *Sei-kagaku*, Fujio Egami, Iwanami Shoten, Tōkyō, 1971.

SN   *Soryūshi no Nazo*, Hideki Yukawa, Asahi Press, Tōkyō, 1972.

SS   *Seimei o Saguru*, Fujio Egami, Iwanami Shoten, Tōkyō, 1967.

The symbols at the left are used in refering to these sources.

4. KANJI LISTS

A list of twenty required *kanji* appears at the beginning of each lesson. The following are explanations and examples of the notation:

1) Identifying numbers, ON and kun readings.

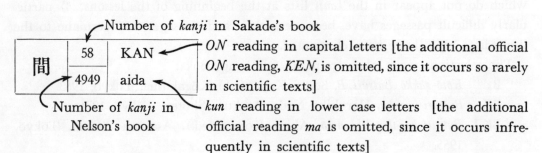

Number of *kanji* in Sakade's book

58 KAN — *ON* reading in capital letters [the additional official *ON* reading, *KEN*, is omitted, since it occurs so rarely in scientific texts]

4949 aida — *kun* reading in lower case letters [the additional official reading *ma* is omitted, since it occurs infrequently in scientific texts]

Number of *kanji* in Nelson's book

2) Verbs and okurigana.

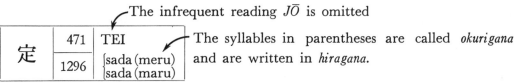

The infrequent reading *JŌ* is omitted

定	471	TEI
	1296	{sada(meru) {sada(maru)

The syllables in parentheses are called *okurigana* and are written in *hiragana*.

The brace indicates a pair of related verbs, the upper always being the *transitive* verb, the lower always being the *intransitive* verb. If there are two verbs not joined by a brace, they are not a transitive-intransitive pair.

3) Unofficial readings.

例	737	REI
	428	[tato(eba)]

Reading enclosed in brackets is not currently an official reading. Since this reading is, however, often encountered in technical Japanese, it is included.

4) Omission of *dakuon* readings.

比	697	HI
	2470	kura(beru)

The pronunciation *PI* as in (反比例 *hanpirei*) is not included, since this is a standard phonetic change replacing ひ by ぴ. Similar phonetic changes, called *dakuon*, such as *ka* (か) to *ga* (が), *su* (す) to *zu* (ず), are also not explicitly included.

5) Omission of verbs derived from ON readings.

熱	490	NETSU
	2797	atsu(i)

No separate entry is given for the verb *nes(suru)*. Similarly in the entry for 応, no separate entry for *ō(zuru)* or *ō(jiru)* will be found.

5. VOCABULARY ENTRIES

In the vocabulary lists which accompany the various readings, generally only the translation of the word which is appropriate in the text at hand has been listed. For example in Supplementary Reading C in Lesson 1, for the entry

大きさ　　　　ōkisa　　　　　magnitude

we have not listed the meanings "largeness, bulk" since they are not appropriate there. Similarly, for the entry

与える　　　　ataeru　　　　to give

we do not include the meanings "present, award, bestow, provide."

ERRATA

Page	Line	Now reads	Should read
8	10	Shimamura	Shinmura
	15	Iinoto	Imoto
	20	Midemichi	Hidemichi
13	25	with the roman	with the italic
34	32	示いす。	示す。
39	12	$(x\text{-}, y\text{-}, z\text{-}$	は $x\text{-}, y\text{-}, z\text{-}$
49	4	taikyō-kei-nai	taiyō-kei-nai
64	22	sōtai suru	aitai suru
85	9	irareu.	irareru.
86	5	kanshite,	hanshite,
91	30	當	当
121	8	The rate of change	The change
143	5	加える	かえる
171	9	反射反線	反射光線
182	15	achromatic lens	achromatic prism
188	21	$(ニュートン)/(クーロン)^2$	$(ニュートン)(メートル)^2/(クーロン)^2$
198	25	解折 (かい)	解析 (かい)
202	9	閉じる tojiru	閉じている tojite iru
224	32	慣用 kan'yō ordinary usage, common use	慣用の kan'yō no usual
229	14	分折	分析
230	14	hundred per cent	percentage
231	23	further, more still	furthermore, still
247	20	see Lesson 11	see Lesson 9
258	2	溶ける tokeru	溶けている tokete iru
288	16–17	主体 shutai primary substance, constituent	…の主体をなす …no shutai o nasu is fundamental in…
298	24	適用しょ (てき)	適用しよ (てき)
309	8	thermoplastic	thermoplasticity
	19	viscoelastic	viscoelasticity
310	25	singly	individual
312	33	乾燥 (そう)	乾燥 (そう)
314	2	ブタジェン	ブタジエン
322	4	dō-bussei	dōbutsu-sei
	4	Shoku-bussei	Shokubutsu-sei
331	25	さまざな	さまざまな
334	20	kō-busshitsu	kōbutsu-shitsu
339	35	kō-busshitsu	kōbutsu-shitsu
348	13, 36	チクトクロム chikutokuromu	チトクロム chitokuromu
402	20	*yadonushti*	*yadonushi*
406	4	グリせリン	グリセリン
407	10	U. Subata	Y. Shibata
	11	O. Shimaura	O. Shimamura

LESSON 1
第 一 課
KANJI

等	484	TŌ		定	474	TEI
	3396	hito(shii) 〔nado, -ra〕			1296	{sada(meru) {sada(maru)
速	453	SOKU		同	295	DŌ
	4700	haya(i)			619	ona(ji)
度	288	DO		距	253a	KYO
	1511				4548	
運	157	UN		離	276a	RI
	4725	hako(bu)			5040	{hana(su) {hana(reru)
動	296	DŌ		時	87	JI
	730	{ugo(kasu) {ugo(ku)			2126	toki
向	213	KŌ		間	58	KAN
	101	mu(ku) mu(kau)			4949	aida
表	309	HYŌ		比	697	HI
	108	omote ara(wasu)			2470	kura(beru)
物	313	BUTSU MOTSU		例	737	REI
	2857	mono			428	〔tato(eba)〕
体	270	TAI		直	472	CHOKU
	405	〔karada〕			775	{nao(su) {nao(ru)
一	1	ICHI ITSU		線	447	SEN
	1	hito(tsu)			3580	

READING SELECTION

速度	sokudo	velocity
等速度	tōsokudo	constant velocity
運動	undō	motion
速さ	hayasa	speed
向き	muki	direction
表わす	arawasu	to show, express, represent
物体	buttai	body
一定の	ittei no	constant
動く	ugoku	to move
(pres. tense)＋ときには	(pres. tense)＋toki ni wa	when…, whenever…

いつも	itsumo	always
同じ	onaji	same
距離	kyori	distance
要した	yō shita	required
時間	jikan	time
…に比例する	…ni hirei suru	to be proportional to…
…をvとすれば	…o v to sureba	if we let v be…
あるいは	aruiwa	or
直線	chokusen	straight line

等速度運動　(B 14)

速度というのは[1]速さ[2]と向き[3]で表わされるものである。物体が一定の速度で動くとき[4]には，運動の向きと速さとはいつも同じであるから，動いた距離 s は，それに[5]要した時間 t に比例する。このとき[4]の速さ[6]を v とすれば

$$s = vt \,^{(7)} \text{あるいは}^{(8)} \ v = \frac{s}{t} \,^{(9)}$$

で表わされる。このように[10]，速度が一定の[11]運動を等速度運動，または等速直線運動という[12]。

TŌSOKUDO UNDŌ

Sokudo to iu no wa[1] hayasa[2] to muki[3] de arawasareru mono de aru. Buttai ga ittei no sokudo de ugoku toki[4] ni wa, undō no muki to hayasa to wa itsumo onaji de aru kara, ugoita kyori s wa sore ni[5] yō shita jikan t ni hirei suru. Kono toki[4] no hayasa[6] o v to sureba

$$s = vt \,^{(7)} \text{ aruiwa}^{(8)} \ v = s/t \,^{(9)}$$

de arawasareru. Kono yō ni,[10] sokudo ga ittei no[11] undō o tōsokudo-undō, mata wa tōsoku-chokusen-undō to iu. [12]

UNIFORM MOTION

Velocity is a quantity which is described by (giving) the speed and direction. When a body moves with constant velocity, the speed and the direction of the motion are always the same, and so the distance s which it has travelled is proportional to the time required t. If we let v be the speed for this case, then

$$s = vt \text{ or } v = s/t.$$

Motion at constant velocity is called uniform (velocity) motion or uniform linear motion.

Explanatory Notes

(1) sokudo to iu no wa　　Literally "the thing called velocity"; translate simply

by "velocity"; although いう is conventionally romanized as *iu*, it is pronounced *yū*.

(2) sokudo vs. hayasa
Sokudo and *hayasa* correspond to the English "velocity" and "speed", the first being the vector quantity and the second being the scalar. In both languages this distinction is not always clearly made. The word *hōkō* (方向) could also be used.

(3) muki (向き)

(4) toki ni wa
"Toki" here is written in *kana* (とき) but may also be written in kanji (時). The present tendency in Japan is to use *kana* rather than *kanji* for prepositions, conjunctions, and adverbial phrases, but the reader should expect to encounter both usages (occasionally in the same paragraph!).
Other examples are:

次に	つぎに	next
従って	したがって	therefore
例えば	たとえば	for example
…の場合	…のばあい	in the case of...
…等	…など	...etc.

(5) Sore ni
Literally "for that" (i.e., for the body to move the distance *s*); in a free translation this can be omitted in English.

(6) kono toki no hayasa
This *toki* refers to the *toki niwa* of the previous sentence.

(7) $s = vt$
Read in Japanese "*s* ikōru *vt*" with the roman letters being pronounced as in English. (See Appendix E, Readings of Mathematical Expressions).

(8) aruiwa
Note that the "wa" is written は and not わ.

(9) $v = s/t$
Read in Japanese: "*v* ikōru *s* ōbā *t*".

(10) kono yō ni
Literally "in this way" (i.e., in the manner above described); in free translation this could be omitted.

(11) sokudo...no
This is a modifying clause telling "what kind of *undō*." It indicates that it is an *undō* for which *sokudo ga ittei de aru*. Here *no* is the copula, taking the place of *de aru*.

(12) A o B to iu
"We designate A by B." More often the phrase will be rendered in English by the passive voice "A is called B."

CONSTRUCTION EXAMPLES

A というのは…である	"A is…"

1. 等速直線運動というのは速度が一定の運動のことである。
2. 時間表というのはタイム・テーブルのことである。
3. 動物というのはじぶんの体を動かすことができるいき物のことである。

時間表	jikan-hyō	time-table
動物	dōbutsu	animal
じぶんの体	jibun no karada	its own body
動かす	ugokasu	to move (an object)
いき物	ikimono	living thing

…ときには	"whenever; when"

1. 物体が直線運動をするときには，運動の向きはいつも同じである。
2. 物体の速さ v が時間 t に比例するときには，動いた距離 s は t^2 に比例する。

…を a とすれば	"if we let… be a"

1. 動物の動いた距離を s とすれば…
2. A, B 間（A と B との間）の距離を s_{AB} とすれば…

A, B 間	A, B kan	between A and B

(verb) とすれば	"if we suppose that"

1. おのおの等速度運動をしている物体 A と物体 B が離れていくとすれば，それぞれの速度は同じではない。
2. 物体が時間 t の間に一定の速度 v で動くとすれば，動いた距離は $s=vt$ である。
3. 物体が一定でない速度で動くとすれば，距離 s は時間 t に比例しない。

おのおの	ono-ono	each
離れていく	hanarete iku	to move apart
それぞれ	sore-zore	their respective

A を B という	"A we call B; A is called B"

1. 速度がいつも一定である運動を等速直線運動という。
2. 向きがいつも同じである運動を直線運動という。

SUPPLEMENTARY READINGS

A.

もちろん	mochiron	of course
ほとんどみられない	hotondo mirarenai	is seldom seen
例えば	tatoeba	for example
おちる	ochiru	to fall
一定していない…	ittei shite inai...	...which is not constant
物体がおちるとき	buttai ga ochiru toki	Literally: (the motion)
の…	no...	when a body falls

　もちろん等速度運動はほとんどみられない。例えば物体がおちるときの運動は直線運動であるが，等速度運動ではない。このように物体が一定していない速さで動くときには動いた距離 s とそれに要した時間 t とは比例しない。

B.

一つ	hitotsu	one
例	rei	an example
…をとってみよう	...o totte miyō	let us consider...
同時に	dōji ni	simultaneously
おのおの	ono-ono	each, individually
…をするとし（て）	...o suru to shi(te)	to suppose that..., (and)
それぞれの	sorezore no	respective
比べる	kuraberu	to compare
それら	sorera	they
比	hi	ratio
…としたら	...to shitara	if we suppose...
そして	soshite	and, then, now
等しい	hitoshii	equal

　一つの例をとってみよう。物体 A と物体 B が同時におのおの等速度運動をするとし，同時間 t で物体 A と物体 B が動いたそれぞれの距離を s_A と s_B とする。s_A と s_B を比べると，いつもそれらの比は物体のそれぞれの速さ v_A と v_B の比に等しい。物体 A と物体 B が同じ距離 s を動いたとしたら，それに要したそれぞれの時間 t_A と t_B の比はなんの比に等しくなるか。

C.

ベクトル	bekutoru	a vector
スカラー	sukarā	a scalar
大きさ	ōkisa	magnitude
方向	hōkō	direction
あたえる	ataeru	to give

単位	tan'i	a unit
毎時	maiji	per hour, every hour
キロメートル	kiromētoru	kilometers
自動車	jidōsha	automobile
…と同じく	...to onajiku	like, similar to...

速度と速さとは同じではない。速度というのはベクトルであるが，速さというのはスカラーである。速度を表わすには，その大きさと方向をあたえなければならない。速度の大きさは速さといい，単位時間に物体が運動した距離で表わす。例えば自動車の速さはキロメートル毎時(km/hr) で表わす。時間も距離も速さと同じくスカラーである。

FINAL TRANSLATION TEST

いま，一つの物体Aが，一定の速度v_AでCから直線運動をはじめたとする。h時間してから物体Bが，一定の速度v_BでCから同じ向きに運動をはじめたとすれば，$v_B > v_A$の時には，BはAに追い付くことができる。追い付くのに要する時間tは

$$t = v_A h / (v_B - v_A)$$

であたえられ，このときの物体A, BのCからの距離sは

$$s = v_A v_B h / (v_B - v_A)$$

で表わされる。このことは，直線運動でなくても，速ささえ一定であれば成り立つ。例えば，ミルウォーキーからシカゴへ向かって1時間まえにでた時速40キロメートルの自動車に，時速80キロメートルで追い付くには，なん時間を要するか，同じように定めることができる。

もちろん，v_Bがv_Aに等しいか，v_Bがv_Aより小さい時には，BはAに追い付くことができない。tはhに比例しているので，例えば，2時間たってからBがでかければ，追い付くのに2ばいの時間を要することになる。

LESSON 2

第 二 課

KANJI

得	850	TOKU
	1622	e(ru)
加	356	KA
	716	{kuwa(eru) {kuwa(waru)
力	148	RIKI RYOKU
	715	chikara
大	22	TAI DAI
	1171	ō(kii)
質	628	SHITSU
	4518	
量	734	RYŌ
	2141	
小	24	SHŌ
	1355	ko chii(sai)
実	233	JITSU
	1297	mi
験	600	KEN
	5220	
観	367	KAN
	4296	

測	668	SOKU
	2632	haka(ru)
結	390	KETSU
	3540	musu(bu)
果	560	KA
	107	
次	227	JI
	638	tsu(gu) [tsugi]
関	365	KAN
	4958	
係	385	KEI
	449	
反	492	HAN
	817	
数	262	SŪ
	2507	kazu kazo(eru)
単	671	TAN
	139	
位	344	I
	401	kurai

READING SELECTION

加速度	kasokudo	acceleration
力	chikara	force
関係	kankei	relation
得る	eru	to get, receive, acquire
大きい	ōkii	large
はたらく	hataraku	to work, to act
…ならば	…naraba	if it is…
質量	shitsuryō	mass
小さい	chiisai	small
実験	jikken	experiment

観測	kansoku	observation
…をもとにして	…o moto ni shite	based on…
結果	kekka	result
AとBとの間に	A to B to no aida ni	between A and B
次の	tsugi no	the following
わかる	wakaru	to understand, find out
大きさ	ōkisa	magnitude
…に反比例する	…ni hanpirei suru	to be inversely proportional to
定数	teisū	constant
単位	tan'i	unit
どのように	dono yō ni	in what way
選ぶ	erabu	to choose
…によって	…ni yotte	according to
定まる	sadamaru	to be decided, determined

加速度と力との関係　(B 23)

　物体の得る加速度は，力が大きいほど大きく，また，はたらく力が同じならば[1]，物体の質量が大きいほど加速度は小さい。実験や観測の結果をもとにして，力と質量と加速度との間には次の関係があることがわかった[2]。

　物体に力がはたらくと，物体はその力の向きに加速度を得る。この加速度の大きさaは，はたらいた力 F に比例し[3]，物体の質量 m に反比例する。

$$a = k\frac{F}{m}$$

ここに k は比例定数であって，m, a, F の単位をどのように選ぶか[4]によって定まる。

KASOKUDO TO CHIKARA TO NO KANKEI

Buttai no eru kasokudo wa, chikara ga ōkii hodo ōkiku, mata, hataraku chikara ga onaji naraba,[1] buttai no shitsuryō ga, ōkii hodo kasokudo wa chiisai. Jikken ya kansoku no kekka o moto ni shite, chikara to shitsuryō to kasokudo to no aida ni wa, tsugi no kankei ga aru koto ga wakatta.[2]

Buttai ni chikara ga hataraku to, buttai wa sono chikara no muki ni kasokudo o eru. Kono kasokudo no ōkisa a wa, hataraita chikara F ni hirei shi,[3] buttai no shitsuryō m ni hanpirei suru.

$$a = k(F/m)$$

Koko ni k wa hirei-teisū de atte, m, a, F no tan'i o dono yō ni erabu ka[4] ni yotte sadamaru.

THE RELATION BETWEEN ACCELERATION AND FORCE

The acceleration which a body acquires is greater as the force is greater; furthermore, if the applied force is the same, the acceleration is smaller as the mass of the body is greater. On the basis of the results of experiments and observations, we know that the following relation exists between force, mass, and acceleration.

If a force acts on a body, the body accelerates in the direction of that force. The magnitude of this acceleration a is proportional to the applied force F and is inversely proportional to the mass m of the body.

$$a = k(F/m)$$

Here k is a proportionality constant and is determined by how we choose the units of m, a, and F.

Explanatory Notes

(1) naraba   Same as *nara* (if it is).

(2) ...koto ga wakatta   This may also be rendered: "it turned out that" or "we have learned that".

(3) hirei shi   One could also write *hirei shite*.

(4) m,...ka   This entire phrase is the object of *ni yotte*.

CONSTRUCTION EXAMPLES

大きいほど…小さい	"the larger......the smaller"

1. 物体に一定の力がはたらくときには，質量が大きいほど加速度は小さい。

2. 等速直線運動では，動いた距離 s が大きいほど，それに要した時間は大きい。

3. 物体にはたらく力が一定ならば，物体の得る加速度は質量が小さいほど大きい。

4. 物体の加速度はそれにはたらく力が大きいほど大きい。

…をもとにして	"based on..."

1. 測定の結果をもとにして，物体の得る加速度は，はたらいた力に比例し，物体の質量に反比例することがわかる。

2. 観測の結果をもとにして，力と加速度との間の関係における比例定数を定めることができる。

3. 加速度と力との観測をもとにして，関数における定数を定める。

4. 実験の結果をもとにして，法則を定める。

測定	sokutei	measurement
…における	…ni okeru	in...

関数	kansū	function
法則	hōsoku	law

···なら（ば）	"if it is"

1. 物体にはたらく力が大きくないなら（ば），加速度も大きくない。

2. 実験の結果がよくないならば，もう一度自動車の加速度を測らなければならない。

3. 加速度が一定ならば，その運動を等加速度運動という。

4. 実験の結果に一定の関係があるならば，その関係を法則という。

Interrogative Clause＋によって	"according to"

1. 力がどのようにはたらくかによって，物体の得る加速度が定まる。

2. 測定をどのようにするかによって，実験の結果が定まる。

3. この実験の結果がいいかわるいかによって，もう一度同じ実験をしなければならないかもしれない。

4. 物体の速度がどのように変わるかによって，物体にはたらいた力の大きさと向きを定める。

もう一度	mō ichido	once more
測る	hakaru	to measure
変わる	kawaru	to vary, change

···ことがわかった	"we know that......"

1. 物体がおちるときにおこる加速度運動は等加速度運動であることが実験の測定からわかった。

2. おちる物体の加速度は質量に関係しないことが実験でわかった。

おこる	okoru	to occur

SUPPLEMENTARY READINGS

A. すなわち	sunawachi	that is, namely
長さ	nagasa	length
用いる	mochi-iru	to use
ダイン	dain	dyne
得させる	esaseru	to give, impart
···として定められている	...to shite sadamerarete iru	is defined as...
ニュートン	nyūton	newton
···とよぶ	...to yobu	is called

…場合	…baai	in cases where…
m/sec²	mētoru-pā-sekondo-jijō	

CGS単位，すなわち長さに cm（センチ），質量に g（グラム），時間に sec（セコンド）を用いる場合，力の単位をダインとよぶ。1ダインは1gの物体にはたらいて，1cm/sec²の加速度を得させる力として定められている。MKS単位，すなわち長さに m（メートル），質量に kg（キログラム），時間に sec を用いる場合，力の単位をニュートンとよぶ。1ニュートンは 1kg の物体にはたらいて，1m/sec² の加速度を得させる力として定められている。このような単位を用いると，比例定数 k は1となって次の関係が得られる。

$$a = F/m$$

B.	一般に（は）	ippan ni (wa)	generally
	もし…としても	moshi…to shite mo	even if…
	その結果として	sono kekka to shite	as a result
	前	mae	before
	あと	ato	after
	したがって	shitagatte	consequently
	…さえ…ば	…sae…ba	if only

一般には物体にはたらく力の向きは，物体が動いていた向きと同じではない。その結果として物体の向きが変わる。したがって，もし物体の速さが一定であるとしても，速度の向きさえ変われば，力がはたらいていたことがわかる。その力のはたらいた向きは，力がはたらく前の物体の速度とはたらいたあとの速度によって定まる。

C.	…の中に	…no naka ni	among…
	瞬間力	shunkan-ryoku	instantaneous force
	測定する	sokutei suru	to measure
	測定できないほど…	sokutei dekinai hodo…	so…as to be immeasurable
	しかし	shikashi	but, yet, however
	…においては	…ni oite wa	as for…, in…
	…にたいして	…ni taishite	in relation to…
	…ないかぎり	…nai kagiri	so long as…is not
	…だけが	…dake ga	only…
	変化	henka	change
	…しやすい	…shiyasui	…is easily (done)
	定められる	sadamerareru	can be determined, to be able to determine
	もとめる	motomeru	to seek
	きゅうに	kyū ni	suddenly
	角度	kakudo	angle

いくらの…	ikura no...	how much
示す	shimesu	to show, point out
はじめの…	hajime no...	original..., initial...

物体にはたらく力の中には瞬間力というのがある。この力は，はたらく時間が測定できないほど小さいので大きさを定めることはできない。しかし，瞬間力だけがはたらく実験においては，その力がはたらかないかぎり，物体が等速度運動をするから，運動の変化は観測しやすい。また速度の変化を測定することによって，はたらいた瞬間力の向きが定められる。

例えば次のような実験から，力の向きをもとめるとする。物体が等速度運動をしていたが，きゅうに速度の向きが変わった。それで瞬間力のはたらいたことがわかった。速度を測定した結果は，速さが一定であって向きが60°の角度だけ変化した。瞬間力のはたらいた向きは，はじめの速度にたいして，いくらの角度を示すか。

D.	かんがえる	kangaeru	to consider
	関数	kansū	function
	…に関する	...ni kansuru	with respect to... pertaining to...
	積分	sekibun	integral
	1次の	ichiji no...	...of the first degree, order
	導関数	dōkansū	derivative

速さが一定でない直線運動をかんがえてみよう。この場合，速さ v は時間 t の関数であり，物体が t_1 から t_2 までの間に動いた距離 s は次のようにあたえられる。

$$s = \int_{t_1}^{t_2} v(t)\, dt$$

すなわち，距離 s は速さ v の時間 t に関する積分である。また，距離と速さとの関係は次のように表わされる。

$$v = \frac{ds}{dt}$$

すなわち，速さは距離の時間に関する1次の導関数である。

FINAL TRANSLATION TEST

物体が等速度で運動しているとき，動いた距離と時間は観測するが，その運動がどうしておこったかということはかんがえない。しかし物体が加速度を得て運動しているとき，どんな結果としてその運動になったかということをかんがえる。すなわち物体にどんな力

がはたらいたかということをかんがえる。

　たとえば，次のような実験をかんがえてみよう。いま，糸のさきに質量1kgの物体をむすびつけて，一定の速さでふりまわしたとする。糸がきれないことをたしかめてから，糸をほどいて，こんどは質量5kgの物体をむすびつけて，前と同じ速さでふりまわすと，糸がきれた。糸がきれたのは，前より大きな力がはたらいたからである。同じ速さでふりまわしたのであるから，物体の得た加速度は同じであるが，質量に大小があるため，糸にはたらく力はちがうわけである。この時の加速度が$1m/s^2$であったとすれば，物体にはたらいた力は，MKS単位をもちいて，それぞれ1N，5Nとなる。一定の速さでまわっている物体の加速度aは，糸のながさrと速度vの関数であって，それらの間には

$$a=v^2/r$$

という関係があり，aはrに反比例している。

LESSON 3
第 三 課

KANJI

積	445	SEKI
	3306	tsu(mu) tsu(moru)
上	20	JŌ ue
	798	a(geru) a(garu)
変	509	HEN
	306	ka(eru) ka(waru)
式	417	SHIKI
	1556	
化	163	KA
	350	
二	2	NI
	273	futa(tsu)
衝	268b	SHŌ
	1638	
突	219b	TOTSU
	3316	tsu(ku)
保	716	HO
	455	tamo(tsu)
存	836	ZON, SON
	1267	

法	513	HŌ
	2535	
則	666	SOKU
	4487	
後	208	GO KŌ
	1610	ushi(ro) nochi
短	466	TAN
	3172	mijika(i)
及	193b	oyo(bi) oyo(bosu) oyo(bu)
	154	
作	82	SA SAKU
	407	tsuku(ru)
用	146	YŌ
	2993	mochi(iru)
対	461	TAI TSUI
	2067	
前	102	ZEN
	595	mae
和	338	WA
	3268	

READING SELECTION

力積	rikiseki	impulse
一直線上	itchokusen-jō	on a straight line
うける	ukeru	to receive, get
…に変わる	…ni kawaru	to change to…
式	shiki	equation
次のように	tsugi no yō ni	as follows; in the following way
かき表わす	kaki-arawasu	to write, express
…あたり	…atari	per…

示す	shimesu	to show, indicate
これより	kore yori	from this
導く	michibiku	to derive
積	seki	product (math.)
変化	henka	change
二つ	futatsu	two
衝突	shōtotsu	collision
…に追いつく	…ni oitsuku	overtake…
衝突後に	shōtotsu-go ni	after the collision
…になる	…ni naru	to become…
運動量	undō-ryō	momentum
ただし…	tadashi…	here…
触れあう	fure-au	to come in contact with; touch each other
（ごく）短い	(goku)mijikai	(extremely) short
及ぼす	oyobosu	to exert, cause
複雑な	fukuzatsu na	complicated
作用	sayō	action, effect
反作用	han-sayō	reaction
…の関係にある	…no kankei ni aru	to be related as…
瞬間	shunkan	instant, moment
反対	hantai	opposite
したがって	shitagatte	therefore, consequently
すなわち	sunawachi	that is (to say); i. e.
…の前後	…no zengo	before and after…
…において	…ni oite	at, as for, concerning, in
和	wa	sum
保存	hozon	conservation
法則	hōsoku	law

力　積　(B 26)

一直線上[1]を速度 v_0 で運動している質量 m の物体が F の力をうけて時間 t の間に速度が v に変わったとすれば[2]，$F=ma$ という式[3]は次のようにかき表わされる。

$$\frac{m(v-v_0)}{t}=F$$

これは単位時間あたりの運動量の変化が力に等しいことを示している。これより

$$mv-mv_0=Ft$$

の関係が導かれる。力 F とそれが[4]はたらいた時間 t の積[5]Ft を「力積」という。この式

は「運動量の変化は力積に等しい」という関係を表わしている。

二つの物体の衝突　(B 26–27)

　速度 u で運動している物体Aが，同じ直線上を v の速度で運動している物体Bに追いつき，衝突したとする。

　A, Bの質量をそれぞれ m_1, m_2 とし[6]，衝突後に速度が u', v' になったとすれば[6]，Aの運動量の変化は力積に等しいので

$$m_1u' - m_1u = F_1t \qquad\qquad (1)\,[7]$$

で表わされる。ただし[8]，t は A, B が触れあっているごく短い時間，F_1は衝突のときにBがAに及ぼす力である。

　衝突のときには複雑な力が作用するが，BがAに及ぼす力 F_1 と，AがBに及ぼす力 F_2 とは，作用・反作用の関係にあるので，どの瞬間でも大きさが等しく向きが反対である。したがって，Bの運動量の変化は力積に等しいので

$$m_2v' - m_2v = F_2t = -F_1t \qquad\qquad (2)$$

(1), (2)式から

$$m_1u + m_2v = m_1u' + m_2v' \qquad\qquad (3)$$

すなわち，衝突の前後において2物体の運動量の和[5]は変わらない。これを運動量保存の法則という。

RIKISEKI

Itchokusen-jō[1] o sokudo v_0 de undō shite iru shitsuryō m no buttai ga, F no chikara o ukete, jikan t no aida ni sokudo ga v ni kawatta to sureba,[2] $F = ma$ to iu shiki[3] wa tsugi no yō ni kaki-arawasareru.

$$\frac{m(v - v_0)}{t} = F$$

Kore wa tan'i-jikan atari no undō-ryō no henka ga chikara ni hitoshii koto o shimeshite iru. Kore yori

$$mv - mv_0 = Ft$$

no kankei ga michibikareru. Chikara F to sore ga[4] hataraita jikan t no seki[5] Ft o *rikiseki* to iu. Kono shiki wa *undōryō no henka wa rikiseki ni hitoshii* to iu kankei o arawashite iru.

FUTATSU NO BUTTAI NO SHŌTOTSU

Sokudo u de undō shite iru buttai A ga, onaji chokusen-jō o v no sokudo de undō shite iru buttai B ni oitsuki, shōtotsu shita to suru.

A, B no shitsuryō o sorezore m_1, m_2 to shi,[6] shōtotsu-go ni sokudo ga u', v' ni

natta to sureba, [6] A no undō-ryō no henka wa rikiseki ni hitoshii no de

$$m_1u' - m_1u = F_1t \tag{1}$$

de arawasareru. Tadashi, [8] t wa A, B ga fure-atte iru goku mijikai jikan, F_1 wa shōtotsu no toki ni B ga A ni oyobosu chikara de aru.

Shōtotsu no toki ni wa fukuzatsu na chikara ga sayō suru ga, B ga A ni oyobosu chikara F_1 to A ga B ni oyobosu chikara F_2 wa, sayō-hansayō no kankei ni aru no de, dono shunkan de mo ōkisa ga hitoshiku muki ga hantai de aru. Shitagatte B no undōryō no henka wa rikiseki ni hitoshii no de

$$m_2v' - m_2v = F_2t = -F_1t \tag{2}$$

(1), (2) shiki kara

$$m_1u + m_2v = m_1u' + m_2v' \tag{3}$$

Sunawachi, shōtotsu no zengo ni oite 2 buttai no undō-ryō no wa [5] wa kawaranai. Kore o *undō-ryō hozon no hōsoku* to iu.

IMPULSE

Let us imagine that a body of mass m, moving rectilinearly with velocity v_0, is acted on by a force F and that its speed changes to v within a time interval t; then the equation $F=ma$ can be written as follows:

$$\frac{m(v-v_0)}{t} = F$$

This shows that the change in momentum per unit time is equal to the force. From this, the relation

$$mv - mv_0 = Ft$$

can be derived. The product of the force F and the time t over which the force acts is called the impulse. This equation states that the *change in momentum is equal to the impulse.*

TWO-BODY COLLISIONS

Let us imagine that a body A moving with velocity u has overtaken a body B moving on the same straight line with velocity v, and that a collision has taken place.

If we let m_1 and m_2 be respectively the masses of A and B, and if we consider that the velocities after collision have become u' and v', then since the change in the momentum of A is equal to the impulse:

$$m_1u' - m_1u = F_1t \tag{1}$$

Here t is the extremely short time interval in which A and B come into contact, and F_1 is the force which B exerts on A at the time of collision.

During the collision complicated forces are acting, but, since the force F_1 which B exerts on A and the force F_2 which A exerts on B are related as action and reaction, they are equal in magnitude and opposite in direction at every

moment. Therefore because the change of momentum of B is equal to the impulse:

$$m_2v' - m_2v = F_2t = -F_1t \tag{2}$$

From Eqns. (1) and (2)

$$m_1u + m_2v = m_1u' + m_2v' \tag{3}$$

That is, the sum of the momenta of the two bodies before and after the collision is unchanged. This is called the *law of conservation of momentum.*

EXPLANATORY NOTES

(1) itchokusen-jō o undō suru — Move along a straight line. Note that this construction is the same as *michi o aruku* (walk along a street).

(2) to sureba — If we suppose that, if we consider (an often encountered expression in scientific texts).

(3) $F=ma$ to iu shiki — The equation (called) $F=ma$ (in the last sentence of this reading selection we also find...... *to iu kankei*).

(4) sore ga — It (that is, the force F).

(5) seki, wa — The elementary mathematical operations are:

和	wa	sum
差	sa	difference
積	seki	product
商	shō	quotient

The corresponding verbs are:

足す	tasu	to add
引く	hiku	to subtract
掛ける	kakeru	to multiply
割る	waru	to divide

(6) ...to shi,...to sureba — Suppose that... and suppose that (*to shi* is the literary equivalent of *to shite*).

(7) u', m₁ — These are read in Japanese as "u-dash" and "m-one".

(8) tadashi — This word at the beginning of a sentence indicates that the meaning of the previous sentence is being elaborated or certain conditions are being specified. When it appears in scientific texts immediately after an equation, it almost always may be translated as "here", e. g.

$$\emptyset = U_x - \frac{m}{r} + \frac{m}{r_1}$$

	Tadashi, r, r_1 wa sorezore O, O_1 kara no kyori de aru.	Here r and r_1 are the distances from O and O_1 respectively.

CONSTRUCTION EXAMPLES

…あたり	"per......"

1. 加速度というのは，単位時間あたりの速度の変化である。
2. 1時間あたりの衝突の数はどのくらいあるかわからない。

…とする	"(we) suppose that..."

1. 物体の速度が積分をせずに得られるとする。
2. 物体 A は動いていない物体 B に衝突して動かなくなったとする。
3. 衝突の前後において 2 物体の運動量の和が変わったとする。

積分をせずに	sekibun o sezu ni	without doing an integration

…において	"in......"

1. 二つの物体の衝突において複雑な力が作用する。
2. すべての衝突において，物体はたがいに作用と反作用の力を及ぼしあう。

すべての	subete no	every, all
たがいに	tagai ni	mutually
及ぼしあう	oyoboshi-au	to exert on each other

どの…でも	"any......"

1. どの物体でも，衝突において力を及ぼす。
2. どの衝突でも，運動量保存の法則にしたがう。

…にしたがう	...ni shitagau	to obey...

SUPPLEMENTARY READINGS

A.	玉突き	tamatsuki	billiards
	ゲーム	gēmu	game
	玉	tama	ball
	キュー	kyū	cue
	突きあてる	tsukiateru	to strike

ごく	goku	extremely
加える	kuwaeru	to add
別々に	betsu-betsu-ni	separately
大変	taihen	very, exceedingly
むずかしい	muzukashii	difficult
それほど	sorehodo	to that extent
必要	hitsuyō	necessary

玉突きというゲームでは，玉にキューを突きあてるときに，玉はごく短い瞬間に運動量を得る。この運動量はキューが玉に加えた力積に等しい。もし玉に作用する力とそれがはたらく時間とを別々に測定したいならば大変むずかしいことになるが，玉の得た運動量は力積で定まるので，それほどむずかしい測定をする必要はない。

B. かならず	kanarazu	necessarily, without fail, always
みたす	mitasu	to satisfy
運動エネルギー	undō enerugii	kinetic energy
かならずしも…ない	kanarazushimo...nai	not always, not necessarily
条件	jōken	conditions
性質	seishitsu	nature, properties
物質	busshitsu	substance, material
少ない	sukunai	few, scarce
弾性	dansei	elasticity
反発係数	hanpatsu-keisū	coefficient of restitution
ともに	tomo ni	together
相対…	sōtai...	relative...
完全な	kanzen na	perfect
なりたつ	naritatsu	to realize, to materialize
…について	...ni tsuite	in connection with..., relating to...
考える	kangaeru	to consider
ダイナマイト	dainamaito	dynamite
ばくはつ	bakuhatsu	explosion
衝動的な	shōdō-teki na	impulsive
化学変化	kagaku-henka	chemical change
による	ni yoru	to depend on
おこる	okoru	to happen, to occur

物体が衝突するときの結果は，かならず運動量保存の法則をみたすが，運動エネルギーはかならずしも保存されない。すなわち，衝突前の条件を同じにしても，物体によって衝

突後の結果は一定ではない。衝突の結果は衝突する物体がどのような性質（せい）をもつかによって変わる。そして，運動エネルギーを保存するような物質はごく少（すく）ない。

衝突の結果は物体の弾性（だんせい）による。それを表わすのに反発係数を用いる。すなわち，二つの物体 A と B が一直線上をともに運動して衝突するとき，衝突前の速度をそれぞれ u, v とし，衝突後の速度をそれぞれ u', v' とすれば，

$$\frac{u'-v'}{u-v}=-e$$

という式で反発係数 e を定める。すなわち，衝突後の相対速度（そう）と衝突前の相対速度（そう）との比が反発係数である。$e=1$ の場合（ばあい）を完全弾性衝突（かんぜんだんせい）というが，この場合（ばあい）だけは運動エネルギー保存がなりたつ。

もちろん，衝突の作用を運動に関する保存法則についてだけ考（かんが）えるときには，ダイナマイトのばくはつのような衝動的（てき）な化学変化（がく）がおこる場合（ばあい）を考（かんが）えない。

FINAL TRANSLATION TEST

運動量保存の法則は，力が質量と加速度の積に等しいという式を積分（ぶん）して得られるものであるから，この関係を用いれば，物体の速度が積分（ぶん）をせずに得られる。したがって，二つの物体の衝突の時に，はたらく力はわからないのに，その運動をとくことができる。二つの物体は，たがいに作用及び反作用を及ぼしあって，速度が変わってしまう。しかし，これらの力がはたらいている時間はごく短いので，その間に物体のある場所（しょ）は変わらない。

質量の大きい物体が運動している時は大きい運動量をもっているから，質量の小さい物体がこれに衝突しても，衝突前後の速度変化は小さい。すなわち，速さも向きもあまり変わらない。一つの物体の質量が大変大きい時，たとえば動かないかべに対してボールがなげつけられ，はねかえる時には，衝突後の速度をもとめるのに，上にのべた法則を用いない。運動量の和が保存されていることに変わりはないが，その大きさはわからないからである。この時は，反発係数さえわかれば，衝突後の速度が定められる。

LESSON 4

第 四 課

K A N J I

重	245	JŪ omo(i)		少	93	SHŌ
	224	{kasa(neru) {kasa(naru)			166	suko(shi) suku(nai)
落	330	RAKU		違	260a	I
	4003	{o(tosu) {o(chiru)			4720	chigau
下	21	KA, GE shita, moto {sa(geru)		由	325	YŪ YU
	9	{sa(garu) kuda(ru)			89	
秒	499	BYŌ		初	428	SHO
	3271				4213	haji(me)
値	229a	CHI		自	229	SHI JI
	488	atai			3841	
地	111	CHI		学	57	GAKU
	1056	JI			1271	mana(bu)
球	188	KYŪ		置	469	CHI
	2941				3644	o(ku)
引	156	IN		原	205	GEN
	1562	hi(ku)			825	
生	34	SEI, SHŌ nama, u(mu) {i(kasu)		点	285	TEN
	2991	{i(kiru)			804	
示	622	SHI JI		軸	253a	JIKU
	3228	shime(su)			4619	

READING SELECTIONS

重力	jūryoku	gravity
落下	rakka	falling, a fall
いろいろな	iroiro na	various
…の結果	…no kekka	as a result of…
重さ	omosa	weight
関係ない	kankei nai	unrelated
およそ	oyoso	about, roughly
秒	byō	second
値	atai	value

もつ	motsu	to have
地球	chikyū	the earth
地上の	chijō no	on the surface of the earth, terrestrial
引く	hiku	to pull
生じる	shōjiru	to produce, bring about, give rise to, cause; to happen, occur, come about
ふつう	futsū	usually
文字	moji	symbol
緯度	ido	latitude (on the earth's surface)
少しずつ	sukoshi-zutsu	bit by bit; little by little
違う	chigau	to be different, vary
鉛直	enchoku	vertical
下向き	shitamuki	downward
初めの	hajime no	initial
自由(落下)	jiyū(rakka)	free(fall)
始める	hajimeru	to begin, start
たつ	tatsu	to elapse, go by
前に	mae ni	before, earlier
学ぶ	manabu	to learn
位置	ichi	position
原点	genten	origin (of coordinates)
y 軸	*y*-jiku	*y*-axis
とる	toru	to take
後の	nochi no	subsequent
座標	zahyō	coordinate

重力の加速度と落下運動

いろいろな実験の結果，落下運動の加速度は，物体の重さに関係なく，およそ9.8m/秒²の値をもっている。この加速度は，地球が地上の物体を引く力，すなわち重力によって生じるので，重力の加速度といわれ[1]，その値をふつう *g* という文字[2]で示いす。

$$g=9.8\text{m}/秒^2 \qquad\qquad (1)$$

g の値は地球上の緯度[3]によって少しずつ[4]違っている。

物体の質量を *m* とすると，それにはたらく力は，鉛直下向きで *mg* である。初めの速さが0で落下する運動を自由落下運動という。

落下し始めて[5]から時間 *t* たったときの速度は，前に学んだように

$$v = gt \qquad (2)$$

で表わされる。

初⁽⁶⁾めの位置を原点とし⁽⁷⁾, 鉛直下向きにy軸をとり⁽⁷⁾, 時間tの後の位置の座標をyとすれば,

$$y = \frac{1}{2}gt^2 \qquad (3)$$

である。

JŪRYOKU NO KASOKUDO TO RAKKA-UNDŌ

Iroiro na jikken no kekka, rakka-undō no kasokudo wa, buttai no omosa ni kankei naku, oyoso kyū ten hachi mētoru-pā-byō-jijō no atai o motte iru. Kono kasokudo wa, chikyū ga chijō no buttai o hiku chikara, sunawachi jūryo- ku ni yotte shōjiru no de, jūryoku no kasokudo to iware,⁽¹⁾ sono atai o futsū g to iu moji⁽²⁾ de shimesu.

$$g = 9.8 \text{ mētoru-pā-byō-jijō} \qquad (1)$$

g no atai wa chikyū-jō no ido⁽³⁾ ni yotte sukoshi-zutsu⁽⁴⁾ chigatte iru.

Buttai no shitsuryō o m to suru to sore ni hataraku chikara wa, enchoku shitamuki de mg de aru. Hajime no hayasa ga 0 de rakka suru undō o jiyū- rakka-undō to iu.

Rakka shi-hajimete⁽⁵⁾ kara jikan t tatta toki no sokudo wa, mae ni mananda yō ni

$$v = gt \qquad (2)$$

de arawasareru. Hajime⁽⁶⁾ no ichi o genten to shi,⁽⁷⁾ enchoku shitamuki ni y-jiku o tori,⁽⁷⁾ jikan t no nochi no ichi no zahyō o y to sureba,⁽⁷⁾

$$y = \frac{1}{2}gt^2 \qquad (3)$$

de aru.

GRAVITATIONAL ACCELERATION AND FALLING MOTION

As a result of various experiments, we know that the acceleration of falling bodies is not related to their weight and has a value of about 9.8m/sec². Since this acceleration results from the force with which the earth attracts terrestrial objects, i.e., gravity, it is called the gravitational acceleration and its value is generally indicated by the symbol g.

$$g = 9.8\text{m/sec}^2 \qquad (1)$$

The value of g on the surface of the earth varies slightly with latitude.

If we let the mass of a body be m, the force acting on it vertically downward is mg. Falling motion with zero initial speed is called freely-falling motion.

As we learned earlier, the velocity after the elapse of a time t since the begin-

ning of the motion is

$$v = gt \qquad (2)$$

If we let the initial position be the origin, take the *y*-axis vertically downward, and let *y* be the position coordinate at a subsequent time *t*, then

$$y = \frac{1}{2}gt^2 \qquad (3)$$

EXPLANATORY NOTES

(1)	iware	Stem of *iwareru*, the passive form of *iu*; note that there is virtually no difference in meaning between AをBという and AはBといわれる。
(2)	*g* to iu moji	"The symbol (called) *g*".
(3)	ido	*Ido*(緯度) is "latitude" and *keido* (経度) is "longitude".
(4)	-zutsu	Note: *hitotsu-zutsu* (一つずつ) one by one; *futatsu-zutsu* (二つずつ) two by two.
(5)	rakka shi-hajimete	*Rakka suru* (to fall); *rakka shihajimeru* (to begin to fall).
(6)	hajime no; hajimeru	Note that the kanji 始 is used for the verbs *haji*(*meru*) and *haji*(*maru*) (the ON-reading is *SHI*); the kanji 初 is used for the noun *haji*(*me*) (the ON reading is *SHO* as in 最初のスライドお願いします "first slide please").
(7)	...shi, ...tori, ...sureba	Note that the provisional ending *eba* applies to the preceding two clauses; hence, *if* we let..., and *if* we take..., and *if* we let... .

CONSTRUCTION EXAMPLES

...の結果	"as a result of..."

1. 落下運動についての実験の結果，物体の加速度はその重さに関係がないことがわかった。

2. いろいろな実験の結果，地球が地上の物体を引く力は一定でなく，地球上の緯度によって少しずつ違っていることがわかった。

...によって	"according to..., depending on..., by means of..."

1. 重力加速度は地球上の位置によって少しずつ違う。

2. この実験によって，重い物体と軽い物体とを同時に落とすと，両方ともほぼ同時に地面につくことがわかる。

3. 物体が重力によって落下するときの運動のことを前に学んだ。

4. 落下運動においては，加速度が重力によって生じる。

重い	omoi	heavy
軽い	karui	light
両方とも	ryōhō tomo	both of them
ほぼ	hobo	almost
地面	jimen	ground; earth's surface
つく	tsuku	to arrive

…ずつ	"...by..."

1. 物理学の保存法則を一つずつ学ぼう。

2. 重力加速度の値は時間がたつにつれて少しずつ変化している。

物理学	butsuri-gaku	physics
…につれて	...ni tsurete	as..., along with...

たつ	"elapse, pass (of time)"

1. 落下運動では，時間 t がたってから鉛直下向きに物体の落ちた距離は t の二乗に比例する。

…の二乗	...no nijō (or:... no jijō) square of...; second power of...

…という文字で示す	"we designate by the symbol..."

1. ふつう（は）質量を m, 速度を v, 距離を s, 時間を t, 加速度を a という文字で示す。

2. 数学では定数を a, b, c, 変数を x, y, z という文字で示す。

変数	hensū	variable

…(verb stem)＋…始める	"begin to＋ (verb)"

1. 物体が動き始めれば，その物体にはかならず力がはたらいている。

2. 自由落下運動をする物体が落ち始めた時刻を O とすれば，それが落ちた距離 s は，いつも t^2 に比例する。

かならず	kanarazu	necessarily
時刻	jikoku	instant, time, moment

…(verb stem)…とすれば	"if we... and if we let..."

1. 鉛直に投げ上げた物体が t_1 時間の後 h の高さに上がり，さらに t_2 時間の後同じ高さ

h の場所におりてきたとすれば, $h=\frac{1}{2}gt_1(t_1+t_2)$ の関係がある。

2.　物体が直線上を一定の速度で動くものとし, 動いた距離を s, 要した時間を t, 速さを v とすれば, $s=vt$.

3.　物体が自由落下運動をするとし, 物体の質量を m, 重力の加速度を g とすれば, 物体にはたらく力は mg である。

投げ上げる	nage-ageru	to toss upwards
高さ	takasa	height
上がる	agaru	to rise
さらに	sara ni	further, again
場所	basho	place, position
おりる	oriru	to descend
おりてくる	orite kuru	to come (falling) down

SUPPLEMENTARY READINGS

A.	真上に	maue ni	directly upward
	投げる	nageru	to throw
	のぼる	noboru	to ascend, to rise
	ふたたび	futatabi	again
	元の	moto no	original, former
	もどる	modoru	to return, to come back
	上向き	uwamuki	upward

　真上に投げた物体はある高さまでのぼると速度が 0 となって, それから自由落下運動が始まり, ふたたび元の位置にもどってくる。物体を投げ上げる位置を原点とし, 鉛直上向きに y 軸をとれば, 物体の加速度は $-g$ である。このとき, 初めの速度を v_0, 投げ上げてから時間 t の後の速度を v, 物体の位置の座標を y とすれば次の式が得られる。

$$v=v_0-gt; \quad s=v_0t-\frac{1}{2}gt^2$$

B.	座標軸	zahyō-jiku	coordinate axes
	すべて	subete	all
	互いに	tagai ni	mutually
	直角に	chokkaku ni	at right angles, perpendicularly
	交わる	majiwaru	to intersect
	に関して	ni kanshite	in relation to
	直角座標	chokkaku-zahyō	rectangular coordinates
	右手	migite	right handed

左手	hidarite	left handed
配置	haichi	arrangement, placement
座標系	zahyō-kei	coordinate system
区別	kubetsu	distinction, differentiation
正の	sei no	positive
親指	oya-yubi	thumb (lit. parent finger)
人さし指	hitosashi-yubi	index finger (lit. person-pointing finger)
中指	naka-yubi	middle finger

座標軸がすべて互いに直角に交わるとき，これに関して表わされる座標を直角座標という。その軸 (Ox, Oy, Oz) の配置によって右手座標系，左手座標系の区別がある。右手座標系で(x-, y-, z- 軸の正の向きがそれぞれ右手の親指，人さし指，中指の関係にある。z 軸の正の方向がこれと反対になるものが左手座標系である。

C.	自然科学	shizen kagaku	the physical sciences, natural science
	ギブズ	Gibuzu	(J. Willard) Gibbs
	自由エネルギー	jiyū enerugii	free energy
	ひろく	hiroku	widely
	とくに	toku ni	especially
	自然に	shizen ni	naturally, spontaneously
	…かどうか	...ka dō ka	whether or not...
	重大な	jūdai na	important
	温度	ondo	temperature
	圧力	atsuryoku	pressure
	条件	jōken	conditions
	の下に	no moto ni	under
	減少	genshō	decrease
	生じ得ない	shōji-enai	cannot occur, happen
	原則として	gensoku to shite	as a fundamental principle
	おこる	okoru	to occur
	原子	genshi	atom
	核分裂	kaku-bunretsu	nuclear fission

自然科学ではギブズの自由エネルギーはひろく用いられて，とくに化学変化が自然に生じるかどうかということを定めるのに重大な関数である。すなわち，ある化学変化において，温度と圧力とが一定という条件の下に，自由エネルギーの減少が生じないと，その化学変化はその条件の下には生じ得ないということがわかる。自然に生じる作用においては

原則として自由エネルギーの減少^{げん}がかならずおこるからである。たとえば，原子核分裂^{しかくぶんれつ}において自由エネルギー変化は減少^{げん}を示す。

D.	1666年に	1666 nen ni	in 1666
	月	tsuki	the moon
	説	setsu	theory
	ためす	tamesu	to test
	数値的に	sūchi-teki ni	quantitatively
	…にそって	…ni sotte	along…
	中心点	chūshin-ten	center
	仮定する	katei suru	to assume
	任意の	nin'i no	any
	半径	hankei	radius
	やく	yaku	approximately
	60倍	rokujū-bai	60 times
	1分	ippun	one minute
	数値	sūchi	numerical value
	同一	dō-itsu	identical, equal
	それなのに	sore na no ni	in spite of that
	自分の	jibun no	his own
	発表する	happyō suru	to announce
	理由	riyū	reason
	全体の	zentai no	total
	集中する	shūchū suru	to be concentrated at
	場合	baai	case
	数学的に	sūgaku-teki ni	mathematically
	証明する	shōmei suru	to prove

　ニュートンは1666年に地球上の物体にはたらく地球の重力によって生じる引力が月^{つき}まで及ぶと考^{かんが}え始^{はじ}めた。この説^{せつ}を数値的^{てき}にためすために，ニュートンは月^{つき}の動きを落下する物体と同じように考^{かんが}えて，それを地球上で自由落下運動をする物体の動きと比べた。すなわち，地球の重力が月^{つき}にはたらくから，月^{つき}が直線にそって動かずに，地球へ落下していると考^{かんが}えた。

　ニュートンは地球の引力によって生じる重力が地球の中心点^{ちゅうしん}からの距離の平方^{へいほう}に反比例すると仮定^かしたので，重力の加速度 g は距離 d によって，次のように変化する。

$$g = \frac{k}{d^2}$$

自由落下運動をする物体が落下した距離 s と時間 t との関係は

$$s = \frac{1}{2}gt^2$$

であるので,

$$s = \frac{1}{2}\,\frac{kt^2}{d^2}$$

という式が得られる。したがって, 自由落下運動をする任意の二つの物体が落下したそれぞれの距離 s_1 と s_2 の比は次の関係で定まる。

$$s_1/s_2 = (t_1/t_2)^2/(d_1/d_2)^2$$

ニュートンは地球の中心点から測った月の距離が地球の半径のやく60倍であることをもとにして, 月の1分間に落下する距離が地球上の自由落体の1秒間に落下する距離に等しくなることを示し, この二つの距離の観測値を比べた。それらの数値はほとんど同一であった。

それなのに, ニュートンは1666年に自分の説を発表しなかった。その理由は, ニュートンが地球の全体の質量が及ぼす引力はその全体の質量が地球の中心点に集中している場合と同じ大きさであることを仮定し, 1666年にはその仮定を数学的に証明することができなかったからである。

SOME FIELDS OF STUDY   学問のいろいろ

Using *kanji* from only the first four lessons you are in a position to understand the names of almost all of the following fields of study.

生物学	seibutsu-gaku	biology
動物学	dōbutsu-gaku	zoology
植物学	shokubutsu-gaku	botany
化学	kagaku	chemistry
生化学	sei-kagaku	biochemistry
化学工学	kagaku-kōgaku	chemical engineering
応用化学	ōyō-kagaku	applied chemistry
力学	rikigaku	mechanics, dynamics
応用力学	ōyō-rikigaku	applied mechanics
運動学	undō-gaku	kinematics
気体力学	kitai-rikigaku	gas dynamics
物理学	butsuri-gaku	physics
数学	sūgaku	mathematics
地質学	chishitsu-gaku	geology
地理学	chiri-gaku	geography
生理学	seiri-gaku	physiology
原子物理学	genshi-butsuri-gaku	atomic physics

FINAL TRANSLATION TEST

　ニュートンによって作り上げられた力学を用いれば，物体に力が作用した時，その結果として生じる運動を解くことができる。もっともよく現われるのは，質量のわかっている物体にはたらく力がわかっていて，その運動をもとめる，すなわち，物体の位置や，速度，加速度が時間とともにどのように変わるかを定めることである。たとえば，地球上ではどのような物体にも重力がはたらいているから，質量かける加速度が重力に等しいという式によって，重力による運動がすべて定められる。物体を鉛直上向きに投げ上げても，ある傾きをもってなげだしても，運動の式は同じで，ただ初めの速度が違うだけである。いずれの場合にも，地表上に原点をとり座標軸を定めた後，運動の式をかいて，これを積分する。エネルギー保存の法則をつかうことができれば，積分せずに速度がもとめられる。

　応用力学において，物体の自重よりもはるかに大きい力が作用している時には，地球の引力は運動の式に現われない。このような時でも，加速度の値をm／秒²の単位ではなく，重力の加速度 g の単位で示すが，これは物体の自由落下とは少しも関係のないことである。

LESSON 5
第 五 課

KANJI

周	632	SHŪ		半	129	HAN	
	622				132		
期	183	KI		径	216a	KEI	
	3785				1602		
的	478	TEKI		図	261	ZU	
	3097				1034	TO	
円	48	EN		角	173	KAKU	
	617				4301	tsuno	
行	73	KŌ GYŌ		絶	828	ZETSU	
	4213	i(ku), yu(ku) oko(nau)			3539	ta(eru)	
糸	83	SHI		増	665	ZŌ	
	3492	ito			1137	ma(su)	
石	44	SEKI SHAKU		合	77	GŌ	
	3176	ishi			383	a(u)	
振	231b	SHIN		組	103	SO	
	1920	fu(ru)			3520	ku(mu) 〔kumi〕	
回	168	KAI		与	194b		
	1028	{mawa(su) {mawa(ru)			6	ata(eru)	
長	116	CHŌ		要	729	YŌ	
	4938	naga(i)			4274		

READING SELECTIONS

周期(的)	shūki(teki)	period(ic)
円周の上	enshū no ue	on the circumference
円運動	en-undō	circular motion
行なう	okonau	to perform, execute
一回りする	hitomawari suru	to go around (one time)
…に要する	...ni yō suru	to be required for...
糸	ito	string, thread
先	saki	end, tip
小石	ko-ishi	pebble, stone

つける	tsukeru	to attach
振り回す	furi-mawasu	to swing around
長さ	nagasa	length
半径	hankei	radius
図 1	zu-ichi	Fig. 1
描く	egaku	to draw, sketch; describe
角度	kakudo	angle
絶えず	taezu	always, continuously, ceaselessly
増大する	zōdai suru	to increase, enlarge
増加する	zōka suru	to increase, add to
割合	wariai	rate
角速度	kaku-sokudo	angular velocity
ラジアン	rajian	radian
増す	masu	to increase
組み合わせる	kumi-awaseru	to combine, join together
与える	ataeru	to give

周期的な運動　　(B 55)

　物体が一つの円周の上を運動するとき，この物体は「円運動」を行なっているといい，物体 [1] が円周を一回りするの [2] に要する時間を円運動の「周期」という。

　糸の先(さき)に小石をつけて振り回すと小石は円運動をする。糸の長さを r とし，小石がいつも同じ速さ v で動くとすれば，v と周期 T との間には，次の関係がある。

$$v = \frac{2\pi r}{T} \tag{1}$$

小石がこのような運動をするとき，動く半径 [3] (図1のOP) の [4] 描(えが)く角度 (∠AOP) は絶えず増大 [5] する。この角が単位時間あたり増加 [5] する割合を角速度といい，ω (オメガ) で表わす。

　小石の速さが変わらないときは，角度は周期 T の間に，ラジアン単位で 2π だけ [6] 増す [5] から，

$$\omega = \frac{2\pi}{T} \tag{2}$$

が得られる。上の二つの式 [7] を組み合わせれば，速さと角速度との関係が次の式 [8] で与えられる。

$$v = r\omega \tag{3}$$

SHŪKI-TEKI NA UNDŌ

Buttai ga hitotsu no enshū no ue o undō suru toki, kono buttai wa "en-undō" o okonatte iru to ii, buttai[1] ga enshū o hitomawari suru no[2] ni yōsuru jikan o en-undō no "shūki" to iu.

Ito no saki ni ko-ishi o tsukete furi-mawasu to, ko-ishi wa en-undō o suru.

Ito no nagasa o *r* to shi, ko-ishi ga itsumo onaji hayasa *v* de ugoku to sureba, *v* to shūki *T* to no aida ni wa, tsugi no kankei ga aru.

$$v = 2\pi r/T \qquad (1)$$

Ko-ishi ga kono yō na undō o suru toki, ugoku hankei[3] (zu-ichi no *OP*) no[4] egaku kakudo (∠AOP) wa taezu zōdai[5] suru. Kono kaku ga tan'i jikan atari zōka[5] suru wariai o kaku-sokudo to ii, *ω* (omega) de arawasu.

Ko-ishi no hayasa ga kawaranai toki wa, kakudo wa shūki *T* no aida ni rajian tan'i de 2π dake[6] masu[5] kara,

$$\omega = 2\pi/T \qquad (2)$$

ga erareru. Ue no futatsu no shiki[7] o kumi-awasereba, hayasa to kaku-sokudo to no kankei ga tsugi no shiki[8] de ataerareru.

$$v = r\omega \qquad (3)$$

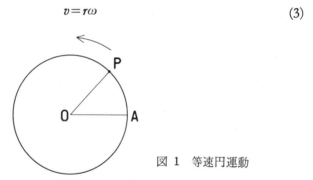

図 1 等速円運動

PERIODIC MOTION

When a body moves along the circumference of a circle, we say that it executes "circular motion." The time needed for the body to go once around the circumference we call the "period" of the circular motion.

If we attach a small stone to the end of a string and swing it around, the stone executes circular motion.

If we let the length of the string be *r* and if we let the stone always move with the same speed *v*, then we have the following relation between *v* and the period *T*:

$$v = 2\pi r/T \qquad (1)$$

When the stone executes this kind of motion, the angle AOP generated by the moving radius (OP in Fig. 1) continuously increases. The rate at which this angle increases per unit time is called angular velocity and is designated by ω (omega)

When the speed of the stone does not change, then, since the angle expressed in radians increases exactly by 2π during the period T, we obtain

$$\omega = 2\pi/T \qquad (2)$$

Combining the above two equations gives the following relation between speed and angular velocity:

$$v = r\omega \qquad (3)$$

EXPLANATORY NOTES

(1) buttai ga enshū ... yō suru   This is the modifying cause for *jikan*.

(2) suru no ni = suru koto ni

(3) hankei (radius); chokkei 直径 (diameter)

(4) hankei no egaku kakudo = hankei ga egaku kakudo (*no* is often used in subordinate clauses)

(5) zōka suru, zōdai suru, masu   Note that these are virtually synonymous in this text.

(6) 2π dake masu   The word *dake* has the basic meaning of "exact amount" and is often translated by expressions such as: "by (the amount of), just (exactly), only."

重量が２キロだけへる

"the weight decreases by 2 kg,"

x 点から△x だけ増すと

"if the value of x increases by △x."

(7) shiki   Often hōteishiki (方程式) is used.

(8) tsugi no shiki   In scientific texts one often encounters also 次式 (jishiki).

(present tense)＋割合	"rate at which..."

1. 変位の時間的変化の割合を速度という。

2. ある量が単位時間あたり増加する割合は，その量の，その時における絶対値に比例する場合がおおい。

変位   hen'i   displacement

| 絶対値 | zettai-chi | the value itself; the actual value |
| ···場合がおおい | ...baai ga ōi | it often happens that... |

| (verb)＋のに要する | "necessary for..." |

1. 等速度運動をしている物体が距離 *s* だけ動くのに要する時間を *t* とすれば, 速さ *v* は, $v=s/t$ で与えられる。

2. 質量 *m* の物体に加速度 *a* を与えるのに要する力は *ma* である。

There is one very important grammatical construction which has not yet appeared in the readings but will be appearing rather frequently in future readings and in final translation tests beginning with this lesson. It is a form not generally encountered except in technical Japanese and consists of the *-eba* verb form plus the adjective *yoi*. It literally means that it is good to do something in the manner just described.

This form is most frequently encountered when directions are given to indicate either the method for solving a problem or the techniques for preparing and conducting an experiment. Appropriate translations are given below.

| -eba yoi | 1. "it is advisable to..." 2. "we need(only)to..." |

1. 物体にいろいろの力がはたらく場合, 図をえがいて物体にはたらくすべての力をかきこんで, その合力をもとめればよい。

2. 物体にいろいろの力がはたらく場合, 物体の運動をとくためには合力だけを考えればよい。

かきこむ	kakikomu	to draw in
もとめる	motomeru	to seek
とく	toku	to solve

See also explanatory note (4), Lesson 11.

SUPPLEMENTARY READINGS

A.	中心	chūshin	center
	向心力	kōshin-ryoku	centripetal force
	いわゆる	iwayuru	what is called; so-called
	慣性	kansei	inertia
	···場合	...baai	when...
	遠心力	enshin-ryoku	centrifugal force

自転する	jiten suru	to rotate
現われる	arawareru	to appear
合力	gōryoku	resultant force

糸の先につけた小石が円運動をするとき，小石は絶えず糸から力を受けていて，その力はいつも円の中心を向いているから，その力を向心力とよんでいる。向心力の大きさは小石の質量 m が大きいほど，また角速度 ω と半径 r が大きいほど大きく，これらの関係は

$$F = mr\omega^2$$

という式で表わされる。

しかし，向心力が小石に加速度を得させるため，小石とともに運動する座標系においては，いわゆる遠心力が小石の慣性によって生じる。小石が円運動をする場合，遠心力は向心力と大きさが等しく，向きは反対である。

地球は自転しているから，地球上では物体の慣性によって遠心力が生じる。したがって地球上に現われる重力は，地球の質量によってはたらく引力に等しくはなく，引力と遠心力との合力である。

B.

ケプラー	Kepurā	Kepler
ティコ・ブラーエ	Tiko Burāe	Tycho Brahe
惑星	wakusei	planets (lit:stars which have gone astray)
特に	toku ni	especially
火星	kasei	Mars
…について	…ni tsuite	relating to…, about…
見いだす	mi-idasu	to discover
太陽	taiyō	sun
焦点	shōten	focus
だ円	da-en	ellipse
結ぶ	musubu	to join, to tie
線分	senbun	line segment
面積	menseki	area
軌道	kidō	orbit
半長径	han-chōkei	semi-major axis
第1・第3	dai-ichi; dai-san	first; third
万有引力	banyū-inryoku	universal gravitation
重要な	jūyō na	important
完全に	kanzen ni	perfectly
一致する	itchi suru	to agree, to be in accord with
および	oyobi	and

ほかの	hoka no	other
二体問題	nitai mondai	two body problem
正しい	tadashii	correct
太陽系内	taikyō-kei-nai	in the solar system
かなり	kanari	rather
精密に	seimitsu ni	accurately, exactly
あてはまる	atehamaru	to hold true, apply, be applicable

ケプラーの法則　(B 59–60)

ケプラーはティコ・ブラーエの惑星（特に火星）の観測数値をもとにして，惑星運動について次の3法則を見いだした。

(1) 惑星は太陽を焦点とするだ円上を運動する。

(2) 太陽と一つの惑星を結ぶ線分が一定時間に描く面積は一定である（面積速度保存の法則）。

(3) 周期をTとし，軌道の半長径をrとすれば，T^2/r^3はすべての惑星について一定である。すなわち

$$T^2/r^3=k$$

ここにkはどの惑星にも同じ比例定数である。

ニュートンが万有引力の法則を見いだすためには，ケプラーの3法則が重要なものであったが，これらの3法則は完全にはニュートンの法則と一致しない。すなわち，第1および第2法則は，ほかの惑星の引力のない場合（いわゆる二体問題），第3法則は惑星の質量が0である場合だけに正しい。しかし太陽系内の惑星は太陽に比べて質量がごく小さいから，かなり精密にあてはまる。

C.	年	nen	year
	による	ni yoru	due to
	…の2乗	…no nijō	the square of…
	知る	shiru	to know
	必要	hitsuyō	necessity, need
	円形の	enkei no	circular
	…の中で	…no naka de	inside of…
	考える	kangaeru	to consider
	円内の	ennai no	within the circle
	正方形	seihō-kei	a square
	想像する	sōzō suru	to imagine, to suppose
	における	ni okeru	in

無数	musū	countless, innumerable
辺	hen	side
正多角形	sei-takaku-kei	regular polygon
あてはめる	atehameru	to apply
推測する	suisoku suru	to infer
平均	heikin	average
関係づける	kankei-zukeru	to relate
導き出す	michibiki-dasu	to derive
結びつける	musubi-tsukeru	to combine, to join
…によると	…ni yoru to	according to…

　ニュートンは1666年に重力による引力が距離の2乗に反比例することを見いだした。そのためには，二つの関係を知る必要があった。その一つは円形の軌道上を運動する物体にはたらく向心力である。ニュートンは円の中で物体が等速度直線運動をして，円周に衝突してから向きだけを変える場合を考えて，円内の正方形の軌道を想像した。正方形の軌道における円周との衝突の場合にはたらく向心力を定めて，それを辺の数が無数に多い正多角形にあてはめることによって，円形の軌道上を運動する物体にはたらく向心力を推測した。このようにして，半径 r をもつ円形に物体が等しい速さ v で運動する場合にはたらく向心力 F は，

$$F = \frac{mv^2}{r}$$

という式で定まることがわかった。

　次にニュートンは向心力の法則をケプラーの第3法則，すなわち惑星の周期 T と太陽からの平均距離 r を関係づける法則と組み合わせて，惑星が太陽に引かれる力の法則を導き出した。

ケプラーの第3法則によると，

$$T^2/r^3 = k$$

また，惑星の平均速度 v は軌道の円周 $2\pi r$ と周期 T との比に等しいから

$$T^2 = \left(\frac{2\pi r}{v}\right)^2$$

　ニュートンは，この式を向心力の法則と結びつけて，太陽の引力の大きさが距離の2乗に反比例するということを見いだした。

反対語 OPPOSITES

Note the following word pairs many of which have appeared thus far in the lessons; read and translate.

1. 大きい 　　　　　　　　 小さい
2. 長い 　　　　　　　　　 短い
3. 上向き 　　　　　　　　 下向き
4. 同じである 　　　　　　 違っている
5. 衝突前 　　　　　　　　 衝突後
6. 比例 　　　　　　　　　 反比例
7. 一定する 　　　　　　　 変化する
8. 重い 　　　　　　　　　 軽い
9. 地上 　　　　　　　　　 地下
10. 増す 　　　　　　　　　 減る
11. 増加する 　　　　　　　 減少する
12. 作用 　　　　　　　　　 反作用
13. 正 　　　　　　　　　　 負
14. 右手 　　　　　　　　　 左手
15. 向心力 　　　　　　　　 遠心力

FINAL TRANSLATION TEST

　糸の一つのはしをなにか動かないものに結びつけ，もう一つのはしには小石をつけると，糸は鉛直の向きを示してとどまる。この時，糸に対して90度をなす向きに，小石に初速度を与えると，小石は円運動を始める。初速度の大きさがあまり大きくなければ，小石は振動し，その周期は，糸の長さと重力加速度 g の関数として与えられる。小石の初速度を増して行ってある大きさになると，糸が鉛直線とある角度をなすところで小石は円運動をやめて，地上であるかたむきをもってなげだした物体の行なう運動と同じ運動を行なう。この時糸は，円運動をしている時のように，はりきってはいなくて，たるんでいる。さらに初速度を増して，小石が初めにあったところの直上まで円運動をつづけるようになると，小石は円にそって一回りするようになり，糸の長さに等しい半径をもった円運動をいつまでもつづける。すなわち，糸のさきに小石をつけて振り回した時と同じ周期的運動が得られ，動く半径のえがく角度は絶えず増大する。

　これらの運動をとくために，たとえば，与えられた初速度に対して上の三つのなかのどの運動が現われるかということをしらべるためには，運動エネルギー保存の法則と，円運

動における半径，角度，角速度，あるいは速度の間になりたつ関係式とを組み合わせてとけばよい。小石が円運動からはずれて地上へ落ちるためには，糸が小石に及ぼす力がどこかで0になることを要する。したがって，この時には，小石の質量と向心加速度との積が半径の向きにはたらく力に等しいという式を用いなければならない。この運動の式を作るには，図をえがいて，小石にはたらくすべての力，すなわち，地球が小石に及ぼす重力と，糸が小石をひっぱる力とをかきこんで，半径の向きにはたらく力をもとめればよい。

LESSON 6
第 六 課
KANJI

正	46	SEI		平	315	HEI
	27	tada(shii)			26	tai(ra) hira(tai)
弦	216a	GEN		相	452	SŌ
	1568	tsuru			2241	ai
波	298	HA		形	200	KEI
	2529	nami			1589	katachi kata
最	402	SAI		進	259	SHIN
	2146	motto(mo)			4709	susu(mu)
幅	247b	FUKU		起	181	KI
	1484	haba			4541	{o(kosu) {o(koru)
音	50	ON		過	562	KA
	5110	oto			4723	{su(gosu) {su(giru)
各	568	KAKU		場	252	JŌ
	1163	ono-ono*			1113	ba
空	65	KŪ		所	246	SHO
	3317	sora			1821	tokoro
気	59	KI		圧	544	ATSU
	2480				818	
方	138	HŌ		水	14	SUI
	2082	kata			2482	mizu

* Note: *ono-ono* is written 各々; the symbol 々 indicates that the preceeding symbol is to be repeated······ for example, 時々＝時時 (tokidoki)

READING SELECTION

正弦波	seigen-ha	sinusoidal wave; sine wave
単振動	tan-shindō	simple harmonic motion
最も	mottomo	most
簡単な	kantan na	simple
振動	shindō	oscillation; vibration
変位	hen'i	displacement
…とともに	...to tomo ni	with...
正弦関数的に	seigen-kansū-teki ni	sinusoidally

振幅	shinpuku	amplitude
音波	onpa	sound wave
…のうち	...no uchi	in...; among...; for...
各点で	kakuten de	at each point
空気	kūki	air
音	oto	sound
くる	kuru	to come
方向	hōkō	direction
…と平行	...to heikō	parallel to...
前後に	zengo ni	back and forth
くり返す	kuri-kaesu	to repeat
相次ぐ	ai-tsugu	to come one after another, be in succession
波形	hakei	wave form, shape of wave
少しずつ	sukoshi-zutsu	little by little
ずれる	zureru	to slip, shift, lag
進む	susumu	to advance
…ことになる	...koto ni naru	it turns out that...
いま	ima	now
縦軸	tatejiku	ordinate
とる	toru	to take
任意の	nin'i no	any arbitrary
経過する	keika suru	to elapse, pass
形	katachi	form
起こる	okoru	to take place, occur, happen
波	nami	wave
よぶ	yobu	to call
進行方向	shinkō-hōkō	direction of propagation
縦波	tatenami	longitudinal wave
…と直角に	...to chokkaku ni	perpendicular to...
横波	yokonami	transverse wave
…として	...to shite	as...
媒質	baishitsu	medium
動き	ugoki	movement
…とした	...to shita	we supposed that...
それに伴って	sore ni tomonatte	along with that, accordingly
場所	basho	place
圧力	atsuryoku	pressure
水	mizu	water
重なる	kasanaru	to be superimposed

一般に	ippan ni	in general
多くの	ōku no	many
考える	kangaeru	to consider

正 弦 波 (B 157–158)

単振動は最も簡単な振動であって，その変位 y は時間 t とともに正弦関数的に変化する。すなわち

$$y=A \sin\frac{2\pi}{T}t \tag{1}$$

ここで，A は振幅，T は周期を示す。

音波のうち最も簡単なものは，各点で，そこの空気が音のくる方向と平行に前後[1]に(1)式のような振動をくり返すものである。相次ぐ点[2]では，波形が少しずつずれて，速さ v で進むことになる[3]。いま，各点 x での変位 y を縦軸にとり，時間，$t, t+\frac{1}{4}T, t+\frac{1}{2}T$ と経過したときの波形を表わすと，図1のようになる。これを式で表わすと

$$y=A \sin\frac{2\pi}{T}(t-\frac{x}{v}) \tag{2}$$

の形で表わされる。この式は $x=0$ の点で(1)式と同じ振動を示し，任意の点 x では時間 x/v だけ経過したとき，同じ形の振動が起こることを示している。(2)式のような形の波を「正弦波」とよんでいる。変位 y が波の進行方向と同じ方向に振動するときは縦波，変位 y が進行方向と直角に振動すれば横波である[4]。ここで変位 y として表わしたものは，音波ではその媒質の1点の小さな動きとしたが，それに伴って，その場所の空気の圧力も図1と同じ形の変化をする。水の波は正弦波ではないが，正弦波の重なったものである。一般に波は多くの正弦波の重なったものと考えることができる。

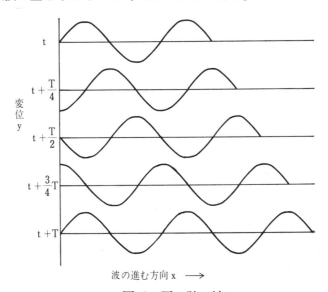

図 1 正 弦 波

SEIGEN-HA

Tan-shindō wa mottomo kantan na shindō de atte, sono hen'i y wa jikan t to tomo ni seigen-kansū-teki ni henka suru. Sunawachi

$$y = A \sin\frac{2\pi}{T}t \tag{1}$$

koko de, A wa shinpuku, T wa shūki o shimesu.

Onpa no uchi mottomo kantan na mono wa, kakuten de, soko no kūki ga, oto no kuru hōkō to heikō ni, zengo[1] ni ichi-shiki no yō na shindō o kurikaesu mono de aru. Ai-tsugu ten[2] de wa, hakei ga sukoshi-zutsu zurete, hayasa v de susumu koto ni naru.[3] Ima, kakuten x de no hen'i y o tatejiku ni tori, jikan t, $t+\frac{1}{4}$T, $t+\frac{1}{2}$T to keika shita toki no hakei o arawasu to zu-ichi no yō ni naru. Kore o shiki de arawasu to

$$y = A \sin\frac{2\pi}{T}(t - \frac{x}{v}) \tag{2}$$

no katachi de arawasareru. Kono shiki wa x=0 no ten de ichi-shiki to onaji shindō o shimeshi, nin'i no ten x de wa, jikan x/v dake keika shita toki, onaji katachi no shindō ga okoru koto o shimeshite iru. Ni-shiki no yō na katachi no nami o "seigen-ha" to yonde iru. Hen'i y ga nami no shinkō-hōkō to onaji hōkō ni shindō suru toki wa tatenami, hen'i y ga shinkō-hōkō to chokkaku ni shindō sureba, yokonami de aru.[4] Koko de hen'i y to shite arawashita mono wa, onpa de wa sono baishitsu no itten no chiisa na ugoki to shita ga, sore ni tomonatte, sono basho no kūki no atsuryoku mo zu-ichi to onaji katachi no henka o suru.

Mizu no nami wa, seigen-ha de wa nai ga, seigen-ha no kasanatta mono de aru. Ippan ni nami wa ōku no seigen-ha no kasanatta mono to kangaeru koto ga dekiru.

SINUSOIDAL WAVES

Simple harmonic oscillation, in which the displacement y changes sinusoidally with the time t, is the simplest vibratory motion. That is,

$$y = A \sin\frac{2\pi}{T}t \tag{1}$$

where A represents the amplitude and T the period.

Among sound waves the simplest case is that for which the air at each location repeatedly oscillates back and forth as in Equation (1), parallel to the direction from which the sound comes. At successive points the wave form shifts little by little such that the wave progresses with a speed v. Now, representing the wave form at each point x by plotting the displacements y as ordinates at elapsed times t, $t +\frac{1}{4}T$, $t+ \frac{1}{2}T$, we obtain Fig. *1*. Expressed by an equation, this becomes

$$y = A \, \sin\frac{2\pi}{T}\left(t - \frac{x}{v}\right) \tag{2}$$

This equation shows that at the point $x=0$ the same oscillatory motion occurs as in Equation (1) and that, at any point x, the same form of vibration occurs whenever a time just equal to x/v has elapsed. Waves having the form of Equation (2) are called sinusoidal. When the displacement y oscillates in the same direction as that of the wave propagation, it is a longitudinal wave; when the displacement y oscillates perpendicularly to the direction of wave propagation, it is a transverse wave. We have supposed here that for sound waves the quantity expressed as the displacement y is a small movement at a given point in the medium and that, accordingly, the pressure of the air at that location will have the same form of variation as that shown in Fig. 1.

A water wave is not a sinusoidal wave, but rather a superposition of sinusoidal waves. In general waves can be regarded as superpositions of many sinusoidal waves.

EXPLANATORY NOTES

(1) zengo ni	Here the meaning is "back and forth." In other contexts *zengo ni* means "before and after" (in time) and "in front of and behind" (in space). See Construction Examples.
(2) aitsugu ten	The word *aitsugu* is somewhat unusual. On the other hand, *aitsuide* (successively) is a frequently encountered word.
(3) susumu koto ni naru	The phrase *koto ni naru*, very common in scientific texts, implies that the statement is a consequence of previously given information or principles. It can sometimes be conveniently translated as "hence," "it turns out that," or "would + verb"; often it is best omitted in translation.
(4) tatenami...yokonami de aru.	Both *tatenami* and *yokonami* have *de aru* as the verb. One could insert *de atte* immediately after *tatenami*.

CONSTRUCTION EXAMPLES

| …と共^{とも}に変化する | "to change with……" |

1. 音波では，圧力 P は距離 s とともに正弦関数的に変化する。
2. 等速円運動をする物体の位置は，時間とともに周期的に変化する。

…の内	"among..."

1. 物理学の法則のうち最も重要なものは保存法則であろう。

2. 数学関数のうち，三角関数，対数関数，べき関数などは，高等学校で学ぶものである。

重要な	jūyō na	important
数学関数	sūgaku-kansū	mathematical function
三角関数	sankaku-kansū	trigonometric function
対数関数	taisū-kansū	logarithmic function
べき関数	beki-kansū	power function
高等学校	kōtō-gakkō	high school

…ことになる	"it turns out that...", "hence..."

1. 音波は縦波であるから，空気は音のくる方向と平行に振動していることになる。

2. 周期関数はすべて正弦関数の和として表わすことができるから，振動はすべて単振動の重なったものということになる。

…として	"as..."

1. CGS単位では，長さ・質量・時間の単位として，それぞれ cm, g, s を用いる。

2. 正弦波は，場所 x を一定にして時間 t の関数としてかんがえても，t を一定にして x の関数としてかんがえても単振動と同じ式で表わされる。

用いる	mochi-iru	to use

…とした	"we supposed that...", "it was supposed that..."

1. 上の式を導く場合，物体間の作用は考えなくてよいものとした。

2. ここに示した波動の式では，正弦波は x 軸の正の向きに進むものとした。

(verb)＋場合	(verb)＋baai	in... -ing, when... -ing
かんがえなくてよい	kangaenakute yoi	we may neglect
波動	hadō	wave motion

…のようになる	"it turns out to be... ", "it is the same as..."

1. x 方向に速度 v で進む正弦波を式で表わすと (2) 式のようになる。

2. 地球の及ぼす引力は，その質量が地球の重心にあつまった場合の引力のようになる。

重心	jūshin	center of gravity
あつまる	atsumaru	to be concentrated, gathered

| …に伴なって | "(along) with..." "in accordance with..." |

1. ニュートンの法則によれば，物体に加わる力の増加に伴なって物体の得る加速度は増大する。

2. 空気の体積は，圧力の増大に伴なって減少する。

…によれば	…ni yoreba	according to...
加わる	kuwawaru	to be added
体積	taiseki	volume
減少する	genshō suru	to decrease

| 前後に | "back and forth"; "before and after"; "in front of and behind" |

1. ピストンは，シリンダーのなかで前後に周期運動を行なっている。

2. 衝突の前後に2物体のもつ運動量はそれぞれ変化するが，その和は変わらない。

3. 一直線上にばねで結合された質点のあつまりにおいて，一つの質点が前後に振動しはじめたとすれば，その前後にある質点に振動がつたわり，振動は次第にひろがって行く。

ピストン	pisuton	piston
シリンダー	shirindā	cylinder
ばね	bane	spring
結合する	ketsugō suru	to join together
質点	shitten	mass point
あつまり	atsumari	collection
つたわる	tsutawaru	to be transmitted, travel, pass
次第に	shidai ni	gradually
ひろがる	hirogaru	to spread
ひろがって行く	hirogatte iku	to spread (and to continue to do so)

SUPPLEMENTARY READINGS

A. 合成(振動)	gōsei(shindō)	resultant(vibration)
常に	tsune ni	always
向かう	mukau	to be directed towards
かつ	katsu	moreover, in addition
正の	sei no	positive
方程式	hōtei-shiki	equation
…となる	…to naru	is..., becomes...

一般解	ippan-kai	general solution
余弦	yogen	cosine
角振動数	kaku-shindō-sū	circular frequency
よぶ	yobu	to call
振動数	shindō-sū	oscillation frequency
同一の	dōitsu no	identical
…について	…ni tsuite	about…, concerning…
述べる	noberu	to explain, mention
合変位	gō-hen'i	resultant displacement
もとの	moto no	original
異なる	kotonaru	to be different, be unlike
横軸	yokojiku	the horizontal axis, abscissa
図の上で	zu no ue de	in the figure (diagram)
加え合わせる	kuwae-awaseru	to combine, add together
曲線	kyokusen	curve
求められた…	motomerareta…	the sought-for…, the desired…

単振動の合成　(BN 83–84)

x 軸上を運動する質量 m の質点が常に原点に向かい, かつ原点からの距離 $|x|$ に比例する力 $-kx$ (k＝正の定数) を受けているとき, 運動方程式は $m\dfrac{d^2x}{dt^2}=-kx$ となる。その一般解は単振動を表わす式

$$x=a\,\sin(\omega t+\varepsilon)\quad (a,\ \varepsilon=定数,\ a>0,\ \omega>0)$$

となる (余弦関数の形で表わすこともできる)。ここに　$\omega=\sqrt{k/m}$ は角振動数とよばれるもので, 振動の周期 T および振動数 v との関係は

$$T=2\pi/\omega,\ v=\omega/2\pi.$$

次に二つの単振動が同一質点に同時に重なる場合の合成振動について述べよう。

(1) 同一直線上の同周期の単振動

　　このような二つの単振動を

$$x_1=\ a_1\sin(\omega t+t_1),\ x_2=a_2\sin(\omega t+t_2)$$

と表わせば, 合変位 $x=x_1+x_2$ は

$$x=a\,\sin\,(\omega t+\varepsilon)$$

となる。これはもとと同じ周期の単振動である。

(2) 同一直線上の周期の異なる単振動

　　横軸に時刻 t を縦軸に変位をとって, それぞれの単振動を表わす正弦曲線をえがき, 各時刻におけるそれらの変位を図の上で加え合わせれば, 合成振動を表わす曲線をえ

がくことができる。このようにして求められた合成振動は一般に単振動とはならない。

B.　変動　　　　　　　　　hendō　　　　　　　　　changes, fluctuation
　　同様に　　　　　　　　dōyō ni　　　　　　　　in the same way;　similarly
　　負の　　　　　　　　　fu no　　　　　　　　　negative
　　一般式　　　　　　　　ippan-shiki　　　　　　general equation
　　偏微分　　　　　　　　hen-bibun　　　　　　　partial differential
　　みたす　　　　　　　　mitasu　　　　　　　　to satisfy
　　特に　　　　　　　　　toku ni　　　　　　　　especially
　　…に対応する　　　　　…ni taiō suru　　　　　to correspond to...
　　導き得る（＝導くことができる）
　　　　　　　　　　　　　michibiki-uru　　　　　can be derived

波を表わす式　（BN 88–89）

　媒質の変動を表わす変数を y とし，波形を変えずに x 軸の正の方向に一定の速さ v で進む波を考え，$t=0$ の波形を $y_0=f(x)$ とする。

　t 秒後には波は vt だけ進むから，時刻 t に座標 x に起きる y の値は座標 $x-vt$ における y_0 に等しい。したがって，

$$y=f(x-vt) \qquad (3.19)$$

となる。同様に x の負の方向に進む波では

$$y=g(x+vt) \qquad (3.20)$$

となる。(3.19), (3.20) は波を表わす一般式であるが次の偏微分方程式をみたす。

$$\frac{\partial^2 y}{\partial t^2} = v^2 \frac{\partial^2 y}{\partial x^2} \qquad (3.21)$$

(3.21) を波動方程式とよぶ。

　特に $t=0$ の波形が正弦曲線 $y_0=a \sin(kx-\varepsilon)$ で与えられるときには，(3.19) に対応する式は $y=a \sin[k(x-vt)-\varepsilon]$ となるが，

$$k=\omega/v \qquad (3.22)$$

と $\sin(-\theta)=-\sin\theta$ の関係を用いると，

$$y=-a \sin\left\{\omega\left(t-\frac{x}{v}\right)+\varepsilon\right\} \qquad (3.23)$$

が得られる。同様にして，(3.20) に対応する式として，

$$y=a \sin\left\{\omega\left(t+\frac{x}{v}\right)-\varepsilon\right\} \qquad (3.24)$$

を導き得る。(3.23), (3.24) は正弦波を表わす式である。

C.　定常波　　　　　　　　teijō-ha　　　　　　　　stationary wave

波長	hachō	wave length
相等しい	ai-hitoshii	equal
…とおけば（=…とすれば）		
	…to okeba	if we take…, if we put…
…とみることができる	…to miru koto ga dekiru	can be thought of as…,
		can be considered as…
位相	isō	phase

定 常 波 (BN 91)

振幅，波長，速さの相等しい二つの正弦波が，同一直線上を反対向きに進んでいるとき，それらを

$$y_1 = a \sin(\omega t - kx)$$

$$y_2 = a \sin(\omega t + kx)$$

と表わせば，合成波 $y = y_1 + y_2$ は

$$y = 2a \cos kx \sin \omega t$$

となる。

$$A = |2a \cos kx|$$

とおけば，A は座標 x の点における合成振動の振幅を表わすとみることができる。この場合，合成波はすべての所で同じ位相で振動し，またその波は進行しない。

D.	われわれの	ware-ware no	our
	耳	mimi	ears
	…に接する	…ni sessuru	to come in contact with…
	感ずる	kanzuru	to feel
	多い	ōi	frequent
	しかし	shikashi	but, yet, however
	流体	ryūtai	fluid
	固体	kotai	solid
	…の中を	…no naka o	through…
	弾性	dansei	elastic
	称する	shōsuru	to call, designate
	人	hito	people
	毎秒	maibyō	per second
	位	gurai	about, approximately
	超音波	chō-onpa	ultrasound wave
	気体中の	kitai-chū no	in a gas
	音速	onsoku	speed of sound
	理論値	riron-chi	theoretical value

1気圧の下で	ichi-kiatsu no moto de	at l atmosphere pressure
実測値	jissoku-chi	actual measured value
水中の	sui-chū no	in water
やく	yaku	approximately
最大値	saidai-chi	maximum value
鉄	tetsu	iron

音　(BN 100–101)

ふつう音波といえば，空気の縦波と考えるが，これはわれわれの耳が空気に接しているので，空気の縦波を音として感ずる場合が多いからである。しかし，一般に流体や固体の中を伝わる弾性縦波をすべて音波と称することができる。人が音として感ずる空気の振動数は，毎秒16から20,000位で，これより振動数の大きい音を超音波とよぶ。気体中の音の速さは，

$$c=\sqrt{\gamma p/\rho} \quad (\gamma=C_p/C_v)$$

で与えられるが，空気中の音速の理論値をこの式から求めれば，0°C, 1 気圧の下で331m/secとなり，実測値は 331.45m/sec である。水中の音速は，やく1500m/secであるが，音速の最大値は固体中に生じる。例えば，鉄では音速がやく 5000m/sec である。

E.   The following reading is taken from the 1958 edition of 理化学辞典 a physical science dictionary. Thus, the description is rather terse and sentences are not always grammatically complete.

円関数	en-kansū	circular functions

(Note: in older texts 関数. is written 函数 We will use this form occasionally without *furigana* so that the reader will learn this character as well.)

正接	seisetsu	tangent
余接	yosetsu	cotangent
正割	seikatsu	secant
余割	yokatsu	cosecant
総称	sōshō	general term, generic name
定義	teigi	definition
仕方	shikata	way, method
指数関数	shisū-kansū	exponential function
実数	jissū	real number
いずれも（＝どれも）	izuremo	everyone of them, any one of them

三 角 函 数　(2RJ 525)

円函数ということもある。sin *x* （正弦函数），cos *x* （余弦函数），tan *x* （正接函数），

cot x (余接函数), sec x (正割函数), cosec x(余割函数) の総称。いろいろの定義の仕方があるが，例えば指数函数 e^{ix} ($i=\sqrt{-1}$, x は実数) を用いれば，

$$\sin x=\frac{1}{2i}(e^{ix}-e^{-ix}),\ \cos x=\frac{1}{2}(e^{ix}+e^{-ix})$$

となる。また $\tan x=\dfrac{\sin x}{\cos x}$, $\cot x=\dfrac{\cos x}{\sin x}$, $\sec x=\dfrac{1}{\cos x}$, $\mathrm{cosec}\,x=\dfrac{1}{\sin x}$ であり，いずれも 2π の周期をもつ。

F. This section consists of brief definitions adapted from *Rika-gaku Jiten* (2RJ) and *Kōjien* (KJE).

1) (正)三角形　　　　(sei)sankakkei　　　　(equilateral) triangle
　　各辺　　　　　　kakuhen　　　　　　every side

正三角形は各辺の長さの相等しい三角形である。等角三角形ともよばれる。
(KJE 1181)

2) 正方形　　　　　sei-hōkei　　　　　a square
　　四つ　　　　　　yottsu　　　　　　four
　　辺　　　　　　　hen　　　　　　　side
　　及び　　　　　　oyobi　　　　　　and
　　内角　　　　　　naikaku　　　　　internal angles
　　四辺形　　　　　shihen-kei　　　　quadrilateral

正方形は四つの辺及び四つの内角がそれぞれ相等しい四辺形である。
(KJE 1190)

3) 平行四辺形　　　heikō-shihen-kei　　parallelogram
　　二組　　　　　　futakumi　　　　　two sets
　　相対する辺　　　sōtai suru hen　　　opposite sides
　　互いに　　　　　tagai ni　　　　　mutually

平行四辺形は，二組の相対する辺がそれぞれ互いに平行する四辺形である。
(KJE 1914)

4) 媒質内　　　　　baishitsu-nai　　　in the (conducting) medium
　　サイクル　　　　saikuru　　　　　cycle
　　(最大) 音圧　　(saidai) on'atsu　　(maximum) sound pressure

音波がない場合に媒質内の点の圧力が P_0, 音波がある場合にその点の圧力が P_0+P であれば，P が音圧である。また1サイクルの間での P の最大値を最大音圧という。
(2RJ 204)

5) 進化論　　　　　shinka-ron　　　　theory of evolution

とは（＝というのは）	to wa	See Explanatory Note 1, Lesson 1.
あらゆる	arayuru	all
生物	seibutsu	living things
最も	mottomo	exceedingly
原始	genshi	primitive
種々に	shuju ni	variously
進化する	shinka suru	to evolve, to develop
説	setsu	view, opinion, theory
種の起源	Shu no Kigen	Origin of Species
本	hon	book
体系づける	taikei-zukeru	to systematize

進化論とはあらゆる生物が最も簡単な原始生物から種々に進化した結果であるという説である。ダーウィンはこの説を「種の起源」という本に体系づけた。

(KJE 1103)

6) 決定する	kettei suru	to determine
空間	kūkan	space
力の場	chikara no ba	force field
万有引力	ban'yū-inryoku	universal gravitation
だけできまる	dake de kimaru	is determined only by
ポテンシャル	potensharu	potential

力の場．物体にはたらく力が物体の位置および速度で決定するとき，その空間を力の場という。万有引力のような場合には力が空間の位置だけできまり，ポテンシャル ϕ を用いて，$-\mathrm{grad}\,\phi$ の形で力の場を表わす。

(2RJ 842)

FINAL TRANSLATION TEST

振幅の小さい水の波が進んで行く場合，時間が過ぎても波形はくずれない。これは，波動の進行速度が振幅の大きさに関係なく一定であるからである。しかしながら，このことは振幅が大きくなるとなりたたなくなる。振幅が大きい場合には，空気のなかの音波でも水の波でもその進行速度は振幅の関数となる。変位の大きい点ほど速く進行するので，波動の進行とともに波形はくずれる。すなわち，初めは一つの周期をもった正弦波であったものでも，周期の違った正弦波の重なった波形になってしまう。相次ぐ点での圧力変化が大きくなりキャビテーションを生じる。物体上でキャビテーションが起こった所は，各点

ではげしい圧力変化と水の衝突のために化学的変化も起こる。

　水のなかで大きな速度で運動する物体に対しては，キャビテーションの起こるのをふせ
ぐ方法と平行して，キャビテーションが起こってもこれにたえる物質を用いることが最も
重要である。

LESSON 7

第 七 課

K A N J I

理	333	RI
	2942	
想	660	SŌ
	1728	
分	133	FUN BUN
	578	wa (keru)
子	31	SHI SU
	1260	ko
温	162	ON
	2634	
明	141	MEI
	2110	aka (rui) aki (raka)
低	677	TEI
	406	hiku (i)
常	642	JŌ
	1364	tsune
有	523	YŪ
	3727	a (ru)
限	601	GEN
	4987	kagi (ru)

導	684	DŌ
	1354	michibi (ku)
全	267	ZEN
	384	matta (ku)
成	439	SEI
	1799	na (ru)
立	149	RITSU
	3343	{ta (teru) {ta (tsu)
状	818	JŌ
	2839	
態	840	TAI
	1743	
特	685	TOKU
	2860	
素	658	SO SU
	3511	
性	645	SEI SHŌ
	1666	
計	201	KEI
	4312	

READING SELECTION

理想気体	risō-kitai	ideal gas
モル	moru	mole
…に対しては	…ni taishite wa	for…, in…
分子	bunshi	molecule
ガス定数	gasu-teisū	gas constant
もし	moshi	if
保つ	tamotsu	to maintain, hold
温度	ondo	temperature
体積	taiseki	volume

絶対温度	zettai-ondo	absolute temperature
確かめる	tashikameru	ascertain, confirm
シャルルの法則	Sharuru no hōsoku	Charles' Law
…にほかならない	…ni hoka naranai	is nothing but…, is just…
ボイルの法則	Boiru no hōsoku	Boyle's Law
上の式	ue no shiki	the above equation
さて	sate	well, now, so
明らかな	akiraka na	clear, distinct
最低の	saitei no	lowest
…においては	…ni oite wa	at…, as for…, by…
少しでも	sukoshi de mo	even a little
(…を)かければ	(…o)kakereba	if we apply…
…はずである	…hazu de aru	it is expected that…; should…
非常に	hijō ni	very
有限の	yūgen no	finite
…限り	…kagiri	as long as…
…得る（＝…ことができる）	…eru (or…uru)	to be able to…
実は	jitsu wa	actually, in fact
導く	michibiku	to derive
限りなく	kagiri-naku	infinitely, extremely
仮定する	katei suru	to suppose, assume, hypothesize
…が完全に成り立つ	…ga kanzen ni naritatsu	…holds exactly
仮想的な	kasō-teki na	hypothetical, imaginary
じゅうぶんに	jūbun ni	sufficiently
希薄な	kihaku na	dilute
状態	jōtai	condition, state
特に	toku ni	in particular
水素	suiso	hydrogen
…の場合には	…no baai ni wa	in the case of…
ほぼ	hobo	almost, nearly
(…と)みなす	(…to)minasu	to regard, consider (as…)
性質	seishitsu	property
利用する	riyō suru	to utilize, use
温度計	ondo-kei	thermometer

理　想　気　体　(B 138)

1 モルの気体に対しては，その分子数[1]を N とすると，

$$pV = NkT = RT \tag{1}$$

となる。R はガス定数といい，その値は $R = 8.317$ [2] ジュール／度・モルである。

この関係は，もし気体の圧力を一定に保ち，温度を変えれば [3]，体積は絶対温度に比例することを示す。これは実験で確かめたシャルルの法則にほかならない。もし温度を一定に保てば，この関係はボイルの法則を示す。したがって上の式で示される関係をボイル・シャルルの法則という。

さて，（1）式から明らかなように，最低の温度 $0°K$ においては [4]，気体の体積は少しでも圧力をかければ 0 になるはずである。

非常に小さいとはいっても，気体分子が有限 [5] の大きさをもつ限り [6]，このようなことはあり得ないが [7]，実は，$p = \frac{1}{3} m\bar{v^2} (N/V)$ という式の関係を導くときに気体分子の大きさは限りなく小さいと仮定していたのである [8]。この関係 [9] が完全に成り立つような仮想的な気体を「理想気体」という [10]。しかし，どんな気体でも，じゅうぶんに希薄 [11] な状態では，特に水素 [12] のような小さい気体分子の場合には，ほぼ理想気体とみなすことができる。このような気体の性質を利用した [13] 温度計が「気体温度計」である。

RISŌ-KITAI

Ichi moru no kitai ni taishite wa, sono bunshi-sū [1] o N to suru to,

$$pV = NkT = RT \tag{1}$$

to naru. R wa gasu teisū to ii, sono atai wa $R = 8.317$ [2] jūru-pā-do-moru de aru.

Kono kankei wa, moshi kitai no atsuryoku o ittei ni tamochi, ondo o kaereba, [3] taiseki wa zettai-ondo ni hirei suru koto o shimesu. Kore wa jikken de tashikameta Sharuru no hōsoku ni hoka naranai. Moshi ondo o ittei ni tamoteba, kono kankei wa Boiru no hōsoku o shimesu. Shitagatte ue no shiki de shimesareru kankei o Boiru-Sharuru no hōsoku to iu.

Sate ichi shiki kara akiraka na yō ni, saitei no ondo reido Kerubin ni oite wa, [4] kitai no taiseki wa sukoshi de mo atsuryoku o kakereba rei (zero) ni naru hazu de aru.

Hijō ni chiisai to wa itte mo kitai-bunshi ga yūgen [5] no ōkisa o motsu kagiri, [6] kono yō na koto wa ari-enai [7] ga, jitsu wa, $p = \frac{1}{3} m\bar{v^2} (N/V)$ to iu shiki no kankei o michibiku toki ni kitai-bunshi no ōkisa wa kagiri naku chiisai to katei shite ita no de aru. [8] Kono kankei [9] ga kanzen ni naritatsu yō na kasō-teki na kitai o "risō-kitai" to iu. [10] Shikashi, donna kitai de mo jūbun ni kihaku [11] na jōtai de wa, toku ni suiso [12] no yō na chiisai kitai-bunshi no baai ni wa, hobo risō-kitai to minasu koto ga dekiru. Kono yō na kitai no seishitsu o riyō shita [13] ondo-kei ga "kitai-ondo-kei" de aru.

THE IDEAL GAS

If we let N be the number of molecules in one mole of gas, then

$$pV = NkT = RT. \tag{1}$$

We call R the gas constant, and its value is 8.317 joules/°K mole.

This relation shows that, if we keep the pressure constant and vary the temperature, the volume will be proportional to the absolute temperature. This is simply the experimentally determined Law of Charles. If we keep the temperature constant, this relation gives Boyle's Law. Therefore, we call the relation denoted by the above equation the Law of Boyle and Charles.

Now as Eq. (1) clearly shows, at the lowest temperature 0°K, the volume of the gas should become zero if even the slightest pressure is applied.

Such a result would be impossible so long as the molecules have a finite size, however tiny we say that may be, and in fact the gas molecules were assumed to be infinitesimally small in deriving the expression $p = \frac{1}{3} m \overline{v^2} (N/V)$. A hypothetical gas for which this relation holds exactly is called an ideal gas. In sufficiently rarefied states, however, any gas, especially one with small gas molecules like hydrogen, can be regarded as essentially ideal. A thermometer employing these properties of gases is called a gas thermometer.

EXPLANATORY NOTES

(1) sono bunshi-sū	*Sono* (literally "its") refers to "ichi-moru no kitai".
(2) 8.317	Read *"hachi-ten-san-ichi-shichi"*.
(3) moshi...tamochi ...kaereba	If we maintain... and if we change....
(4) ni oite wa	Literary construction; in spoken language one would say *saitei no ondo de wa*.
(5) yūgen	The opposite of *yūgen* 有限 (having a limit, i.e. finite) is *mugen* 無限 (no limit, i.e., infinite).
(6) kagiri	When *kagiri* follows an affirmative or negative verb it may be translated "as long as"; after a negative verb, an alternative translation is "unless + affirmative verb".
(7) ari-enai	The verb stem + *eru* is equivalent to the plain present + *koto ga dekiru*; e.g., *kaki-eru = kaku koto ga dekiru*.
(8) ...shite ita no de aru	The *no de aru* is used to emphasize the statement; it can be omitted in translation.
(9) kono kankei, etc.	*Kankei* is the subject of *naritatsu*.
(10) *A o B to iu*	"we designate *A* by *B*," or "we call *A*, *B*".

(11) kihaku　　　　　　　The opposite of *kihaku* 希薄 (dilute) is *nōkō* 濃厚 (concentrated).

(12) suiso　　　　　　　A few other elements:

　　　　　　　　　　　tanso　　炭素　(carbon)
　　　　　　　　　　　sanso　　酸素　(oxygen)
　　　　　　　　　　　chisso　窒素　(nitrogen)
　　　　　　　　　　　enso　　塩素　(chlorine)

(13) riyō shita　　　　　This is past tense in Japanese, but is best translated by the present tense in English.

CONSTRUCTION EXAMPLES

| …に対しては | "for…" |

1. 理想気体に対しては，ボイル・シャルルの法則が成り立つ。
2. 速さ v, 周期 T, 半径 r, の円運動に対しては $v=2\pi r/T$。
3. この法則は理想気体に対してのみ用いるべきである。

　　　　のみ　　　　　　　　nomi　　　　　　　only
　　　　(verb)べきである　(*verb*) beki de aru　ought to (verb)

| …となる | "becomes……" |

1. 理想気体の法則は，温度一定の場合，ボイルの法則となる。
2. x 方向に速度 v で進行する音波を式で表わすと，$y=A\sin\dfrac{2\pi}{T}\left(t-\dfrac{x}{v}\right)$ となる。

| もし…ば | "if…" |

1. もし気体の体積を一定に保ち，温度を上げれば，圧力は増大する。
2. もし空気がなければ，生物は生存できない。

　　　　生存する　　　　　seizon suru　　　　　to live, exist

| …にほかならない | "is nothing but…" |

1. 加速度とは，単位時間あたりの速度変化にほかならない。
2. 等速円運動は，周期的運動の一つにほかならない。

| …においては | "at…, for…" |

1. 絶対温度の 0°K においては，ヘリウムは気体ではない。
2. 単振動においては，加速度は変位に比例する。

| 少しでも | "even a little" |

1. 気体分子が少しでもひろがりをもつ限り，理想気体とはいえない。

2. 化学変化においては，少しでも自由エネルギーが減少すれば反応がその方向に進行する。

ひろがり	hirogari	extent
…とはいえない	…to wa ienai	it is impossible to call…
反応	hannō	reaction

| …ば，…はずである | "if…, …would (be expected to)…" |

1. 地球の引力がもっと小さければ，地球上の物体はもっとかるいはずである。

2. (1)式を(2)式に用いれば，最後の結果が得られるはずである。

| もっと | motto | more |
| 最後の | saigo no | the last |

| …とはいっても | "even if we say that…" |

1. 温度が大変低いとはいっても，絶対温度の $0°K$ でない限り，分子運動はとまらない。

2. 物体が重いとはいっても，質量が限りなく大きいのでなければ，力を加えれば加速度を生じる。

大変	taihen	very
とまる	tomaru	to stop
加える	kuwaeru	to apply

| …限り | "as long as" |

1. どんな運動でも，周期運動である限り，単振動を重ね合わせて表わすことができる。

2. 大変少なくても気体分子がある限り，気体の体積は0にはならない。

| 重ね合わせる | kasane-awaseru | to superpose |

| …ない限り | "unless+affirmative verb," "as long as+negative verb" |

1. 気体分子の大きさが0にならない限り，圧力を加えて気体の体積が0になるということはあり得ない。

2. 力が作用しない限り，物体の速度は一定である。

3. ボイル・シャルルの法則は，理想気体に対してのみ用いるべきものであるが，温度

が特に低くない限り，常に成り立つと考えてよい。

…と考えてよい	…to kangaete yoi	we may consider that

---

verb stem＋得ない	"cannot..."

1. 力を加えても変形しないような物体はあり得ない。

2. 衝突の前後において，2物体の運動量の和が変化するということは起こり得ない。

変形	henkei	deformation

…は（を）…とみなす	"we regard...as..."

1. 地球全体の質量が及ぼす引力をもとめる場合には，その全質量が地球の重心にあつまっているとみなすことができる。

2. 0⁰ C, 1気圧における空気1gの体積をもとめよ。ただし，空気を理想気体とみなす。

もとめる	motomeru	to seek
重心	jūshin	center of gravity
あつまる	atsumaru	to be collected

SUPPLEMENTARY READINGS

A.	状態（方程）式	jōtai-(hōtei)-shiki	equation of state
	実在の	jitsuzai no	real, actual
	…のうち	...no uchi	among...
	アルゴン	arugon	argon
	等	nado	and so forth; such as
	みたす	mitasu	to satisfy
	標準	hyōjun	standard
	高温（圧）	kō-on(atsu)	high temperature(pressure)
	低温（圧）	tei-on(atsu)	low temperature(pressure)
	ずれを生ずる	zure o shōzuru	to show deviations
	…を除いて	...o nozoite	excepting...
	運動論	undō-ron	kinetic theory
	実際の	jissai no	real, actual
	質点	shitten	mass point
	さらに	sara ni	further
	分子間の	bunshi-kan no	intermolecular
	相互（の）	sōgo(no)	mutual
	中心	chūshin	center
	…までしか近寄れない	...made shika chika-yorenai	can approach only as far as...

容器の中に	yōki no naka ni	inside the container
空間	kūkan	space
全体では	zentai de wa	in all, in the whole
占める	shimeru	to occupy
全体積	zen-taiseki	entire volume
4倍	yonbai	four times
内部	naibu	within
周囲の	shūi no	surrounding
釣り合う	tsuri-au	to balance
表面	hyōmen	surface
内方に	naihō ni	inwardly
壁	kabe	wall
減る	heru	to decrease
影響	eikyō	influence
数	kazu	number
密度	mitsudo	density
結局	kekkyoku	in the end, finally
…より…小さくなる	…yori…chiisaku naru	becomes smaller than…
ゆえに（＝したがって）	yue ni	consequently, therefore
…の代（わ）りに	…no kawari ni	instead of…
入れる	ireru	to insert
そこで	soko de	then

VAN DER WAALS の状態式　(BN 132–133)

実在の気体のうち，空気，水素，アルゴン等は標準状態(0⁰C, 1気圧）でほぼ Boyle や Charles の法則をみたすが，低温高圧ではずれを生ずるし，どんな気体でも高温低圧の場合を除いて，一般には Boyle-Charles の法則をみたさない。気体運動論では分子の大きさを考えていなかったが，実際の分子は質点ではなくて大きさをもち，さらに分子間の相互作用がある。

分子に大きさがあれば，二つの分子の中心は分子の直径の距離までしか近寄れない。容器の中にある分子が運動できる空間はそれだけ小さくなり，全体では各分子の体積の和に関係するある値 b だけ小さくなる。（分子の半径を r，分子数を N とすると，$b=4N\frac{4}{3}\pi r^3$，すなわち分子の占める全体積の4倍である。）

気体の内部では，一つの分子に対してその周囲の分子が及ぼす力は全体として釣り合っているが，気体の表面にある分子は内部の分子に引かれて内方に向う加速度を受け，したがって分子が壁に及ぼす圧力は減る。この引力が圧力に及ぼす影響は表面分子の内方にあって，引力を及ぼす分子の数，したがって気体の密度 ρ に比例し，また衝突する表面分子

の数（これも ρ に比例する）に比例するから，結局 ρ^2 に比例するが，ρ は体積 V に反比例するから，実在気体について測定される圧力 P は理想気体の圧力 P_{id} より a/V^2（a は比例定数）だけ小さくなる（$P=P_{\mathrm{id}}-a/V^2$）。ゆえに，理想気体の状態式の P_{id} の代りに $(P+a/V^2)$ を入れなければならない。そこで実在気体の状態式は 1 モルについて

$$\{P+(a/V^2)\}(V-b)=RT$$

となる。

B.	気体中では	kitai-chū de wa	within a gas
	多数	tasū	many
	飛び回る	tobi-mawaru	to fly about
	考える	kangaeru	to imagine
	性質	seishitsu	property
	説明する	setsumei suru	to explain
	まず	mazu	first of all
	考えてみよう	kangaete miyō	let us consider (and see how it turns out)
	一辺	ippen	one side
	立方体	rippō-tai	cube
	容器中に	yōki-chū ni	inside a container
	閉じこめる	toji-komeru	to confine
	壁	kabe	wall
	垂直な	suichoku na	perpendicular
	直交座標（=直角座標）	chokkō-zahyō	rectangular coordinates
	飛ぶ	tobu	to fly
	飛んできた分子	tonde kita bunshi	molecules which come (flying)
	ぶつかる	butsukaru	to strike
	成分	seibun	component
	壁面	hekimen	wall surface
	影響	eikyō	influence
	効果	kōka	effect
	残る	nokoru	to remain
	1個	ikko	one
	はね返る	hane-kaeru	to recoil, bounce back
	平均	heikin	average; arithmetic mean
	起こる	okoru	to occur, happen
	総数	sōsū	total number
	t 秒間に1回の割合で	t byōkan ni ikkai no wari-ai de	at a rate of once every t seconds

…における	…ni okeru	in…
着目する	chakumoku suru	to fix one's attention on
他の	ta no	another
何回も	nankai mo	many times; frequently
ふたたび	futatabi	again
帰ってくる	kaette kuru	to come back
わからないわけである	wakaranai wake de aru	we cannot know, do not know
回数	kaisū	frequency
面積	menseki	area
全く	mattaku	entirely; completely
(不)規則	(fu)kisoku	(ir)regular
勝手の	katte no	arbitrary
一様に	ichiyō ni	uniformly
入りまじる	iri-majiru	to be mixed with
…の2乗の平均	…no nijō no heikin	mean-square…
断わる	kotowaru	to warn
条件	jōken	condition
いいかえると	ii-kaeru to	(to say it) in other words
ただ	tada	merely, simply

気体の分子運動とボイルの法則　(B 134–136)

　気体中では多数の分子が絶えず飛び回っていると考えれば，気体のいろいろな性質を説明することができる。

　まず，気体の体積と圧力との関係を考えてみよう。図1のように一辺 L の立方体の容器中に一定量の気体が閉じこめられているとする。壁Aに垂直な方向を x 軸として直交座標 x, y, z をとる。いろいろの方向から飛んできた分子がこの壁にぶつかって力を及ぼす。各分子の速度成分のうち，壁面に平行な成分 v_y, v_z の影響はないから，壁に垂直な成分 v_x の効果だけが残る。

　1個の分子の質量を m とすれば，衝突前の運動量は mv_x，はね返った後の運動量は $-mv_x$ であるから，1個の分子の衝突によって，平均としては $2mv_x$ だけの運動量の変化が起こる。容器中の分子の総数を N とし，壁に対するこのような分子の衝突が，すべての分子についてそれぞれ平均 t 秒間に1回の割合で起こるとすれば，単位時間における運動量の変化は力に等しいから，壁に垂直の方向に及ぼす力は $N \cdot 2mv_x/t$ となる。

　さて，この t については，もし1個の分子に着目すれば，壁からはね返った後，他の分子と何回も衝突をするから，いつふたたびこの壁に帰ってくるかわからないわけであるが，

多数の分子についての平均をとれば，その時間 t は $t=2L/v_x$ 秒になる。したがって1秒間に壁Aに衝突する回数は $1/t=v_x/2L$ になる。

すなわち，この壁に及ぼす力は $Nmv_x{}^2/L$ となる。壁の面積は L^2 であるから，壁に及ぼす圧力Pは $Nmv_x{}^2/L^3$ である。L^3 は容器の体積Vにほかならない。すなわち

$$P=mv_x{}^2\frac{N}{V} \tag{1}$$

さて，分子の平均速度 v とその速度成分 v_x, v_y, v_z の間には，図2からわかるように，次の関係がある。

$$v^2=v_x{}^2+v_y{}^2+v_z{}^2 \tag{2}$$

分子の運動は全く不規則で，勝手の方向のものが一様に入りまじっていると考えられるから，多数の分子について速度の2乗の平均$(\overline{v_x{}^2}, \overline{v_y{}^2}, \overline{v_z{}^2}, \overline{v^2})$ をとれば次の関係が成り立つ。

$$\overline{v_x{}^2}=\overline{v_y{}^2}=\overline{v_z{}^2}=\frac{1}{3}\overline{v^2} \tag{3}$$

したがって，容器の壁に及ぼす圧力Pは次のように表わされる。

$$P=\frac{1}{3}m\overline{v^2}\frac{N}{V} \tag{4}$$

初めに特に断わらなかったが，ここで質量mの分子が平均速度 v で飛び回っているとしたが，これにはある一定の温度でという条件があったのである。いいかえると，$\frac{1}{3}m\overline{v^2}$ はただ温度だけによって定まる量である。

したがって，(4) 式は温度一定のとき，一定量の気体の体積は圧力に反比例することを示す。これはボイルの法則にほかならない。

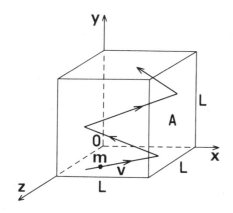

図 1. 壁に衝突する気体分子

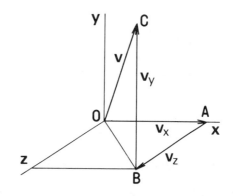

図 2. 分子の速度と速度成分

C. エネルギー等分配　　　　enerugii tō-bunpai　　　　equipartition of energy

単原子分子　　　　　　tan-genshi-bunshi　　　　monatomic molecule

…から成る　　　　　　…kara naru　　　　　　to consist of…

きめる　　　　　　　　kimeru　　　　　　　　to decide

ため　　　　　　　　　tame　　　　　　　　　for (the sake of)

三つ　　　　　　　　　mittsu　　　　　　　　three

考えればよい　　　　　kangaereba yoi　　　　we need only to consider

自由度　　　　　　　　jiyū-do　　　　　　　degrees of freedom

とは（＝というのは）　to wa　　　　　　　　(see Lesson 1, Explanatory
　　　　　　　　　　　　　　　　　　　　　　　Note 1)

配置　　　　　　　　　haichi　　　　　　　　arrangement, configuration

必要な　　　　　　　　hitsuyō na　　　　　　necessary

二原子分子　　　　　　ni-genshi-bunshi　　　diatomic molecule

質量中心　　　　　　　shitsuryō-chūshin　　center of mass

…を通る　　　　　　　…o tōru　　　　　　　to pass through…

互いに　　　　　　　　tagai ni　　　　　　　mutually

直交　　　　　　　　　chokkō　　　　　　　　orthogonal

…のまわり　　　　　　…no mawari　　　　　　around…

回転　　　　　　　　　kaiten　　　　　　　　rotation

総計（＝合計）　　　　sōkei　　　　　　　　the sum total

証明できる　　　　　　shōmei dekiru　　　　can be proved,
　　　　　　　　　　　　　　　　　　　　　　　demonstrated

三原子分子　　　　　　san-genshi-bunshi　　triatomic molecule

…以上　　　　　　　　…ijō　　　　　　　　upwards of…; more
　　　　　　　　　　　　　　　　　　　　　　　than…

余り　　　　　　　　　amari　　　　　　　　too

…に対応する　　　　　…ni taiō suru　　　　to correspond to…

近似的に　　　　　　　kinji-teki ni　　　　approximately

多原子分子　　　　　　ta-genshi-bunshi　　polyatomic molecule

分子振動　　　　　　　bunshi-shindō　　　　molecular vibration

…に比して　　　　　　…ni hishite　　　　　compared to…;
　　　　　　　　　　　　　　　　　　　　　　　in comparison with…

はるかに　　　　　　　haruka ni　　　　　　by far, far and away

エネルギー等分配の法則

　単原子分子から成る理想気体の分子は，その運動をきめるための座標として x, y, z の三つを考えればよい。この場合分子の自由度は3である。一般に分子の自由度とは分子の位置とその分子内における原子の配置とをきめるのに必要な座標の数である。

単原子分子から成る理想気体の分子のもつエネルギー U は運動エネルギーだけから成るから

$$U = N\left[\frac{1}{2}m\overline{v^2}\right]$$

となる。理想気体の状態式を次の二つの形

$$PV = NkT$$

$$PV = \frac{1}{3}Nm\overline{v^2}$$

で表わせば，

$$U = \frac{3}{2}kT$$

という関係が導き得られる。そして，気体運動論において

$$\overline{v_x^2} = \overline{v_y^2} = \overline{v_z^2}$$

という関係が成り立つので

$$\frac{1}{2}m\overline{v_x^2} = \frac{1}{2}m\overline{v_y^2} = \frac{1}{2}m\overline{v_z^2} = \frac{1}{2}kT$$

を得る。すなわち一つの自由度当りの平均のエネルギーは $\frac{1}{2}kT$ に等しい。これをエネルギー等分配の法則という。

　二原子分子の場合には，原子の中心を結ぶ方向を z 方向とすると，分子の質量中心を通って互いに直交する x 軸と y 軸のまわりの回転があり，一つの軸のまわりの回転について自由度が一つ増すから，質量中心の運動の自由度 3 と合せて総計 5 である。そしてこの場合 x 軸，y 軸のまわりの運動エネルギーの平均値も $\frac{1}{2}kT$ であることが証明できる。したがって二原子分子の平均の運動エネルギーは $\left(\frac{5}{2}\right)kT$ となる。三原子分子以上では，原子数が余り大きくない限り，一般に x, y, z 軸のまわりの回転に対応する三つの自由度を加えればよく，平均の運動エネルギーは近似的に $\left(\frac{6}{2}\right)kT$ で表わされる。一般に多原子分子は分子振動があるが，その振動のエネルギーは $\left(\frac{1}{2}\right)kT$ に比して，はるかに小さい。

SOUND-ALIKE KANJI 同音異議の漢字

The following groups of *kanji* have the same *ON* readings. Identify each *kanji* by giving a sample compound (*jukugo*) in which the *kanji* appears. For example, in the pair "音, 温" we can identify the *kanji* as follows:

音：音波の音　　　　onpa no on　　　the *on* of *onpa*

温：温度の温　　　　ondo no on　　　the *on* of *ondo*

The Japanese frequently use ths method for identifying *kanji* in conversations when there may be some chance for misunderstanding. Hence, in addition to being a useful exercise for beginners, this type of drill will be found indispensable in learning how to communicate with Japanese people.

1. 間・関・観
2. 相・想
3. 測・則・速
4. 小・少・衝
5. 値・置・地
6. 加・化・過
7. 体・対・態
8. 用・要

FINAL TRANSLATION TEST

　ボイル・シャルルの法則は，気体温度，圧力，体積という三つの状態量と質量のうち三つの量が与えられて，のこりの一つをもとめる時有用である。最もよく現われるのは，質量，温度，圧力が与えられて体積をもとめる場合で，たとえば，0℃，1気圧における空気 1g の体積はいくらかというような時である。空気は，酸素と窒素とから成り立ち，酸素は全体の体積の $\frac{1}{5}$，窒素は $\frac{4}{5}$ を占めるものとして計算すればよい。もともとこの法則は，理想気体に対してのみ用いるべきものであるが，温度が特に低い場合をのぞいて常に成り立つと考えてよい。気体の 0°K ちかくの低温特性をとりあつかう場合に，この法則を用いてはならないことは明らかで，この時には，分子間の力を考えに入れ，分子の大きさは有限であるとして導かれた式を用いなければならない。ボイル・シャルルの法則は気体に関する問題をとりあつかう限り，かならずといってよいほどよく現われる，最も重要な法則の一つである。

LESSON 8
第 八 課
KANJI

程	846	TEI		減	775	GEN	
	3285	〔hodo〕			2637	{he(rasu) / he(ru)	
容	730	YŌ		密	239a	MITSU	
	1309				1316		
固	393	KO		取	238	SHŪ	
	1036	{kata(meru) / kata(maru)			3699	to(ru)	
構	785	KŌ		入	125	NYŪ	
	2343				574	{i(reru) / i(ru)	
考	74	KŌ		曲	381	KYOKU	
	3684	kanga(eru)			103	{ma(geru) / ma(garu)	
際	612	SAI		調	471	CHŌ	
	5018				4392	shira(beru)	
壁	270a	HEKI		極	382	KYOKU	
	1148	kabe			2305	〔kiwa(mete)〕	
近	195	KIN		個	603	KO	
	4671	chika(i)			489		
部	504	BU		界	170	KAI	
	4767				2998		
内	489	NAI		面	322	MEN	
	82	uchi			5087		

READING SELECTION

状態方程式	jōtai-hōtei-shiki	equation of state
不完全気体	fu-kanzen-kitai	imperfect gas
容積	yōseki	volume
広く	hiroku	widely
物質	busshitsu	substance
固有な	koyū na	characteristic
構成する	kōsei suru	to comprise, constitute, form
かたい	katai	rigid, hard
動き回る	ugoki-mawaru	to move around
実際の	jissai no	true

影響	eikyō	influence, effect
考慮する	kōryo suru	to consider, bear in mind
…の代りに	…no kawari ni	instead of…
…とおく	…to oku	we put…
さらに	sara ni	furthermore
分子間	bunshi-kan	between molecules
触れ合う	fure-au	to touch each other
壁	kabe	wall
近い	chikai	near
部分	bubun	part, portion
内側	uchigawa	inside
減ることになる	heru koto ni naru	turns out to be less
量	ryō	quantity
密度	mitsudo	density
内部	naibu	interior
従って	shitagatte	therefore
取り入れる	tori-ireru	to insert
計算	keisan	calculation
省略する	shōryaku suru	to omit
4倍	yonbai	four times
v に関して3次の	v ni kanshite sanji no	third order with respect to v
乗ずる	jō-zuru	to multiply
p を v に対して描く	p o v ni taishite egaku	to plot p versus v
第一	dai-ichi	first
曲線	kyokusen	curve
高い	takai	high
単調	tanchō	monotone
常に	tsune ni	usually
…に反して	…ni hanshite	in contrast to…
極大（小）値	kyokudai (shō)-chi	maximum (minimum) value
もつ	motsu	to have
範囲	han'i	extent, region, limits
3個の実数	sanko no jissū	three real numbers (個 is a counter)
存在する	sonzai suru	to exist
境目	sakaime	boundary line
臨界温度	rinkai-ondo	critical temperature
呼ぶ	yobu	to call
臨界温度より下の	rinkai-ondo yori shita no	below the critical temperature

極値	kyokuchi	extremum
圧縮する	asshuku suru	to compress
かえって	kaette	instead, on the contrary
減少する	genshō suru	to decrease
(不)安定	(fu)antei	(un)stable
実現する	jitsugen suru	to come true, be realized

…し得ない＝…することができない

そこで (＝ところで)	soko de	then
線分	senbun	line segment
交わる	majiwaru	to intersect
しかも	shikamo	furthermore
上(下)部	jō(ka)bu	upper (lower) part
囲む	kakomu	to surround
面積	menseki	area
端	hashi	end, tip
同一	dōitsu	identical
…に対応する	…ni taiō suru	to correspond to…
何となれば	nan to nareba	the reason for this is that…
積分	sekibun	integral
差	sa	difference
零	rei	zero
位相	isō	phase
互いにつり合う	tagai ni tsuri-au	to be in equilibrium (literally, to balance each other)

液体	ekitai	liquid
一方…他方	ippō…tahō	the one…the other
解釈する	kaishaku suru	to explain; interpret
飽和蒸気圧	hōwa-jōki-atsu	saturation vapor pressure
気(液)相	ki (eki) sō	gas (liquid) phase
著しい	ichijirushii	remarkable
同様に	dōyō ni	in the same way

VAN DER WAALS の状態方程式　(FK9–11)

不完全[1]気体の状態方程式として van der Waals の式

$$\left(p+\frac{a}{v^2}\right)(v-b)=kT \tag{1}$$

(p＝圧力,　v＝一分子あたりの容積[2]　k＝Boltzmann 定数,　T＝絶対温度) は広く用いら

れる。ここに *a* と *b* とは物質に固有な定数である。

この関係式は次のようにして導かれる。気体を構成する分子は有限[1]な直径 σ のかたい球であると考えれば，分子が理想気体の分子のように自由に動き回ることのできる空間の容積は実際の容積より小さい。この影響を考慮して，理想気体の状態式 $pv=kT$ の v の代りに $v-b$ とおく。さらに分子間には，分子が触れ合わない距離では引力が作用し，壁に近い部分の分子は内側に引かれる。その結果，実際の圧力 p は理想気体の圧力 p' より減ることになるが，その量は壁の近くにある分子の密度と，内部の分子の密度と[3]の積に比例すると考えられる。すなわち，$p=p'-a/v^2$。従って理想気体の状態式の p の代りに $p'=p+a/v^2$ を取り入れることになる。

分子の直径 σ と定数 b と[3]の間の関係は，ここでは計算を省略するが

$$b=\frac{2}{3}\pi\sigma^3 \tag{2}$$

すなわち，b は分子の容積の4倍である。

(1)は v に関して3次の方程式である。すなわち，v^2/p を乗ずれば，

$$v^3-\left(\frac{kT}{p}+b\right)v^2+\frac{a}{p}v-\frac{ab}{p}=0 \tag{3}$$

T を一定にして，p を v に対して描けば第1図の曲線が得られる。高い温度では曲線は単調であり，常に $(\partial p/\partial v)_T<0$ が成り立っている。これに反して，低い温度では曲線は極大値と極小値と[3]を一つずつもち，その範囲の p の値に対して方程式 (3) には3個の実数の v が存在する。その境目になる温度は「臨界温度」T_c と呼ばれ，$T>T_c$ では曲線は単調，$T<T_c$ では極値をもつ。

臨界温度より下の等温曲線については，極大と極小との間では $(\partial p/\partial v)_T>0$ となるが，これは圧縮すればかえって圧力が減少するという不安定な状態であり，実現し得ない。そこで図に示したように v 軸に平行な線分ABを引いて，3点で曲線と交わらせる。しかも，もとの曲線の内，この線分の上部にある部分と線分と[3]で囲まれる面積が，下部にある部分と線分とで囲まれる面積に等しいように描く。そうすれば，線分で結ばれた二つの端の点 A，B は，同一の Gibbs 自由エネルギー G （一分子あたり）をもつ二つの状態に対応する。何となれば[4]

$$\left(\frac{\partial G}{\partial p}\right)_T=v; \quad G_A-G_B=\int_B^A v\,dp \tag{4}$$

であるが，この積分は線分 AB の上部に囲まれた面積と下部に囲まれた面積との差に等しく，零となるからである。

従って，点 A と点 B と[3]に対応する二つの位相は，その圧力 p_s の下に互いにつり合い，一方は液体，他方は気体の状態と解釈される。p_s は温度 T における飽和蒸気圧である。圧

力がp_sより減少すれば自由エネルギーも減少するが，$(\partial G/\partial p)_T=v$ の関係によって，v の大きい気相の方が自由エネルギーの減少が著しく，安定になる。同様に $p>p_\mathrm{s}$ の圧力の下では，v の小さい液相の方が安定となる。

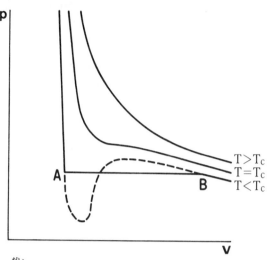

第1図　van der Waals 気体の等温曲線

VAN DER WAALS NO JŌTAI-HŌTEI-SHIKI

Fu-kanzen-kitai [1] no jōtai-hōtei-shiki to shite van der Waals no shiki

$$(p+a/v^2)\,(v-b)=kT \tag{1}$$

(p=atsuryoku, v=ichi-bunshi atari no yōseki, [2] k=Boltzmann teisū, T=zettai-ondo) wa hiroku mochi-irareru. Koko ni a to b to wa busshitsu ni koyū na teisū de aru.

Kono kankei-shiki wa tsugi no yō ni shite michibikareru. Kitai o kōsei suru bunshi wa yūgen [1] na chokkei σ no katai kyū de aru to kangaereba, bunshi ga risō-kitai no bunshi no yō ni jiyū ni ugoki-mawaru koto no dekiru kūkan no yōseki wa jissai no yōseki yori chiisai. Kono eikyō o kōryo shite, risō-kitai no jōtai-shiki $pv=kT$ no v no kawari ni $v-b$ to oku. Sara ni bunshi-kan ni wa, bunshi ga fure-awanai kyori de wa inryoku ga sayō shi, kabe ni chikai bubun no bunshi wa uchigawa ni hikareru. Sono kekka, jissai no atsuryoku p wa risō-kitai no atsuryoku p' yori heru koto ni naru ga, sono ryō wa kabe no chikaku ni aru bunshi no mitsudo to, naibu no bunshi no mitsudo [3] to no seki ni hirei suru to kangaerareru. Sunawachi $p=p'-a/v^2$. Shitagatte risō-kitai no jōtai-shiki no p no kawari ni $p'=p+a/v^2$ o tori-ireru koto ni naru.

Bunshi no chokkei σ to teisū b to [3] no aida no kankei wa, koko de wa keisan o shōryaku suru ga

$$b=2/3\pi\sigma^3. \tag{2}$$

Sunawachi b wa bunshi no yōseki no yonbai de aru.

Ichi wa v ni kanshite sanji no hōtei-shiki de aru. Sunawachi v^2/p o jō-zureba

$$v^3 - (kT/p+b)v^2 + (a/p)v - ab/p = 0 \tag{3}$$

T o ittei ni shite, p o v ni taishite egakeba dai-ichi-zu no kyokusen ga erareru. Takai ondo de wa kyokusen wa tanchō de ari, tsune ni $(\partial p/\partial v)_T < 0$ ga naritatte iru. Kore ni kanshite, hikui ondo de wa kyokusen wa kyokudai-chi to kyokushō-chi to [3] o hitotsu-zutsu mochi, sono han'i no p no atai ni tai-shite hōtei-shiki (3) ni wa sanko no jissū no v ga sonzai suru. Sono sakaime ni naru ondo wa "rinkai-ondo" T_C to yobare, $T > T_C$ de wa kyokusen wa tanchō, $T < T_C$ de wa kyokuchi o motsu.

Rinkai-ondo yori shita no tō-on-kyokusen ni tsuite wa, kyokudai to kyokushō to no aida de wa $(\partial p/\partial v)_T > 0$ to naru ga, kore wa asshuku sureba kaette atsuryo-ku ga genshō suru to iu fu-antei na jōtai de ari, jitsugen shi-enai. Soko de zu ni shimeshita yō ni v jiku ni heikō na senbun A B o hiite santen de kyokusen to majiwaraseru. Shikamo, moto no kyokusen no uchi, kono senbun no jōbu ni aru bubun to senbun to [3] de kakomareru menseki ga, kabu ni aru bubun to senbun to de kakomareru menseki ni hitoshii yō ni egaku. Sō sureba, senbun de musu-bareta futatsu no hashi no ten A, B wa, dō-itsu no Gibbs jiyū enerugii G (ichi-bunshi atari) o motsu futatsu no jōtai ni tai-ō suru. Nan to nareba [4]

$$(\partial G/\partial p)_T = v; \quad G_A - G_B = \int_B^A v\,dp \tag{4}$$

de aru ga, kono sekibun wa senbun A B no jōbu ni kakomareta menseki to kabu ni kakomareta menseki to no sa ni hitoshiku, rei to naru kara de aru.

Shitagatte ten A to ten B to [3] ni tai-ō suru futatsu no isō wa, sono atsuryoku p_s no moto ni tagai ni tsuriai, ippō wa ekitai, tahō wa kitai no jōtai to kaishaku sareru. p_s wa ondo T ni okeru hōwa-jōki-atsu de aru. Atsuryoku ga p_s yori genshō sureba, jiyū enerugii mo genshō suru ga, $(\partial G/\partial p)_T = v$ no kankei ni yotte, v no ōkii kisō no hō ga jiyū enerugii no genshō ga ichijirushiku antei ni naru. Dōyō ni $p > p_s$ no atsuryoku no moto de wa, v no chiisai ekisō no hō ga antei to naru.

VAN DER WAALS EQUATION OF STATE

The van der Waals equation

$$(p+a/v^2)(v-b) = kT \tag{1}$$

(p=pressure, v=volume per molecule, k=the Boltzmann constant, T=absolute temperature) is widely used as an equation of state for imperfect gases. Here a and b are constants characteristic of the substance.

The equation can be derived as follows. If we think of the molecules which constitute a gas as hard spheres of finite diameter σ, then the volume of space in which the molecules can move about freely, as molecules of ideal gases do, is smaller than the actual volume. Considering this effect, we introduce $v-b$ in place of v in $pv=kT$, the equation of state for an ideal gas. Moreover, attractive forces

operate between the molecules at distances where they do not touch each other, and the molecules in that portion of the gas near the walls are attracted inwards. As a result, the actual pressure p is less than the pressure p' of an ideal gas by an amount that is thought to be proportional to the product of the density of the molecules near the walls and the density of the molecules in the interior, i.e. $p = p' - a/v^2$. Consequently, $p = p' + a/v^2$ replaces p in the equation of state for an ideal gas.

Although the calculation is omitted here, the relation between the molecular diameter σ and the constant b is

$$b = 2/3\pi\sigma^3 \tag{2}$$

namely, four times the volume of a molecule.

Equation (1) is of third order with respect to v, i.e. if we multiply through by v^2/p, then

$$v^3 - (kT/p + b)v^2 + (a/p)v - ab/p = 0 \tag{3}$$

If T is fixed and p is plotted versus v, the curves in Figure 1 are obtained. At high temperatures, the curves are monotonic and $(\partial p/\partial v)_T < 0$. At low temperatures, however, the curves have both a maximum and a minimum, and for values of p in that range there exist three real roots for v in equation (3). The boundary-line temperature is called the critical temperature T_C, the curves being monotonic for $T > T_C$ and having extrema for $T < T_C$.

Below the critical temperature in the range between the minimum and the maximum on an isothermal, there is an unrealizable state for which $(\partial p/\partial v)_T > 0$, namely, an unstable state where compression would actually result in a decrease in pressure.

We draw line segment A B parallel to the v-axis, as shown in the figure, and make it intersect the curve at 3 points. Furthermore, we draw it such that the area enclosed by the line segment and that part of the original curve above the line segment is equal to the area enclosed by the line segment and that part of the curve below it. By so doing, the two extremities A and B joined by the line segment will correspond to two states which have identical Gibbs free energies (per molecule). The reason for this is

$$(\partial G/\partial p)_T = v; \quad G_A - G_B = \int_B^A v\,dp \tag{4}$$

and this integral is zero, since it is equal to the difference between the area enclosed above line segment A B and that enclosed below.

Consequently, the two phases corresponding to point A and point B are in equilibrium at the pressure p_s and may be interpreted as liquid on the one hand and gas on the other. p_s is the saturation vapor pressure at temperature T. If the pressure decreases below p_s, the free energy also decreases and, according to the relation $(\partial G/\partial p)_T = v$, it is the vapor phase with its large v which markedly

decreases in free energy and becomes stable. Similarly, at pressures $p > p_s$, it is the liquid phase with its small v which becomes stable.

EXPLANATORY NOTES

(1) fu-kanzen

The prefixes *fu-* (不), *mu-* (無), and *hi-* (非) correspond to English "un-", "non-", "in-".
For example,

(不)導体	(fu) dōtai	(non) conductor
(不)等式	(fu) tōshiki	(in) equality
(無)極性	(mu) kyokusei	(non) polar
(非)線形	(hi) senkei	(non) linear

For words prefixed with *mu-* (無) the opposite is often prefixed with *yū-* (有).

有限	yūgen	finite
無限	mugen	infinite
有機化学	yūki-kagaku	organic chemistry
無機化学	muki-kagaku	inorganic chemistry

(2) ichi bunshi atari no yōseki

"Volume (available) per molecule." The word *yōseki* is always used to indicate the volume of a container, that is, the "volume available" for the contents. The word *taiseki* always refers to the "volume occupied by" a body, but *yōseki* may also be used. (*cf. bunshi no yōseki* "the volume of a molecule," just after Eq. (2)).

(3) ...to...to no seki — product of...and...

...to...to no aida no kankei — relation between...and...

...to...to no hitotsu-zutsu motsu — possesses one each of...and...

...to...to de kako-mareru — which is surrounded by...and...

...to...to ni taiō suru — which correspond to...and...

(4) nan to nareba

Almost equivalent expressions are:
Naze nareba and
Naze ka to ieba
It generally precedes an explanation for a previous statement.

CONSTRUCTION EXAMPLES

| …について（は） | "as for..., concerning..., for..." |

1. 実在の気体については，ファン・デル・ワールス状態方程式のような式を用いなければならない。

2. ボイル・シャルルの法則は理想気体について成り立つ法則であって，不完全気体については成り立たない。

実在の	jitsuzai no	real

| …に対応する | "to correspond to..., to be equivalent to..., to balance, match" |

1. 二つの合同な3角形の対応する頂点をそれぞれ A, A′; B, B′; C, C′ とする。

2. ホドグラフ面上の速度ベクトルは物理面上の加速度ベクトルに対応する。

3. 物体を真上に投げ上げるためには少なくとも重力に対応するだけの力を加えなければならない。

合同な	gōdō na	congruent
3角形	sankaku-kei	triangle
頂点	chōten	vertex
ホドグラフ	hodogurafu	hodograph
真上に	maue ni	directly upwards
投げ上げる	nage-ageru	to toss upwards
少なくとも	sukunaku-tomo	at least

| …における | "in..., at..., on..." |

1. 一定圧力の気体の温度 0°C, t°C における体積を v_0, v とすれば，$v=v_0\{1+(t/273)\}$。
2. 界面における現象の一つに表面張力がある。

界面	kaimen	interface
現象	genshō	phenomenon
表面張力	hyōmen-chōryoku	surface tension

| …に対しては | "for..." (See also Lesson 7) |

1. 1モルの気体に対しては $pv=RT$. 従って 0°C においては $pv=273\times8.317$ ジュール/モル。

2. 不完全気体に対しては，ファン・デル・ワールスの状態方程式を用いるが，この式においては分子の容積が考えに入れられている。

考えに入れる　kangae ni ireru　　　　to take into consideration

| …に反して | "in contrast to…", "contrary to…" |
| …に対して | "against …," "in contrast to…," "for…" |

1.　理想気体については，ボイル・シャルルの法則が成り立つ。これに対して，不完全
　気体については，ファン・デル・ワールスのような状態方程式を用いなければならな
　い。これに反して，ドルトンの分圧の法則はどんな気体に対しても適用できる。

2.　物体 A が物体 B に対して作用を及ぼせば，B は A に対して反作用を及ぼす。この
　法則に反して力がはたらくことはあり得ない。

| 分圧 | bun'atsu | partial pressure |
| 適用する | tekiyō suru | to apply |

SUPPLEMENTARY READINGS

A.	対応状態	taiō-jōtai	corresponding states
	比較する	hikaku suru	to compare
	これより	kore yori	from this; whence
	…の如く	…no gotoku	as…
	係数	keisū	coefficient
	通常の	tsūjō no	ordinary, usual
	代入する	dainyū suru	to substitute
	…を通じて	…o tsūjite	by means of…
	物質定数	busshitsu-teisū	physical constants
	含む	fukumu	to include
	普遍的な	fuhen-teki na	universal
	特定の	tokutei no	special
	一般化する	ippan-ka suru	to generalize
	種々の	shuju no	various

対応状態の法則　(FK 11–12)

van der Waals の式の v に関する 3 次の方程式，すなわち

$$v^3 - \left(\frac{kT}{p} + b\right)v^2 + \frac{a}{p}v - \frac{ab}{p} = 0$$

という式は $T = T_c$ において

$$(v - v_c)^3 = v^3 - 3v_c v^2 + 3v_c^2 v - v_c^3 = 0$$

という形をとらなければならない。この二式を比較して，

$$v_c^3 = \frac{ab}{p_c}, \quad 3v_c^2 = \frac{a}{p_c}, \quad 3v_c = \frac{kT_c}{p_c} + b$$

の関係が得られ，これより van der Waals の式の二つの定数は $a=3p_cv_c{}^2$, $b=v_c/3$ の如く，臨界点における値で表わされ，さらに

$$\frac{kT_c}{p_cv_c}=\frac{8}{3}$$

なる関係が得られる。$\frac{kT_c}{p_cv_c}$ は臨界係数と呼ばれ，通常の気体で測定された値は，この値よりも20％ほど大きい。

臨界点における値で表わされた a と b を代入して，さらに臨界係数を利用すれば，van der Waals の方程式は，

$$\left\{\frac{p}{p_c}+\frac{3}{(v/v_c)^3}\right\}\left\{\frac{v}{v_c}-\frac{1}{3}\right\}=\frac{8}{3}\frac{T}{T_c}$$

の形に表わされる。この式においては，圧力，容積，温度は臨界点におけるそれらの値との比を通じて現われ，関数式はその他の物質定数を含まない普遍的なものである。

すなわち，$\frac{p}{p_c}$ と $\frac{v}{v_c}$ と $\frac{T}{T_c}$ それぞれを p_r, v_r, T_r とすれば，van der Waals の方程式は特定の物質定数を含まない次の普遍的な形をとる。

$$\left\{p_r+\frac{3}{v_r{}^3}\right\}\left\{v_r-\frac{1}{3}\right\}=\frac{8}{3}T_r$$

この結果を一般化すると，状態方程式において，臨界点における温度 T_c，一分子あたりの容積 v_c，圧力 P_c を単位として，温度 T_r, 容積 v_r, 圧力 p_r を表わすとき，種々の物質の状態方程式が同じ形となるはずである。すなわち，普遍的な関数形 F を用いて，状態方程式が

$$p_r=F(T_r, v_r)\qquad[F(1, 1)=1]$$

の形に表わされることになる。これを対応状態の法則という。

B. The following three readings are adapted from the highly authoritative Japanese science dictionary 理化学辞典 It is an excellent resource for determining the essential vocabulary necessary for discussing any particular scientific topic. Note that the law of corresponding states is treated in terms of the reduced characteristic equation of state.

1)

均質な	kinshitsu na	homogeneous
等方性の	tōhō-sei no	isotropic
状態量	jōtai-ryō	quantity of state, state function
必然的に	hitsuzen-teki ni	necessarily, inevitably
…に相当する	...ni sōtō suru	to correspond to..., be equivalent to...
ファン・デル・ワールス	fan-deru-Wārusu	van der Waals

ならびに（＝および）	narabi-ni	and; as well as
ディエテリーチ	Dieteriichi	Dieterici
クラウジウス	Kuraujiusu	Clausius
これらの	korera no	these
高圧	kōatsu	high pressure
以上の	ijō no	above
多くの	ōku no	many
あるいは…あるいは	aruiwa...aruiwa	either...or
理論的に	riron-teki ni	theoretically
提出する	teishutsu suru	to offer, introduce
ビリアル	biriaru	virial
展開	tenkai	expansion (math.)
液体	ekitai	liquid
固体	kotai	solid
最近	saikin	recently, lately
物性論	bussei-ron	theory of matter
発達	hattatsu	development, progress
…につれて	...ni tsurete	along with...

状 態 式　(2RJ 657)

　均質な等方性の物体に対して，その状態量である温度 T，圧力 P，体積 V の間に成り立つ一定の関係式を状態式という。三つの量のうち二つを定めればほかは必然的に定まる。理想気体の状態式はボイル・シャルルの法則に相当する $PV=RT$（R は気体定数，1 mol について）である。理想気体に近い気体に対してはファン・デル・ワールスの状態式ならびにディエテリーチの状態式，クラウジウスの状態式などがある。これらの式は高圧でなく，また低温でない場合に実際の気体に対して用いられる。以上のほかに多くの状態式が，あるいは理論的にあるいは実験的に提出され，ビリアル展開式もその一つである。液体および固体の状態式も最近は物性論の発達につれて明かにされてきている。

2)	ビリアル係数	biriaru keisū	virial coefficients
	…によらない	...ni yoranai	independent of...
	第二，第三，…第 n	dai-ni, dai-san,...dai-en	2nd, 3rd...nth
	外部ビリアル	gaibu-biriaru	external virial
	…に由来する	...ni yurai suru	to originate in..., to be derived from...
	求める	motomeru	to seek

ビリアル係数　（2RJ 107）

気体の状態式を $Pv = RT(1 + B/v + C/v^2 + \cdots)$ （P は圧力，v はモル体積，R は気体定数，T は絶対温度，$B, C, \cdots$ は体積によらない T の関数）と表わすとき，$B, C, \cdots$ をそれぞれ第二，第三，$\cdots$ 第 n ビリアル係数と呼ぶ。ビリアル係数と呼ぶのは，Pv が外部ビリアルに比例することに由来する。特に第二ビリアル係数については，$\phi(r)$ を r の距離にある分子間力のポテンシャルとするとき，

$$B = 2\pi N \int_0^\infty \left(1 - \exp\frac{-\phi(r)}{kT}\right) r^2 dr$$

（N はモル分子数，k はボルツマン定数）であって，B の温度変化の実験値から分子間力を求めることができる。

3) 換算状態式　　　　　　　kansan-jōtai-shiki　　　　　reduced equation of state
（換算する means to convert, e.g. to convert one currency to another.）

比体積	hi-taiseki	specific volume
適当な	tekitō na	suitable
尺度	shakudo	measure, standard, scale
選ぶ	erabu	to select, to choose
異なる	kotonaru	to be different
統一した	tōitsu shita	unified
書き直す	kaki-naosu	to rewrite

換算状態式　（3RJ 275）

実在気体の状態式において，圧力 P, 比体積 V, 温度 T のかわりに，臨界状態での圧力 P_c. 比体積 V_c, 温度 T_c との比，$\pi = P/P_c$, $\nu = V/V_c$, $\theta = T/T_c$ を変数にとれば，たとえばファン・デル・ワールスの状態式は，

$$\left(\pi + \frac{3}{\nu^2}\right)(3\nu - 1) = 8\theta$$

と書かれる。同様に，一般の状態式についても，状態変数に適当な尺度を選ぶことによって異なる物質についての状態式を統一した形に表わすことができる場合，書き直された状態式を換算状態式といい，換算状態式によって対応する状態を対応状態という。

FINAL TRANSLATION TEST

物体の性質を調べる場合，あらゆる物体は原子や分子からできているから，物質のすべての性質はこれらの原子や分子の位置と運動，すなわちその力学的性質で定まると考えられる。このような考え方をミクロの立場という。これに対して，分子や原子を考えずに直

接測れる量の間の関係だけを取りあつかう場合にはマクロの立場という。容器の壁に及ぼされる気体の圧力を気体分子の衝突によるものと考えて圧力を計算するのは，ミクロの考え方の一例である。

いま，同じ分子からできている気体と固体との界面を考えてみよう。気体内部で界面の近くにある分子は固体内部へはいって行き，固体分子も気体内部へはいって行く。温度が低ければ固体から気体へはいって行く分子の個数の方が少なく，温度が高ければ気体から固体へはいって行く分子の方が少ない。すなわち，気体は凝縮し，あるいは固体は昇華する。

このような物質の状態変化を，ミクロの考え方を取り入れて説明すると次のようになる。ある温度，圧力の下で，ある容積をもっている気体の状態は，その構成分子がいろいろ違った，極めて多くの力学的状態をとる場合に同じように現われる。このように一つのマクロ状態になるようなミクロ状態の数の多いほど，そのマクロ状態は実際に現われる程度，すなわち確率が高い。この確率は，実はその状態のエントロピーと密接に関係しているのであって，エントロピーは確率の対数曲線で表わされる。そこで，与えられた温度，圧力，容積において気体と固体の状態になるようなミクロ状態の数をそれぞれもとめて，その大小によって変化の進む方向を定めればよい。エントロピーの減少する方向には変化はおこり得ないのである。

LESSON 9

第 九 課

KANJI

流	334	RYŪ		断	841	DAN
	2576	naga(su) naga(reru)			2078	kotowa(ru)
中	23	CHŪ		研	204	KEN
	81	naka			3180	
察	406	SATSU		究	185	KYŪ
	1334				3314	
管	573	KAN		確	570	KAKU
	3416	kuda			3217	tashi(kameru)
細	218	SAI		知	112	CHI
	3522	hoso(i) koma(kai)			3169	shi(ru)
三	3	SAN		抵	216b	TEI
	8	mit(tsu)			1878	
側	667	SOKU		抗	210a	KŌ
	509	kawa			1852	
高	76	KŌ		粘	242b	NEN
	5248	taka(i)			3472	neba(ru)
太	269	TAI		摩	266b	MA
	1172	futo(i)			5392	
液	552	EKI		擦	273b	SATSU
	2599				2025	

READING SELECTIONS

流れ	nagare	flow, stream
…の中	…no naka	in…, inside…
観察	kansatsu	observation
ガラス管	garasu-kan	glass tube
一部	ichibu	one part
細くする	hosoku suru	to make thin, make narrow
三つ	mittsu	three
側管	sokkan	side tube
つける	tsukeru	to affix, put on, attach

水平に	suihei ni	horizontally
左の方から	hidari no hō kara	from the left
流す	nagasu	to cause... to flow
水面	suimen	surface of the water
変える	kaeru	to change
高低	kōtei	height
調べる	shiraberu	investigate
…の結果	...no kekka	as a result of...
…によらず	...ni yorazu	without regard to..., independently of...
太い	futoi	wide, fat
部分	bubun	part, portion
高い	takai	high
液体	ekitai	liquid
ようす	yōsu	appearance
定常流	teijō-ryū	steady-state flow, stationary flow
一定時間に	ittei-jikan ni	in a fixed time
細い	hosoi	thin, narrow
断面積	dan-menseki	cross-sectional area
面	men	surface
押し縮める	oshi-chijimeru	to compress
性質	seishitsu	property, nature
おそい	osoi	slow
いい表わす	ii-arawasu	to express
所	tokoro	place
詳しい	kuwashii	detailed
研究	kenkyū	research
密度	mitsudo	density
確かめる	tashikameru	to ascertain, confirm
アルミニウム	aruminiumu (usually pronounced *aruminyūmu*)	aluminum
粉末	funmatsu	powder, dust
まく	maku	to scatter, sow
粉	kona	powder, dust; flour
みち	michi	path
みちすじ	michisuji	course, trajectory
流線	ryūsen	streamline
囲む	kakomu	to surround
流管	ryūkan	stream tube

管内の流れ	kannai no nagare	tube flow
…に限らず	…ni kagirazu	not limited to…
成立する	seiritsu suru	to be valid, be applicable
ベルヌーイの定理	Berunūi no teiri	Bernoulli's theorem
用いる	mochiiru	to use
風	kaze	wind
測る	hakaru	to measure

流れの中の圧力　(B 98–99)

観察　図1のようなガラス管の一部を細くした[1]ものに A, B, C 三つの側管をつけ，ガラス管を水平にして[2]，左[3]の方から水を流してみよ[4]。A, B の側管の水面はどうなるか。また，水の流れの向きを変えて水面の高低[5]を調べよ[4]。

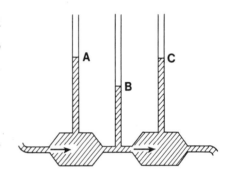

図1　流れの中の圧力

　このような実験の結果，流れの向きによらずガラス管の太い部分の側管の水面の方が高いことがわかる。

　液体の流れのようすが時間的に変化しない場合，この流れを「定常流」という。上の図のような定常流の場合には，一定時間に流れる液体の量は管の太い部分でも[6]，細い部分でも[6]同じである。いま，管の断面積を S, その面における流れの速さを v とすれば

$$vS＝一定 \qquad (1)$$

となる。これは押し縮めることのできない液体[7]の性質を示している。

　このことから，管の太い部分では流れがおそく，細い部分では流れが速いことがわかる。したがって，上の実験の結果を次のようにいい表わすことができる。

　定常流において流れの速い所では圧力は小さく，おそい所では圧力が大きい。詳しい研究の結果，液体の定常流の速さを v, 圧力を P, 密度を ρ とするとき，水平な管のどの部分でも

$$P+\frac{1}{2}\rho v^2＝一定 \qquad (2)$$

という関係が成り立つ[8]ことが確かめられている。

　定常流の中にアルミニウムなどの粉末をまくと，粉の運動していく[9]みちは，流れのみちすじを示す。このみちすじを「流線」という。流線によって囲まれた管を「流管」という。

　上の関係は，ガラス管内の流れに限らず，すべての水平な定常流の流管について成立

し⁽⁸⁾，「ベルヌーイ⁽¹⁰⁾の定理」とよばれる。

　ベルヌーイの定理は気体にも成り立ち，これを用いれば，運動している流体，たとえば風_{かぜ}の及ぼす圧力を測って⁽¹¹⁾，その速さを知ることができる。

抵抗	teikō	resistance
バケツ	baketsu	bucket
回す	mawasu	to turn, rotate
中の水	naka no mizu	the water inside
しだいに	shidai ni	gradually
引きずる	hiki-zuru	to drag (along)
粘性	nensei	viscosity
種類	shurui	type, kind
グリセリン	guriserin	glycerine
…では…では	…de wa… de wa	for… whereas for…
エーテル	ēteru	ether
…の中で	…no naka de	in…
静かに	shizuka ni	slowly (lit., quietly)
…にもとづく	…ni motozuku	based on…, owing to…, due to…
付近の	fukin no	neighboring, adjacent
次々に*	tsugi-tsugi ni	one after another, successively
摩擦	masatsu	friction
…に似る	…ni niru	to resemble…
細かい	komakai	fine, minute
雨粒	amatsubu	raindrop
上空	jōkū	sky
互いに	tagai ni	mutually, together

流体の抵抗　(B 100)

　水のはいったバケツ⁽¹²⁾を回すと，中の水もしだいに回り始_{はじ}める。このように流体はその近くの部分の運動に引きずられる性質がある。

　この性質を流体の粘性という。粘性の大きさは流体の種類_{しゅるい}によって違い，グリセリンのようなものでは大きく，エーテルのようなものでは小さい。

　流体の中で，小さい物体が静_{しず}かに運動するときには粘性にもとづく力がはたらく。すなわち，物体が付_ふ近の流体を次々に引きずり，引きずられた流体が物体に摩擦に似_にた力を及

---

*The symbol 々 indicates a repetition of the previous *kanji*.

ぼすようになる。粘性による抵抗は物体の速さに比例して増す。

　細かい雨粒が上空から落ちてくる[9]とき，雨粒には重力と空気の粘性による抵抗力とが互いに反対向きにはたらき，雨粒は一定の速さ，すなわち，重力と抵抗とがつり合うときの速さで落下しているのである。

NAGARE NO NAKA NO ATSURYOKU

Kansatsu: Zu-ichi no yō na garasu-kan no ichibu o hosoku shita[1] mono ni *A, B, C* mittsu no sokkan o tsuke, garasu-kan o suihei ni shite,[2] hidari[3] no hō kara mizu o nagashite miyo.[4] *A, B* no sokkan no suimen wa dō naru ka. Mata, mizu no nagare no muki o kaete suimen no kōtei[5] o shirabeyo.[4]

　Kono yō na jikken no kekka, nagare no muki ni yorazu, garasu-kan no futoi bubun no sokkan no suimen no hō ga takai koto ga wakaru.

　Ekitai no nagare no yōsu ga jikan-teki ni henka shinai baai, kono nagare o *teijō-ryū* to iu. Ue no zu no yō na teijō-ryū no baai ni wa, ittei-jikan ni nagareru ekitai no ryō wa kan no futoi bubun de mo,[6] hosoi bubun de mo[6] onaji de aru. Ima, kan no danmenseki o *S*, sono men ni okeru nagare no hayasa o *v* to sureba

$$vS = \text{ittei} \tag{1}$$

to naru. Kore wa oshi-chijimeru koto no dekinai ekitai[7] no seishitsu o shimeshite iru.

　Kono koto kara, kan no futoi bubun de wa nagare ga osoku, hosoi bubun de wa nagare ga hayai koto ga wakaru. Shitagatte ue no jikken no kekka o tsugi no yō ni ii-arawasu koto ga dekiru.

　Teijō-ryū de wa, nagare no hayai tokoro de wa atsuryoku wa chiisaku, osoi tokoro de wa atsuryoku ga ōkii.

　Kuwashii kenkyū no kekka, ekitai no teijō-ryū no hayasa o *v*, atsuryoku o *p*, mitsudo o *ρ* to suru toki, suihei na kan no dono bubun de mo

$$p + \left(\frac{1}{2}\right)\rho v^2 = \text{ittei} \tag{2}$$

to iu kankei ga naritatsu[8] koto ga tashikamerarete iru.

　Teijō-ryū no naka ni aruminiumu nado no funmatsu o maku to, kona no undō shite iku[9] michi wa, nagare no michisuji o shimesu. Kono michisuji o *ryūsen* to iu. Ryūsen ni yotte kakomareta kan o *ryūkan* to iu.

　Ue no kankei wa, garasu-kan-nai no nagare ni kagirazu, subete no suihei na teijō-ryū no ryūkan ni tsuite seiritsu shi,[8] *Berunūi no*[10] *teiri* to yobareru.

　Berunūi no teiri wa kitai ni mo naritachi, kore o mochiireba, undō shite iru ryūtai, tatoeba kaze no oyobosu atsuryoku o hakatte[11], sono hayasa o shiru koto ga dekiru.

RYŪTAI NO TEIKŌ

Mizu no haitta baketsu [12] o mawasu to, naka no mizu mo shidai ni mawari–hajimeru. Kono yō ni ryūtai wa sono chikaku no bubun no undō ni hiki-zurareru seishitsu ga aru.

Kono seishitsu o ryūtai no nensei to iu. Nensei no ōkisa wa ryūtai no shurui ni yotte chigai, guriserin no yō na mono de wa ōkiku, ēteru no yō na mono de wa chiisai.

Ryūtai no naka de, chiisai buttai ga shizuka ni undō suru toki ni wa, nensei ni motozuku chikara ga hataraku. Sunawachi, buttai ga fukin no ryūtai o tsugi-tsugi ni hiki-zuri, hikizurareta ryūtai ga buttai ni masatsu ni nita chikara o oyobosu yō ni naru. Nensei ni yoru teikō wa buttai no hayasa ni hirei shite masu.

Komakai amatsubu ga jōkū kara ochite kuru toki, amatsubu ni wa jūryoku to kūki no nensei ni yoru teikō-ryoku to ga tagai ni hantai-muki ni hataraki, amatsubu wa ittei no hayasa, sunawachi, jūryoku to teikō to ga tsuri-au toki no hayasa de rakka shite iru no de aru.

PRESSURE IN FLUID FLOW

Observation: Attach three side tubes to a glass tube with a narrow section as shown in Figure 1, and then let water flow through it from the left. What happens to the water levels in side-tubes *A* and *B*? Then examine the water levels when the direction of flow is changed.

As a result of this kind of experiment we find that, whatever the direction of flow, the water level is highest in the side tubes attached to the wide part of the tube.

When the appearance of the flow of the liquid does not change with time, we speak of "steady-state flow." For steady state flow of the type shown in the above figure, the quantity of fluid which flows in a given time interval is the same both in the wide part and in the narrow part of the tube. Now, if we let the cross-sectional area be *S*, and the flow velocity at that cross section be *v*, then

$$vS = \text{constant} \tag{1}$$

which expresses the nature of an incompressible fluid.

From this relation, we see the flow is slow in the wide part of the tube but rapid in the narrow part. Therefore the results of the above experiment can be expressed as follows.

In steady-state flow the pressure is small at points where the flow is rapid, and large where the flow is slow.

As a result of detailed research, it has been established that the following

relation holds for any part of a horizontal tube

$$p + \left(\frac{1}{2}\right)\rho v^2 = \text{constant} \qquad (2)$$

where v is the speed of the steady-state flow of the liquid, p is the pressure, and ρ is the density.

If we scatter some powder, such as aluminum powder, into a steady-state flow, the path followed by the powder shows the flow trajectory. These trajectories are called "stream lines." The tubes which are surrounded by streamlines are called "stream tubes."

The above relation is not restricted to flow in glass tubes but applies to all horizontal steady-state stream tubes; it is called "Bernoulli's theorem."

Bernoulli's theorem applies also to gases, and by using it we can ascertain the speed of a moving fluid, e. g. the wind, by measuring the pressure which it exerts.

FLUID RESISTANCE

If we rotate a bucket of water, the water in it also gradually begins to revolve. Thus, a fluid has the property of being dragged along by the movement of adjacent material.

This property is called the viscosity of the fluid. The magnitude of viscosity differs with the type of fluid, being large for fluids like glycerine and small for those like ether.

When a small body moves slowly through a fluid, there is a force acting which depends on the viscosity. That is to say, the body drags along successively the neighboring fluid, and the fluid thus dragged along exerts a force akin to friction on the body. The resistance due to viscosity increases in proportion to the speed of the body.

When small raindrops fall from the sky, gravity and the resisting force due to viscosity of the air act in opposite directions on the drops, so that they fall at constant speed, that is, at that speed for which gravity and fluid resistance are in balance.

EXPLANATORY NOTES

(1) hosoku suru "To make · · · narrow"; compare *hosoku naru* "to become narrow".

(2) suihei ni suru "To make · · · horizontal"; compare *suihei ni naru* "to become horizontal".

(3) hidari The opposite of *hidari* 左 (left) is *migi* 右 (right).

(4) miyo, shirabeyo These are plain imperatives; do not confuse with *miyō, shirabeyō*.

(5) kōtei The word *kōtei* (height) is an abstraction formed

from combining the *kanji* for "high" 高 and "low" 低. The word *kōtei* is synonymous with *takasa* (高さ). Other examples of this kind of word formation are:

Compound		Formed from			
深浅	*shinsen* (depth) :	深い	*fukai* (deep)	浅い	*asai* (shallow)
大小	*daishō* (size) :	大きい	*ōkii* (big)	小さい	*chiisai* (small)
長短	*chōtan* (length) :	長い	*nagai* (long)	短い	*mijikai* (short)
遅速	*chisoku* (speed) :	遅い	*osoi* (slow)	速い	*hayai* (fast)
強弱	*kyōjaku* (strength)	強い	*tsuyoi* (strong)	弱い	*yowai* (weak)
明暗	*meian* (brightness) :	明るい	*akarui* (bright)	暗い	*kurai* (dark)
寒暑	*kansho* (temperature) :	寒い	*samui* (cold)	暑い	*atsui* (hot)

The nouns in the left column are synonymous with *fukasa, ōkisa, nagasa, hayasa, tsuyosa, akarusa, ondo*. Sometimes the compound words are best translated as 深浅 deep and shallow, 寒暑 hot and cold, climate; i.e., they may signify the combination of the ideas embodied in the individual *kanji*.

(6) ...de mo ...de mo   "both... and..."

(7) oshi-chijimeru koto no dekinai ekitai   It would be more concise to say 非圧縮性液体 *hi-asshuku-sei-ekitai*, "incompressible liquid".

(8) nari-tatsu; seiritsu suru   Note that these words use the same *kanji*, one making use of *kun*-readings and the other of *on*-readings; the meanings are substantially the same here.

Similar comments apply to *mochi-iru* (用いる) and *yō-suru* (用する).

(9) undō-shite iku; ochite kuru   The *-te iku** construction with verbs of motion usually implies motion *away* from the observer or speaker; similarly the *-te kuru* construction implies motion *towards* the observer or speaker. Hence *kona no undō shite iku michi* means "the path of the powder as it goes moving off" (i.e., away from the place where we put the powder into the liquid). *Amatsubu ga ochite kuru* means "raindrops come falling down" (i. e., towards us).

Note also that *-te iku* and *-te kuru* may also be used with temporal, rather than spatial, distinctions: *-te iku* has the idea of continuation of the motion (same as verb-stem + *tsuzukeru*), and *-te kita* contains the idea of an action which begins and continues to the present (in contrast to verb-stem + *hajimeru* which

---

*sometimes *-te yuku* (more formal).

contains only the idea of the beginning of the action.)
Note the following sentence:

Kyō wa ame ga furi-hajimete, ima made futte kita no de,
kore kara mo futte iku darō (or: *furi-tsuzukeru darō*).
"Today it started to rain, it has been raining up
until now, and it will probably go on raining."

(10) Berunūi — In research texts and scholarly journals proper names
are usually written in *Rōmaji*. However the *katakana*
versions are not infrequently encountered, particularly
when a name is firmly attached to an equation or a
piece of equipment; hence one encounters 非ニュー
トン流体 "non-Newtonian fluid" and ヴェンチュリ管
(*Venchurikan*) "Venturi tube". Note the use of ゛ on
the *wa* row of the *kana* table to make a *v*-row.

For "Torricelli", in the transcription トリチェッリー,
small ツ is used to simulate the doubling of the "l"
in Italian! There tends to be some diversity in
transcribing foreign names into *katakana*, because of
the limited number of sounds in Japanese.

(11) hakaru — Several different *kanji* may be used for *hakaru* "to
measure": 測る, 計る, 量る The first of these is the
most common, and the third *kanji* should be used
only for volume or weight. In compounds (*jukugo*),
the most common word is 測定する *sokutei suru*. For
time measurement 計時する *keiji suru* may be used;
for volume, 計量する *keiryō suru*; for distance, 測量す
る *sokuryō suru*.

(12) mizu no haitta — Lit. "a bucket (into which) water has entered,"
baketsu (=mizu ga — hence freely "a bucket containing water," or "a
haitta baketsu) — bucket with water in it." Note also: *nensei o motta*
ekitai ("a fluid which has viscosity" or "a viscous
fluid"); *ittan no hiraita kan* ("a tube (which is) open
at one end"). Note the Japanese use of the past tense
in these sentences; to an English-speaking person a
present tense would seem more usual.

CONSTRUCTION EXAMPLES

| …によると | "according to…" |

| …によらず | "independently of…," "regardless of…",
"not due to…,"* "rather than…"** |

| …によって | "in accordance with…," "by…," "due to…" |

1. ベルヌーイの定理によると，管中を流れる水の圧力は，流れの向きによらず，流れ
    の速さによって定まる。
2. 物体が水に浮くかどうかは，物体の重さによらず，密度によって定まる。
3. 環境庁によると，東京地方の光化学スモッグは，工場排煙によらず，自動車の排
    気ガスによっておこっている。
4. 実在気体の圧力を求めるには，理想気体の方程式によらず van der Waals の方程
    式によって計算するのがふつうである。

浮く	uku	to float
環境庁	Kankyō-chō	Environmental Agency
東京地方	Tokyō-chihō	Tokyo area
光化学…	kō-kagaku…	photochemical…
工場排煙	kōba-haien	exhaust smoke from factories
自動車	jidōsha	automobile
排気ガス	haiki-gasu	exhaust gases
実在気体	jitsuzai-kitai	real gas
計算する	keisan suru	to calculate

| …場合（には） | "when…", "for the case that…" |

| …とき（には） | "when…", "for the case that…" |

1. 野球において打者がボールを打つ〔場合／とき〕には，ボールがベースの真上に来たときに
    打つのがよい。
2. 不完全気体を取りあつかう〔場合／とき〕には，ファン・デル・ワールスの方程式のような
    式を用いなければならない。
3. 信号灯の所に来た〔場合／とき〕には，緑色に変わるときまで発車してはならない。

---

*The meaning "not due to" is illustrated in sentence 3.
**The meaning "rather than" is illustrated in sentence 4.

野球	yakyū	baseball
打者	dasha	batter
打つ	utsu	to hit
ベース	bēsu	base
来る	kuru	to come
取りあつかう	tori-atsukau	to deal with
信号灯	shingō-tō	(traffic) signal light
緑色	midori-iro	green
発車する	hassha suru	to start the car

| …ていく | | …てくる | | …てきた | | (See Explanatory Note (9)) |

1. 物体が空気中を上昇していく場合でも下降してくる場合でも，重力は一定の向きにはたらいている。

2. 生物は地球上に生きてきたし，これからも生きていくであろう。

3. 次々と新しい問題が出てくるので，議論はいつまでも続いていく。

4. 自動車が走っていくためには，抵抗に打ち勝つだけの動力が必要である。

上昇する	jōshō suru	to ascend
下降する	kakō suru	to descend
生きる	ikiru	to live
次々と	tsugi-tsugi to	one after another
新しい	atarashii	new
出て来る	dete kuru	to arise, come up
議論	giron	argument, discussion
続く	tsuzuku	to continue
いつまでも	itsu made mo	indefinitely
走る	hashiru	to run
打ち勝つ	uchi-katsu	to overcome
動力	dōryoku	motive power
必要	hitsuyō	necessity

| …でも…でも | "both...and..." |

1. ガリレオは重い物体でも軽い物体でも同じ速さで落ちてくると主張した。

2. 二つの物体の衝突に関する運動量保存の法則は，物体が金属であってもプスラチックであっても成り立つ。

軽い	karui	light
主張する	shuchō suru	to affirm, insist
金属	kinzoku	metal

| …にもとづく | "based on…," "owing to…," "due to…" |

1. 金属の弾性は原子間の引力にもとづき，塑性は格子欠陥にもとづく。

2. 静力学では，力とモーメントのつり合いにもとづいて未知の力をもとめる。

3. 保存力場においては，エネルギー保存の原理にもとづいて問題を解くことができる。

弾性	dansei	elasticity
塑性	sosei	plasticity
格子	kōshi	lattice
欠陥	kekkan	defect
静力学	sei-rikigaku	statics
未知の	michi no	unknown
保存力場	hozon-rikijō	conservative force field
原理	genri	principle

SUPPLEMENTARY READINGS

A.   *Selections from Rikagaku-Jiten, 2nd Edition:*

1)	縮む	chijimu	to contract, shrink
	縮まない流体	chijimanai ryūtai	incompressible fluid
	任意の	nin'i no	arbitrary
	一般化する	ippan-ka suru	to generalize
	外力	gairyoku	external force

ベルヌーイの定理   (2RJ 1245)

粘性のない縮まない流体の定常な流れでは，一つの流線について

$$\frac{1}{2}v^2 + \frac{p}{\rho} + gz = \text{const} \tag{1}$$

(vは流速，pは圧力，ρは密度，gは重力の加速度，zはある任意の水平面からの高さ）が成り立つ。これは流体の運動についてエネルギー保存の法則を表わすもので，ベルヌーイの定理という。縮む流体ではρがpだけの関数の場合，(1)は

$$\frac{1}{2}v^2 + \int \frac{dp}{\rho} + \Omega = \text{const.} \tag{2}$$

の形に一般化される（Ωは外力のポテンシャル）。

2)	容器	yōki	container
	穴をあける	ana o akeru	to make a hole
	流れ出る	nagare-deru	to flow out

トリチェッリーの定理　(2 RJ　971)

　容器に入れた液体が壁にあけた小さい穴から流れ出るとき，その速度は，$v=\sqrt{2gh}$ で与えられる。ここで g は重力の加速度，h は穴から液面までの高さである。すなわち v は質点が h の高さから自由に落下するときに得る速度に等しい。これをトリチェッリー (Torricelli) の定理という。

3) ヴェンチュリ管	Venchuri-kan	Venturi tube
中央	chūō	center, middle
くびれる	kubireru	to be constricted
流速	ryūsoku	speed of the current
くびれ	kubire	constriction
計算する	keisan suru	to calculate
なお	nao	furthermore, moreover
低下	teika	lowering
…を通して	…o tōshite	through…, via…
吸い出す	sui-dasu	to aspirate
現象	genshō	phenomenon
最初の	saisho no	first
観察者	kansatsu-sha	observer
信じられている	shinjirarete iru	believed to be
名	na	name
因む	chinamu	to be associated with

ヴェンチュリ管　(2RJ 111)

　図のように中央のくびれた管で流速の測定に用いられる。管を流れに平行におくと，くびれの部分では流れが速く，したがってベルヌーイの定理によって圧力が下る。その値を測れば，流速が計算される。なお，この圧力低下を利用して，くびれ部につけた側管を通して空気を吸い出したり側管内に定常な気流を作ることなども行なわれる。この現象の最初の観察者と信じられている G. B. Venturi (ヴェントゥーリ, 1746-1822)*の名に因む。

4) ピトー管	Pitō-kan	Pitot tube
一端	ittan	one end
開らく	hiraku	to open

* Note that the *kana* transcription is different for the name "Venturi" and for the name in the expression "Venturi tube."

よどみ点	yodomi-ten	stagnation point
総圧	sōatsu	total pressure
装置	sōchi	apparatus
２重の	nijū no	double
側壁	sokuheki	sidewall
穴	ana	hole
静圧	seiatsu	static pressure
差	sa	difference
直接(に)	chokusetsu(ni)	directly
簡単に	kantan ni	simply

ピトー管

一端Aの開いた管（第一図）を流れに平行におくと，A点はよどみ点になるので，管内の圧力を測れば流れの総圧がわかる。このようにして総圧を測る装置をピトー管または総圧管という。第二図のような２重の管の側壁にあけた穴Bから静圧Pをとり，Aからとった総圧 $P+\dfrac{\rho}{2}v^2$（ρは密度，vは流速）との差を直接測定し，流速vを求めるようにしたものをピトー静圧管，または簡単にピトー管ということがある。

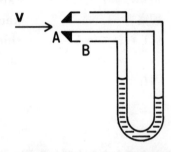

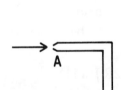

第一図　総圧管　　　　　　　　　　　　　　第二図　ピトー静圧管

B. 層流	sōryū	laminar flow
乱流	ranryū	turbulent flow
粒子	ryūshi	particles
混じる	konjiru	to mix
模様	moyō	pattern
動揺する	dōyō suru	to swirl
直線状に	chokusen-jō ni	rectilinearly
だんだん	dandan	gradually
突然	totsuzen	suddenly
激しい	hageshii	violent
混乱する	konran suru	to be in disorder, chaotic
前者	zensha	the former

相互に	sōgo ni	mutually
軌跡	kiseki	locus
画く	egaku	to trace
いわば	iwaba	in a sense, as it were
層状の	sōjō no	stratified, lamellar
後者	kōsha	the latter
工学上	kōgaku-jō	in engineering
あらわれる	arawareru	to appear
高粘度	kō-nendo	high viscosity
見られる	mirareru	is seen in, occurs in
転移	ten'i	transition
いかなる…	ikanaru…	what kind of…
（＝どんな…）		
彼によれば	kare ni yoreba	according to him
慣性力	kansei-ryoku	force of inertia
いずれ（＝どちら）	izure	which one
支配的	shihai-teki	controlling
レイノルズ数	Reinoruzu-sū	Reynolds number
決定の	kettei no	determining, decisive
尺度	shakudo	measure, criterion
以下	ika	below, in what follows
略記する	ryakki suru	to abbreviate
平均	heikin	average
次元	jigen	dimensions
無次元量	mu-jigen-ryō	dimensionless quantity
各因子	kaku-inshi	each factor
統一した単位系	tōitsu shita tan'i-kei	unified system of units
使用する	shiyō suru	to use
境界	kyōkai	boundaries
幾何学的に	kikagaku-teki ni	geometrically
相似の	sōji no	similar
移る	utsuru	to move
…際の	…sai no	at which…
臨界速度	rinkai-sokudo	critical velocity
称する	shōsuru	to call, name
上限	jōgen	upper limit
下限	kagen	lower limit
必ずしも…とはいえない	kanarazushimo… **to wa** ienai	cannot always say that…; cannot necessarily say that…

大体	daitai	generally
約	yaku	approximately
大型の	ō-gata no	large-sized
水槽	suisō	water tank
流入する	ryūnyū suru	to flow in
入口	iriguchi	entrance
滑らかな	nameraka na	smooth
ラッパ形	rappa-gata	bell-shaped
乱れ	midare	disturbance
注意する	chūi suru	to be careful, take care
…以上	…ijō	more than…
なお	nao	still
わずかの	wazuka no	slight
鋭い	surudoi	sharp
少々	shōshō	slightly
存在する	sonzai suru	to exist
流入後	ryūnyū-go	after entering
まもなく	ma mo naku	before long, soon after
消える	kieru	to disappear
特別の	tokubetsu no	special
注意をはらう	chūi o harau	to take care, to pay attention to
なんらかの	nanra ka no	some kind of
原因	gen'in	cause, source
判定	hantei	judgment, decision
…を基準にする	…o kijun ni suru	to take…as standards
過渡状態	kato-jōtai	transition state

層流と乱流　(KK 31–32)

　ガラス管の中に水を流し，これに水と密度のほぼ等しい粒子を混じて流れの模様を観察すると，速度がごく小さい間は粒子は動揺しないで直線状に流れるが，だんだん速度を増すとある大きさになって突然流れに直角方向の運動を生じ，粒子は激しく混乱しながら流れるようになる。前者のように流体部分が相互にまた管壁面に対しても平行な軌跡を画いて，いわば層状になって流れるのを層流といい，後者のような混乱した流れを乱流という。工学上あらわれるのは主として乱流であって，層流はきわめて細い管内の流れや高粘度の流体の低速度の流れに見られる。

　層流から乱流への転移がいかなる量に関係するかは，Osborne Reynolds が1883年に

初めて明らかにした。彼によれば，管内の流れの模様は流体にはたらく慣性力と粘性力とのいずれが支配的であるかによって定まるもので，この2つの力の比に比例するいわゆるレイノルズ数 (Reynolds number) が決定の尺度になる。レイノルズ数（以下 Re と略記する）は管内の流れの場合では，管の内径を D, 断面平均速度を $\bar{u}$, 流体の密度を ρ, 粘性係数を μ とすれば，

$$Re = D\bar{u}\rho/\mu$$

であらわされる。したがって Re が大きければ乱流となり，小さければ層流となる。Re 式の次元を計算すると Re は無次元量であることがわかり，したがって各因子の値を統一した単位系であらわせば，いかなる単位系を使用しても同一の数値を得る。また2つの管内の流れにおいてその Re が等しいときは流体の境界が幾何学的に相似である限り運動状態も力学的に相似である。

　層流から乱流へ移る際の Re を臨界レイノルズ数とよび，このときの断面平均速度を臨界速度と称する。臨界レイノルズ数（以下 (Re)c と略記する）の値はその上限は必ずしも一定とはいえないが，下限は大体一定しており約 2,300 である。たとえば大型の水槽から直線管に液が流入する場合，管の入口が滑らかなラッパ形になり液にもできるだけ乱れがないように注意して流すと，Re が 10,000 以上においてもなお層流状態を保たせることができるが，このような状態はきわめて不安定であって，わずかの振動を与えても流れは乱流状態に変わる。しかし下限の方はほぼ明らかであって，Re が 2,300 以下となると直線管の入口が鋭くて乱れが少々存在しても，管へ流入後まもなくその乱れは消え層流状態になる。特別の注意をはらわない限り，なんらかの乱れの原因は存在するから，実際の管内流の層流か乱流かの判定は次を基準にすればよい。

$$Re < 2300 \quad 層流$$
$$Re > 3000 \quad 乱流$$
$$2300 < Re < 3000 \quad 過渡状態$$

政府所管の研究所のいろいろ
Some National Research Laboratories in Japan

　Here are the names of a few of the famous National Research Laboratories in Japan. Read them aloud, and then try to see how the names in Japanese correspond to the official English translations.

1.　理化学研究所　　　　　The Institute of Physical and Chemical Research
2.　金属材料技術研究所　　National Research Institute for Metallic Materials
3.　国立遺伝学研究所　　　National Institute for Genetics

4. 統計数理研究所   Institute of Statistical Mathematics
5. 国立予防衛生研究所   National Institute of Health
6. 農業技術研究所   National Institute of Agricultural Science
7. 電子技術総合研究所   General Electronic Technology Research Laboratories
8. 微生物工業技術研究所   Fermentation Research Institute
9. 繊維高分子材料研究所   Research Institute for Polymers and Textiles
10. 電波研究所   Radio Research Laboratory
11. 土木研究所   Public Works Research Institute
12. 建築研究所   Building Research Institute

FINAL TRANSLATION TEST

　流体力学の研究における最大の目的は，流体中を運動する物体にはたらく力を知ることである。流体の性質の内，粘性を考えに入れない完全流体では，物体のうける抵抗は0であるというダランベールのパラドックスが現われる。そこで，少なくとも抵抗を論ずる限りは，粘性を考えに入れなければならない。

　粘性流体の運動方程式，すなわちナヴィエー・ストークスの方程式において，レイノルズ数が大きい場合，物体表面の近くでだけ流体摩擦を考えて，物体から離れた所では完全流体の流れとするのがプラントルの境界層の理論である。物体を流線形にしておけば，圧力を全表面にわたって積分して得られる抵抗，いわゆる圧力抵抗(drag)は0になり，物体のうける抵抗は境界層内の粘性によるもの，いわゆる摩擦抵抗(drag)のみとなる。物体の上側と下側とで流管の太さが違い，たとえば上側で細く下側で太い場合には，下側の圧力が上側より高くなって，物体には上向きの力が作用する。境界層は理論のみならず実験的にも気体や液体について観察され確かめられている。

　流体力学の三つの方程式，すなわちナヴィエー・ストークスの方程式，連続の方程式，ならびに圧力と密度の関係を表わす状態方程式を連立にとくということが困難なことは断るまでもない。

LESSON 10
第 十 課

KANJI

板	305	HAN		非	698	HI	
	2213	ita			5080		
応	556	Ō		目	25	MOKU	
	1504				3127	me	
微	255b	BI		現	602	GEN	
	1631				2943	ara (wareru)	
差	399	SA		出	90	SHUTSU	
	3662	sa (su)			97	{da (su) / de (ru)	
種	423	SHU		必	497	HITSU	
	3295	tane			129	kanara (zu)	
受	240	JU		率	878	RITSU	
	2826	u (keru)			319		
垂	214b	SUI		熱	490	NETSU	
	211				2797	atsu (i)	
接	652	SETSU		伝	681	DEN	
	1951				379	{tsuta (eru) / tsuta (waru)	
般	235b	HAN		移	547	I	
	3865				3282	{utsu (su) / utsu (ru)	
弾	247b	DAN		象	663	SHŌ	
	1575				4472		

READING SELECTIONS

粘性係数	nensei-keisū	coefficient of viscosity
広い	hiroi	broad, wide
平板	heiban	flat plate
固定する	kotei suru	to fix (in place)
…に応じる	…ni ōjiru	in response to…
微小な	bishō na	infinitesimal
両側	ryōgawa	both sides
差	sa	difference
前方・後方	zenpō, kōhō	front side, back side

遅い	osoi	slow
引きもどす	hiki-modosu	to pull back, draw back
境界	kyōkai	boundary
一種の	isshu no	a kind of, a variety of
接線力	sessen-ryoku	tangential force
剪断応力	sendan-ōryoku	shear(ing) stress
受ける	ukeru	to receive
粘性力	nensei-ryoku	viscous force
垂直な	suichoku na	perpendicular
割合	wariai	rate
勾配	kōbai	gradient
次式	jishiki	following equation
粘度	nendo	viscosity
動的物性	dōteki-bussei	dynamical property
知られており（＝知られていて）		is known, and...
一般に	ippan ni	in general
通常の	tsūjō no	ordinary, normal
適用する	tekiyō suru	to apply
(非)ニュートン流体	(hi)Nyūton-ryūtai	(non)Newtonian fluid
扱う	atsukau	to deal with, handle, treat
高分子物質	kō-bunshi-busshitsu	macromolecular materials
…に近い	...ni chikai	near..., akin to...
従う	shitagau	to obey
…の代りに	...no kawari ni	instead of...
目的の…	mokuteki no...	...which we have as our object
表現する	hyōgen suru	to express, represent
提出する	teishutsu suru	to present, offer
変形	henkei	deformation
科学	kagaku	science
流動学	ryūdō-gaku	rheology
流性学	ryūsei-gaku	rheology
主として	shu to shite	mainly, principally
…に応じる	...ni ōjiru	to meet..., satisfy...
下記の	kaki no	following, (listed) below
文献	bunken	literature, bibliography
参照	sanshō	reference
もどる	modoru	to return
粘度	nendo	viscosity
粘性率	nensei-ritsu	(coefficient of) viscosity

系	kei	system
上記の	jōki no	(listed) above
動粘性係数	dō-nensei-keisū	(coefficient of) kinematic viscosity
活動粘度	katsudō-nendo	kinematic viscosity
定義	teigi	definition
ほとんど	hotondo	almost
溶液	yōeki	solution
溶媒	yōbai	solvent
…のほか	…no hoka	besides…, in addition to…
溶質	yōshitsu	solute
種類	shurui	sort, kind
濃度	nōdo	concentration

粘性係数　(I 1–3, BM 79, 2RJ 128)

　二つの平行な広い平板の間に流体があり，固定した下の平板に対して上の平板が一定速度で x 方向に動き，流体もそれに応じて平行に流れるとする。流体中において，平板に平行する微小な面 dS を考えると，この面の両側の部分に速度の差があり，上面が速い側に前方に引きずられ，下面が遅い側に後方に引きもどされる。したがって境界の微小面は一種の接線力，すなわち剪断応力を受けることになる。これを粘性力という。この面に垂直な方向を y とし，流体の速度を u とすると，y 方向に関する速度の変化の割合[1]，すなわち速度勾配は du/dy である。そしてこのような境界面が流体から受ける x 方向への単位面積あたりの剪断応力[2] τ_{yx} は速度勾配 du/dy に比例して次式であらわされる。

$$\tau_{yx} = -\mu \frac{du}{dy} \tag{1}$$

　上式の比例定数 μ は粘性係数（粘度）と呼ばれ，流体の動的物性として重要な物理定数である。上式は「粘性に関するニュートンの法則」として知られており，一般に気体や通常の液体に適用される。このような流体をニュートン流体と呼び流体力学・水力学で扱っているものである。実際には，たとえば高分子物質などのように弾性の性質に近い流体も重要であるが (1) には従わない。このように (1) に従わない流体は，非ニュートン流体と呼ばれ (1) の代りに目的の[3] 流体における du/dy と τ_{yx} の関係を表現するいろいろな式が提出されている。なお，このような物質の流れに関しては，「物質の変形と流れの科学」である「流動学または流性学（レオロジー）」が主として取り扱っているから，必要に応じて下記の文献を参照されたい[4]。

　さて (1) にもどり粘性係数（粘度，粘性率） μ の単位を考えれば，CGS 系においては

$$[\mu] = \left[\frac{\mathrm{dyn/cm^2}}{\mathrm{(cm/s)/cm}}\right] = \left[\frac{\mathrm{g}}{\mathrm{cm \cdot s}}\right]$$

上記の単位で 1g/cm·s を 1 ポアズ (poise, p)，また 0.01p を 1 センチポアズ (centipoise, cp) と呼んでいる。

いま流体の密度を ρ とし，次式で動粘性係数（活動粘度）ν を定義してみる[5]。

$$\nu = \mu/\rho \tag{2}$$

動粘性係数の単位は cm²/s である。

気体の粘性は小さく[6]，温度とともに増加し[1]，圧力によってはほとんど変わらない[1]。液体では一般に温度を上げると粘性は減少し[1]，圧力とともに増加する[1]。溶液の粘性は溶媒の粘性のほか，溶質の種類，濃度などによって変化する[1]。

熱伝導度	netsu-dendō-do	thermal conductivity*
厚さ	atsusa	thickness
両(面)	ryō(men)	both (surfaces), the two (surfaces)
任意の	nin'i no	arbitrary
(非)定常状態	(hi)teijō-jōtai	(un)steady state
事実	jijitsu	fact
熱流と直角	netsuryū to chokkaku	perpendicular to the flow of heat
(熱)移動速度	(netsu)idō-sokudo	rate of (heat) transport
熱流束	netsu-ryūsoku	heat flux
時刻	jikoku	(instant of) time
瞬間	shunkan	moment, instant
微分	bibun	differentiation
記号	kigō	symbol
負号	fugō	minus sign
1 次元熱伝導	ichi-jigen netsu-dendō	one-dimensional heat conduction
本式	honshiki	this equation
現象	genshō	phenomenon
説明	setsumei	explanation

熱伝導度　(I 10–12)

厚さ L の広い固体平板を考えよう。両境界面の温度がそれぞれ T_1, T_2 に保たれ，任意の位置 x における温度 T が時間に対して変化しない[1]状態すなわち定常状態においては

---

*Chemical engineers use 熱伝導度 whereas mechanical engineers and physicists use 熱伝導率

次の事実が実験的に確かめられている。

$$\left.\begin{array}{c}\text{熱流と直角な単位断面積}\\\text{あたりの熱移動速度}\\\text{すなわち熱流束 } q\end{array}\right\} \propto \left\{\dfrac{\text{温度差}}{\text{距離}}\right\} \tag{1}$$

いま比例定数を k とすると，

$$q = k\frac{\varDelta T}{L} \tag{2}$$

上の式で定義される k は cal/cm·s·°C または kcal/m·hr·°C の単位をもち，熱伝導度（熱伝導率）とよばれる。

さて，(2) は定常状態の場合の式であるが，時間とともに温度が変化する[1]非定常状態の場合はどうであろうか。ある時刻において x 方向の微小距離 $\varDelta x$ に対し $\varDelta T$ の温度差が生じている場合，その瞬間においては (2) の関係が成立すると考えれば，x に垂直な断面の単位断面積あたり x 方向に流れる熱の移動速度は $-k(\varDelta T/\varDelta x)$ となる。よって微分記号を用い[7]，

$$q_x = -k\frac{dT}{dx} \tag{3}$$

ここに温度の減少する方向に熱が流れることを考えて負号をつけている。上式は1次元熱伝導におけるフーリエの法則とよばれ，本式[8]を積分した式は実際の非定常伝導現象をよく説明する。もし温度 T が x, y, z の3方向に変化する[1]ならば次式のようになる。

$$\vec{q} = -k\nabla T \tag{4}$$

NENSEI KEISŪ

Futatsu no heikō na hiroi heiban no aida ni ryūtai ga ari, kotei shita shita no heiban ni taishite ue no heiban ga ittei sokudo de x hōkō ni ugoki, ryūtai mo sore ni ōjite heikō ni nagareru to suru. Ryūtai-chū ni oite, heiban ni heikō-suru bishō na men dS o kangaeru to, kono men no ryōgawa no bubun ni sokudo no sa ga ari, jōmen ga hayai gawa ni zenpō ni hiki-zurare, kamen ga osoi gawa ni kōhō ni hiki-modosareru. Shitagatte kyōkai no bishō-men wa isshu no sessen-ryoku, sunawachi sendan-ōryoku o ukeru koto ni naru. Kore o nensei-ryoku to iu. Kono men ni suichoku na hōkō o y to shi, ryūtai no sokudo o u to suru to, y hōkō ni kansuru sokudo no henka no wariai,[1] sunawachi sokudo kōbai wa du/dy de aru. Soshite kono yō na kyōkai-men ga ryūtai kara ukeru x hōkō e no tan'i-menseki atari no sendan-ōryoku[2] τ_{yx} wa sokudo kōbai du/dy ni hirei shite jishiki de arawasareru.

$$\tau_{yx} = -\mu\, du/dy \tag{1}$$

Jōshiki no hirei-teisū μ wa nensei-keisū (nendo) to yobare, ryūtai no dōteki-bussei to shite jūyō na butsuri-teisū de aru. Jōshiki wa "nensei ni kan-suru Nyūton no hōsoku" to shite shirarete ori, ippan ni kitai ya tsūjō no ekitai ni tekiyō sareru. Kono yō na ryūtai o Nyūton ryūtai to yobi, ryūtai-rikigaku, sui-rikigaku de atsukatte iru mono de aru. Jissai ni wa tatoeba kōbunshi-busshitsu nado no yō ni dansei no seishitsu ni chikai ryūtai mo jūyō de aru ga (1) ni wa shitagawanai. Kono yō ni (1) ni shitagawanai ryūtai wa, hi-Nyūton ryūtai to yobare (1) no kawari ni mokuteki no[3] ryūtai ni okeru du/dy to τ_{yx} no kankei o hyōgen suru iroiro na shiki ga teishutsu sarete iru. Nao, kono yō na busshitsu no nagare ni kanshite wa, "busshitsu no henkei to nagare no kagaku" de aru "ryūdō-gaku mata wa ryūsei-gaku (reorojii)" ga shu to shite tori-atsukatte iru kara, hitsuyō ni ō-jite kaki no bunken o sanshō saretai.[4]

Sate (1) ni modori nensei-keisū (nendo, nensei ritsu) μ no tan'i o kangaereba, CGS kei ni oite wa

$$[\mu] = \left[\frac{\text{dyn/cm}^2}{(\text{cm/s})/\text{cm}} \right] = [\text{g/cm} \cdot \text{s}] \tag{2}$$

Jōki no tan'i de ichi g/cm·s o ichi Poazu (Poise, p), mata 0.01 p o ichi senchi-poazu (centipoise, cp) to yonde iru.

Ima ryūtai no mitsudo o ρ to shi, jishiki de dō-nensei-keisū (katsudō-nendo) ν o teigi shite miru.[5]

$$\nu = \mu/\rho \tag{3}$$

Dō-nensei-keisū no tan'i wa cm²/s de aru.

Kitai no nensei wa chiisaku,[6] ondo to tomo ni zōka shi,[1] atsuryoku ni yotte wa hotondo kawaranai.[1] Ekitai de wa ippan ni ondo o ageru to nensei wa genshō shi,[1] atsuryoku to tomo ni zōka suru.[1] Yōeki no nensei wa yōbai no nensei no hoka, yōshitsu no shurui, nōdo nado ni yotte henka suru.[1]

NETSU-DENDŌ-DO

Atsusa L no hiroi kotai-heiban o kangaeyō. Ryō-kyōkai-men no ondo ga sorezore T_1, T_2, ni tamotare, nin'i no ichi x ni okeru ondo T ga jikan ni taishite henka shinai[1] jōtai, sunawachi teijō-jōtai ni oite wa tsugi no jijitsu ga jikken-teki ni tashikamerarete iru.

$$\left\{ \begin{array}{l} \text{netsuryū to chokkaku na} \\ \text{tan'i-dan-menseki atari no} \\ \text{netsu-idō-sokudo} \\ \text{sunawachi netsu-ryūsoku } q \end{array} \right\} \propto \left\{ \frac{\text{ondo-sa}}{\text{kyori}} \right\} \tag{1}$$

Ima hirei-teisū o k to suru to

$$q = k\Delta T/L \tag{2}$$

Ue no shiki de teigi sareru k wa cal/cm·sec·°C mata wa k cal/m·hr·°C no tan'i o mochi, netsu-dendō-do (netsu-dendō-ritsu) to yobareru.

Sate (2) wa teijō-jōtai no baai no shiki de aru ga, jikan to tomo ni ondo ga henka suru[1] hi-teijō-jōtai no baai wa dō de arō ka. Aru jikoku ni oite, x hōkō no bishō-kyori $\varDelta x$ ni taishi $\varDelta T$ no ondo-sa ga shōjite iru baai, sono shunkan ni oite wa (2) no kankei ga seiritsu suru to kangaereba, x ni suichoku na danmen no tan'i-dan-menseki atari x hōkō ni nagareru netsu no idō-sokudo wa $-k(\varDelta T/\varDelta x)$ to naru. Yotte bibun-kigō o mochi-i, [7]

$$q_x = -k\, dT/dx \qquad (3)$$

koko ni ondo no genshō suru hōkō ni netsu ga nagareru koto o kangaete fugō o tsukete iru. Jōshiki wa ichi-jigen-netsu-dendō ni okeru Fūrie no hōsoku to yobare, honshiki[8] o sekibun shita shiki wa jissai no hi-teijō-dendō-genshō o yoku setsumei suru. Moshi ondo T ga x, y, z no san-hōkō ni henka suru[1] naraba jishiki no yō ni naru.

$$\vec{q} = -k\nabla T \qquad (4)$$

THE COEFFICIENT OF VISCOSITY

Consider a fluid located between a pair of wide, parallel flat plates; the upper plate moves in the x-direction at constant velocity with respect to the lower plate, which is fixed. In response to the motion of the upper plate, the fluid also flows parallel to the plates. Let us now consider a differential surface element dS moving with the fluid, this element being parallel to the flat plates; then there will be a velocity difference on the two sides of dS, the upper part of the surface being dragged forward by the rapidly-moving fluid on the top side and the lower part of the surface being drawn backwards by the slowly-moving fluid on the underside. Thus the infinitesimal bounding surface experiences a kind of tangential force, that is to say, a shear(ing) stress. This called a "viscous force." If we take the y direction perpendicular to the surface and let u be the fluid velocity, then the rate of change of velocity in the y direction, that is the velocity gradient, is du/dy. Furthermore, the shearing stress τ_{yx} per unit area exerted on the boundary surface by the fluid in the x direction is proportional to the gradient du/dy and is expressed by the following equation.

$$\tau_{yx} = -\mu du/dy \qquad (1)$$

The proportionality constant in the above equation is called the coefficient of viscosity and, as a dynamic fluid property, is an important physical constant. The above equation is known as Newton's law of viscosity and is in general applicable to gases and ordinary liquids. Such fluids are called Newtonian and are treated in fluid mechanics and hydraulics. Actually there are also important fluids, having essentially elastic properties, such as macromolecular substances, which do not obey (1). Such fluids that do not obey (1) are called non-Newtonian, and to replace (1) a variety of equations have been proposed for expressing the relation between τ_{yx} and du/dy for the fluid concerned. Since problems related to the flow

of these materials are treated primarily in rheology, the science of deformation and flow, the references below should be consulted as occasion demands.

Returning now to (1) and considering the units of viscosity μ we have, for the CGS system,

$$[\mu] = \left[\frac{\text{dyn/cm}^2}{(\text{cm/s})/\text{cm}}\right] = \left[\frac{\text{g}}{\text{cm} \cdot \text{s}}\right]$$

and, for the above units, we call 1 g/cm·s one poise (p) and 0.01p one centipoise, cp.

Now if we let the density of the fluid be ρ, we may define the coefficient of kinematic viscosity ν with the following equation,

$$\nu = \mu/\rho$$

The units of kinematic viscosity are cm²/s.

The viscosity of a gas is small, increases with temperature but changes hardly at all with pressure. The viscosity of liquids generally decreases with rising temperature and increases with pressure. The viscosity of a solution varies not only with the viscosity of the solvent but also with the type of solute and the concentration.

THERMAL CONDUCTIVITY

Let us consider a broad, solid flat plate of thickness L. When the temperatures of the two boundary surfaces are maintained at T_1 and T_2 respectively, then at steady state (i.e., the state in which the temperature T at any point x does not change with time), the following fact has been experimentally confirmed:

$$\left\{\begin{array}{l}\text{The heat flux } q, \text{ that is the rate} \\ \text{of heat transport per unit area} \\ \text{perpendicular to the flow of heat}\end{array}\right\} \propto \frac{\text{temperature difference}}{\text{distance}} \qquad (1)$$

Now if k is the proportionality constant, then

$$q = k\,\Delta T/L \qquad (2)$$

The constant k defined by the above equation is called the thermal conductivity and has the units cal/cm·sec°C or kcal/m·hr·°C.

Now (2) is the equation for the steady state case, but what would it be for the unsteady state case where the temperature changes with time? If we consider the relation in (2) to be valid for that instant where there is a temperature difference ΔT in the x direction over an infinitesimal distance Δx, then the rate of heat transport in the x direction per unit cross-sectional area perpendicular to x is $-k$ $(\Delta T/\Delta x)$. Accordingly, if we use differential symbols and introduce a negative sign in consideration of the fact that heat flows in the direction of decreasing temperature, then we have

$$q_x = -k\,dT/dx \qquad (3)$$

The above equation is called Fourier's Law for one-dimensional heat conduction,

and the integrated form of this equation well explains the actual phenomena in unsteady state conduction. If the temperature T varies in the three dimensions x, y, z, then the following equation holds.

$$\vec{q} = -k\nabla T \tag{4}$$

EXPLANATORY NOTES

(1) Note the many ways in which change and dependence can be stated in Japanese:

y-hōkō ni kansuru sokudo no henka	The rate of change of velocity in the *y*-direction
nensei wa ondo to tomo ni zōka suru	The viscosity increases with temperature
nensei wa atsuryoku ni yotte hotondo kawaranai	The viscosity is almost independent of the pressure
ondo o ageru to nensei wa genshō suru	If we raise the temperature, the viscosity decreases
nensei wa nōdo ni yotte henka suru	The viscosity depends on the concentration
T ga jikan ni taishite henka shinai	T does not change with time
jikan to tomo ni ondo ga henka suru	The temperature changes with time
T ga x, y, z, no 3 hōkō ni henka suru naraba...	If T changes in the three directions x, y, and z...

(2) ryūtai kara ukeru;
   x-hōkō e no;
   tan'i menseki atari no

These three phrases all modify *sendan-ōryoku*. Note the juxtaposition of the two particles *e* and *no*. In Japanese "the force in the *x*-direction" is *x-hōkō e no chikara* and the *no* cannot be omitted. *x-hōkō e* describes the kind of *chikara* we are dealing with.

(3) mokuteki no ryūtai

Same as *sono ryūtai* or *kangaete iru ryūtai* (i. e., that fluid which we have as the aim of our study.)

(4) sanshō saretai

"We wish you to consult." The form *sanshō saretai*, used only in the written language, is the desiderative form (*-tai* ending) of the verb *sareru* (the honorific equivalent of suru).

Compare: *sanshō seyo* "consult!" (brusque imperative); *sanshō shite itadakitai* "we should like to request that you consult" (polite conversational usage).

Other examples:

Kono hōkoku o yomaretai: We'd like you to read this report.

Kongetsu no kaigi ni shusseki saretai: I'd like you to attend this month's conference.

(5) teigi shite miru — Literally "define it and see how it turns out." In this case the expression can be replaced by *teigi suru.*

(6) chiisaku — In conversation, one would be more apt to say *chiisakute;* in either case the meaning is "is small, and."

(7) mochi-i — In conversation, one would use *mochi-ite;* in either case the meaning is "we use…, and."

(8) honshiki — Same as *kono shiki* ("this equation"); the use of *hon-* as a prefix meaning "this" is often used.

CONSTRUCTION EXAMPLES

| …に関する | "concerned with…," "with respect to…," "related to…" |

1.   2 変数 x, y の関数 z の微分 dz は，x に関する微分 $\frac{\partial z}{\partial x}dx$ と，y に関する微分 $\frac{\partial z}{\partial y}dy$ を用いて，$dz = \frac{\partial z}{\partial x}dx + \frac{\partial z}{\partial y}dy$ で表わされる。

2.   流体中を運動する物体が受ける抵抗の中には，流体の圧力に関する部分と粘性に関する部分とがある。

3.   環境保存は人類の存亡に関する重大な問題である。

変数	hensū	variable
関数	kansū	function
環境	kankyō	environment
人類	jinrui	mankind
存亡	sonbō	destiny
問題	mondai	problem

| …に関しては | "about…", "with regard to…", "as for…" |

1.   熱伝導に関しては，移動現象一般に関する専門書を参照されたい。

2.   本学会誌掲載の論文の内容に関しては本学会は責任を負いません。

3.   粘性の分子的考察に関しては後章で詳述する。

| 専門書 | senmon-sho | specialized works |

本学会誌掲載の	hon-gakkai-shi keisai no	which appeared in the journal of this society
論文	ronbun	article, paper
内容	naiyō	contents
責任	sekinin	responsibility
負う	ou	to bear, assume (responsibility)
考察	kōsatsu	consideration, inquiry
後章	kōshō	later chapter
詳述する	shōjutsu suru	to explain fully, enter fully into

| …に応じて | "in accordance with…", "depending on…" |

1. 球のまわりの定常流れの場合には，レイノルズ数の大小に応じて，圧力抵抗と粘性抵抗との大小関係が定まる。

2. 空間に固定して流体の運動を記述（きじゅつ）するか，流体に固定して記述（きじゅつ）するかに応じて，オイラーの式あるいはラグランジュの式が現われる。

大小	daishō	magnitude
圧力抵抗	atsuryoku-teikō	pressure drag
記述する	kijutsu suru	to describe
オイラー	Oirā	Euler
ラグランジュ	Raguranju	Lagrange

| 主として | "mainly", "principally" |

1. ある量の変化の割合（わり）を表わす場合，ベクトル量に対しては主（しゅ）として「グラジエント」スカラー量に対しては主（しゅ）として「傾（かたむ）き」を用いる。

2. 流体力学では主（しゅ）としてニュートン流体を取り扱（あつか）う。

| グラジエント | gurajiento | gradient (of a vector) |
| 傾き | katamuki | gradient (of a scalar) |

SUPPLEMENTARY READINGS

A.	等モル	tō-moru	equimolar
	(相互)拡散	(sōgo)kakusan	(counter) diffusion
	簡単な	kantan na	simple
	隔壁	kakuheki	partition
	容器	yōki	container, vessel
	別々に	betsu-betsu ni	separately

満たす	mitasu	to fill
保持する	hoji suru	to maintain
まま	mama	as it is
中間の	chūkan no	in the middle
取りはずす	tori-hazusu	to remove
ただし	tadashi	moreover
巨視的	kyoshi-teki	macroscopic
対流	tairyū	convection
仮定する	katei suru	to assume
濃度分布ができる	nōdo bunpu ga dekiru	a concentration distribution results
分圧	bun'atsu	partial pressure
…を通じる	…o tsūjiru	to pass through…
正(負)方向	sei (fu) hōkō	positive (negative) direction
移る	utsuru	to move
しかた	shikata	way, type
液系	ekikei	liquid system
多孔性の	takō-sei no	porous
よく見られる	yoku mirareru	often seen
さて	sate	now
以上の	ijō no	the above
モル量	moru-ryō	molar amount, mols
移動	idō	transport
流束	ryūsoku	flux
勾配	kōbai	gradient
負号	fugō	negative sign
フィック	Fikku	Fick
知られている	shirarete iru	is known
比較する	hikaku suru	to compare

等モル相互拡散 (I 18–19)

　もっとも簡単な場合として隔壁をもつ容器内に気体Aと気体Bを別々に満たし，温度・圧力を同じに保持したまま中間の隔壁を瞬間的に取りはずしたとしよう。ただし両気体の分子量は近い値であって，巨視的な対流はないものと仮定する。この場合は図1に示したように気体Aの分子は気体Bの方へ，気体Bの分子は気体Aの方へ拡散してゆくので，ある瞬間では図1のような濃度分布ができる。この場合，容器内の圧力はりの位置によらず一定P(atm)とすると

$$P_A + P_B = P \tag{1}$$

気体 A, B の分圧 P_A, P_B と，そのモル濃度 C_A, C_B は次の関係にある。

$$C_i = \frac{P_i}{P_0} \cdot \frac{1\,(\text{mol})}{22.4 \times 10^3\,(\text{cm}^3)} \cdot \frac{273}{T}, \qquad i = A, B \tag{2}$$

ここに P_0 は 1 気圧，T は温度 (°K) である。上式と (1) とから，

$$C_A + C_B = \frac{P}{P_0} \cdot \frac{1\,(\text{mol})}{22.4 \times 10^3\,(\text{cm}^3)} \cdot \frac{273}{T} = C = \text{constant} \tag{3}$$

すなわち断面を考えればその面を通じてAの分子が y の正方向に移る数と，Bの分子が y の負方向に移る数とは常に等しいことになる。このような拡散のしかたを等モル相互拡散といい，気体に限らず液系および多孔性の固体内においてもよく見られる現象である。

さて，以上の2成分系において，ある断面を考え，その場所におけるA成分の拡散する単位断面積あたりのモル量移動速度すなわち流束を $\mathcal{N}_A$ (mol/cm²·s) とするとこの値は y 方向の濃度勾配に比例して，次の式であらわされている。

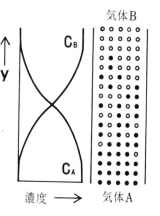

$$\mathcal{N}_A = -D_{AB} \frac{dC_A}{dy} \tag{4}$$

負号がついているのは，Aの濃度が減少する方向へ拡散することをあらわす。上式はフィックの拡散第一法則として知られているものであり，比例定数 D_{AB} (cm²/s) は拡散係数と呼ばれている。さて図1における気体Bのモル流束 $\mathcal{N}_B$ は y と反対の方向であるから，負の値として

$$\mathcal{N}_B = -D_{BA} \frac{dC_B}{dy} \tag{5}$$

等モル相互拡散の場合は $\mathcal{N}_A + \mathcal{N}_B = 0$ であり，また (3) から

$$\frac{-dC_A}{dy} = \frac{dC_B}{dy} \tag{6}$$

となるから，(4) と (5) を比較して

$$D_{AB} = D_{BA} \tag{7}$$

A, B が液体の場合でも上式の関係は成立する。

B.	一方拡散	ippō-kakusan	unidirectional diffusion
	条件	jōken	condition
	…場合が多い	…baai ga ōi	it frequently happens that…
	静止（状態）	seishi(jōtai)	stationary(state)

気体B中に	kitai-B-chū ni	in gas B
蒸発する	jōhatsu suru	to evaporate, to vaporize,
接触する	sesshoku suru	to contact
蒸気	jōki	vapor
与えられた…	ataerareta...	given...
平衡状態	heikō-jōtai	equilibrium condition, state
任意の	nin'i no	any (arbitrary)
逆方向	gyaku-hōkō	reverse direction
総括的に見て	sōkatsu-teki ni mite	viewed over-all, seen in total
分子群	bunshi-gun	collection of molecules
介在する	kaizai suru	to lie within
当然	tōzen	naturally
やはり	yahari	of course
…に乗る	...ni noru	to ride on...
前述した	zenjutsu shita	aforementioned
外側の	sotogawa no	outside
静止している観測者	seishi shite iru kansokusha	stationary observer
モル分率	moru bunritsu	mol fraction
重畳する	chōjō suru	superimposed, piled on one another
記述できる	kijutsu dekiru	can be expressed
昇華	shōka	sublimation
吸収	kyūshū	absorption
吸着	kyūchaku	adsorption
反応する	hannō suru	to react (chemically)
付近	fukin	neighborhood, vicinity
起る	okoru	to occur, happen

一方拡散　(I 19–21)

以上は等モル相互拡散の場合であり，A, B 全体として見た場合にはモル量の移動がない条件である。しかし実際の拡散現象には巨視的に見た場合，たとえば気体Aがｙ方向に流れながら気体Bと相互拡散を行なう場合が多い。そのもっとも簡単な例として巨視的には静止状態にある気体B中に，液A中の表面から蒸発した気体Aが拡散する図2を考えよう。ここで液表面に接触する気体中の蒸気（気体）Aの濃度は与えられた温度と圧力のもとで液面と平衡状態にあると仮定する。いま任意の位置ｙにおいて，ある瞬間における気体AおよびBのモル流束をN_A, N_Bとする。ただしモル流束で正の値はｙ方向，負の値は

y の逆方向の流束を表わす。さて，図2で液面から蒸発した蒸気すなわち気体Aの分子はy方向に移動するから総括的に見てy方向に質量あるいはモル量の流れが生ずることになる。いま単位断面積あたり気体Aが移動するモル量の流れ速度すなわちモル流束を N_A としよう。このようにAの分子群が総括的に見てy方向に流れるとき，その中に介在している気体Bの分子は当然これに引きずられてやはりy方向に流れる。このモル流束を N_B とすると，気体 A と B を合わせて $N_A + N_B$ の流れがy方向に生ずることになる。

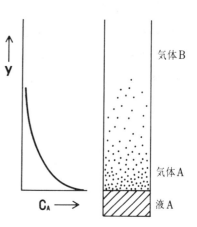

気体B

気体A

液A

$C_A \longrightarrow$

　いま $N_A + N_B$ のモル流束をもつ流れに乗ったままで観測すると考えれば，観測場所断面の前後には前述したような相互拡散が行なわれているはずである。すなわち外側の静止している観測者から見れば次式が成立する。

$$\begin{Bmatrix} \text{Aの移動す} \\ \text{るモル流束} \end{Bmatrix} = \begin{Bmatrix} \text{全体として} y \text{方向} \\ \text{に流れるモル流束} \end{Bmatrix} \begin{Bmatrix} \text{A成分の} \\ \text{モル分率} \end{Bmatrix} + \begin{Bmatrix} \text{総括の流れに重　畳する相} \\ \text{互分子拡散によるモル流束} \end{Bmatrix}$$

(4)を用いて記号で示せば

$$N_A = (N_A + N_B)x_A - D_{AB}\frac{dC_A}{dy} \tag{8}$$

このような拡散のしかたを一方拡散といい，相互拡散係数 D_{AB} によって記述できる現象である。一方拡散の例としては蒸発に限らず固体の昇華の場合，気体中の1成分が液体に吸収したり固体に吸着したりする場合，あるいは気体中の1成分が固体と反応して固定される場合に，境界面付近の気相中では以上のような一方拡散が起っている。

FINAL TRANSLATION TEST

　固体の内部での温度の変化は一般に熱の伝導によるが，液体や気体中での熱の移動という現象は少しこみいっている。例えば液体の一部が熱を受けると，その体積が増大するため，その部分の密度はまわりの部分の密度より小さくなる。この密度の差のために高温の部分が上昇して，液体の中に流れができ，熱は液体とともに運ばれる。上昇する部分があれば必ず下降する部分がなければ液体のない所が出現するので，流れは対をなして現われ，これを対流という。液体や気体の熱伝導率は非常に低いので，対流がなければ熱の移動に長時間を要する。

　いま，熱せられた平板を水平に置き，シュリーレン法によって平板に接する空気の動きを観察したとする。シュリーレン法は，空気の微小な密度差が目にみえるようにする方法

で，密度の小さい部分が平板に垂直に上昇して行くのがわかる。この場合，上向きの空気の流れの速度は，平板とまわりの空気の温度差に応じて定まる。

種々の物質について熱伝導率の測定値が得られているが，体積弾性率と同じく，固体より液体，液体より気体の方が小さい値を示す。

LESSON 11

第十一課

KANJI

仕	221	SHI		巻	221b	KAN
	362				1466	ma(ku)
事	230	JI		器	372	KI
	272	koto			994	utsuwa
転	479	TEN		銀	196	GIN
	4615				4855	
当	290	TŌ		利	528	RI
	1359	{a(teru) {a(taru)			3264	
飛	493	HI		盛	242a	
	5152	{to(basu) {to(bu)			3116	saka(ri) mo(ru)
散	407	SAN		決	202	KETSU
	2056	{chi(rasu) {chi(ru)			2509	{ki(meru) {ki(maru)
車	88	SHA		端	263a	TAN
	4608	kuruma			3363	hashi
止	220	SHI		以	342	I
	2429	{to(meru) {to(maru)			348	
使	224	SHI		油	522	YU
	432	tsuka(u)			2534	abura
装	252a	SŌ		外	56	GAI
	4234				1168	hoka soto

READING SELECTIONS

仕事	shigoto	work
力学的エネルギー	rikigaku-teki enerugii	mechanical energy
なす	nasu	to perform, do
著しい	ichijirushii	noticeable, significant
といし	toishi	grindstone
ナイフ	naifu	knife
押し当てる	oshi-ateru	to push (hold) against
とぐ	togu	to whet, grind
火花	hibana	spark

飛び散る	tobi-chiru	to fly off (in various directions)
ブレーキ	burēki	brake
止める	tomeru	to stop
車輪	sharin	wheel
熱い	atsui	hot
上げる	ageru	to raise, elevate
方法	hōhō	method, way
高温	kōon	high temperature
熱	netsu	heat
流入	ryūnyū	influx
…と限らない	…to kagiranai	is not limited to…
流れこむ	nagare-komu	to flow in
生ずる（＝生じる）	shōzuru	to produce, bring about
上昇する	jōshō suru	to rise
同等	dōtō	equality
ジュール	Jūru	Joule
使う	tsukau	to use
装置	sōchi	apparatus
略図	ryakuzu	sketch
おもり	omori	weight
下がる	sagaru	to hang down; descend
糸巻き	itomaki	spool
回る	mawaru	to rotate
入れる	ireru	to insert
容器	yōki	container, vessel
羽根車	hane-guruma	impeller, paddle-wheel
回転する	kaiten suru	to rotate
かき回す	kaki-mawasu	to stir
羽根	hane	blade, vane
ぶつかる	butsukaru	to hit, collide with
…につれて	…ni tsurete	as…
このほか	kono hoka	besides (this), moreover
当量	tōryō	equivalent
別の	betsu no	different
目盛り	memori	scale
数値	sūchi	numerical value
低温	teion	low temperature
結論	ketsuron	conclusion
後に	nochi ni	later

総和	sōwa	sum total
内部エネルギー	naibu enerugii	internal energy
まとめて	matomete	together, collectively
…の前後を通じて	…no zengo o tsūjite	throughout…
孤立系	koritsu-kei	isolated system
合わせる	awaseru	to combine
…に際して	…ni saishite	in case of…
総量	sōryō	total amount
物理	butsuri	physics
基礎的な	kiso-teki na	fundamental

エネルギー保存の法則　(B 126–127)

　摩擦や抵抗のない場合には，物体に仕事をすると，その物体は仕事に等しいだけの力学的エネルギーを得る。摩擦や抵抗のあるときには，力学的エネルギーの増加はなされた仕事量より少ないが，摩擦された部分の温度は著しく上がっている[1]。たとえば回転といしにナイフを押し当ててとぐときには火花が飛び散り，ブレーキをかけて自動車を止めるときには，車輪やブレーキが熱[2]くなっている。

　このように，物体の温度を上げる[1]方法は，高温の物体からの熱[3]の流入だけとは限らない。仕事によっても温度を上げることができる。

　熱が流れこむことによる温度上昇が，仕事すなわち力学的エネルギーの変化によって生ずる温度上昇と同等であることを示すために，ジ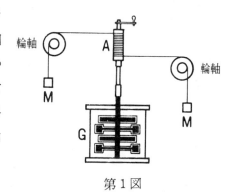ュールによっていろいろの実験が行なわれた。図1はその実験に使われた装置の略図である。二つのおもりMが重力に引かれて下がることによって糸巻きAが回り，水を入れた容器の中の羽根車Gが回転して水をかき回すが，水の運動は容器の内側に固定した羽根にぶつかって止められ，おもりが下がるにつれて水の温度が上がる。

第1図

　これから重力がおもりにした仕事，あるいはおもりの位置エネルギーの減少Wと，水の温度上昇に要する熱量Qとの間に

$$W = JQ \tag{1}$$

の関係が成り立つことが示された。このほかいろいろの実験が行なわれたがJの値はいつの場合も一定で，その値は

$$J = 4.2 \text{ ジュール/cal} \tag{2}$$

である。これを「熱の仕事当量」という。

Ｊがいつも一定であることから，ＷとＱとは同じ量を別の目盛りで測った数値と考えてよい⁽⁴⁾。したがって，熱は高温の物体から低温の物体に流れるエネルギーであることが結論される。これが熱エネルギーである。

物体に熱が流れこむと，その物体のエネルギーが増す。後に学ぶように，このエネルギーは物体を構成している分子のもつ力学的エネルギーの総和である⁽⁵⁾と考えられている。このエネルギーを物体の「内部エネルギー」という。状態の変化がないときは，内部エネルギーが増加すると，物体の温度が上がり，内部エネルギーが減少すると，温度が下がる。

ジュールの実験で，おもり・羽根車および容器内の水をまとめて考えれば，おもりの位置エネルギーの減少Ｗが水の内部エネルギーの増加になったと考えられるから，実験の前後を通じて内部エネルギーと力学的エネルギーの総和は変わらないことになる。すなわち「孤立系のもつ内部エネルギーと力学的エネルギーとを合わせて考えれば，その状態の変化に際してエネルギーの総量は常に一定に保たれる。」

これを「エネルギー保存の法則」といい，物理においては最も基礎的な法則の一つである。

暖かさ	atatakasa	warmth
冷たさ	tsumetasa	coolness
数量的に	sūryō-teki ni	quantitatively
ふつうに	futsū ni	generally
水銀	suigin	mercury
冷暖	reidan	warmth and coldness
…に伴う	…ni tomonau	to accompany…
利用する	riyō suru	to utilize
ぬく	nuku	to remove
まず	mazu	first of all
標準	hyōjun	standard
決める	kimeru	to decide, fix, set
1気圧	ichi-kiatsu	one atmosphere
…のもとで	…no moto de	at…, under…
とける	tokeru	to melt
沸騰する	futtō suru	to boil
(verb stem)＋つつある	(verb stem)＋tsutsu aru	is…-ing
氷	kōri	ice
水蒸気	sui-jōki	water vapor
氷点	hyōten	melting point
沸点	futten	boiling point
上端	jōtan	upper end
等分する	tōbun suru	to divide equally
以上；以下	ijō; ika	above; below

割合	wariai	proportion
刻む	kizamu	to mark off, score
石油エーテル	sekiyu-ēteru	petroleum ether
ぐらい	gurai	approximately
…以外	…igai	outside of…
示度	shido	reading
相違	sōi	discrepancy
トルオール (also written トルエン)	toruōru	toluene

温 度 計 (B 114–115)

暖かさ[6]冷たさ[6][7]を数量的に表わしたものを温度という。温度を測る温度計にはいろいろのものがあるが，ふつうに用いられるのは水銀温度計である。これは水銀の体積が冷暖に伴って変化する性質を利用したもので，空気をぬいた細いガラス管の中に水銀を入れたものである。

温度の目盛りをするために，まず二つの標準点を決める。それには，

(1) 1気圧のもとでとけつつある[8]氷

(2) 1気圧のもとで沸騰しつつある[8]水の上の水蒸気

の温度を，それぞれ 0°（氷点），100°（水の沸点）と決める。このときの水銀の上端の位置を 0, 100 とする。0, 100 の間を 100 等分しさらに 0 以下，100 以上も同じ割合で刻む。このようにして定めた[9]温度目盛りを C 目盛りとよぶ。

水銀のかわりに石油エーテルを用いた温度計もあり，−30°C から 200°C ぐらいの間で使われる。このとき，0°C と 100°C 以外では温度の示度に相違が起こるが，その差は小さい。トルオールを入れた温度計では，−90°C ぐらいまでの低い温度が測られる。

ENERUGII HOZON NO HŌSOKU

Masatsu ya teikō no nai baai ni wa, buttai ni shigoto o suru to, sono buttai wa shigoto ni hitoshii dake no rikigaku-teki enerugii o eru. Masatsu ya teikō no aru toki ni wa, rikigaku-teki enerugii no zōka wa nasareta shigoto-ryō yori sukunai ga, masatsu sareta bubun no ondo wa ichijirushiku agatte iru.[1] Tatoeba kaiten-toishi ni naifu o oshi-atete togu toki ni wa hibana ga tobi-chiri, burēki o kakete jidōsha o tomeru toki ni wa, sharin ya burēki ga atsuku[2] natte iru.

Kono yō ni, buttai no ondo o ageru[1] hōhō wa, kō-on no buttai kara no netsu[3] no ryūnyū dake to wa kagiranai. Shigoto ni yotte mo ondo o ageru koto ga dekiru.

Netsu ga nagare-komu koto ni yoru ondo-jōshō ga, shigoto sunawachi rikigaku-teki enerugii no henka ni yotte shō-zuru ondo-jōshō to dōtō de aru koto o shimesu tame ni, Jūru ni yotte iroiro no jikken ga okonawareta.

Zu-ichi wa sono jikken ni tsukawareta sōchi no ryakuzu de aru. Futatsu no omori M ga jūryoku ni hikarete sagaru koto ni yotte itomaki A ga mawari, mizu o ireta yōki no naka no hane-guruma G ga kaiten shite mizu o kaki-mawasu ga, mizu no undō wa yōki no uchigawa ni kotei shita hane ni butsukatte tomerare, omori ga sagaru ni tsurete mizu no ondo ga agaru.

Kore kara jūryoku ga omori ni shita shigoto, aruiwa omori no ichi enerugii no genshō *W* to, mizu no ondo-jōshō ni yō suru netsuryō *Q* to no aida ni

$$W = JQ \tag{1}$$

no kankei ga nari-tatsu koto ga shimesareta. Kono hoka, iroiro no jikken ga oko-nawareta ga *J* no atai wa itsu no baai mo ittei de, sono atai wa

$$J = 4.2 \text{ Joule/cal} \tag{2}$$

de aru. Kore o "netsu no shigoto-tōryō" to iu. *J* ga itsu mo ittei de aru koto kara, *W* to *Q* to wa onaji ryō o betsu no memori de hakatta sūchi to kangaete yoi[4]. Shitagatte, netsu wa kō-on no buttai kara tei-on no buttai ni nagareru enerugii de aru koto ga ketsuron sareru. Kore ga netsu enerugii de aru.

Buttai ni netsu ga nagare-komu to, sono buttai no enerugii ga masu. Nochi ni manabu yō ni, kono enerugii wa buttai o kōsei shite iru bunshi no motsu riki-gaku-teki enerugii no sōwa de aru[5] to kangaerarete iru. Kono enerugii o buttai no "naibu-enerugii" to iu. Jōtai no henka ga nai toki wa naibu-enerugii ga zōka suru to, buttai no ondo ga agari, naibu-enerugii ga genshō suru to ondo ga sagaru.

Jūru no jikken de, omori, hane-guruma, oyobi yōki-nai no mizu o matomete kangaereba, omori no ichi-enerugii no genshō *W* ga mizu no naibu-enerugii no zōka ni natta to kangaerareru kara, jikken no zengo o tsūjite naibu enerugii to rikigaku-teki enerugii no sōwa wa, kawaranai koto ni naru. Sunawachi "Koritsu-kei no motsu naibu-enerugii to rikigaku-teki enerugii to o awasete kangaereba, sono jōtai no henka ni saishite enerugii no sōryō wa, tsune ni ittei ni tamotareru."

Kore o "enerugii hozon no hōsoku" to ii, butsuri ni oite wa mottomo kiso-teki na hōsoku no hitotsu de aru.

ONDO-KEI

Atatakasa[6] tsumetasa[6] [7] o sūryō-teki ni arawashita mono o ondo to iu. Ondo o hakaru ondo-kei ni wa iroiro no mono ga aru ga, futsū ni mochi-irareru no wa suigin-ondo-kei de aru. Kore wa suigin no taiseki ga reidan ni tomonatte henka suru seishitsu o riyō shita mono de, kūki o nuita hosoi garasu-kan no naka ni suigin o ireta mono de aru.

Ondo no memori o suru tame ni, mazu futatsu no hyōjun-ten o kimeru. Sore ni wa

(1) Ichi-kiatsu no moto de toke-tsutsu aru[8] kōri

(2) Ichi-kiatsu no moto de futtō shi-tsutsu aru[8] mizu no ue no sui-jōki

no ondo o, sorezore rei-do (hyōten), hyaku-do (mizu no futten) to kimeru. Kono

toki no suigin no jōtan no ichi o rei, hyaku to suru. Rei, hyaku no aida o hyaku-tōbun shi, sara ni rei ika, hyaku ijō mo onaji wariai de kizamu. Kono yō ni shite sadameta [9] ondo-memori o C memori to yobu.

Suigin no kawari ni sekiyu-ēteru o mochi-ita ondo-kei mo ari, mainasu sanjū-do kara nihyaku-do gurai no aida de tsukawareru. Kono toki, rei-do to hyaku-do igai de wa ondo no shido ni sōi ga okoru ga, sono sa wa chiisai. Toruōru o ireta ondo-kei de wa, mainasu kyūjū-do gurai made no hikui ondo ga hakara-reru.

THE LAW OF THE CONSERVATION OF ENERGY

When work is done on a body in the absence of friction and resistance, that body receives (an amout of) mechanical energy exactly equal to the work. When friction and resistance are present, the increase in mechanical energy is less than the amount of work performed, but the temperature of the parts subjected to friction rises significantly. For example, when we press a knife against a rotating grindstone, sparks fly off, and when we apply the brakes to stop a car, the wheels and the brakes become hot.

Thus, the way to raise the temperature of a body is not limited only to the influx of heat from a high temperature object. Temperature can also be raised by means of work.

In order to show that the rise in temperature due to the influx of heat is equal to the temperature rise which occurs due to work, i.e.. to a change in mechanical energy, various experiments were performed by Joule.

Figure 1 is a sketch of the apparatus used in the experiments. Spool A revolves due to the falling of the two weights M pulled by gravity, and the paddle wheel G in the vessel filled with water rotates and stirs the water. The motion of the water is stopped by striking against the blades fixed to the inner surface of the container and, as the weights fall, the temperature of the water rises.

It was shown by these experiments that the relation

$$W = JQ \tag{1}$$

holds between the work performed by gravity on the weights, i. e., the decrease in potential energy W of the weights, and the amount of heat Q required to raise the temperature of the water.

Various other experiments were done and the value of J for every case was constant, that value being

$$J = 4.2 \text{ joules/cal.} \tag{2}$$

This is called the mechanical equivalent of heat. Because J is always constant, we may consider W and Q to be numerical values of the same quantity measured by different scales. Consequently, we conclude that heat is an energy which flows from a high temperature body to a low temperature body. This is "thermal

energy."

If heat flows into a body, the energy of that body increases. As we will learn later, this energy is thought of as the sum total of the mechanical energy possessed by the molecules which constitute the body. This energy is called the internal energy of the body. If the internal energy of a body increases without a change of state, the temperature of the body rises, and if the internal energy of the body decreases, the temperature drops.

If we consider collectively the weights, paddle wheel, and water in the container in Joule's experiments, then, since the decrease in the potential energy of the weights W can be thought of as having become the increase in the internal energy of the water, the sum of the internal and mechanical energy throughout the experiment will not have changed. In other words, if we consider together the mechanical and internal energies which an isolated system possesses, then in cases of change in its state, the total amount of energy will always be maintained constant.

This is called the law of the conservation of energy and is one of the most fundamental laws in physics.

THERMOMETERS

Temperature is the quantitative expression of warmth and coldness. There are various kinds of thermometers which measure temperature, but the mercury thermometer is ordinarily used. It utilizes the property that the volume of mercury changes according to warmth and coldness, and it consists of mercury inserted into a fine glass tube from which the air has been removed.

In order to make a temperature scale, two standard points are first fixed; the temperature of melting ice at 1 atmosphere pressure and that of steam above boiling water at 1 atmosphere pressure are set respectively at 0° (the ice point) and 100° (the boiling point of water), The positions of the upper end of the mercury for these cases are made 0 and 100. The space between 0 and 100 is divided into a hundred equal parts, and those regions below 0 and above 100 are further marked off in the same proportions. The temperature scale determined in this way is called the Centigrade scale.

There is also a thermometer which employs petroleum ether in place of mercury and which is used in the range from −30°C to about 200°C. In this case discrepancies arise for temperature readings other than those at 0°C and 100°C, but the differences are small. With thermometers filled with toluene low temperatures can be measured to about−90°C.

EXPLANATORY NOTES

(1) agaru, ageru   Note that *agaru* is intransitive and means "to rise",

whereas *ageru* is transitive and means "to raise." Correspondingly, *sagaru* (下がる) is intransitive, meaning "to descend," "to hang down", whereas *sageru* (下げる) is transitive and means "to lower". For further comments on *-aru*, *-eru* verb pairs, see Explanatory Notes of Lesson 13.

(2) atsui   Note that "hot" may be translated by 熱い (*atsui*) or by 暑い (*atsui*); the latter is used only for describing hot weather. Note that a homonym 厚い (*atsui*)—used in Lesson 10—means "thick".

(3) kōon no buttai kara no netsu   "The heat from a high-temperature body." The *no* serves to indicate that *kōon no buttai kara* modifies *netsu*. Other examples of the juxtaposition of two particles are:

Kyōto de no kaigi	A conference in Kyōto
Shūi to no netsu-kōkan	Heat exchange with the surroundings
Kenkyū-jo e no dōro	The road to the research center

(4) kangaete yoi   The-*te yoi* construction can usually be translated by "may". The following comparison of several related constructions should be helpful for future reference with verbs other than *kangaeru*.

Kono jikken de wa garasukan o   In this experiment,

a) tsukawanakereba naranai	a) you must use	
b) tsukau to yoi	b) you had better use*	
c) tsukaeba yoi	c) it is advisable to use**	
d) tsukatte yoi	d) you may use***	a glass
e) tsukatte mó yoi	e) you may use (if necessary)****	tube
f) tsukawanakute yoi	f) you need not use	
g) tsukatte wa ikenai	g) you must not use	

*   i.e., if you want to get good experimental results
**   i.e., glass is quite adequate for the experiment
*** i.e., it makes no difference, really, whether you use glass or copper
****i.e., if you can't find the proper copper tubing and end up having to use glass, then use it!

(5) kono enerugii wa ...de aru   *buttai...iru* modifies *bunshi*, which in turn is the subject of *motsu*; *bunshi no motsu=bunshi ga motsu* "which the molecules have".

(6) atatakasa, tsumetasa   These are nouns formed from the corresponding ad-

jectives *atatakai* ("warm") and *tsumetai* ("cold"). In previous lessons we have encountered *hayasa, takasa, omosa, ōkisa,* and *atsusa* ("thickness") similarly formed.

(7) tsumetai vs. samui — Both *tsumetai* (冷たい) and *samui* (寒い) mean cold; the latter refers primarily to the weather. *Tsumetai* would be used in referring to a cold wind, cold water, iced tea, etc.; it is used to indicate the individual's perception of coldness.

(8) toke-tsutsu aru; futtō-shi-tsutsu aru — "which is melting" and "which is boiling"; these are literary forms which correspond to the present progressive forms *tokete iru* and *futtō shite iru* used in the spoken language. The suffix-*tsutsu* sometimes has the same meaning as -*nagara*, indicating the simultaneous occurence of two actions:

> Netsu-rikigaku no dai-ichi hōsoku o manzoku shi-tsutsu, shizen ni hannō ga okoru.
>
> Reactions proceed spontaneously, and at the same time satisfy the first law of thermodynamics.

(9) sadamaru, sadameru — *Sadamaru* means "to be decided, to be determined," whereas *sadameru* means "to decide, to determine." Hence *kono yō ni shite sadameta ondo-memori* is "the temperature scale which we fix in this fashion."

CONSTRUCTION EXAMPLES

| …に際して | "in the case of…," "on the occasion of…", "at the time of…" |

1. ジュールは熱エネルギーの実験に際して羽根車を用いた。
2. 物体の衝突に際して運動量の和は保存される。
3. 2気体の等モル相互拡散に際して巨視的な対流はないものと仮定した。
4. 開会に際して大会委員長のあいさつがある。

相互拡散	sōgo-kakusan	counter diffusion
巨視的な	kyoshi-teki na	macroscopic
対流	tairyū	convection
仮定する	katei suru	to suppose, postulate
開会	kaikai	the opening of a meeting
大会委員長	taikai-iin-chō	chairman of the convention committee
あいさつ	aisatsu	introduction

…につれて	"with…," "as…"

1. ブレーキをかけると時間がたつ（の）につれてブレーキが熱くなってくる。

2. 高分子物質では，分子量の増大につれて粘度が増大する。

…を通じて	"throughout…," "through…"

1. 観測の全期間を通じて異常は見出されなかった。

2. 物体の衝突の前後を通じて運動量の和は一定である。

全期間	zen-kikan	entire duration
異常	ijō	abnormality; anything unusual
見出す	mi-idasu	to discover

…を通して	"passing through…," "by means of…"

1. 熱は外部から容器を通して内部の液体に伝えられた。

2. 糸の一端を物体に結んで自由端を引っ張れば，糸を通して物体に力を及ぼすことができる。

伝える	tsutaeru	to transmit, transfer
引っ張る	hipparu	to pull

SUPPLEMENTARY READINGS

A. Selections from Rikagaku Jiten

1)

きわめて	kiwamete	very
精密な	seimitsu na	precise, exact
考案する	kōan suru	to devise, design
二重管	nijū-kan	annular tube
細管	saikan	narrow tube
…とならべて	…to narabete	side by side with…
約	yaku	approximately
範囲	han'i	extent, limit, range
目盛る	memoru	to mark off (a scale), graduate
スケール	sukēru	scale
接続する	setsuzoku suru	to connect, join
使用する	shiyō suru	to use
あたためる	atatameru	to warm up
逆さにする	sakasa ni suru	to turn upside down

軽く	karuku	lightly
振る	furu	to shake
適量	tekiryō	suitable amount
…をCにおくように	…o C ni oku yō ni	after putting…in C
してから	shite kara	
…にする	…ni suru	to cause…, bring about…
正立させる	seiritsu saseru	to set upright
零点	reiten	zero point
望みの	nozomi no	desired
調整できる	chōsei dekiru	can adjust, regulate
付近	fukin	neighborhood

ベックマン温度計　(2RJ 1230)

　熱量や温度の変化のきわめて精密な測定に用いられる図のような水銀の液体温度計で，E. O. Beckmann が考案した。球部Ａの体積は，1−2 cm³ でふつうの水銀温度計より大きい。B部は二重管で内部のものはきわめて細い。細管とならべて約 6 deg の範囲を 0.01deg まで目盛ったスケールがおかれ，細管の上部には太いガラス管Ｃが接続してある。使用したい温度より数 deg 高い温度にあたためて，逆さにし，軽く振って適量の水銀をＣにおくようにしてから正立させれば目盛りの零点を望みの温度に調整できて，その温度付近の温度変化を測定することができる。

2)			
	転移点	ten'i-ten	transition point
	転移温度	ten'i-ondo	transition temperature
	現われる	arawareru	to manifest itself, appear
	鉄	tetsu	iron
	としていい表わす	to shite ii-arawasu	to refer to as, speak of as

転移点と転移温度　(2RJ 905)

　ある物質の転移現象は各物質に固有な一定の圧力，温度のもとで現われる。例えば鉄は 1atm, 910°C において α 状態から γ 状態に転移する。転移点を定める状態変数としては圧力および温度がとられるが，主として圧力を一定にして温度の変化だけを考えるから，このような場合には転移温度を単に転移点としていい表わす。

3)			
	熱拡散	netsu-kakusan	thermal diffusion
	混合気体	kongō-kitai	gas mixture
	各成分	kaku seibun	each component
	相対的に	sōtai-teki ni	relatively

図　1
ベックマン
温度計

わずかながら	wazuka nagara	although very slight
通常	tsūjō	usually
移行する	ikō suru	to move
濃度	nōdo	concentration
普通の	futsū no	ordinary

熱　拡　散　(2RJ 1017)

　混合気体の内部で温度の差があれば，各成分は気体全体に対して相対的にわずかながら一方の向きに流れる。通常重い気体が温度の低い方に移行する。その結果，場所によって濃度の差を生ずるが，濃度の差があれば，普通の拡散が熱拡散と反対の方向におこり，定常状態が成り立つ。

4)	熱力学	netsu-rikigaku	thermodynamics
	第三法則	daisan-hōsoku	third law
	ネルンスト	Nerunsuto	Nernst
	定理	teiri	theorem
	確立する	kakuritsu suru	to establish
	相	sō	phase
	極限	kyokugen	limit
	炭素	tanso	carbon
	グラファイト	gurafaito	graphite
	ダイヤモンド	daiyamondo	diamond
	結晶	kesshō	crystal
	…をとりうる	…o tori-uru	can adopt..., can take...
	異なる…	kotonaru...	different...
	相等しい	ai-hitoshii	equal
	決定できる	kettei dekiru	can determine
	有限回数	yūgen-kaisū	finite number of cycles
	過程	katei	process
	到達する	tōtatsu suru	to reach
	純粋な	junsui na	pure
	いかなる…も	ikanaru...mo	whatever...
	仮定する	katei suru	to assume, postulate
	意味	imi	meaning
	限界	genkai	limitation
	統計力学	tōkei-rikigaku	statistical mechanics
	意義	igi	meaning
	考慮する	kōryo suru	to consider

熱力学の第三法則 (2RJ 1024)

ネルンストの熱定理ともいう。Nernst によって確立された法則で(1906)，その内容は始め次のように表わされた。気体，液体，固体の相での，あるいはそれらの相の間での等温変化におけるエントロピーの変化を ΔS とすれば，これは絶対温度零度の極限で0になる。例えば炭素は絶対温度 $T=0$ において，グラファイトとダイヤモンドの二つの結晶状態をとりうると考えられるが，この二つの状態のエントロピーが等しいというのである。グラファイトのエントロピーとダイヤモンドのエントロピーはそれぞれ異なる状態関数であるが，これらが $T=0$ において相等しい値をとるかということは熱力学の第一法則，第二法則からは決定できない内容である。

この法則はまた有限回数の過程によっては $T=0$ の状態に到達することはできないという形に表わすことができる。

Planck はさらに進んで純粋な物質のエントロピーはそれがいかなる種類のものであっても，絶対温度零度においては0になると仮定した。これらの法則の意味と限界はエントロピーの統計力学的意義を考慮すれば明らかになる。

B.

われわれの	wareware no	our
経験	keiken	experience
…に基づく	…ni motozuku	to be based on…, to be founded on…
やはり	yahari	also
事柄	kotogara	circumstance, situation
異なった	kotonatta	different
接触させる	sesshoku saseru	to put in contact
失なう	ushinau	to lose
他方	tahō	the other
…ところである (=…ことである)	…tokoro de aru	is what…
依然	izen	as it was before
満足する	manzoku suru	to satisfy
…に向って流れる	…ni mukatte nagareru	to flow towards…
化学種	kagaku-shu	chemical species
自然に	shizen ni	naturally, spontaneously
反応	hannō	reaction
発熱(の)	hatsunetsu (no)	exothermic
他の	ta no	other
生成する	seisei suru	to produce, create
平衡の	heikō no	equilibrium

推進力	suishin-ryoku	driving force
(不) 可逆的	(fu) kagyaku-teki	(ir) reversible
逆にする	gyaku ni suru	to reverse
多くの	ōku no	many
加える	kaeru	to convert
制限	seigen	limit
有する	yū suru	to have
蒸気	jōki	vapor
1成分2相系	ichi-seibun-nisō-kei	1-component-2-phase system
無視する	mushi suru	to disregard
おもり	omori	a weight
無限大の	mu-gendai no	infinitely great
容量	yōryō	capacity
恒温槽	kōon-sō	constant temperature reservoir
凝縮する	gyōshuku suru	to condense
…に相当する	…ni sōtō suru	to correspond to…
周囲	shūi	surroundings
系	kei	system
静止する	seishi suru	to rest, stand still
降下	kōka	fall, lowering
吸収する	kyūshū suru	to absorb
蒸発する	jōhatsu suru	to vaporize
元の…にもどる	moto no…ni modoru	to return to the original…
サイクル	saikuru	cycle
完結する	kanketsu suru	to complete
取り出す	tori-dasu	to remove
全く	mattaku	completely, perfectly
条件	jōken	conditions
更に	sara ni	still more
仕事をなす	shigoto o nasu	to perform work
有効	yūkō	available
導き出す	michibiki-dasu	to deduce
循環…	junkan…	cyclical…
なんら	nanra	any
助け	tasuke	aid, help, assistance
借りる	kariru	to borrow
正味の	shōmi no	net
(不) 可能	(fu) kanō	(im) possible

熱力学の第二法則　(N 49–50)

　エネルギー保存則というのはわれわれの経験に基づくものであるが，このほかにやはり経験に基づく事実で，第一法則では説明できない事柄がある。

　異なった温度の2つの物体を接触させると，熱は常に高温から低温に移動し，高温部が失なった熱量と，低温部が得た熱量とは相等しくなる。この一つの失なった量が他方の得た量に等しいということは第一法則が説明するところであるが，もしこれが低温から高温に流れたとしても，全エネルギーが一定であれば第一法則は依然満足されていることになる。

　したがって，この第一法則を満足しつつ，さらに自然におこる変化においては，もう一つの法則が成り立つ必要がある。例えば発熱反応によって，他の化学種を生成する現象等，自然に変化のおこる方向は第一法則では説明できない新しい経験事実である。すなわち，自然現象は平衡の状態になるように変化している場合，変化の方向を説明する自然の法則があるはずである。自然におこる変化は，ある推進力によっておこり，この推進力の極限が0であると可逆的プロセスであった。不可逆なプロセスでは，常にある推進力を必要とし，外部からエネルギーを与えなければその方向を逆にすることはできない。

　熱と仕事の場合を例にとって考えると，多くの実験結果から仕事は完全に熱にかえることができるが，熱を仕事にかえるについては，ある制限がある。しかし，それは熱が完全に仕事にかえられないというのではない。例えば，摩擦のないピストンを有するシリンダー中に，小量の液と，その蒸気がある(1成分2相系)。しかも，ピストンの重さが無視でき，その上にのせられているおもりは，液の蒸気圧と釣合っている。この系全体を，無限大の容量の恒温槽中にいれて，ピストンに無限小の重さを加えると，一定温度で蒸気は凝縮して液となり，蒸気の凝縮熱 Q に相当する熱が，系から周囲に与えられて，ピストンは液面上で静止する。このプロセスではピストンの降下による仕事は完全に熱にかえることができる。

　次にピストンの上のおもりを，液の蒸気圧より無限小だけ小さくすると，一定温度で，系は周囲から熱を吸収して蒸発しピストンは元の状態にもどり，サイクルを完結する。このプロセスでは，系が吸収した熱は最初のプロセスで，系から取り出された熱 Q と全く相等しく，この熱はピストンを元の状態にあげる仕事に使用される。

　この事柄は，ある条件の下では，熱は完全に仕事にかえられることを示しているが，更に重要なことは最初のプロセスで系になされた仕事と，次のプロセスで系がなした仕事とは相等しいから，サイクル中になした有効仕事は0になっていることである。

　以上の事柄からして，第二法則が導き出される。すなわち，ある方法によれば理想的プロセスで，熱を完全に仕事にかえることはできるが，循環プロセスを使用して，周囲から

なんら助けを借りないで熱エネルギーを完全に正味の有効仕事にかえることは不可能である。

FINAL TRANSLATION TEST

　重い物体を一つの地点から他の地点へ運ぶ場合，物体につなを巻きつけて地面上を引きずって行けば，物体と地面との間の摩擦に抗して仕事をしなければならない。この仕事をなるべく小さくするために，車が考え出された。これによってすべり摩擦を回転摩擦に変え，大いに力を利することができた。さらに，軸受けでの摩擦を減ずるために油を使用する。一般の軸受けでは，すべり面と軸との間に $20kg/mm^2$ 程度の油圧をもった膜が形成されて摩擦を減ずる。ところで，このような油は使用中空気中へ飛散したり，軸受け以外の部分に流出したりして減少するので，その分だけ常に油を加える必要を生じる。そこで最近では，非常に多くの細かい穴があって，その中に油を保持している含油軸受け (self-lubricating bearing) がよく用いられる。軸の回転が始まると，摩擦熱のために，穴の中の油や空気がふくれて穴から盛り上がり，軸受けに当たっている面にしみ出してくる。摩擦熱による油粘性の減少もこの作用をたすけている。軸の回転が止まると温度が下がって，油はまた穴の中へもどる。このことは次のような実験装置で観察することができる。すなわち，一端を閉じた細いガラス管の中に空気と油を入れ，容器内に逆さに立てる（第1図）。ガラス管を熱すると油が出て行くが，温度が下がればまたもどってくることがわかる。同じくガラス管を用いて液体を入れたものに気圧計があるが，この場合には，一端を閉じたガラス管から空気をのぞいて水銀が入れてあるので，以上のような現象は決して起こらない。

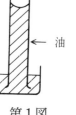

← 空気

← 油

第1図

LESSON 12

第十二課

KANJI

膨	272a	BŌ
	3818	
張	675	CHŌ
	1570	ha(ru)
多	108	TA
	1169	ō(i)
鉄	283	TETSU
	4844	
両	336	RYŌ
	34	
伸	206a	SHIN
	403	{no(basu) no(biru)}
棒	249a	BŌ
	2302	
晶	248b	SHŌ
	2137	
異	738	I
	3008	koto(naru)
様	328	YŌ
	2341	

急	186	KYŪ
	1667	iso(gu)
縮	274a	SHUKU
	3608	{chiji(meru) chiji(maru)}
逆	758	GYAKU
	485	saka(rau)
他	459	TA
	361	
発	303	HATSU
	3092	
放	512	HŌ
	2084	hana(su)
源	257a	GEN
	2656	
機	373	KI
	2379	
効	782	KŌ
	722	
蒸	258b	JŌ
	4002	mu(su)

READING SELECTIONS

(熱)膨張	(netsu)bōchō	(thermal) expansion
多くの	ōku no	many, a number of
…に従って	…ni shitagatte	as…
鉄	tetsu	iron
相当	sōtō	rather, fairly
著しい	ichijirushii	noticeable
鉄橋	tekkyō	iron bridge
両端	ryōtan	both ends
寒暑	kansho	heat and cold, temperature

差	sa	difference, variation
鉄材	tetsuzai	iron (material)
伸び縮み	nobi-chijimi	expansion and contraction
余裕	yoyū	allowance (for)
棒	bō	rod
…ごとに	…goto ni	each…, at an interval of…
伸びる	nobiru	to expand
線膨張率	sen-bōchō-ritsu	coefficient of linear expansion
木材	mokuzai	wood (material)
縦と横とで	tate to yoko to de	longitudinally and transversely
結晶（軸）	kesshō(jiku)	crystal (axis)
異なる	kotonaru	to be dissimilar, unlike
上昇する	jōshō suru	to rise
各辺	kakuhen	every edge; every side
体膨張率	tai-bōchō-ritsu	coefficient of volume expansion
一様に	ichiyō ni	uniformly

固体の熱膨張　(B 115–117)

水銀や石油などに限らず，多くの固体も温度が上がるに従って膨張する。

鉄も相当 著しい熱膨張を示すので，鉄橋の両端などは固定せず[1]，寒暑[2] の差によって鉄材の伸び縮み[3] が起こる余裕をもたせてある。

一般に，固体の熱膨張は液体や気体に比べて小さい。

いま，$t°C$ のときの棒の長さ[5]を l，$t'°C$ のときの長さを l' とすると，温度が t と t' の間で1度上がるごとに，棒が $t°C$ のときの長さに比べて伸びる割合 α は，

$$\alpha = \frac{(l'-l)/l}{t'-t} \tag{1}$$

で示される。これを線膨張率という。したがって，

$$l' = l\ \{1 + \alpha(t'-t)\} \tag{2}$$

となる。

木材は縦と横とで線膨張率が違っている。また，結晶でも結晶軸の方向によって，性質が異なることがある[6]ので，伸び方も方向によって違う。

温度が上昇するにつれて，固体の各辺が伸びるので体積も膨張する。いま $t°C$ のときの体積を v，$t'°C$ のときの体積を v' とすれば，温度が1度上がるごとに体積が $t°C$ のときに比

べて増加する割合を体膨張率といい β で表わす。すなわち，

$$\beta = \frac{(v'-v)/v}{t'-t} \quad \text{したがって} \quad v' = v\{1+\beta(t'-t)\} \tag{3}$$

各方向に一様に伸びる固体では

$$\beta \fallingdotseq 3\alpha \tag{4}$$

の関係がある。

断熱(変化)	dannetsu (henka)	adiabatic (change)
急(激)に	kyū (geki) ni	quickly
圧縮する	asshuku suru	to compress
ぬく	nuku	to pull out, draw out
押し下げる	oshi-sageru	to push down, depress
熱容量	netsu-yōryō	heat capacity
いっぱいに	ippai ni	as much as possible
さしこむ	sashi-komu	to thrust in
放す	hanasu	to release
外	soto	outside, surroundings
逃げる	nigeru	to escape
逆に	gyaku ni	on the contrary, conversely
外部	gaibu	surroundings
出入り	de-iri	going in and out; exchange

断熱変化　(B 128–129)

実験：空気を急激に圧縮したり，膨張させたりする [7] と，その温度がどう変わるか，次のようにして調べてみよう。

1) 初めピストンを上の方にぬいておく [8]。このピストンを急に押し下げて中の空気を圧縮する。このとき，熱容量の小さい温度計で空気の温度を測ると，数度上昇したことがわかる。

2) 初めピストンをいっぱいにさしこんでおく [8]。ピストンを急に放して中の空気を急に膨張させると，その温度は数度下がる。

このように，熱が外へ逃げないようにして気体を急激に圧縮すると，その温度が上がり，逆に気体を急激に膨張させると，温度が下がる。一般に外部との間に熱の出入り [9] のない状態の変化を「断熱変化」といい，その変化が圧縮の場合を「断熱圧縮」，膨張の場合を「断熱膨張」という。

このように熱の出入りがないようにして，外から仕事を加えると，その仕事は物体の内部エネルギーの増加になるので，物体の温度は上昇する。また，物体が外に仕事をする場

合には内部エネルギーが減少するので温度が下がる。

カルノー・サイクル	Karunō saikuru	Carnot cycle
他の…	ta no…	another…
経る	heru	to pass through
再び	futatabi	again, once more
もとの（元の）	moto no	original
帰る	kaeru	to return
循環	junkan	cycle
循環過程	junkan-katei	cyclical process
出発する	shuppatsu suru	to depart, start
（不）可逆的	(fu) kagyaku-teki	(ir) reversible
吸収する	kyūshū suru	to absorb
放出する	hōshutsu suru	to release, discharge
…てきた	…te kita	has come to be…
終わる	owaru	to end
不変である	fuhen de aru	to be unchanged
…により	…ni yori	according to…
熱源	netsugen	heat reservoir
（熱）機関	(netsu) kikan	(heat) engine
有効な	yūkō na	effective
効率	kōritsu	efficiency
蒸気	jōki	vapor (since 水蒸気 is implied here, translate as "steam")
内燃	nainen	internal combustion
内外	naigai	about, approximately

カルノー・サイクル

　物体が一つの状態から他の状態を経て，再びもとの状態に帰るのをサイクルあるいは循環過程という。いま図のようにABとDCを一定量の気体の温度 T_2 および T_1（$<T_2$）の等温曲線とし，ADとBCを断熱曲線とする。まずAから出発して，AB, BC, CD, DAの可逆的変化を経て再びAに帰る可逆循環過程（またはその逆の過程）をカルノー・サイクルという。

　このサイクルにおいて気体は温度 T_2 の等温膨張 A→B の間に熱量 Q_2 を吸収し，温度 T_1 の等温圧縮 C→D の間に熱量 Q_1 を放出するものとする。そして一回のサイクルで気体が外部にした仕事の大きさを $-W$ とする（外からされる仕事を正としてきた）[10]。サイクルを一回終わったときに気体はもとの状態に帰るので，その内部エネルギーは不変であるから第一法則により

$$Q_2 - Q_1 = -W \tag{5}$$

である。

気体は温度の高い熱源（高熱源）から熱エネルギー Q_2 をとり温度 T_1 の低熱源に熱エネルギー Q_1 を与え，その間に外へ仕事 $-W$ をしている。このように熱エネルギーを仕事に変える装置を熱機関という。熱機関が外にした有効な仕事と高熱源から得た熱エネルギーとの比を熱効率あるいは効率とよび，これを η とすれば，可逆熱機関であるカルノーのサイクルの効率は

$$\eta = \frac{-W}{Q_2} = \frac{Q_2 - Q_1}{Q_2} = \frac{T_2 - T_1}{T_2} \tag{6}$$

となる。一般に η の値は小さく，蒸気機関や蒸気タービンで15％，内燃機関で25％内外[11]である。

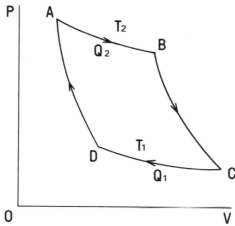

KOTAI NO NETSU-BŌCHŌ

Suigin ya sekiyu nado ni kagirazu, ōku no kotai mo ondo ga agaru ni shita-gatte bōchō suru.

Tetsu mo sōtō ichijirushii netsu-bōchō o shimesu no de, tekkyō no ryōtan nado wa kotei sezu, [1] kansho [2] no sa ni yotte tetsuzai no nobi-chijimi [3] ga okoru yoyū o motasete aru. [4]

Ippan ni, kotai no netsu-bōchō wa ekitai ya kitai ni kurabete chiisai.

Ima, t-do no toki no bō no nagasa [5] o l, t'-do no toki no nagasa o l' to suru to, ondo ga t to t' to no aida de, ichido agaru goto ni, bō ga t-do no nagasa ni kurabete nobiru wari-ai α wa

$$\alpha = \frac{(l'-l)/l}{t'-t} \tag{1}$$

de shimesareru. Kore o sen-bōchō-ritsu to iu. Shitagatte,

$$l' = l[1 + \alpha(t'-t)] \tag{2}$$

to naru.

Mokuzai wa tate to yoko to de sen-bōchō-ritsu ga chigatte iru. Mata, kesshō de mo kesshō jiku no hōkō ni yotte, seishitsu ga kotonaru koto ga aru[6] no de, nobi-kata mo hōkō ni yotte chigau.

Ondo ga jōshō suru ni tsurete, kotai no kakuhen ga nobiru no de taiseki mo bōchō suru. Ima t-do no toki no taiseki o V, t'-do no toki no taiseki o V' to sure-ba, ondo ga ichi-do agaru goto ni taiseki ga t-do no toki ni kurabete zōka suru wari-ai o tai-bōchō-ritsu to ii, β de arawasu.

Sunawachi $\beta = \dfrac{(V'-V)/V}{t'-t}$ shitagatte $V' = V[1+\beta(t'-t)]$ \hfill (3)

Kaku hōkō ni ichiyō ni nobiru kotai de wa

$$\beta \fallingdotseq 3\alpha \hfill (4)$$

no kankei ga aru.

DANNETSU-HENKA

Jikken: Kūki o kyūgeki ni asshuku shitari, bōchō sasetari suru to, sono ondo ga dō kawaru ka, tsugi no yō ni shite shirabete miyō.

(1) Hajime pisuton o ue no hō ni nuite oku.[8] Kono pisuton o kyū ni oshi-sagete naka no kūki o asshuku suru. Kono toki, netsu-yōryō no chiisai ondo-kei de kūki no ondo o hakaru to, sūdo jōshō shita koto ga wakaru.

(2) Hajime pisuton o ippai ni sashi-konde oku.[8] Pisuton o kyū ni hanashite naka no kūki o kyū ni bōchō saseru to, sono ondo wa sūdo sagaru.

Kono yō ni, netsu ga soto e nigenai yō ni shite kitai o kyūgeki ni asshuku suru to, sono ondo ga agari, gyaku ni kitai o kyūgeki ni bōchō saseru to, ondo ga sagaru. Ippan ni gaibu to no aida ni netsu no de-iri[9] no nai jōtai no henka o "dannetsu-henka" to ii, sono henka ga asshuku no baai o "dannetsu-asshuku", bōchō no baai o "dannetsu-bōchō" to iu.

Kono yō ni netsu no de-iri ga nai yō ni shite, soto kara shigoto o kuwaeru to, sono shigoto wa, buttai no naibu-enerugii no zōka ni naru no de, buttai no ondo wa jōshō suru. Mata, buttai ga soto ni shigoto o suru baai ni wa naibu-enerugii ga genshō suru no de, ondo ga sagaru.

KARUNŌ SAIKURU

Buttai ga hitotsu no jōtai o hete, futatabi moto no jōtai ni kaeru no o saikuru aruiwa junkan-katei to iu. Ima, zu no yō ni AB to DC o ittei-ryō no kitai no ondo T_2 oyobi T_1 ($<T_2$) no tōon-kyokusen to shi, AD to BC o dannetsu-kyokusen to suru. Mazu A kara shuppatsu shite AB, BC, CD, DA no kagyaku-teki-henka o hete futatabi A ni kaeru kagyaku-junkan-katei (mata wa sono gyaku no katei) o Karunō saikuru to iu.

Kono saikuru ni oite kitai wa ondo T_2 no tōon-bōchō A→B no aida ni netsuryō

Q_2 o kyūshū shi ondo T_1 no tōon-asshuku C→D no aida ni netsuryō Q_1 o hōshutsu suru mono to suru. Soshite ikkai no saikuru de kitai ga gaibu ni shita shigoto no ōkisa o $-W$ to suru (soto kara sareru shigoto o sei to shite kita).[10] Saikuru o ikkai owatta toki ni kitai wa moto no jōtai ni kaeru no de, sono naibu-enerugii wa fuhen de aru kara daiichi-hōsoku ni yori

$$Q_2 - Q_1 = -W \qquad (5)$$

de aru.

Kitai wa ondo no takai netsugen (kō-netsugen) kara netsu-enerugii Q_2 o tori, ondo T_1 no tei-netsugen ni netsu-enerugii Q_1 o atae, sono aida ni soto e shigoto $-W$ o shite iru. Kono yō ni netsu-enerugii o shigoto ni kaeru sōchi o netsu-kikan to iu. Netsu-kikan ga soto ni shita yūkō na shigoto to kō-netsugen kara eta netsu-enerugii to no hi o netsu-kōritsu arui wa kōritsu to yobi, kore o η to sureba, ka-gyaku-netsu-kikan de aru Karunō no saikuru no kōritsu wa

$$\eta = -W/Q_2 = (Q_2 - Q_1)/Q_2 = (T_2 - T_1)/T_2 \qquad (6)$$

to naru. Ippan ni η no atai wa chiisaku, jōki-kikan ya jōki-tābin de 15%, nainen-kikan de 25% naigai[11] de aru.

THE THERMAL EXPANSION OF SOLIDS

Not only mercury and petroleum but also many solids expand with rising temperature.

Since iron also exhibits a rather noticeable thermal expansion, the two ends and other parts of iron bridges are not rigidly fixed but given play to allow for the expanding and contracting of the iron material which occurs due to variations in temperature.

In general, the thermal expansion of solids is small compared to liquids and gases.

If now we let l be the length of a rod at $t°C$ and l' be the length at $t'°C$, then the rate α at which the rod expands for each degree of temperature between temperatures t and t', in comparison to the length at $t°C$, is expressed by

$$\alpha = \frac{(l' - l)/l}{t' - t} \qquad (1)$$

This is called the coefficient of linear expansion. If follows that

$$l' = l[1 + \alpha(t' - t)] \qquad (2)$$

The coefficient of linear expansion of wood differs longitudinally and transversely. Likewise there are also crystals which, having differing properties along the directions of their crystal axes, expand differently in those directions.

Since every edge of a solid block expands with rising temperature, the volume also expands. If now we let V be the volume when at $t°C$ and V' the volume when at t' °C, then the rate at which the volume increases for each degree rise in temperature, compared to the volume at $t°C$, is called the coefficient of vol-

ume expansion and is called β.

In other words,

$$\beta = \frac{(V'-V)/V}{t'-t} \text{ and, accordingly, } V' = V[1+\beta(t'-t)] \tag{3}$$

For a solid which expands uniformly in every direction, the relation

$$\beta = 3\alpha \tag{4}$$

holds.

ADIABATIC CHANGE

Experiment: Let us examine the question of how the temperature changes when air is suddenly compressed or expanded in the following way.

1) First withdraw the piston to an upper position. Then compress the air by suddenly pushing the piston downwards. If, at that time, you measure the temperature of the air with a thermometer of small heat capacity, you will find the temperature has risen several degrees.

2) First thrust the piston in fully. Then, when you allow the air to expand suddenly by quickly releasing the piston, the temperature will drop several degrees.

Thus, if you compress a gas suddenly so that heat does not escape to the surroundings, the temperature rises and, conversely, if you cause a gas to expand suddenly, the temperature falls. We call those general changes of state in which no heat is exchanged with the surroundings adiabatic changes, and for the case of those changes by compression, adiabatic compression, for the case of expansion, adiabatic expansion.

Thus, if work is added from without and no exchanges of heat occur, the temperature of the substance rises because the work increases the internal energy of the substance. Moreover, when the substance performs work on the surroundings, the temperature falls because the internal energy decreases.

THE CARNOT CYCLE

A process in which a body passes from one state to another and returns once more to the original state is called a cycle or a cyclical process. Now take AB and DC in the figure as isotherms at temperatures T_2 and T_1 ($<T_2$) for a fixed quantity of gas, and AD and BC as adiabatic curves. A reversible cyclical process which begins first at A, then passes through reversible changes AB, BC, CD, and DA to return again to A is called a Carnot cycle.

Suppose the gas in this cycle absorbs an amount of heat Q_2 during the isothermal expansion at temperature T_2 from A to B and releases an amount of heat Q_1 during the isothermal compression at temperature T_1 from C to D. Furthermore take the amount of work done by the gas on the surroundings as $-W$ (work

done by the surroundings is conventionally taken as positive). When a single cycle has been completed, then since the gas has returned to its original state, the internal energy is unchanged, and according to the first law

$$Q_2 - Q_1 = -W \tag{5}$$

The gas takes thermal energy Q_2 from the high temperature heat reservoir, gives an amount of thermal energy Q_1 to the low temperature heat reservoir, and in the process performs work $-W$. A device which thus transforms thermal energy into work is called a heat engine. The ratio of the actual work performed by the heat engine and the thermal energy received from the high temperature heat source is called the thermal efficiency (or efficiency) and, if we let this be η, then the efficiency of a reversible heat engine in a Carnot cycle becomes

$$\eta = -W/Q_2 = (Q_2 - Q_1)/Q_2 = (T_2 - T_1)/T_2. \tag{6}$$

In general the value of η is small, being about 15% for a steam engine or steam turbine, and about 25% for an internal combustion engine.

EXPLANATORY NOTES

(1) kotei sezu — "is not fixed, and"; this is the negative analog of *kotei shi* "is fixed, and".

(2) kansho — "hot and cold" or "temperature," used only for weather or climate; see the Explanatory Notes for Lesson 9 for other examples of the formation of an abstract noun from the juxtaposition of two contrasting *kanji*.

(3) nobi-chijimi — "expansion and contraction" or "extension and compression". Note that the word *shinshuku* (伸縮), that is, the corresponding *ON*-reading, appears in the Supplementary Reading on *Bō no shindō* in this lesson. The meaning of both words is about the same.

(4) motasete aru — The *-te aru* construction usually is most easily rendered by the passive voice in English; for example *hōteishiki ga kokuban ni kaite aru* "the equation is written on the blackboard." Note: *motsu* "has"; *motaseru* "causes to have"; *motasete aru* "is caused to have", or, less literally, "is given".

(5) $t°C$ no toki no bō no nagasa — *toki* here does not have any particular temporal significance; it has the idea of *baai* "case, condition, occasion." Translate as "length of the bar at $t°C$.".

(6) (present tense verb) + koto ga aru — "there are cases for which..." or "it sometimes happens that..." are standard renditions of this phrase. Hence, "there are crystals for which the properties differ, etc."

(7) ...tari...tari suru — Indicates several actions occuring, possibly in alternation.

(8) nuite oku; sashikonde oku — The *-te oku* construction gives the idea of (a) doing something beforehand for future need or use, or (b) doing something to get it out of the way. In descriptions of experimental procedures where one prepares equipment or chemicals for use in a subsequent step in the experiment, the *-te oku* is a convenient expression. The *-te oku* is seldom translated into English, since there is no construction which conveys the same implications.

(9) gaibu to no aida ni netsu no de-iri — "heat exchange with the surroundings". This can be regarded as an abbreviated version of *gaibu to kei to no aida ni netsu no de-iri* "heat exchange between the system and the surroundings"

(10) gaibu kara sareru shigoto o sei to shite kita — For comments on the *-te kuru* construction see Explanatory Notes of Lesson 9. The expression here means literally, "We (physical scientists) began (at some time) to take the work done by the surroundings as positive and have continued to do so." Hence the translation, "work done by the surrondings is conventionally taken as positive."

(11) naigai — "approximately." Several other synonymous words are *yaku* (約), *oyoso* (およそ), *gurai* (位)

CONSTRUCTION EXAMPLES

| …に限らず | "not only...but also...," "not just...but..." |

1. 鉄や銀に限らず一般に固体の熱膨張は液体や気体より小さい。
2. 熱の移動に限らず移動現象一般について多くの研究を行なった。

| verb＋に従って | "according as...," "as..." |

1. 振動数が固有振動数に近づくに従って振幅が増大した。
2. 油に限らず一般に液体では，温度を上げるに従って粘度が下がる。

| (固有)振動数 | (koyū)shindō-sū | (characteristic) frequency |
| 近づく | chikazuku | to approach |

| …ごとに | "each...," "at an interval of..." |

1. 一定時間ごとに同じ状態がくりかえされる運動を周期運動という。

2. 一定体積の気体の圧力は，温度1℃上がるごとに0℃のときの圧力の1/273ずつ増加する。

| くりかえす | kuri-kaesu | to repeat |

| …に比べて | "compared to..." |

1. 一般に気体の熱伝導率は固体や液体に比べて小さい。

2. 分子や原子の大きさは，一般の物体に比べて非常に小さい。

| …せず | "without... -ing" |

1. 気体の圧力を変化せず，熱を加えて温度を上げた場合の比熱を定圧比熱という。

2. 考えている気体と外部との間に熱を出入りさせず，気体を圧縮することを断熱圧縮という。

| (定圧)比熱 | (teiatsu) hinetsu | specific heat (at constant pressure) |
| 出入りさせる | de-iri saseru | to permit exchange |

| …てある | (see Explanatory Note No. 4) |

1. 実験台の上に置いてある温度計は比熱を測定するためのものである。

2. 蒸気機関では調速機をつけて速度が一定になるように考えてある。

3. ジュールの実験装置では温度変化が測定できるようにしてある。

実験台	jikken-dai	laboratory bench
調速機	chōsoku-ki	governor (Literally: control-speed-device)
考えてある	kangaete aru	it is planned
してある	shite aru	it is arranged

| …ことがある | "there are cases for which...," "it sometimes happens that..." |

1. ステンレス鋼でもさびることがある。

2. 水を1気圧の下で100℃まで熱しても沸騰しないことがある。

ステンレス鋼	sutenresu-kō	stainless steel
でも	de mo	even
さびる	sabiru	to rust

熱する	nessuru	to heat

…ておく (see Explanatory Note No. 8)
---

1. ジュールの実験装置では，容器を通して外部と熱の出入りがないようにしておく必要がある。

2. 以下の考察においては，空気を理想気体としていることを断わっておく。

考察	kōsatsu	consideration, study
断わっておく	kotowatte oku	to warn, remind

SUPPLEMENTARY READINGS

A. *Selections from Rikagaku Jiten*

1)

ジェット機	jetto-ki	jet (plane)
推進	suishin	propulsion
飛行する	hikō suru	to fly
航空機	kōkū-ki	aircraft
ジェット・エンジン	jetto-enjin	jet engine
開く	hiraku	to open
両方開いた筒	ryōhō hiraita tsutsu	an open-ended tube
燃料	nenryō	fuel
注入する	chūnyū suru	to inject
燃焼	nenshō	combustion
噴出する	funshutsu suru	to exhaust, blow out
推力	suiryoku	thrust
口	kuchi	entrance
ラムジェット	ramu-jetto	ram jet
混合する	kongō suru	to mix
タービン・ジェット	tābin-jetto	turbine jet
ターボ・ジェット	tābo-jetto	turbo jet
実用的に	jitsuyō-teki ni	in actual practice
後者	kōsha	the latter
プロペラ	puropera	propeller
ターボ・プロップ	tābo-puroppu	turbo prop
ロケット	roketto	rocket
酸素	sanso	oxygen
供給	kyōkyū	supply
不可能	fu-kanō	impossible
遷音速の	sen-onsoku no	transsonic
超音速の	chō-onsoku no	supersonic

ジェット機　(3RJ 544)

　ジェット推進によって飛行する航空機をジェット機という。ジェット推進装置すなわち
ジェット・エンジンは両方開いた筒の前方から空気をとりいれて圧縮し，ガソリンなどの
燃料を注入して燃焼させ，高速気体を後方に噴出して推力を得る装置である。開いた口か
らとり入れた空気を，飛行速度だけによって圧縮する方法をラム・ジェットという。圧縮
機によって空気を圧縮し，燃料と混合して燃焼，噴出させ，燃焼気体のエネルギーの一部
でタービンをまわし，タービンの力によって圧縮機をまわす方法をタービン・ジェットま
たはターボ・ジェットという。実用的にはほとんど後者が用いられている。また，タービ
ンの力でさらにプロペラをまわす装置をターボ・プロップという。ロケット推進との相違
は空気(中の酸素)の供給を必要とするところにある。プロペラ推進では音速近くの飛行
は不可能なので，遷音速・超音速の航空機は主としてジェット機である。

2)			
	作動流体	sadō-ryūtai	working fluid
	自身	jishin	itself
	含む	fukumu	to include
	気筒	kitō	cylinder
	弁	ben	valve
	クランク	kuranku	crank
	機構	kikō	mechanism
	往復	ōfuku	reciprocating
	指す	sasu	to indicate
	方式	hōshiki	method
	分類する	bunrui suru	to classify
	吸入する	kyūnyū suru	to take in, suck in
	電気火花	denki-hibana	electric spark
	点火する	tenka suru	to ignite
	噴射する	funsha suru	to inject
	吸排気	kyūhai-ki	intake and exhaust of gases
	行程	kōtei	stroke
	完了する	kanryō suru	to complete
	重油・軽油	jūyu; keiyu	heavy oil; light oil
	いわゆる	iwayuru	so-called
	ディーゼル	Diizeru	Diesel
	オットー	Ottō	Otto
	馬力	bariki	horsepower
	してすむ	shite sumu	can get by with doing
	特長	tokuchō	strong point, merit

内燃機関 (2RJ 979)

熱機関の一種で，作動流体に熱を与えるのに，作動流体自身の中で燃料を燃焼させるものを内燃機関という。ガス・タービンのような回転機関を含めることもあるが，普通は気筒，弁，ピストンおよびクランクなどの機構をもつ往復機関を指す。燃焼方式により分類すれば，空気と燃料との混合気体を気筒に吸入，圧縮し，電気火花で点火して燃焼させる火花点火機関と，空気だけを気筒に吸入，圧縮し，その中に燃料を噴射して燃焼させる圧縮点火機関とがある。吸排気方式により分類すれば，クランク軸の一回転，ピストンの2行程で1サイクルを完了する2サイクル機関と，クランク軸の2回転，ピストンの4行程で1サイクルを完了する4サイクル機関とがある。圧縮点火機関では，低速のものは重油が用いられるので重油機関ともいわれるが，高速のものは軽油が用いられる。低速圧縮点火機関では，いわゆるディーゼル・サイクル機関ともいっているが，高速の方のサイクルはむしろオットー・サイクルになる。内燃機関は蒸気機関などにくらべて熱効率が高く，1馬力あたりの重量も体積も小さくてすむという特長がある。

3)	異性	isei	isomerism
	分子式	bunshi-shiki	molecular formula
	化合物	kagō-butsu	chemical compound
	異性体	isei-tai	isomers
	有機・無機	yūki; muki	organic; inorganic
	構造式	kōzō-shiki	structural formula
	立体配置	rittai-haichi	spatial configuration
	立体異性	rittai-isei	stereoisomerism
	幾何異性	kika-isei	geometrical isomerism
	回転異性	kaiten-isei	rotational isomerism
	光学異性	kōgaku-isei	optical isomerism
	大別する	taibetsu suru	to classify broadly

異 性 (3RJ 76)

同一の分子式で表わされながら性質の異なる化合物が存在することを異性といい，異性の関係にある化合物を異性体という。有機化合物では，構造式が異なる構造異性，分子式と構造式は同じであるが原子の立体配置が異なる立体異性（幾何異性，回転異性，光学異性）とに大別される。

4)	多形	takei	polymorphism
	組成	sosei	composition, constitution
	結晶(形)	kesshō(kei)	crystal (shape)

二形・三形	nikei, sankei	dimorphism, trimorphism
異にする	koto ni suru	to be dissimilar
原因	gen'in	source, cause
主に	omo ni	chiefly
条件	jōken	conditions
…支配される	…shihai sareru	to be influenced by…
多形間	takei-kan	between polymorphic substances
グラファイト-ダイヤモンド転移	gurafaito-daiyamondo ten'i	graphite-diamond transition
本質的に	honshitsu-teki ni	essentially
石英	sekiei	quartz
配置関係	haichi-kankei	configurational relationship
対称性	taishō-sei	symmetry

多　形　(3RJ 785)

　同一の化学組成をもちながら，異なる結晶構造をもち，異なる結晶形を示す現象，またはその現象を示すものを多形という。その数によって二形，三形などという。結晶形を異にする原因は主に温度，圧力であるが，そのほかの物理的，化学的条件によっても支配される。多形間の転移にはグラファイト・ダイヤモンド転移のように結晶構造が本質的にかわる転移と，低温石英・高温石英転移のように配置関係はかわらずに結晶の対称性だけが変化する転移とがある。

5) 伸縮する	shinshuku suru	to expand and contract
縦振動	tate-shindō	longitudinal vibration
ねじれ振動	nejire-shindō	torsional vibration
横方向	yoko-hōkō	transverse direction
たわむ	tawamu	to bend
横振動	yoko-shindō	transverse vibration
まっすぐな	massugu na	straight
ヤング率	Yangu-ritsu	Young's modulus
中央	chū-ō	center

棒の振動　(2RJ 1281)

　弾性棒の行なう振動には軸方向に伸縮する縦振動，軸のまわりのねじれ振動，および横方向にたわむ横振動の三つがある。一様なまっすぐな棒については，棒の長さを l，密度を ρ，ヤング率を E とすれば，縦振動の振動数は $v_S = \dfrac{Ms}{2l}\sqrt{E/\rho}$ の形で表わされる。ここ

でM_Sは両端自由の場合には$M_S=S$; 中央固定，両端自由の場合 $M_S=2S-1$; 一端固定，一端自由の場合には $M_S=S-\frac{1}{2}$である。 ($S=1, 2, 3...$)

B.	平衡	heikō	equilibrium
	純粋な	junsui na	pure
	…のみ	…nomi	only…
	蒸発熱	jōhatsu-netsu	heat of vaporization
	それ故	sore yue	therefore
	…に対し目盛った	…ni taishi memotta	plotted versus…
	傾斜	keisha	slope
	求まる	motomaru	is obtained
	範囲	han'i	range
	より（正確な）	yori(seikaku na)	more (accurate)
	液体を閉管中にとる	ekitai o heikan-chū ni toru	to take the liquid (and put it) into the closed tube
	除く	nozoku	to remove
	液体…のみにし＝液体とその蒸気のみがある状態にし， or 液体とその蒸気のみがのこるようにし，		
	…にする	…ni suru	to cause…, bring about…
	…静的方法と…動的方法とがある	…seiteki-hōhō to…dōteki-hōhō to ga aru	there is a static method in which…and a dynamic method in which…
	前者…後者	zensha…kōsha	the former…the latter
	代表的な	daihyō-teki na	representative
	実施	jisshi	execution
	容易	yōi	easy, not difficult
	器具	kigu	apparatus
	トラップ	torappu	trap
	フラスコ	furasuko	flask
	有機化合物	yūki-kagō-butsu	organic compounds
	アセトン	aseton	acetone
	クロロホルム	kurorohorumu	chloroform
	ベンゼン	benzen	benzene
	アルコール	arukōru	alcohol
	四塩化炭素	shi-enka-tanso	carbon tetrachloride
	組み立て	kumi-tate	assembly
	枝付きフラスコ	edatsuki-furasuko	distilling flask (Lit. a branched flask)
	分液漏斗	bun'eki-rōto	separatory funnel
	下端	katan	lower end

細工をする	saiku o suru	to make
球部	kyūbu	bulb
ガーゼ	gāze	gauze
しばる	shibaru	to tie, fasten
接続する	setsuzoku suru	to connect, join
すり合わせ部分	suri-awase bubun	adjoining moving parts (parts which rub each other)
グリース	guriisu	grease
ケイ素	keiso	silicon
樹脂	jushi	resin
水流ポンプ	suiryū ponpu	tap aspirator
排気する	haiki suru	to exhaust
閉じる・開く	tojiru;hiraku	to close;to open
漏れ	more	leak
約	yaku	approximately
放置する	hōchi suru	to leave as it is
できるだけ低圧に	dekiru dake teiatsu ni	at as low a pressure as possible
徐々に	jojo ni	slowly, gradually
布	nuno	cloth
滴	teki	drop
底	soko	bottom
滴下する	tekika suru	to drip
水浴	suiyoku	water bath
蒸発してしまう	jōhatsu shite shimau	to vaporize completely (See Explanatory Note 1, Lesson 15)
調節する	chōsetsu suru	to adjust, regulate
読み	yomi	reading
記録する	kiroku suru	to record
毛細管	mōsai-kan	capillary tube
加熱する	kanetsu suru	to heat (up)
繰り返す	kuri-kaesu	to repeat
…に達する	...ni tassuru	to reach...
今度は	kondo wa	this time
注意	chūi	precaution, N.B.
円滑に	enkatsu ni	smoothly
ヤスリ	yasuri	a file
みぞ	mizo	groove
枝	eda	side-arm

連結する	renketsu suru	to connect
上下	jōge	above and below
気密	kimitsu	air-tight
十分	jūbun	thoroughly, fully
注意する	chūi suru	to be careful

液体の蒸気圧の測定　(BKJ 104–106)

　液体と平衡にある蒸気の圧力をその液体の蒸気圧といい，純粋液体では温度のみによって変わるが，溶液においては温度の外に溶液の組成にもえいきょうされる。純粋液体の蒸気圧を異なる温度で測定すれば，その液体の蒸発熱 L は次式で与えられる。

$$\frac{d\log P}{dT} = \frac{L}{2.303RT^2}$$

それ故，$\log P$ を $1/T(°\mathrm{K})$ に対し目盛った線の傾斜から L が求まる。（L は温度によっても変化するから T の広い範囲で直線にならない。蒸気圧と温度との間のより正確な関係に関しては，Felsing and Durban, J. Am. Chem. Soc. 48, 2885 (1926) 参照）。

　液体の蒸気圧を求めるには，その液体を閉管中にとり，内部の空気を除いて液体とその蒸気のみにし，その時の圧力を求める静的方法と，種々の圧力の下で液体の沸点を測定し，温度・蒸気圧関係を知り，それから逆にその温度における蒸気圧を知る動的方法とがある。前者の代表的なものは Smith-Menzies 法であり，後者は Ramsay-Young 法であり，この方が実施が容易である。

[実験20]　Ramsay-Young 法により各種液体の蒸気圧を測定せよ。

使用器具：Ramsay-Young 装置，水銀圧力計，トラップ，10 l フラスコ，液体有機化合物 2 種（アセトン，クロロホルム，ベンゼン，アルコール，四塩化炭素等）。

装置の組み立て：Ramsay-Young 装置及び全体の組み立ては第 1 図に示す。F は 250ml 位の枝付きフラスコ，P は 100ml 位の分液漏斗でその下端を図に示すように細工をしておく。温度計は 1/10 または 1/15 度目盛りのものを使用し，その球部に図のようにガーゼを巻き付けてしばっておく。この装置を図に示すように約 100ml のトラップ C, 水銀圧力計 M, 10 l フラスコ B に接続する。すり合わせ部分のグリースはケイ素樹脂を使用する。

測定法：まず水流ポンプで全装置を排気した後，コック H を閉じ装置に漏れがあるかどうかを調べる。約 20 分間放置しても M の水銀面に変化がなければ完全であるとしてよい。

　次に測定する液体約 40ml を分液漏斗にとり，ふたたび全装置をできるだけ低圧になるまで排気し，H を閉じる。分液漏斗のコックを徐々に開き，液体が温度計に巻いた布から 1 分間 4〜5 滴の割合でフラスコの底へ滴下するようにする。水浴 D を熱して，その温度が管中の温度計より約 20° 高くなる程度にしておいて，液の滴下の速さを各滴下液が次の滴

の落下する前蒸発してしまうように調節する。温度計の読みが一定したならば温度と圧力計の読みを記録する。

　次にコックCから毛細管を通して空気を入れて圧力を約30mm上げ，水浴の温度を内部の温度より20°ぐらい高くなるように加熱し，上と同様に平衡になった時の温度と圧力を記録し，以下同様な測定を繰り返して大気圧まで測定する。ただし 50℃以上では圧力を100mm ずつ上げて測定する。

　大気圧に達したならば，今度は逆に圧力を下げながら上と同じような測定を繰り返す。このようにして各温度 $T°$K における蒸気圧 P を求め，$\log P$ と$1/T$ の関係を図にえがき，これより蒸発熱を計算せよ。

注意：液体の滴下量の調節を円滑にするために，分液漏斗のコックにヤスリで図のようなみぞを作っておくとよい。また同じ目的で分液漏斗の上部をフラスコの枝の部分とガラス管で連結しておくと，液の上下の圧力差が小さくなって調節が容易になる。ただし，気密には十分注意しなければならない。

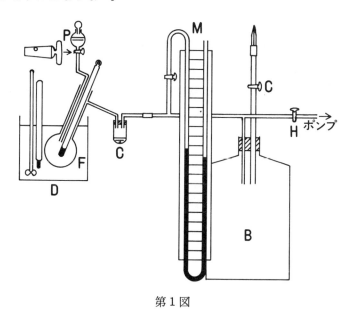

第1図

FINAL TRANSLATION TEST

　大気の性質が明らかになるにつれて，これを利用して仕事をさせようという考えが生まれてきた。ピストン・シリンダー機構において，ピストンの一方の側を真空にすれば，反対側からはたらく大気圧によってピストンは大きな力を受けるから，これによって，例えばポンプを作動させることができるわけである。最初に発明された Newcomen の蒸気機

関では，水蒸気を凝縮して水にすることによって真空を得るため，シリンダーに水を噴射して冷却していたので，効率が低く，熱源から与えられた熱量の多くの部分は無益に放出されていた。そこで Watt は，シリンダーを常に高温に保ち，凝縮器を別につけて，ここで水蒸気を凝縮し，行程の初期において水蒸気の供給を断ち，その後は水蒸気の膨張によって仕事がなされるようにしたので，高い効率が得られた。さらに，ピストンに加えられる力が一方向だけでなく，他方向からも加わるように，すなわち複動としたので，効率は大いに向上した。

　蒸気機関は，シリンダー，シリンダー内にゆるくはめこまれて自由にすべり動く円板状のピストン，ピストン棒，ピストン棒の直線運動を回転運動に変えるための機構から成り立っている。シリンダーとピストンがあまりぴったりはめこまれると動かなくなり，ゆるければ蒸気が漏れてしまう。そこでピストンに，鉄でできた細いピストンリングをはめて，すきまをふさいでいる。ピストンにはかたさが必要であるが，ピストンリングは目的が異なり，よく伸び縮みしてシリンダーの内面との間にすきまを作らぬよう，結晶の大きさなどを加減したものを用いる。

　ピストンが直線上を周期運動するこの種の機関では，行程の両端で急に運動方向が逆になるため振動を生じ，また出力が低下する。この点を合理化したものが Wankel 機関，すなわち回転ピストン発動機である。この機関は，まるみをもった三角形の回転ピストンの一様な回転運動を利用し，自動車用原動機として最近用いられている。

LESSON 13
第十三課

K A N J I

光	72	KŌ		紫	242b	SHI
	1358	hika(ru) [hikari]			3534	murasaki
干	194b	KAN		射	230b	SHA
	1492				4603	
渉	241a	SHŌ		屈	215b	KUTSU
	2591				1386	
折	651	SETSU		写	419	SHA
	1855	{o(ru) o(reru)			626	utsu(su)
遠	160	EN		見	67	KEN
	4733	tō(i)			4284	mi(ru)
強	192	KYŌ tsuyo(i)		鏡	378	KYŌ
	1521	{tsuyo(meru) tsuyo(maru)			4912	kagami
通	281	TSŪ		焦	250a	SHŌ
	4703	{tō(su) tō(ru)			5029	
像	664	ZŌ		右	19	U, YŪ
	540				878	migi
色	94	SHOKU SHIKI		左	18	SA
	3889	iro			1455	hidari
赤	35	SEKI		心	95	SHIN
	4534	aka aka(i)			1645	kokoro

READING SELECTIONS

光	hikari	light
干渉（じま）	kanshō(jima)	interference (fringes)
回折	kaisetsu	diffraction
光源	kōgen	light source
遠方	enpō	a great distance
到達する	tōtatsu suru	to reach, arrive at
しくみ（仕組）	shikumi	arrangement
野球	yakyū	baseball
かたまり	katamari	lump

粒	tsubu	grain, particle
…か…かのいずれかである	…ka …ka no izure ka de aru	is either… or…
基本的な	kihonteki na	fundamental
強い	tsuyoi	strong
レンズ	renzu	lens
…を通す	…o tōsu	to pass through…
像を結ばせる	zō o musubaseru	to focus an image
スリット	suritto	slit
先に	saki ni	ahead
当てる	ateru	to strike, hit
すりガラス	suri-garasu	frosted glass
明暗	meian	bright and dark
しま	shima	bands, fringes
位相	isō	phase
送り出す	okuri-dasu	to send forth
重なる	kasanaru	to be superimposed
条件	jōken	condition
満足する	manzoku suru	to satisfy
強め合う	tsuyome-au	to reinforce each other
明るい	akarui	bright
暗い	kurai	dark
隣あう	tonari-au	to adjoin each other
計算する	keisan suru	to calculate
ヤング	Yangu	(Thomas) Young
はじめて（初めて）	hajimete	for the first time; originally
…の程度である	…no teido de aru	is of the order of magnitude of…
精密な	seimitsu na	accurate, precise
色	iro	color
…のとうり（…の通り）	…no tōri	in the manner of… (here: "as shown in")
ミリミクロン	miri-mikuron	millimicron
赤	aka	red
だいだい	daidai	orange
黄	ki	yellow
緑	midori	green
青	ao	blue
紫	murasaki	purple

光の干渉と回折　(B 178–180)

　光は光源から出て遠方まで到達する。光の伝わる ⁽¹⁾しくみは，野球のボールのように何か ⁽²⁾一つのかたまりすなち「粒」が動いていく ⁽³⁾のか，または，音のように「波」が伝わるのかのいずれか ⁽⁴⁾である。

　波の最も基本的な性質は干渉や ⁽⁵⁾回折のあることである。光が波であるといわれるのは，次のように光も干渉・回折を行なうからである。

観察　図1のように強い光源Sから出た光を，レンズLを通して ⁽⁶⁾スリットS₁上 ⁽⁷⁾に像を結ばせ，次にS₁から出る光をおよそ0.5m先にあるスリット S₂, S₃ に当てる。S₂, S₃ から出た光を，これからまた0.5〜1mぐらいの距離にあるすりガラス板G上に当てると，明暗のしまが現われるのを観察せよ ⁽⁸⁾。

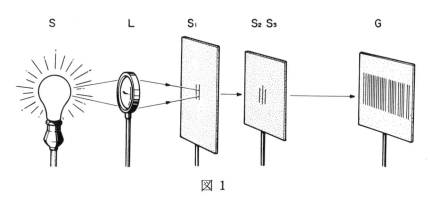

図 1

　スリット S₂, S₃ からは光の回折の結果，同じ位相の波が図2のように次々に送り出されている。この二つの波の重なる ⁽¹⁾所で干渉が起こる ⁽⁶⁾。いま，この光の波長を λ とすると，すりガラス板G上の1点 x で

$$S_2x - S_3x = N\lambda \quad N=0, \ \pm1, \ \pm2, \dots$$

という条件が満足されると，この点では波が強めあって ⁽⁹⁾明るくなる。また，

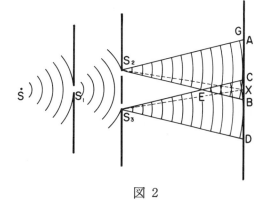

図 2

$$S_2x - S_3x = \left(N+\frac{1}{2}\right)\lambda$$

が成立すると暗くなる。したがって，明暗の線が隣あって ⁽⁹⁾，干渉じまを作ることになる。

　この実験で S₂x − S₃x を測れば，光の 波長 λ を計算することができる。ヤングは，このような方法ではじめて ⁽¹⁰⁾光の波長を測定し，それが10⁻⁴cm の程度であることを確かめ

た。その後，干渉を利用してもっと精密な方法で波長を測定することができるようになり，光の波長と色との関係は表1のとおりであることが知られた。

表1 光の波長と色	
波長（ミリミクロン）	色
700—610	赤
610—590	だいだい
590—570	黄（き）
570—500	緑（みどり）
500—450	青（あお）
450—400	紫

反射	hansha	reflection
屈折	kussetsu	refraction
前方の	zenpō no	in front, ahead
景色	keshiki	scenery
写る	utsuru	to be reflected, mirrored
見える	mieru	to be able to see
鏡	kagami	mirror
姿	sugata	figure
写す	utsusu	to reflect, mirror
曲がる	magaru	to bend
浮き上がる	uki-agaru	to float; rise to the surface
浮き上がって見える	uki-agatte mieru	it appears to be lifted towards the surface
…このためである	…kono tame de aru	this is why…
境界面	kyōkai-men	boundary surface
垂線	suisen	perpendicular
入射光線	nyūsha-kōsen	incident ray
なす（＝する）	nasu	to do, make
入射角	nyūsha-kaku	angle of incidence
同一平面内に	dōitsu-heimen-nai ni	in the same plane
屈折側	kussetsu-gawa	refracting side
媒質	baishitsu	medium
屈折率	kussetsu-ritsu	index of refraction
全く	mattaku	entirely
強さ	tsuyosa	strength, intensity
ふれる	fureru	to touch upon, deal with

光の反射と屈折　(B 183–184)

　光が空気中[7]から他の物質の表面に進んでくる[3]と，一部分はその物質の中にはいり，他の部分は反射する。

　静かな水面に前方の景色が写って見えたり[11]，鏡によって自分の姿を写すことができたりするのは，光の反射による。

　光が他の物質の中にはいるとき，光は曲がって進む。水中[7]にある物体が浮き上がって見えたり[11]するのはこのためである。

反射・屈折の法則

　光が反射・屈折するとき，境界面の垂線が入射光線・反射反線および屈折光線となす[12]角をそれぞれ入射角(i)，反射角(i')，および屈折角(r)という。

(1) 入射光線・反射光線および屈折光線は境界面に垂直な同一平面内にある。

(2) $i = i'$

(3) $\dfrac{\sin i}{\sin r} = \dfrac{v_1}{v_2} = 一定 = n$

これを反射および屈折の法則という。この n は屈折側の媒質の入射側の媒質に対する屈折率である。ここで v_1, v_2 はそれぞれ入射側および屈折側における光の速さである。

　光の反射および屈折の法則は，波の反射および屈折の法則と全く等しい。反射・屈折の法則は光の進み方[13]に関する法則であって，反射光および屈折光の強さについてはふれていない。それらの強さは，反射する物質の種類によって異なるが，同じ物質でも入射角が大きくなると，反射光が強くなる。

凸レンズ	totsu-renzu	convex lens
光軸	kōjiku	optical axis
通過する	tsūka suru	to pass through, be transmitted
焦点	shōten	focus
中心	chūshin	center
焦点距離	shōten-kyori	focal length
左方	sahō	the left
右方	uhō	the right
互いに	tagai ni	mutually
対称の	taishō no	symmetrical
プリズム	purizumu	prism
頂角	chōkaku	vertex angle
そのまま	sono mama	as it is (without changing or disturbing it)

厚い	atsui	thick
直進する	chokushin suru	to move straight ahead
逆進する	gyakushin suru	to move in reverse
まとめる	matomeru	to summarize, collect

凸レンズにおける光の進み方　(B 200–201)

　平行光線を凸[14]レンズの光軸に平行に当てると，レンズを通過した光線は図3のように1点を通る。この点を凸レンズの焦点といい，レンズの中心と焦点との距離を焦点距離という。

　図3では平行光線をレンズの左方から当てたのであるが，右方から当てた場合にもレンズを通過した光線は1点Fを通り，この点も焦点である。このように，レンズの焦点は二つあり，レンズに対して互いに対称の位置にある。

　凸レンズの光軸の部分は小さいプリズムとしての頂角は0であるから，光軸上を進む光線はそのまま直進する。また，レンズの中心に入射する光線はレンズに垂直でないときでもレンズがあまり厚くない限り[15]図4のように直進していく。[3]

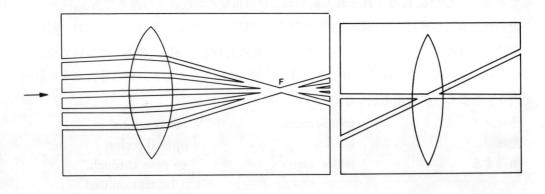

図3　凸レンズの焦点　　　　　　　　図4　レンズの中心を通る光線

以上のことと，光は初めに進んだ道を逆進することが可能であることなどから，凸レンズに入射した光線の進み方を次のようにまとめることができる。

(1) レンズの光軸に平行に進む光線は，レンズ通過後焦点Fを通る。

(2) レンズの中心Oを通る光線はそのまま直進する。

(3) 焦点F′を通る光線は，レンズ通過後[7]光軸に平行に進む。

HIKARI NO KANSHŌ TO KAISETSU

Hikari wa kōgen kara dete enpō made tōtatsu suru. Hikari no tsutawaru[1] shikumi wa, yakyū no bōru no yō ni nani ka[2] hitotsu no katamari sunawachi "tsubu" ga ugoite iku [3] no ka, mata wa, oto no yō ni "nami" ga tsutawaru no ka no izure ka[4] de aru.

Nami no mottomo kihon-teki na seishitsu wa kanshō ya[5] kaisetsu no aru koto de aru. Hikari ga nami de aru to iwareru no wa, tsugi no yō ni hikari mo kanshō, kaisetsu o okonau kara de aru.

Kansatsu: Zu-ichi no yō ni tsuyoi kōgen S kara deta hikari o, renzu L o tōshite[6] suritto S_1 jō[7] ni zō o musubase, tsugi ni S_1 kara deru hikari o oyoso 0.5m saki ni aru suritto S_2, S_3 ni ateru. S_2, S_3 kara deta hikari o, kore kara mata 0.5－1m gurai no kyori ni aru suri-garasu-ita G jō ni ateru to, meian no shima ga arawareru no o kansatsu seyo.[8]

Suritto S_2, S_3 kara wa hikari no kaisetsu no kekka, onaji isō no nami ga zu-ni no yō ni, tsugi-tsugi ni okuri-dasarete iru. Kono futatsu no nami no kasanaru[1] tokoro de kanshō ga okoru.[6] Ima, kono hikari no hachō o λ to suru to, suri garasu-ita G jō no itten x de

$$S_2x - S_3x = N\lambda \qquad N = 0, \pm 1, \pm 2, \ldots$$

to iu jōken ga manzoku sareru to, kono ten de wa nami ga tsuyome-atte[9] akaruku naru. Mata,

$$S_2x - S_3x = \left(N + \frac{1}{2}\right)\lambda$$

ga seiritsu suru to kuraku naru. Shitagatte, meian no sen ga tonari-atte,[9] kanshō-jima o tsukuru koto ni naru.

Kono jikken de, $S_2x - S_3x$ o hakareba, hikari no hachō λ o keisan suru koto ga dekiru. Yangu wa, kono yō na hōhō de hajimete[10] hikari no hachō o sokutei shi, sore ga 10^{-4}cm no teido de aru koto o tashikameta. Sono nochi, kanshō o riyō shite, motto seimitsu na hōhō de hachō o sokutei suru koto ga dekiru yō ni nari, hikari no hachō to iro to no kankei wa hyō-ichi no tōri de aru koto ga shirareta.

Hyō Ichi. Hikari no Hachō to Iro

Hachō (mirimikuron)	Iro
700－610	aka
610－590	dai-dai
590－570	ki
570－500	midori
500－450	ao
450－400	murasaki

HIKARI NO HANSHA TO KUSSETSU

Hikari ga kūki-chū [7] kara ta no busshitsu no hyōmen ni susunde kuru [3] to, ichi-bubun wa sono busshitsu no naka ni hairi, ta no bubun wa hansha suru.

Shizuka na suimen ni zenpō no keshiki ga utsutte mietari, [11] kagami ni yotte jibun no sugata o utsusu koto ga dekitari suru no wa, hikari no hansha ni yoru.

Hikari ga ta no busshitsu no naka ni hairu toki, hikari wa magatte susumu. Suichū [7] ni aru buttai ga uki-agatte mietari [11] suru no wa kono tame de aru.

Hansha, Kussetsu no Hōsoku: Hikari ga hansha, kussetsu suru toki, kyōkai-men no suisen ga nyūsha-kōsen, hansha-kōsen oyobi kussetsu-kōsen to nasu [12] kaku o sorezore nyūsha-kaku(i), hansha-kaku(i') oyobi kussetsu-kaku (r) to iu.

(1) Nyūsha-kōsen, hansha-kōsen oyobi kussetsu-kōsen wa kyōkai-men ni suichoku na dōitsu-heimen-nai ni aru

(2) $i=i'$

(3) $\dfrac{\sin i}{\sin r} = \dfrac{v_1}{v_2} = \text{ittei} = n$

Kore o hansha oyobi kussetsu no hōsoku to iu. Kono n wa kussetsu-gawa no baishitsu no nyūsha-gawa no baishitsu ni taisuru kussetsu-ritsu de aru. Koko de v_1, v_2 wa sorezore nyūsha-gawa oyobi kussetsu-gawa ni okeru hikari no hayasa de aru.

Hikari no hansha oyobi kussetsu no hōsoku wa, nami no hansha oyobi kussetsu no hōsoku to mattaku hitoshii.

Hansha, kussetsu no hōsoku wa hikari no susumikata [13] ni kansuru hōsoku de atte, hansha-kō oyobi kussetsu-kō no tsuyosa ni tsuite wa furete inai. Sorera no tsuyosa wa, hansha suru busshitsu no shurui ni yotte kotonaru ga, onaji busshitsu demo nyūsha-kaku ga ōkiku naru to, hansha-kō ga tsuyoku naru.

TOTSU-RENZU NI OKERU HIKARI NO SUSUMIKATA

Heikō-kōsen o totsu-renzu [14] no kōjiku ni heikō ni ateru to, renzu o tsūka shita kōsen wa zu-san no yō ni, itten o tōru. Kono ten o totsu-renzu no shōten to ii, renzu no chūshin to shōten to no kyori o shōten-kyori to iu.

Zu-san de wa, heikō-kōsen o renzu no sahō kara ateta no de aru ga, uhō kara ateta baai ni mo renzu o tsūka shita kōsen wa itten F o tōri, kono ten mo shōten de aru. Kono yō ni, renzu no shōten wa futatsu ari, renzu ni taishite tagai ni taishō no ichi ni aru.

Totsu-renzu no kōjiku no bubun wa chiisai purizumu to shite no chōkaku wa rei de aru kara, kōjiku-jō o susumu kōsen wa sono mama chokushin suru. Mata, renzu no chūshin ni nyūsha suru kōsen wa, renzu ni suichoku de nai toki de mo, renzu ga amari atsuku nai kagiri [15] zu-yon no yō ni chokushin shite iku. [3]

Ijō no koto to, hikari wa hajime ni susunda michi o gyakushin suru koto ga

kanō de aru koto nado kara, totsu-renzu ni nyūsha shita kōsen no susumikata o tsugi no yō ni matomeru koto ga dekiru.

(1) Renzu no kōjiku ni heikō ni susumu kōsen wa, renzu tsūka-go, shōten F o tōru.

(2) Renzu no chūshin O o tōru kōsen wa sono mama chokushin suru.

(3) Shōten *F'* o tōru kōsen wa, renzu-tsūka-go, [7] kōjiku ni heikō ni susumu.

INTERFERENCE AND DIFFRACTION OF LIGHT

Light emanating from a luminous source will reach to great distances. The mechanism by which light is transmitted may be by the motion of some kind of lump or "particle" (like a baseball) or by the propagation of a "wave" (like sound).

The most fundamental characteristics of waves are diffraction and interference. Light is said to be a wave because light also manifests diffraction and interference as follows.

Observation: Light which leaves a strong luminous source S, as shown in Figure 1, passes through lens L, then is focussed on slit S_1 and proceeds on to strike slits S_2 and S_3 which are located about 0.5m ahead. When the light which has left slits S_2 and S_3 strikes the plate of frosted glass G located at a distance of about 0.5−1 m, observe the bright and dark bands which appear.

As a consequence of the diffraction of light, waves of the same phase are sent forth successively from slits S_2 and S_3 as shown in Figure 2. Where these two waves are superimposed, interference occurs. If now we let λ be the wave length of light and if at a single point x on the frosted glass plate G the condition

$$S_2x - S_3x = N\lambda \qquad N = 0, \ \pm 1, \ \pm 2, \ldots$$

is satisfied, then the waves reinforce each other at this point and it becomes bright. Moreover, if

$$S_2x - S_3x = \left(N + \frac{1}{2}\right)\lambda$$

holds, then it becomes dark. Consequently, bright and dark lines adjoin each other and interference bands are formed.

If you measure $S_2x - S_3x$ in this experiment, you can calculate the wavelength λ of light. (Thomas) Young was the first one to measure the wavelength of light by this method and established that it was of the order of 10^{-4}cm. Subsequently, it became possible to measure the wavelength by a more precise method using interference, and it was learned that the relation between color and the wave length of light is that in Table *I*.

Table I. Color and the Wavelength of Light

Wavelength (millimicrons)	Color
700—610	Red
610—590	Orange
590—570	Yellow
570—500	Green
500—450	Blue
450—400	Purple

REFLECTION AND REFRACTION OF LIGHT

When light moves through air and comes to the surface of another substance, a part enters the substance and the other part is reflected.

The fact that we can see scenery in front of us mirrored on the surface of still water and can reflect our own figure by means of a mirror is due to the reflection of light.

When light enters another substance, it bends and moves on. This is why bodies in water appear to be lifted towards the surface.

The Laws of Reflection and Refraction: In the reflecting and refracting of light, we call the angles which the incident ray, reflected ray, and refracted ray make with the perpendicular to the boundary surface the angle of incidence (i), the angle of reflection (i') and the angle of refraction (r) respectively.

(1) The incident ray, reflected ray and the refracted ray lie in the same plane perpendicular to the boundary surface.

(2) $i = i'$

(3) $\dfrac{\sin i}{\sin r} = \dfrac{v_1}{v_2} = $ a constant $= n$

These are called the laws of reflection and refraction. The constant n is the index of refraction of the refracting medium with respect to the incident medium. Here v_1 and v_2 are the speeds of light in the incident and refraction sides respectively.

The laws of the reflection and refraction of light are exactly the same as the laws of the reflection and refraction of waves.

The laws of reflection and refraction are laws concerning the propagation of light and do not deal with the intensities of the reflected and refracted light. These intensities vary with the type of substance but, as the angle of incidence becomes larger for any one substance, the reflected light becomes intensified.

THE MOVEMENT OF LIGHT AND CONVEX LENSES

When parallel light rays strike a convex lens parallel to the optical axis, the light rays transmitted through the lens will pass through a single point as shown in Figure 3. This point is called the focus of the convex lens and the distance

from the center of the lens to the focus is called the focal length.

In Figure 3 the parallel light rays strike the lens from the left; but also for light rays striking from the right, those transmitted through the lens will pass through a single point F and this point also is a focus. Hence, a lens has two foci and they are in symmetrical positions with respect to the lens.

Since the region of the convex lens at the optical axis, considered as a small prism, has a vertex angle of zero, the light rays proceeding along the optical axis move undeflected. Moreover, even if the light rays incident at the center of the lens are not perpendicular to the lens, as long as the lens is not too thick, they will continue to move in a straight line as in Figure 4.

From the above facts and the fact that it is possible for light to travel in reverse on the path by which it originally came, the movement of incident light rays in convex lenses may be summarized as follows

(1) Rays which proceed parallel to the optical axis of the lens will, after transmission, pass through focus F.

(2) Rays passing through the center of the lens 0 will proceed undeflected.

(3) Rays passing through the focus F' will, after transmission through the lens, proceed parallel to the optical axis.

EXPLANATORY NOTES

(1) tsutawaru, tsutaeru	It was pointed out in Lesson 11 that, for verb pairs ending in *-aru* and *-eru*, the *-aru* verb is intransitive and the *-eru* verb is transitive. Hence *tsutawaru* is "to be transmitted, to move," whereas *tsutaeru* means "to transmit, transfer". Similar comments apply to *kasanaru* and *kasaneru*.
(2) nani ka	As a substantive, *nani ka* means "something, anything" as in the sentence *ano yōki no naka ni nani ka aru ka* ("Is there anything in that container?"). In the text here it has the meaning of "some kind of".
(3) ugoite iku, susunde kuru	For *-te kuru* and *-te iku*, see Lesson 9, Explanatory Note 9.
(4) ...(verb) no ka...... (verb) no ka no izure ka de aru	"is either...or..." This construction implies that one or the other of the statements is true.
(5) ya	Remember that *ya* (as opposed to *to*) implies an incomplete listing.
(6) tōru, tōsu	For verb pairs ending in *-ru* and *-su*, the *-ru* verb is intransitive, whereas the *-su* verb is transitive. Hence *tōsu* means "to pass something through," *tōru* "to pass

through." Other such pairs are:

kieru	to go out
kesu	to extinguish
okoru	to happen
okosu	to start (something)
utsuru	to be reflected
utsusu	to copy, photograph, reflect

(7) suritto S_1 jō ni   "on slit S_1". Note that one could also say *suritto S_1 no ue ni* by using the extra particle *no*. Other examples in this lesson are:

kūki-chū kara=kūki no naka kara

sui-chū ni aru=mizu no naka ni aru

tsūka-go=tsūka no nochi

heimen-nai ni=heimen no uchi ni

Generally the first expression corresponds to the written style, whereas the second is used in conversation.

(8) seyo   Imperative of *suru*

(9) tsuyome-au   The compound verbs with *-au* as the second element usually indicate some kind of mutual interaction and can be translated by "(verb) + each other" or "(verb) + one another"

tsuyome-au	to strengthen (reinforce) one another
hiki-au	to attract each other
oyoboshi-au	to exert on each other; to influence one another
hanpatsu shi-au	to repel one another
tonari-au	to adjoin one another

(10) hajimete   This has the meaning of "for the first time," but usually sentences containing this word are best rearranged in English. Thus,

Koko wa hajimete desu ka?

"Is this the first time you've been here?"

Tanaka kyōju wa hajimete kono riron o rombun to shite happyō shita

"Prof. Tanaka was the first to publish this theory (in an article)."

(11) utsutte mietari;   In the first case *mieru* means "to be visible" ("the
uki-agatte mietari   scenery is seen reflected" or more naturally "we can

see the scenery reflected"). In the second case *mieru* means "appears, looks like" ("the body appears to be lifted towards the surface"). In both instances the *-tari* forms indicate that there are other examples of similar phenomena which could be cited.

(12) kyōkai-men...to nasu	This entire phrase modifies *kaku*.
(13) susumi-kata	Addition of *-kata* to the verb stem is a standard way to express "way of...ing." Other examples: *ugoki-kata* "way of moving"; *nagare-kata* "way of flowing."
(14) totsu-renzu	The opposite of *totsu-renzu* "convex lens" (凸レンズ) is *ō-renzu* "concave lens" (凹). These *kanji* are not *Tōyō kanji* but are particularly useful in optics. Their *kun* readings appear in the equally graphic word *deko-boko* (凸凹) "bumpy, uneven, rough".
(15) amari atsuku nai kagiri	"as long as it is not too thick," "unless it is too thick" (See also Note in Lesson 7).

CONSTRUCTION EXAMPLES

…はこのためでめる	"this is why..."; "for that reason..."

1. 光は波動としての性質をもっている。光が干渉したり回折したりするのはこのためでめる。
2. 光の速さは媒質によって異なる。二つの異なった媒質の境界面で光が屈折するのはこのためである。

何か…	"some kind of..."

1. 光は真空中でも伝わるので，真空中にも何か光を伝える媒質があると考えられ，エーテルと名づけられた。
2. アクリル樹脂を高圧下におくと何かガス状のものが出てきたので，よく調べてみると解重合が行なわれていた。

真空	shinkū	vacuum
名づける	na-zukeru	to call, name
アクリル樹脂	akuriru-jushi	acrylic resin
解重合	kai-jūgō	depolymerization

AがBと角をなす	"A makes an angle with B"

1. 正三角形の相隣る2辺は互いに60度の角をなす。
2. 入射光線が境界面に立てた垂線となす角は，反射光線がこの垂線となす角と等しい。

相隣る	ai-tonaru	to be adjacent
立てる	tateru	to erect

見える	"can be seen" or "appears"

1. ガラス壁をもった水槽を暗い部屋に入れて，光を入射すれば，光の通るみちが見える。
2. 水中に入れた棒は水面のところで折れて見える。

水槽	suisō	water tank

SUPPLEMENTARY READINGS

A. *Selections from Rikagaku Jiten*

1)

単レンズ	tan-renzu	simple lens
ときとしては	toki to shite wa	sometimes, in some cases
凹面鏡	ōmen-kyō	concave mirror
凸面鏡	totsumen-kyō	convex miror
含む	fukumu	to contain
…から成る	…kara naru	to be made of…
光学系	kōgaku-kei	optical system
光線束	kōsen-soku	pencil of light rays
発する	hassuru	to emanate
集合させる	shūgō saseru	to cause to converge
発散させる	hassan saseru	to cause to diverge
実像	jitsuzō	real image
虚像	kyozō	virtual image

レンズ (2RJ 1456)

一個または数個の単レンズ（ときとしては凹面鏡，凸面鏡をも含む）から成る光学系で，物体（ときにはほかの光学系の作った像）から発する光線束を集合あるいは発散させて実像あるいは虚像を結ばせるものをレンズという。

2)

偏光	henkō	polarized light
顕微鏡	kenbi-kyō	microscope
通常の	tsūjō no	ordinary, usual
岩石	ganseki	rocks

鉱物	kōbutsu	minerals
薄片	hakuhen	lamina
砕片	saihen	fragment, splinter
ニコル・プリズム	nikoru purizumu	Nicol prism
人造の	jinzō no	artificial, man-made
偏光子	henkō-shi	polarizer
備える	sonaeru	to provide, equip
載物台	saibutsu-dai	table, stage (of microscope)

偏光顕微鏡　(2RJ 1249)

偏光を使う顕微鏡で，通常岩石学，鉱物学で岩石や鉱物の薄片や砕片の光学的観察に使用するから，鉱物あるいは岩石顕微鏡ともいう。普通の顕微鏡と違う所は2個のニコル・プリズム（あるいは人造偏光子）を備え，また普通は載物台が回転できることである。

3)	位相差顕微鏡	isō-sa-kenbi-kyō	phase contrast microscope
	部分的に	bubun-teki ni	in different regions
	無色の	mushoku no	colorless
	透明な	tōmei na	transparent
	むずかしい	muzukashii	difficult
	透過光	tōka-kō	transmitted light
	見やすい	mi-yasui	easy to see

位相差顕微鏡　(2RJ 76)

屈折率または厚さが部分的に違う無色透明な物体の構造を普通の顕微鏡で見ることはむずかしいが，位相差顕微鏡は各部分の透過光の間に生じた位相差を像面で明暗の差に変えて構造を見やすくしたものである。

4)	望遠鏡	bōen-kyō	telescope
	対物レンズ	taibutsu-renzu	objective lens
	凹面の	ōmen no	concave
	適当な	tekitō na	suitable
	集束させる	shūsoku saseru	to focus
	誘導する	yūdō suru	to conduct, lead
	様式	yōshiki	style, form
	区別する	kubetsu suru	to differentiate

反射望遠鏡　(2RJ 1075)

屈折望遠鏡の対物レンズの代りに凹面反射鏡を使用し，物体から来る光をこの鏡で反射

させ，さらに第二の鏡でこの光を観測に適当な場所に集束させるものをいう。光を誘導する方法によって種々の様式が区別される。

5)	写真用	shashin-yō	photographic
	撮影する	satsuei suru	to take a photograph
	乾板	kanpan	dry plate
	有効な	yūkō na	effective
	色収差	iro-shūsa	chromatic aberration
	実視…	jisshi...	visual...
	接眼レンズ	setsugan renzu	ocular lens
	写真機	shashin-ki	camera

写真用望遠鏡　(2RJ 608)

写真撮影の目的に用いられる望遠鏡。写真乾板に有効な青，紫の光に対して，色収差のないように作られた対物レンズをもち，実視望遠鏡の接眼レンズのつく位置に写真機が置かれている。

6)	色消しプリズム	iro-keshi purizumu	achromatic lens
	偏角	henkaku	deflection
	クラウンガラス	kuraun garasu	crown glass
	フリントガラス	furinto garasu	flint glass
	前者…後者	zensha...kōsha	the former...the latter
	分散	bunsan	dispersion
	打ち消す	uchi-kesu	to cancel

色消しプリズム　(2RJ 90)

屈折率により光線の方向を曲げるのに，色によって偏角の差がないようにしたプリズム系。クラウンガラスのプリズムにそれと逆の方向に光を曲げるフリントガラスのプリズムを組み合わせ，前者による色の分散を後者のそれで打ち消すようにする。

7)	回折格子	kaisetsu-gōshi	diffraction grating
	スペクトル	supekutoru	spectrum
	等間隔	tō-kankaku	equally spaced
	刻む	kizamu	to notch, score
	針金	harigane	wire
	張る	haru	to stretch
	強まる	tsuyomaru	to be strengthened, intensified

回折格子　(2RJ 214)

　光を回折させてスペクトルを得るのに用いられる装置。平面上に等間隔に多数の平行線の格子を刻み，または多数の針金を平面上に平行に張った平面格子および平面の代りに凹面鏡を用いた凹面格子がある。いずれも等間隔の格子線の周期的な性質により反射光または通過光の回折したものが互いに干渉して一定の方向に一定の波長の光が強まり全体としてスペクトルを表わす。

B. 1)

太陽	taiyō	the sun
白色光	haku-shokkō	white light
…から…に至る	…kara… ni itaru	from… to…
連続した	renzoku shita	continuous
色帯	shikitai	a band of colors
連続スペクトル	renzoku-supekutoru	continuous spectrum
白熱電燈	hakunetsu dentō	incandescent electric lamp
炭火	sumibi	charcoal fire
何本かの…	nanbon ka no…	some number of…

　(本 is the counter for long, slender objects, e. g. pencils, trees, etc.)

線スペクトル	sen-supekutoru	line spectrum
…に特有な	…ni tokuyū na	characteristic of…
型	kata	pattern
未知	michi	unknown
分光器	bunkō-ki	spectroscope
輝線	kisen	bright line
所々	tokoro-dokoro	here and there, in places
密集する	misshū suru	to be close together
帯状	taijō	in the form of bands
帯スペクトル	tai-supekutoru	band spectrum
遷移	sen'i	transition

(Note: used for changes in energy level outside the nucleus.)

全域	zen'iki	the entire range
…にわたって	…ni watatte	throughout…
黒線	kokusen	black lines
フラウンホーファー線	Furaunhōfā-sen	Fraunhofer lines
順に	jun ni	in order
命名する	meimei suru	to designate, call
自身	jishin	it itself
吸収する	kyūshū suru	to absorb
吸収スペクトル	kyūshū-supekutoru	absorption spectrum

付近	fukin	vicinity, neighborhood
特定の	tokutei no	particular

スペクトル　(BN 180)

　太陽光線のような白色光のスペクトルは赤から紫に至る連続した色帯でこれを連続スペクトルとよぶ。白熱電燈，炭火などすべて高温固体を光源とした場合にこのようなスペクトルが得られる。これに反して，高温の気体から発する光のスペクトルは何本かの明るい線からできているのでこれを線スペクトルという。これは気体原子のエネルギー状態の変化によって生ずるものと考えられ，各元素に特有な型を示すので未知成分の気体のスペクトルをしらべることによりその気体の成分を知ることができる。（スペクトルを作って，これをしらべる装置を一般に分光器という。）輝線が所々に密集して帯状になっているスペクトルを帯スペクトルとよぶが，これは分子状態の遷移によって生ずるものと考えられる。

　太陽光線のスペクトルは完全に連続したスペクトルでなく，よく見ると全域にわたって多数の黒線のあることがわかる。この黒線をフラウンホーファー線といい，その赤の方から順に A, B, C, D, …線と命名されている。気体は高温において自身が発するスペクトル線と同じ波長の光を低温では吸収する性質がある。フラウンホーファー線は太陽付近の気体によって太陽光線中の特定の波長のものが吸収されて生ずるもので，このように黒線の現われるスペクトルを吸収スペクトルという。

2)	赤外線	sekigai-sen	infrared ray
	紫外線	shigai-sen	ultra violet ray
	…域	…iki	…region
	範囲	han'i	range
	われわれ	ware-ware	we
	感じる	kanjiru	to sense; experience
	可視光線	kashi-kōsen	visible rays, visible light
	…外	…gai	beyond…, outside of…
	赤色光	seki-shokkō	red light
	熱効果	netsu-kōka	heat effect
	輻射	fukusha	radiation
	熱線	nessen	heat rays
	岩塩	gan'en	rock salt
	透過する	tōka suru	to transmit
	紫色光	shi-shokkō	violet light
	発見する	hakken suru	to discover
	水晶	suishō	rock crystal, crystallized quartz

赤外線と紫外線　(BN 181)

　波長域がおよそ 0.8μ から 0.4μ の範囲の光線はわれわれが赤から紫までの色として感じるもので，これを可視光線という。可視域外で赤色光より波長が長いところに著るしく熱効果を示す輻射線のあることが知られて，これが赤外線と名づけられた。その範囲は大体 0.5cm～0.8μ とされる。赤外線はまた熱線ともよばれ，ガラスや水などによって吸収されるが岩塩はほとんどこれを透過する。次に紫色光よりさらに波長が短く，写真作用その他の化学作用を有する輻射線が発見されて紫外線と名づけられたが，これはふつうのガラスで吸収されるので，その実験には紫外線をよく通す水晶が用いられる。紫外線域は 0.38μ～0.01μ のところにある。

3)　眼	manako	eye
感度	kando	sensitivity
黄色光	ō-shokkō	yellow light
混合する	kongō suru	to mix
作り出す	tsukuri-dasu	to produce, create
三原色	san-genshoku	three primary colors
補色	hoshoku	complementary color
余色	yoshoku	complementary color

光の色　(BN 181–182)

　光として眼に感ずる光線の波長は，大体 0.38μ～0.81μ の範囲であるが，この範囲でも色光に対する感度は一様でない。われわれの眼は D 線付近の黄色光に最も強く感ずる。色光を二種以上混合して他の色の光を得ることができるが，実験によれば，赤・緑・青の三つの単色光を適当な割合に混合するとほとんどすべての色光を作り出すことができるのでこの三つの色を光の三原色という。この三原色を同じ割合で混合すると白色光となるが，一般に適当な二つの色光を混合して，白色光が得られるときの二色光を互に補色（余色ともいう）であるという。

FINAL TRANSLATION TEST

　光の反射・屈折の法則に明らかなように，入射角の正弦と屈折角の正弦との比は物質及び光の波長によって定まる定数となるから，レンズを用いて光を屈折させれば，単色光でない限り光は分散してしまい一つの焦点にはあつまらない。すなわち，赤から紫にいたるスペクトルに分かれて，それぞれ異なったみちを取る。これをさけるために鏡が用いられる。ふつう鏡は一方の側を厚く銀めっきしたガラス板で，光をガラスの面から入射させる

と，ガラスの表面で反射した光と，めっき面で反射した光とがいっしょに目にはいって像が2重に見えるので光学機器ではめっきした面に光を入射する。鏡を用いれば光の屈折にもとづく分散はさけられるが，写った像の左右は逆になっている。しかしこの事は非常に遠くの物体を見る場合にはあまり気にならない。レンズのかわりに鏡を用いた反射望遠鏡でも，光の干渉にもとづく現象はやはり起こる。例えば星を見る場合，ふつうの星は非常に遠い所にあるのでその像は点として現われるはずである。ところが，実際に望遠鏡を通して星を見ると，その像は点にはならず，ある大きさの明るい円輪になる。これは光の回折のためであって，光が波である以上，どうしてもさけることのできないものである。このように回折によって像がある大きさをもつため，第2の星の像が第1の星の像に非常に近いと，二つの強く光った円輪が重なり合って，二つの異なった星の像だか一つの星の像だか見分けがつかなくなる。大体同じ明るさの二つの星の場合には，第2の星の像の中心が第1の星の像の円輪の外になければ二つとして観測できない。

LESSON 14
第十四課
KANJI

帯	669	TAI
	1474	o(biru)
電	286	DEN
	5050	
互	194a	GO
	14	taga(i)
荷	165	KA
	3956	
真	438	SHIN
	783	ma
約	726	YAKU
	3499	
問	520	MON
	4944	to(u)
題	464	DAI
	2164	
金	16	KIN
	4815	kane
属	835	ZOKU
	1400	

縁	268a	EN
	3585	
並	219b	HEI nara(bini) {nara(beru) {nara(bu)
	589	
静	442	SEI JŌ
	5077	shizu(ka)
誘	264a	YŪ
	4371	saso(u)
負	312	FU
	4488	
基	755	KI
	1098	moto(zuku)
本	45	HON
	96	
列	537	RETSU
	2438	
路	540	RO
	4561	
算	219	SAN
	3415	

READING SELECTIONS

帯電体	taiden-tai	charged body
異種の	ishu no	of a different kind
同種の	dōshu no	of the same kind
電気	denki	electricity
引き合う	hiki-au	to attract one another
互いに	tagai ni	mutually
反発し合う	hanpatsu shi-au	to repel one another
クーロン	Kūron	Coulomb
ねじればかり	nejire-bakari	torsion balance

及ぼし合う	oyoboshi-au	to exert on one another
精密に	seimitsu ni	accurately
2乗	nijō	second power; square
決まる	kimaru	to be determined
電荷	denka	electric charge
真空	shinkū	vacuum
約	yaku	approximately
問題	mondai	problem
隔てる	hedateru	to separate

帯電体の間にはたらく力　(B 223–224)

　異種の電気は互いに引きあい[1]，同種の電気は互いに反発しあう[1]。この力の大きさはどのくらい[2]になるであろうか。

　クーロンはねじればかりを作り，二つの帯電体が及ぼしあう[1]力を精密に測定した。その結果によれば，二つの帯電体の間にはたらく力 F は，それぞれの電気量 q, q' に比例し，2物体間の距離 r の2乗に反比例している。すなわち

$$F = k\frac{qq'}{r^2} \tag{1}$$

これを電気力に関するクーロンの法則という。比例定数 k は帯電体の間にある物質によって変わるが，物質が決まれば一定の値をとる。

　1クーロンの電荷（電気量）をもつ二つの物体を，真空中で 1m の距離に置いたとき，互いに及ぼしあう力は約 9×10^9 ニュートンである。したがって， q をクーロン， r をメートルで表わすとき， k は 9×10^9 ニュートン／（クーロン）^{2} となる。

問題。真空中 10cm 隔てて置いた二つの物体が等しく帯電しているとき， その間に 0.9 ニュートンの力がはたらいた。その電気量はいくらか。（10^{-6} クーロン）

コンデンサー	kondensā	condenser
2枚	ni-mai	two
金属板	kinzoku-ban	metal sheets
絶縁体	zetsuen-tai	insulator
はさむ	hasamu	to insert between
狭い	semai	narrow
間隔	kankaku	space
並べる	naraberu	to arrange
つなぐ	tsunagu	to connect
一方…他方	ippō…tahō	the one...the other
静電誘導	seiden-yūdō	electrostatic induction
逃げる	nigeru	to escape

ためる	tameru	to store
役目をする	yakume o suru	perform a function
電位差	den'i-sa	electric potential difference
電気容量	denki-yōryō	electric capacity (capacitance)
ファラド	farado	farad
ずっと小さい	zutto chiisai	much, much smaller
マイクロファラド	maikuro-farado	microfarad
…からなる	...kara naru	to be made of...
電極	denkyoku	electrode
極板	kyokuban	electrode plates
誘電率	yūden-ritsu	dielectric constant
パラフィン	parafin	paraffin
一端…他端	ittan...tatan	one end...the other end
引き寄せる	hiki-yoseru	to attract, draw near
誘電分極	yūden-bunkyoku	dielectric polarization
…のつなぎ方	...no tsunagikata	method of connecting...
並列	heiretsu	parallel
直列	chokuretsu	series
合成の	gōsei no	resultant

コンデンサー　 (B 227–230)

コンデンサーは，2枚の金属板を，絶縁体をはさんで狭い間隔で並べたものである。一方[3]の金属板に正の電気を与えると，地球につないだ他方の金属板に静電誘導によって負の電気が生じ，互いに引きあって外に逃げずに止まっている。このようにコンデンサーは電気をためておく[4]役目をする。

コンデンサーにためられる電荷 q をしだいに増していくと，それに比例して2枚の金属板の電位差 V は大きくなる。すなわち，

$$q=CV \qquad\qquad (2)$$

の関係がある。C はコンデンサーによって決まる比例定数で，コンデンサーの電気容量という。電気容量が大きいほど，小さい電位差で多量の電荷がためられることになる。

コンデンサーに1クーロンの電荷を与えて，1ボルトの電位差を生じるとき，その電気容量を1ファラド($\mathbf{F}$)であるという。ふつうのコンデンサーの電気容量は1ファラドよりずっと小さいので $10^{-6}\mathrm{F}$ を1マイクロファラド ($\mu\mathrm{F}$) とよび，これを単位として用いることが多い[5]。

2枚の平行な金属板からなるコンデンサーの1枚の電極の面積を S,電極の間隔を d とす

れば，電気容量 C は S に比例し，d に反比例する。すなわち

$$C=KS/d \tag{3}$$

となる。K は2枚の極板の間にある絶縁体の種類によって決まる値であって[6]，絶縁体があるときには，ないときよりも電気容量が大きくなる[7]。真空中での K の値を K_0 とするとき，K/K_0 を誘電率という。

空気の誘電率はほとんど1であるが，ガラスでは 5〜8，パラフィンでは 1.9〜2.4 という値をもっているので，それだけ[8]電気量が大きくなる。極板の間に絶縁体を入れると電気容量が増すのは，絶縁体の分子の一端[3]に正，他端に負の電気が現われるので，極板にそれだけ多くの電気量が引き寄せられているからである。絶縁体がこのようになることを誘電分極または単に分極するという。

コンデンサーのつなぎ方

実際にコンデンサーを用いるときには，いくつかのコンデンサーをつないで用いる場合が多い[5]。基本的なつなぎ方としては並列と直列との二つがある。電気容量 C_1, C_2 の二つのコンデンサーを並列につないだときには，二つのコンデンサーの電位差 V は等しく，全電荷はそれぞれのコンデンサーの電荷 q_1, q_2 の和になる。したがって，合成の容量 C は

$$C=\frac{q_1+q_2}{V} \quad \therefore C=C_1+C_2 \tag{4}$$

で与えられる。また，直列につないだときには，二つのコンデンサーにたまる電荷 q が等しく，全電位差は V_1+V_2 となるので，合成容量 C は

$$\frac{q}{C}=V=V_1+V_2=\frac{q}{C_1}+\frac{q}{C_2} \qquad \therefore \frac{1}{C}=\frac{1}{C_1}+\frac{1}{C_2} \tag{5}$$

で与えられる。

電子計算機	denshi-keisan-ki	electronic computer
回路	kairo	circuit
素子	soshi	element
真空管	shinkū-kan	vacuum tube
ちょうど	chōdo	precisely, exactly
細胞	saihō, saibō	cell
に似る	ni niru	to be similar to
人	hito	man, people
眼	manako	eyes
耳	mimi	ears
手	te	hands
拡張する	kakuchō suru	to extend
最近	saikin	recently
頭脳	zunō	brain

盛に	sakan ni	widely, extensively
このよい例	kono yoi rei	a good example of this
そろばん	soroban	Japanese abacus
玉	tama	bead
上げ下げ	age-sage	raising and lowering
電流	denryū	electric current
非常に	hijō ni	exceptionally
…と比較にならない	...to hikaku ni naranai	cannot compare with...
複雑な	fukuzatsu na	complicated
英語	Eigo	English
日本語	Nihongo	Japanese
翻訳する	hon'yaku suru	to translate
試みる	kokoromiru	to try, attempt
エレクトロニクス	erekutoronikusu	electronics
発展	hatten	development
進歩する	shinpo suru	to progress
今後	kongo	in the future
応用	ōyō	application

電子計算機　(B 334)

　電子装置のはたらきはいろいろ違っているが，みな同じような回路素子や真空管などを組み合わせて作られている。これはちょうど生物がいろいろの細胞から作られているのに [9] 似ている。人の眼や耳や手のはたらきを拡張する電子装置のほかに，最近は頭脳のはたらきをするものが作られ，盛んに用いられている。

　このよい例 [10] が電子計算機である。そろばんは玉の上げ下げで数を表わす。電子計算機では電流が流れるか流れないかによって数を表わす。真空管などでの電子のはたらきが非常に速いので，電子計算機はそろばんとは比較にならないほど高速度で非常に複雑な計算もできる。ふつうには計算とは考えられないようなこと，たとえば英語を日本語に翻訳 [11] するようなことまで試みられている。電子計算機は固体エレクトロニクスの発展に伴って急速に進歩しているので今後その応用はいろいろの方面に発展するだろう。

TAIDEN-TAI NO AIDA NI HATARAKU CHIKARA

Ishu no denki wa tagai ni hiki-ai [1] dōshu no denki wa tagai ni hanpatsu shi-au. [1] Kono chikara no ōkisa wa, dono kurai [2] ni naru de arō ka.

　Kūron wa, nejire-bakari o tsukuri, futatsu no taiden-tai ga oyoboshi-au [1] chikara o seimitsu ni sokutei shita. Sono kekka ni yoreba, futatsu no taiden-tai no aida ni hataraku chikara F wa, sorezore no denki-ryō q, q' ni hirei shi, ni-buttai-

kan no kyori *r* no nijō ni hanpirei shite iru. Sunawachi

$$F = kqq'/r^2 \qquad (1)$$

Kore o denki-ryoku ni kansuru Kūron no hōsoku to iu. Hirei-teisū *k* wa taiden-tai no aida ni aru busshitsu ni yotte kawaru ga, busshitsu ga kimareba ittei no atai o toru.

Ichi kūron no denka (denki-ryō) o motsu futatsu no buttai o, shinkū-chū de ichi mētoru no kyori ni oita toki, tagai ni oyoboshi-au chikara wa yaku kyū kakeru jū no kyūjō nyūton de aru. Shitagatte, *q* o kūron, *r* o mētoru de arawasu toki *k* wa kyū kakeru jū no kyūjō nyūton mētoru no jijō pā kūron no jijō to naru.

Mondai: Shinkū-chū jussenchi hedatete oita futatsu no buttai ga hitoshiku taiden shite iru toki, sono aida ni rei ten kyū nyūton no chikara ga hataraita. Sono denki-ryō wa ikura ka. (jū no mainasu rokujō kūron)

KONDENSĀ

Kondensā wa, nimai no kinzoku-ban o zetsuen-tai o hasande semai kankaku de narabeta mono de aru. Ippō[3] no kinzoku-ban ni sei no denki o ataeru to, chikyū ni tsunaida tahō no kinzoku-ban ni seiden-yūdō ni yotte fu no denki ga shōji, tagai ni hiki-atte soto ni nigezu ni tomatte iru. Kono yō ni kondensā wa denki o tamete oku[4] yakume o suru.

Kondensā ni tamerareru denka *q* o shidai ni mashite iku to, sore ni hirei shite, nimai no kinzoku-ban no den'i-sa *V* wa ōkiku naru. Sunawachi

$$q = CV \qquad (2)$$

no kankei ga aru. *C* wa kondensā ni yotte kimaru hirei-teisū de, kondensā no denki-yōryō to iu. Denki-yōryō ga ōkii hodo, chiisai den'i-sa de taryō no denka ga tamerareru koto ni naru.

Kondensā ni ichi kūron no denka o ataete, ichi boruto no den'i-sa o shōjiru toki, sono denki-yōryō o ichi-farado (F) de aru to iu. Futsū no kondensā no denki-yōryō wa ichi-farado yori zutto chiisai no de jū no mainasu rokujō o ichi-maikurofarado (μF) to yobi, kore o tan'i to shite mochi-iru koto ga ōi.[5]

Nimai no heikō na kinzoku-ban kara naru kondensā no ichimai no denkyoku no menseki o *S*, denkyoku no kankaku o *d* to sureba, denki-yōryō *C* wa *S* ni hirei shi, *d* ni hanpirei suru. Sunawachi

$$C = KS/d \qquad (3)$$

to naru. *K* wa nimai no kyokuban no aida ni aru zetsuen-tai no shurui ni yotte kimaru atai de atte[6], zetsuen-tai ga aru toki ni wa, nai toki yori mo denki-yōryō ga ōkiku naru.[7] Shinkūchū de no *K* no atai o K_0 to suru toki, K/K_0 o yūden-ritsu to iu.

Kūki no yūden-ritsu wa hotondo ichi de aru ga, garasu de wa go naishi hachi, parafin de wa ichi-ten-kyū naishi ni-ten-yon to iu atai o motte iru no de, sore

dake[8] denki-yōryō ga ōkiku naru. Kyokuban no aida ni zetsuen-tai o ireru to denki-yōryō ga masu no wa, zetsuen-tai no bunshi no ittan ni[3] sei, tatan ni fu no denki ga arawareru no de, kyokuban ni sore dake ōku no denki-ryō ga hiki-yoserarete iru kara de aru. Zetsuen-tai ga kono yō ni naru koto o yūden-bunkyoku mata wa tan ni bunkyoku suru to iu.

Kondensā no tsunagikata: Jissai ni kondensā o mochiiru toki ni wa, ikutsu ka no kondensā o tsunaide mochi-iru baai ga ōi.[5] Kihon-teki na tsunagi-kata to shite wa heiretsu to chokuretsu to no futatsu ga aru. Denki-yōryō C_1, C_2 no futatsu no kondensā o heiretsu ni tsunaida toki ni wa, futatsu no kondensā no den'i-sa V wa hitoshiku, zen-denka wa sorezore no kondensā no denka q_1, q_2 no wa ni naru. Shitagatte, gōsei no yōryō C wa

$$C = (q_1 + q_2)/V \quad \therefore C = C_1 + C_2 \tag{4}$$

de ataerareru. Mata, chokuretsu ni tsunaida toki ni wa, futatsu no kondensā ni tamaru denka q ga hitoshiku, zen-den'i-sa wa $V_1 + V_2$ to naru no de, gōsei-yōryō C wa

$$q/C = V = V_1 + V_2 = (q/C_1) + (q/C_2) \quad \therefore 1/C = 1/C_1 + 1/C_2 \tag{5}$$

de ataerareru.

DENSHI-KEISAN-KI

Denshi-sōchi no hataraki wa iroiro chigatte iru ga, mina onaji yō na kairo-soshi ya shinkū-kan nado o kumi-awasete tsukurarete iru. Kore wa chōdo seibutsu ga iroiro no saihō kara tsukurarete iru no ni[9] nite iru. Hito no manako ya mimi ya te no hataraki o kakuchō suru denshi-sōchi no hoka ni, saikin wa zunō no hataraki o suru mono ga tsukurare, sakan ni mochi-irarete iru.

Kono yoi rei[10] ga denshi-keisan-ki de aru. Soroban wa tama no age-sage de kazu o arawasu. Denshi-keisan-ki de wa, denryū ga nagareru ka, nagarenai ka ni yotte kazu o arawasu. Shinkū-kan nado de no denshi no hataraki ga hijō ni hayai no de, denshi-keisan-ki wa soroban to wa hikaku ni naranai hodo kō-sokudo de hijō ni fukuzatsu na keisan mo dekiru. Futsū ni wa keisan to wa kangaerarenai yō na koto, tatoeba Eigo o Nihongo ni hon'yaku[11] suru yō na koto made koko-romirarete iru. Denshi-keisan-ki wa kotai-erekutoronikusu no hatten ni tomonatte kyūsoku ni shinpo shite iru no de kongo sono ōyō wa iroiro no hōmen ni hatten suru darō.

THE FORCES ACTING BETWEEN CHARGED BODIES

Different kinds of electricity (mutually) attract each other, but identical kinds (mutually) repel. How large are these forces?

Coulomb constructed a torsion balance and measured accurately the forces which two charged bodies exert on one another.

According to his results, the force F acting between the two bodies is pro-

portional to their respective electrical charges q and q' and inversely proportional to the square of the distance r between them.

$$F = kqq'/r^2 \qquad (1)$$

This is called Coulomb's law of electrical force.

The proportionality constant k varies with the substance between the charged bodies but, for any given substance, it has a constant value.

When two bodies each carry an electric charge of 1 Coulomb and are placed in a vacuum at a distance of 1 meter, they exert a force on each other of about 9×10^9 Newtons. Consequently, if q is expressed in Coulombs and r in meters, k is 9×10^9 Newtons m²/Coulomb².

Problem:

If two equally charged bodies placed in a vacuum at a separation of 10 cm. have a force of 0.9 Newtons acting between them, how large is their electrical charge?

(10^{-6} Coulomb)

CONDENSERS

A condenser consists of two narrowly separated metal plates with an insulator between them. If one of the metal plates is charged positively, negative electricity will be produced by electrostatic induction on the other plate which is connected to the earth, and these charges will mutually attract each other and become stabilized. Thus, a condenser performs the function of storing electricity.

If the electrical charge q stored by a condenser is increased continuously, the potential difference V between the two metal plates increases in direct proportion, that is, the relation

$$q = CV \qquad (2)$$

is obtained. C is a proportionality constant determined by the condenser and is called the electric capacity of the condenser. The larger the electric capacity, the larger the amount of electricity which can be stored at low potential differences.

If a potential difference of 1 volt is produced by giving a 1 Coulomb charge to a condenser, the electric capacity is said to be 1 Farad. Since the electric capacity of the usual condenser is far less than 1 Farad, the unit more frequently used is $10^{-6}F$, the microfared (μF).

If we let S be the area of an electrode in a parallel metal plate condenser and d their separation, then the electric capacity C is proportional to S and inversely proportional to d, that is,

$$C = KS/d \qquad (3)$$

The value of K is determined by the variety of insulator present between the electrodes, and the capacity will be larger with an insulator than without one. If

we take K_0 as the value of K in a vacuum, then K/K_0 is called the dielectric constant.

The dielectric constant for air is approximately 1 and, since glass has a value of 5–8 and paraffin of 1. 9—2. 4, they will increase the electric capacity by those factors. The increase in the electric capacity upon inserting an insulator between the electrode plates is due to the fact that positive electricity arises at one end of an insulator molecule and negative at the other, thus permitting much more electricity to be attracted by the electrode plates. We call this change in the insulator dielectric polarization or simply polarization.

Methods of Connecting Condensers: In the actual use of condensers, they are more frequently used in connected combinations. The two main methods are to connect them in parallel or in series. When two condensers with electric capacities C_1 and C_2 are connected in parallel, their potential differences are equal and the total electric charge is the sum of their respective charges q_1 and q_2. The resultant capacity C is given by

$$C=C_1+C_2$$

since
$$C=(q_1+q_2)/V \tag{4}$$

When connected in series the electric charge q stored on each of the two condensers is the same, and the total potential difference is V_1+V_2. Thus, the resultant capacity C is given by

$$1/C=1/C_1+1/C_2$$

since
$$q/C=V=V_1+V_2=q/C_1+q/C_2 \tag{5}$$

ELECTRONIC COMPUTERS

Electronic devices have various different functions, but they are all produced by combining the same circuit elements, vacuum tubes and other parts. This is exactly similar to living things which are made from various cells.

Electronic devices have been devised which extend the functions of human eyes, ears, and hands, and more recently the brain, and these (devices) are being widely used. A good illustration of this (development) is the electronic computer. The abacus indicates numbers by the raising and lowering of beads, whereas an electronic computer indicates numbers according to whether or not an electric current is flowing. Since the functioning of electrons in such things as vacuum tubes is extremely fast, electronic computers are able to do even complicated computations at such high speeds that there is no comparison with the abacus. Even activities that we do not usually consider as calculating, for example, the translating of English into Japanese, are being attempted. Since electronic computers are progressing extremely rapidly with the development of solid state electronics, applications will be developing in a variety of directions in the future.

EXPLANATORY NOTES

(1) hiki-au, hanpatsu shi-au, oyoboshi-au	See Note 9 of Lesson 13. The addition of *tagai ni* emphasizes the idea of mutual action.
(2) dono kurai (*or* dono gurai)	This can mean "how much," "how long," "how far," etc., depending on the context.
(3) ippō...tahō	"the one...the other." A similar construction occurs later (*ittan...tatan* "one end...the other end"). Note that *chikyū ni tsunaida* modifies *tahō no kinzoku ban*.
(4) tamete oku	For the *-te oku* construction see the Notes of Lesson 12.
(5) koto ga ōi; baai ga ōi	These are standard Japanese idioms for "often."
(6) K wa...de atte	K is the subject of *de atte*, with *nimai...kimaru* modifying *atai:* "K is the value which is determined by..."; *nimai...aru* is a phrase modifying *zetsuen-tai* "the dielectric which is between the two electrode plates." 枚 (*mai*) is a counter for flat objects.
(7) zetsuen-tai ga...ōkiku naru	*zetsuen-tai* is the subject of *aru* and of *nai; denki-yōryō* is the subject of *naru*. Note that *yori* is used to compare *aru toki* ("when it is present") with *nai toki* ("when it is absent").
(8) sore dake	Same as *sore hodo* "to that extent" (i.e., by factors of 5–8 or 1. 9–2. 4).
(9) (verb) + no ni	Do not confuse with the *no ni* which, when appearing at the end of a phrase, means either (1) "in spite of", or (2) "for the purpose of". In this sentence the *no* is the equivalent of *koto*, and the *ni* occurs in the expression...*ni nite iru* "to resemble".
(10) kono yoi rei	"a good example of this." The *kono* refers back to the main idea of the foregoing sentence. An additional illustration of this use of *kono* is: *Kono kaisetsu ni tsuite wa...o sanshō saretai.* "For an explanation of this we should like the reader to consult...."
(11) hon'yaku suru	"to translate" (in written form). The expression for "to translate" (in oral form) is *tsūyaku suru* 通訳する。

CONSTRUCTION EXAMPLES

どのくらい	"how much (long, far, etc.)"

1. 電子の質量がどのくらいあるか知るためには, どのような実験をすればよいだろうか。

2. 電子１個のもつ電気量で１クーロンをわれば，１アンペアの電流の流れている導体の断面を通って１秒間にどのくらいの数の電子が移動するかがわかる。

| …でわる | …de waru | to divide...by |
| 導体 | dōtai | conductor |

…か…かによって   "according to whether...or (whether)..."

1. 二つの帯電体は，その電荷が同種であるか異種であるかによって反発しあいあるいは引きあう。
2. そろばんは玉が上がっているか下がっているかによって数を表わす。

…から成る   "to be made of..."

1. ２個の質点から成る質点系の力学を２体問題という。
2. 多くの回路素子や真空管から成る電子装置は，いろいろの細胞から成る生物とよく似ている。

| 系 | kei | system |
| 力学 | rikigaku | mechanics |

(verb)＋ことが多い   or   (verb)＋場合が多い   "often＋(verb)"

1. 電気工学ではMKS絶対単位を用いる場合が多いが，機械工学では重力単位を用いることが多い。
2. 空気中における重量測定においては，空気の浮力に対する補正は無視することが多い。
3. 電気計算では空気の誘電率は１ととることが多い。

機械工学	kikai-kōgaku	mechanical engineering
浮力	furyoku	buoyant force
補正	hosei	correction
無視する	mushi suru	to neglect, ignore

SUPPLEMENTARY READINGS

A. *Selections from Rikagaku Jiten*

1)
ディジタル	dijitaru	digital
信号	shingō	signal
離散的	risan-teki	discrete
数字	sūji	numeral, figure
表現する	hyōgen suru	to represent

方式	hōshiki	type
卓上計算機	takujō-keisan-ki	desk calculator
金銭登録加算機	kinsen-tōroku-kasan-ki	cash register

ディジタル計算機 (3RJ 863)

ディジタル信号すなわち離散的数字を組み合わせて数値を表現する方式の計算機である。電子計算機のほか，そろばん，卓上計算機，金銭登録加算機などがある。

2)	アナログ	anarogu	analog
	連続的な	renzoku-teki na	continuous
	機械的な	kikai-teki na	mechanical
	計算尺	keisan-jaku	slide rule
	微分解析器	bibun-kaiseki-ki	differential analyzer
	さす	sasu	indicate
	線形	senkei	linear
	常微分	jō-bibun	ordinary differential
	従属変数	jūzoku-hensū	dependent variable
	解	kai	solution
	表示する	hyōji suru	to indicate
	…ようにする	…yō ni suru	to do(something)such that…
	受動	judō	passive
	増幅器	zōfuku-ki	amplifier
	基本形	kihon-kei	fundamental type
	オシログラフ	oshirogurafu	oscillograph

アナログ計算機 (3RJ 27)

アナログ信号すなわち連続的な物理量によって数値を表現する方式の計算機である。機械的変位によって数値を表わす計算尺や微分解析器などもあるが，ふつうは電気的量を用いるものをさす。定数係数の線形常微分方程式の従属変数を電圧または電流で表わし，解をオシログラフで表示できるようにしておいて，線形受動素子と線形増幅器の組み合わせ回路を用いて対応する微分方程式の解を求めるのが基本形である。

二体問題 (3RJ 979)

ふつう互いに力を及ぼしあう２つの物体の相対運動に関する問題。とくに万有引力を及ぼしあう２質点の相対運動をさす場合が多い。

3)	イオン	ion	ion
	原子団	genshi-dan	group of atoms

中性の	chūsei no	neutral
失う	ushinau	to lose
過剰に	kajō ni	in excess
電離	denri	ionization, electrolytic dissociation
イオン化	ion-ka	ionization
電気素量	denki-soryō	elementary charge
整数倍	seisū-bai	integral multiple
意味	imi	meaning
ギリシア語	Girishia-go	Greek
ことば	kotoba	word
…にちなんで命名する	…ni chinande meimei suru	to name after…
カソード	kasōdo	cathode
陰極	inkyoku	cathode
カチオン	kachion	cation
陽イオン	yō-ion	cation
アノード	anōdo	anode
陽極	yōkyoku	anode
アニオン	anion	anion
陰イオン	in-ion	anion

(Note that the pair of characters 陰 and 陽 used to represent negative and positive, are the characters used in Taoism for dark and bright, feminine and masculine, i. e. the opposite forces found in the world.)

イ オ ン (3RJ 69)

電荷をもつ原子または原子団（分子を含む）をイオンという。中性の原子または原子団が１個または数個の電子を失うか，あるいは過剰に電子を得て生ずるもので，このような過程でイオンになることをイオン化または電離という。イオンのもつ電気量は電気素量の整数（正または負）倍に等しい。ファラデーがイオンと名づけたが，「行く」という意味のギリシア語のことばにちなんで命名し，さらにカソード（陰極）に向かう正電荷のイオンをカチオン（陽イオン），アノード（陽極）に向かう負電荷のイオンをアニオン（陰イオン）とよんだ。

4)	誘導時間	yūdō-jikan	induction time
	反応物	hannō-butsu	reactant
	接触	sesshoku	contact
	開始	kaishi	beginning
	刺激	shigeki	stimulus
	時間の経過	jikan no keika	lapse of time

生成物	seisei-butsu	products
延長	enchō	extension
切る	kiru	to cut
精製する	seisei suru	to purify
塩素	enso	chlorine
認める	mitomeru	to recognize, perceive
存在	sonzai	existence
不純物	fu-junbutsu	impurity
抑制剤	yokusei-zai	inhibitor
混入する	konnyū suru	to mix
共存する	kyōson suru	to coexist
負触媒	fu-shokubai	negative catalyst; inhibitor
消費する	shōhi suru	to consume

誘導時間

化学反応において，反応物の接触その他，反応開始の刺激を加え始めた時刻t_0から，反応がいちじるしく現われるまでに，ある時間の経過を必要とすることがある。この時間を誘導時間という。実際には生成物の量の時間的変化を曲線で表わし，この曲線の延長が時間軸を切る点とt_0との差を誘導時間とする。この現象は，たとえばふつうに精製された水素と塩素との光化学反応の場合などにいちじるしく認められる。誘導時間の存在は反応物中の不純物として抑制剤が混入したり負触媒が共存してそれが消費されるまで誘導時間となる場合などがある。

B.	電場	denba	electric field
	数学的形式	sūgaku-teki-keishiki	mathematical form
	相似である	sōji de aru	is similar, analogous
	クーロン力	Kūron-ryoku	Coulomb force
	周辺	shūhen	surroundings
	重力場	jūryoku-ba	gravitational field
	保存的な力	hozon-teki na chikara	conservative force
	定義する	teigi suru	to define
	もしくは	moshiku wa	or
	電界 (＝電場)	denkai	electric field
	点電荷	ten-denka	point charge
	正負に応じて	seifu ni ōjite	depending on the sign
	静電場	sei-denba	electrostatic field
	振動電流	shindō-denryū	oscillating current
	非定状な	hi-teijō na	unsteady
	区別する	kubetsu suru	to differentiate

すでに	sude ni	previously
述べる	noberu	to relate, tell
媒質	baishitsu	medium
弱わめる	yowameru	to weaken
最も極端な…	mottomo kyokutan na...	the most extreme...
…と，直ちに	...to, tadachi ni	if,...then immediately
正負の電荷	seifu no denka	the positive and negative charges
残存する	zanson suru	to remain
やむ	yamu	to cease, stop
誘電体	yūden-tai	dielectric
…に沿って	...ni sotte	along..., in line with...
結局	kekkyoku	finally, eventually
打ち消す	uchi-kesu	to cancel, eliminate
終局状態	shūkyoku-jōtai	final state, terminal state
直交する	chokkō suru	to intersect at right angles

電　　場　(BN 198–200)

　クーロンの法則はその数学的形式が万有引力の法則と全く相似であるから（電気量と質量，クーロン力と万有引力がそれぞれ対応する），電荷の周辺の空間に重力場と同様な保存的なクーロン力の場を定義することができる。これを電場もしくは電界とよび，ある一点におけるそれの強さはその点に点電荷 e を置いたときに生ずるクーロン力を $\vec{F}$ として，

$$\vec{E}=\vec{F}/e$$

というベクトルで表示する。したがって e の正負に応じて，$\vec{F}$ と $\vec{E}$ の向きは同一または逆になる。電場の強さ（たんに電場ともいう）の単位は Newton/coulomb である。

　E が時間的に変化しないような場を特に静電場とよんで，振動電流などによる非定常な場と区別することがある。

　すでに述べたようにクーロン力は媒質の存在によって弱められるから電場の強さも物体中では減少する。最も極端な例として電場内に導体を入れると，ただちに正負の電荷が互いに反対側の表面に現われ，導体内部の電場は 0 となる。この現象を静電誘導とよぶ。導体の内部には電場によって自由に移動し得る電荷が存在するので，電場が残存する間は電荷の移動がつづき，電場が 0 となって始めてやむのである。これに対して，電場内に置かれたとき内部の電場が 0 にならない物質を誘電体または絶縁体という。理想的な絶縁体は真空である。

　導体の表面では，もし電場 $\vec{E}$ が表面の接線方向の成分を持っていると，これに沿って電荷が動かされ，結局場を打ち消すようになるはずだから，終局状態においては $\vec{E}$ は常に表

面と直交する。

C.	導線に沿って	dōsen ni sotte	along the conductor
	切り口	kiri-kuchi	cross-section
	粒子	ryūshi	particle
	電解質(溶液)	denkai-shitsu (yōeki)	electrolyte (solution)
	加え合う	kuwae-au	add together
	道筋	michi-suji	route
	なんらかの形で	nanraka no katachi de	in some form or other
	閉じる	tojiru	to be closed
	任意の	nin'i no	arbitrary
	直流	chokuryū	direct current
	定常電流	teijō-denryū	stationary current

電　流　(BN 210–211)

　電荷の流れを電流といい，一般にベクトル$\vec{I}$をもって表わす。このベクトルの大きさ$|\vec{I}|$＝I，すなわち電流の強さは例えばそれが導線に沿って流れている場合には導線の切り口を単位時間に一方向に通過する正電気量（と逆方向に流れる負電気量の絶対値との和）で測られる。MKS系では，

$$1\ \text{coulomb/sec} = 1\ \text{ampere}（アンペア）$$

という単位を用いる。ベクトル$\vec{I}$の方向は正電荷の運動方向を正とするから，金属導線とか真空管などのように負の電荷をもつ電子が運動している場合には帯電粒子の運動方向と電流の方向とは逆になる。電解質溶液などのように陰イオン（－）と陽イオン（＋）とが同時に反対方向へ移動するときには両方を加え合わせたものが電流の強さになる。

　電流の通る道筋は必ずなんらかの形で閉じているので，これを回路という。回路上の任意の一点における$\vec{I}$の向きが時間的に不変の電流を直流とよび，さらにその大きさが不変ならば定常電流という。

FINAL TRANSLATION TEST

　物質の中を電流が流れるのは，電荷をもってしかも動きやすい状態にあるキャリアが物質の中にあるからである。金属の場合には電子の一部が個々の原子を離れて原子全体の間を動きまわるようになる。これが金属のキャリアである。非金属の場合には互いに電子を引きつけあっているために，電子は原子を離れて自由に動きまわることができないので電圧をかけても静止している。すなわち，キャリアをもたないので絶縁体である。一般に電子はエネルギー準位が低い程安定であって，高いエネルギーをもつものはエネルギーの一部を他のものに与えて低いエネルギー準位におちつこうとする。すなわち，電子はゆるさ

れたエネルギー帯の下の方をうずめて行く。しかし、パウリの原理によって一定のエネルギーをもつ電子の数は限られている。それで電子はだんだん高いエネルギーを取り、あるエネルギー帯が電子でいっぱいになると、次にはその上のエネルギー帯にはいって行く。こうして電子を納めてしまうまで、エネルギー帯を下から次々にうずめて行く。

　金属に電圧をかけると電子は加速され、エネルギーは少し大きくなる。ただし、こういうことのできるのは、フェルミエネルギーの近くにある電子だけであって、それよりエネルギーの低い電子にとっては、上がつかえているので高エネルギーの列にはいることはできない。しかし、上の方の電子がエネルギーのより高い状態に移れば、初めにしめていたエネルギーの所に電子がなくなるから、それより少し低いエネルギーにあった電子がそこへ上ってきて、エネルギーを増すことができるようになる。こうして一つのエネルギー帯をしめていた電子が次々にエネルギーを増し、キャリアになって行く。

　誘電体の場合には、電子があるエネルギー帯をみたしていて、それよりわずかに高いエネルギーは禁制帯になっている。すなわち、誘電体のフェルミエネルギーは、電子がつまっている帯とあいている帯とにはさまれた禁制帯の中程にある。これに対して金属では、フェルミエネルギーがエネルギー帯の中にあるのである。

　どうして誘電体の中の電子はキャリアになれないかという問題は、基本的に以上のように考えられている。最近電子計算機等固体エレクトロニクスを利用した電子回路によく用いられている半導体は誘電体に近い性質をもっているが、禁制帯の幅のせまいものである。少し温度が上がると自由電子は禁制帯を飛びこえて伝導帯に移る。負の電気をもった電子が飛び出して行けば、後には正の電気をもった穴ができるのと同じ事になり、この伝導帯の電子並びに自由電子の中にできた正の穴が半導体のキャリアとなる。半導体にはこのような真性半導体以外のものもあるが、その機構の大約は以上の通りである。

LESSON 15
第十五課

K A N J I

池	110	CHI
	2489	ike
解	567	KAI
	4306	to(ku)
銅	683	DŌ
	4853	
亜	206a	A
	43	
鉛	260a	EN
	4842	namari
希	575	KI
	1470	
硫	250b	RYŪ
	3191	
酸	618	SAN
	4789	
針	236b	SHIN
	4817	hari
続	456	ZOKU
	3544	tsuzu(keru) / tsuzu(ku)

溶	257a	YŌ
	2659	to(kasu) / to(keru)
陽	527	YŌ
	5012	
陰	245a	IN
	5006	
交	212	KŌ
	290	maji(waru) / ma(jiru)
暗	154	AN
	2154	kura(i)
*燈	485	TŌ
	2800	
手	28	SHU
	1827	te
何	51	
	409	nan / nani
磁	263a	JI
	3209	
偏	237a	HEN
	511	

*Also written 灯 (280b / 2745)

READING SELECTIONS

電池	denchi	battery, electric cell
電解	denkai	electrolysis
分解	bunkai	decomposition
その例	sono rei	an example of that (See Explanatory Note 10, Lesson 14)
ボルタの	boruta no	voltaic
銅	dō	copper
亜鉛	aen	zinc

希硫酸	ki-ryūsan	dilute sulfuric acid
浸す	hitasu	to immerse, moisten
できる	dekiru	to be made, be produced
針金	harigane	wire
続けて	tsuzukete	continuously
…を伝わる	…o tsutawaru	to be transmitted along…, move along…
溶ける	tokeru	to dissolve
陽電気（＝正電気）	yō-denki	positive electricity
流れ込む	nagare-komu	to flow into
陰極（＝負電極）	inkyoku	cathode
陽極（＝正電極）	yōkyoku	anode
イオン化	ion-ka	ionization
傾向	keikō	tendency
電解質	denkai-shitsu	electrolyte
起電力	kiden-ryoku	electromotive force
まもなく	ma mo naku	in no time, shortly
その原因	sono gen'in	the cause of that, the reason for that
正常の	seijō no	normal
さからう	sakarau	to oppose
水溶液	sui-yōeki	aqueous solution
直流	chokuryū	direct current
1 グラムイオン	ichi-guramu-ion	one gram ion
価数	kasū	magnitude of the charge
割る	waru	to divide
有する	yū suru	to have
1 ファラデー	ichi-faradē	one faraday
アボガドロ数	Abogadoro-sū	Avogadro number
含む	fukumu	to contain

電池と電解 （3K 169–172）

化学変化によって電流を得る装置が電池である。また，電流によって化学変化を起こさせることができる。電気分解（電解）はその例である。

ボルタの電池：銅と亜鉛とを希硫酸に浸すと，ボルタの電池ができる。両方の金属を針金でつなぐと，次の変化が続けて起こり，電子が針金を伝わってたえず亜鉛から銅へ流れる。亜鉛の表面で亜鉛イオン Zn^{2+} ができ，これが希硫酸に溶ける。

$$Zn \rightarrow Zn^{2+} + 2e^-$$

銅の表面で水素イオンが電子と結合して水素ができる。

$$2e^- + 2H^+ \rightarrow H_2$$

　電流は電子の流れであるが，電子の流れる方向と反対の方向に陽電気が流れるといい，陽電気の流れる方向を電流の方向という。電池では，電流が針金から流れ込むほうの金属を負電極（陰極）といい，電流が針金へ流れ出るほうの金属を正電極（陽極）という。イオン化傾向の違う二つの金属を電解質の水溶液に浸すと電池ができ，イオン化傾向の大きいほうの金属が負電極，イオン化傾向の小さいほうの金属が正電極となる。

　電池が電気を流す力を起電力という。ボルタの電池は約 1.3V の起電力があるが，電流を流し始めると，まもなく，起電力は 0.4V ぐらいに減ってしまう[1]。その原因は，電池がはたらくと，電極で化学変化が起こり，その結果，正常の起電力にさからう起電力が生じるからである。この現象を電池の分極という。

電気分解：電解質の水溶液に電極を入れて直流の電気を通すと，電気分解が起こる。電池の負電極につないだ電極を陰極，正電極につないだ電極を陽極という。

　あるイオンの1グラムイオンの重さを，そのイオンの価数で割ったものが，イオンの1グラム当量である。1グラム当量のイオンの有する電気量は，どのイオンでも等しく，その電気量を1ファラデーという。1ファラデーの電気が通ると，どの電極でも1グラム当量のイオンの変化が起こる。これをファラデーの電気分解の法則という。

　1グラムイオンはアボガドロ数のイオンを含むから，1ファラデーは 6×10^{23} 個の電子と同じ量の陰電気，または陽電気に相当する。1ファラデーは約 96500 クーロンで，1クーロンは1アンペアの電流が1秒間通るときに流れる電気量である。

交流	kōryū	alternating current
暗い	kurai	dark
ネオンランプ	neon ranpu	neon light
光る	hikaru	to light up, shine
電燈	dentō	electric light
ソケット	soketto	socket
点燈する	tentō suru	to turn on a light
手を振る	te o furu	to wave a hand
電燈線	dentō-sen	electric light cord
明滅する	meimetsu suru	to flicker
交互に	kōgo ni	alternately
電圧	den'atsu	voltage
発電機	hatsuden-ki	electric generator
わが国	waga kuni	our country (i.e., Japan)
関東	Kantō	the Kantō area (Tōkyō)
関西	Kansai	the Kansai area (Kyōto-Ōsaka-Kōbe)

それなのに	sore na no ni	in spite of that; nevertheless
何	nani	what
…を意味する	…o imi suru	to signify…
発生する	hassei suru	to generate
毎秒	maibyō	every second; per second
平均発熱量	heikin-hatsunetsu-ryō	average quantity of heat produced
ちょうど	chōdo	precisely, exactly
実効値	jikkō-chi	effective value

交　　流　(B 271–273)

観察：へやを暗くして[2]，ネオンランプを約100ボルトの電池につなぐと，負極だけ光っている。次にネオンランプを電燈のソケットにつけて点燈して，その前で手を大きく振ってみよ。

　ネオンランプを電燈線につけたときは，絶えず明滅している。これは両方の電極が同時に点燈せず[3]，交互に短時間だけ光るからである。直流電源で点燈したときはネオンランプはいつでも負の極だけが光るから，電燈線の電圧は向きが絶えず変わっていることがわかる。すなわち，電燈線の電流は交流であることがわかる。

　発電機から得られる交流の電圧は，図1のように正弦曲線を示し，これを式で表わせば，

$$V = V_0 \sin 2\pi ft \qquad (1)$$

となる。ここで V は各瞬間の電圧，V_0 は最大電圧（振幅）である。f は周波数（単振動の振動数と同じ）で，わが国では50サイクル（主として関東），または60サイクル（主として関西）である。

　交流では，このように電圧は絶えず向

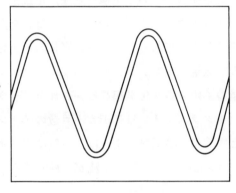

図 1　交流波形

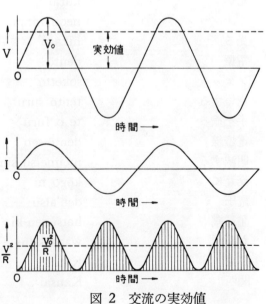

図 2　交流の実効値

きと大きさとが変化している。それなのに100ボルトの交流などというのは何を意味するのか。(1)式で与えられる電圧 V が抵抗 R にかかると，抵抗には $I=V/R$ の電流が流れる。熱の発生する割合は，$VI=V^2/R$ で 図2の下の図のようになる。すなわち，電力は0と $\dfrac{V_0{}^2}{R}$ との間で変化し，そのときの毎秒の平均発熱量は，図に示したように最大発熱量のちょうど半分，すなわち $\dfrac{V_0{}^2}{2R}$ になっている。これは抵抗 R に $\dfrac{V_0}{\sqrt{2}}$ ボルトの直流電圧を加えたときの発熱量に相当する。

そこで $\dfrac{1}{\sqrt{2}}V_0$ すなわち，最大値の $\dfrac{1}{\sqrt{2}}=0.707$倍を実効値とよぶ。ふつう100ボルトの交流といえばこの実効値が100ボルトであることを意味する。したがって，このとき最大電圧は $100×\sqrt{2}=141$ ボルトである。

地磁気	chi-jiki	terrestrial magnetism
磁針	jishin	magnetic needle
南北	nanboku	north and south
さす	sasu	to point
何かの原因で	nani ka no gen'in de	for some reason or other
磁石	jishaku	magnet
磁界	jikai	magnetic field
必ずしも…ない	kanarazu-shimo...nai	not necessarily...
重心	jūshin	center of gravity
ささえる	sasaeru	to support
東京	Tōkyō	Tokyo
傾く	katamuku	to incline
伏角	fukkaku	magnetic dip, inclination
真の	shin no	true
いくぶん	ikubun	somewhat, partly
東	higashi	east
西	nishi	west
日本内地	Nihon-naichi	within Japan
偏角	henkaku	declination
付近	fukin	neighborhood
わけにはいかない	wake ni wa ikanai	cannot
完全に	kanzen ni	completely
要素	yōso	main element

地 磁 気 (B 255-256)

地球上では小さい磁針がおよそ南北⁽⁴⁾の方向をさす。これは地球が何かの原因で磁石になっているために生じる磁界によるものだと考えられる。これを地磁気という。地磁気の極が地球の内部にあるために磁界の方向が必ずしも水平でなく，磁針を重心でささえると，

東京ではＮ極側が水平方向より約49°下に傾く。このときの磁針のＮ極の方向と水平面とのなす角度を伏角という。ふつうの磁針は重心より少しＮ極より⁽⁵⁾の方でささえられているのでだいたい水平になっている。

また，水平面内で自由に回転できる磁針のさす方向は真の南北ではなく，いくぶん東または西にかたよっている。たとえば日本内地ではＮ極が5〜9°西に向いている。この角度を偏角という。地球の両極の付近では偏角が非常に大きいので，磁針の方向で南北をすぐ知るわけにはいかない⁽⁶⁾。地球磁界の水平方向の成分と地磁気の偏角，伏角を知れば地球上のある点の磁界が完全に決まるので，これらを地磁気の三要素という。

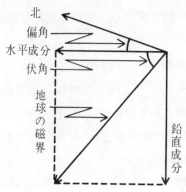

北
偏角
水平成分
伏角
地球の磁界
鉛直成分

DENCHI TO DENKAI

Kagaku-henka ni yotte denryū o eru sōchi ga denchi de aru. Mata, denryū ni yotte, kagaku-henka o okosaseru koto ga dekiru. Denki-bunkai (denkai) wa sono rei de aru.

Boruta no denchi: Dō to aen to o ki-ryūsan ni hitasu to, boruta no denchi ga dekiru. Ryōhō no kinzoku o harigane de tsunagu to, tsugi no henka ga tsuzukete okori, denshi ga harigane o tsutawatte, taezu aen kara dō e nagareru.

Aen no hyōmen de aen ion Zn^{2+} ga deki, kore ga ki-ryūsan ni tokeru.

$$Zn \rightarrow Zn^{2+} + 2e^-$$

Dō no hyōmen de suiso ion ga denshi to ketsugō shite, suiso ga dekiru.

$$2e^- + 2H^+ \rightarrow H_2$$

Denryū wa denshi no nagare de aru ga, denshi no nagareru hōkō to hantai no hōkō ni yō-denki ga nagareru to ii, yō-denki no nagareru hōkō o denryū no hōkō to iu. Denchi de wa denryū ga harigane kara nagare-komu hō no kinzoku o fu-denkyoku (inkyoku) to ii, denryū ga harigane e nagare-deru hō no kinzoku o sei-denkyoku (yōkyoku) to iu. Ion-ka-keikō no chigau futatsu no kinzoku o denkai-shitsu no sui-yōeki ni hitasu to denchi ga deki, ion-ka-keikō no ōkii hō no kinzoku ga fu-denkyoku, ion-ka-keikō no chiisai hō no kinzoku ga sei-denkyoku to naru.

Denchi ga denki o nagasu chikara o kiden-ryoku to iu. Boruta no denchi wa yaku ichi ten san boruto no kiden-ryoku ga aru ga, denryū o nagashi-hajimeru to, ma mo naku, kiden-ryoku wa rei-ten-yon boruto gurai ni hette shimau. ⁽¹⁾ Sono gen'in wa, denchi ga hataraku to, denkyoku de kagaku-henka ga okori, sono kekka, seijō no kiden-ryoku ni sakarau kiden-ryoku ga shōjiru kara de aru. Kono genshō o denchi no bunkyoku to iu.

Denki-bunkai: Denkai-shitsu no sui-yōeki ni denkyoku o irete chokuryū no denki o tōsu to, denki-bunkai ga okoru. Denchi no fu-denkyoku ni tsunaida denkyoku o inkyoku, sei-denkyoku ni tsunaida denkyoku o yōkyoku to iu.

Aru ion no ichi-guramu ion no omosa o, sono ion no kasū de watta mono ga, ion no ichi-guramu tōryō de aru. Ichi-guramu tōryō no ion no yūsuru denki-ryō wa, dono ion de mo hitoshiku, sono denki-ryō o ichi-faradē to iu. Ichi-faradē no denki ga tōru to, dono denkyoku de mo ichi-guramu tōryō no ion no henka ga okoru. Kore o Faradē no denki-bunkai no hōsoku to iu.

Ichi-guramu ion wa Abogadoro-sū no ion o fukumu kara, ichi-faradē wa roku kakeru jū no nijū-san-jō ko no denshi to onaji ryō no in-denki, mata wa yō-denki ni sōtō suru. Ichi-faradē wa yaku kyūman-rokusen-gohyaku-kūron de, ichi-kūron wa, ichi-anpea no denryū ga ichi-byōkan tōru toki ni nagareru denki-ryō de aru.

KŌRYŪ

Kansatsu: Heya o kuraku shite,[2] neon ranpu o yaku hyaku boruto no denchi ni tsunagu to, fukyoku dake hikatte iru. Tsugi ni, neon ranpu o dentō no soketto ni tsukete tentō shite, sono mae de te o ōkiku futte miyo.

Neon ranpu o dentō-sen ni tsuketa toki wa, taezu meimetsu shite iru. Kore wa ryōhō no denkyoku ga dōji ni tentō sezu,[3] kōgo ni tan-jikan dake hikaru kara de aru. Chokuryū-dengen de tentō shita toki wa neon ranpu wa itsu de mo fu no kyoku dake ga hikaru kara, dentō-sen no den'atsu wa muki ga taezu kawatte iru koto ga wakaru. Sunawachi, dentō-sen no denryū wa kōryū de aru koto ga wakaru.

Hatsuden-ki kara erareru kōryū no den'atsu wa, zu-ichi no yō ni seigen-kyoku-sen o shimeshi, kore o shiki de arawaseba

$$V = V_0 \sin 2\pi ft. \qquad (1)$$

to naru. Koko de V wa kaku-shunkan no den'atsu, V_0 wa saidai-den'atsu (shinpuku) de aru. f wa shūha-sū (tan-shindō no shindō-sū to onaji) de, wagakuni de wa gojū-saikuru (shu to shite Kantō), mata wa rokujū-saikuru (shu to shite Kansai) de aru. Kōryū de wa, kono yō ni den'atsu wa taezu muki to ōkisa to ga henka shite iru. Sore na no ni hyaku-boruto no kōryū nado to iu no wa nani o imi suru no ka. Ichi-shiki de ataerareru den'atsu V ga teikō R ni kakaru to, teikō ni wa $I=V/R$ no denryū ga nagareru. Netsu no hassei suru wariai wa $VI=V^2/R$ de zu-ni no shita no zu no yō ni naru.

Sunawachi, denryoku wa rei to V_0^2/R to no aida de henka shi, sono toki no maibyō no heikin-hatsunetsu-ryō wa, zu ni shimeshita yō ni saidai-hatsunetsu-ryō no chōdo hanbun, sunawachi $V_0^2/2R$ ni natte iru. Kore wa teikō R ni $V_0/\sqrt{2}$ boruto no chokuryū-den'atsu o kuwaeta toki no hatsunetsu-ryō ni sōtō suru.

Soko de $V_0/\sqrt{2}$ sunawachi, saidai-chi no $1/\sqrt{2} = 0.707$ bai o jikkō-chi to yobu. Futsū hyaku-boruto no kōryū to ieba kono jikkō-chi ga hyaku-boruto de aru koto o imi suru. Shitagatte, kono toki saidai-den'atsu wa

$$100 \times \sqrt{2} = 141 \text{ boruto}$$

de aru.

CHI-JIKI

Chikyū-jō de wa chiisai jishin ga oyoso nanboku[4] no hōkō o sasu. Kore wa chikyū ga nani ka no gen'in de jishaku ni natte iru tame ni shōjiru ji-kai ni yoru mono da to kangaerareru. Kore o chi-jiki to iu. Chi-jiki no kyoku ga chikyū no naibu ni aru tame ni jikai no hōkō ga kanarazushimo suihei de naku, jishin o jūshin de sasaeru to, Tōkyō de wa N-kyokugawa ga suihei-hōkō yori yaku yonjū-kyū-do shita ni katamuku. Kono toki no jishin no N kyoku no hōkō to sui-heimen to no nasu kakudo o fukkaku to iu. Futsū no jishin wa jūshin yori sukoshi N-kyoku-yori[5] no hō de sasaerarete iru no de daitai suihei ni natte iru.

Mata, sui-heimen-nai de jiyū ni kaiten dekiru jishin no sasu hōkō wa shin no nanboku de wa naku, ikubun higashi mata wa nishi ni katayotte iru. Tatoeba Nihon-naichi de wa N-kyoku ga go-do naishi kyū-do nishi ni muite iru. Kono kakudo o henkaku to iu. Chikyū no ryōkyoku no fukin de wa, henkaku ga hijō ni ōkii no de, jishin no hōkō de nanboku o sugu shiru wake ni wa ikanai.[6]

Chikyū-jikai no suihei-hōkō no seibun to chi-jiki no henkaku, fukkaku o shireba chikyū-jō no aru ten no jikai ga kanzen ni kimaru no de korera o chi-jiki no san-yōso to iu.

ELECTRIC CELLS AND ELECTROLYSIS

An electric cell is a device which yields an electric current by means of a chemical change. It is also possible for an electric current to cause a chemical change. An example of this is electrolysis.

Voltaic Cell: If copper and zinc are immersed in dilute sulfuric acid, a voltaic cell is produced. If the two metals are joined by a wire, the following continuous change occurs, namely, electrons flow ceaselessly through the wire from the zinc to the copper.

Zinc ions Zn^{2+} form at the zinc surface and dissolve in the dilute sulfuric acid.

$$Zn \rightarrow Zn^{2+} + 2e^-$$

At the copper surface, hydrogen ions combine with electrons to produce hydrogen.

$$2e^- + 2H^+ \rightarrow H_2$$

An electric current is a flow of electrons, but we say that the direction of cation flow is the direction of the current and cations flow in the opposite direction to that of electrons. In an electric cell, the metal into which electric current flows from the wire is called the negative electrode (cathode), and the metal from which electric current flows out into the wire is called the positive

electrode (anode). If two metals with different ionization tendencies are immersed in an aqueous solution of an electrolyte, an electric cell is formed. The metal with the greater ionization tendency is the negative electrode, and the metal with the smaller ionization tendency is the positive electrode.

The force with which an electric cell causes an electric current is called electromotive force. The electromotive force of a voltaic cell is about 1.3V, but if a current begins to flow, it soon decreases to about 0.4V. The reason for this is that when an electric cell is working, chemical changes occur at its electrodes and, as a result, an electromotive force arises which is counter to the normal electromotive force. This phenomenon is called polarization of the cell.

Electrolysis: If electrodes are placed in an aqueous solution of an electrolyte and a direct current is passed through, electrolysis occurs. The electrode connected to the negative electrode is called the cathode, the one joined to the positive electrode is called the anode.

The weight of one gram ion of any ion divided by its charge number is one gram equivalent of that ion. The amount of electricity carried by one gram equivalent ion is the same for all ions and is called 1 faraday. If 1 faraday of electricity passes through a cell, then 1 gram equivalent of ionic change occurs at either electrode. This is called Faraday's Law of electrolysis.

Since 1 gram ion contains as many ions as Avogadro's number, 1 faraday corresponds to as much negative or positive electricity as 6×10^{23} electrons. One faraday is about 96500 coulombs, and 1 coulomb is the amount of electricity which passes in one second when a current of 1 ampere is flowing.

ALTERNATING CURRENT

Observations: If a room is darkened and a neon light is connected to a 100 volt battery, only the cathode lights up. Now, connect the neon light to a light socket, turn it on, and wave your hand vigorously before it.

When a neon light is connected to an electric light cord, it constantly flickers. This is because the two electrodes do not light up at the same time, but light up alternately for only short periods of time. Since it is always only the cathode which lights up when the neon light is lit by direct current, we realize that the voltage in the electric light cord is constantly changing direction. That is, we learn that the current in the electric light cord is an alternating current.

The voltage of an alternating current coming from a generator is a sine curve, as shown in Figure 1, and when expressed by an equation is

$$V = V_0 \sin 2\pi f t. \qquad (1)$$

V is the instantaneous voltage and V_0 the maximum voltage (amplitude). f is the frequency (the same as the frequency of a simple vibration) and in our country this is either 50 cycles (chiefly in the Kantō area) or 60 cycles (mainly in the Kansai

area).

Thus, with an alternating current, the voltage is constantly changing in magnitude and direction. What is the meaning, then, when we speak of 100 volts of alternating current?

If we apply the voltage V given by equation 1 to a resistance R, a current $I = V/R$ flows in the resistance. The rate of heat production will be $VI = V^2/R$ as shown in the bottom figure.

As the electric power varies from 0 to V_0^2/R, the average amount of heat produced, as shown in the figure, is exactly one-half of the maximum amount of heat evolved, namely, $V_0^2/2R$. This corresponds to the amount of heat which would be produced if a direct current voltage of $V_0/\sqrt{2}$ were applied to a resistance R.

Here, $(1/\sqrt{2})V_0$, that is $1/\sqrt{2} = 0.707$ times the maximum value is called the effective value. Generally, when we speak of 100 volts of alternating current, we mean that the effective value is 100 volts. Therefore, the maximum voltage is

$$100 \times \sqrt{2} = 141 \text{ volts.}$$

TERRESTRIAL MAGNETISM

On earth a magnetic needle points approximately in the north-south direction. This is believed to be caused by a magnetic field which arises because the earth is for some reason a magnet. We call this terrestrial magnetism. Since the terrestrial magnetic poles are located within the earth, the direction of the magnetic field is not necessarily horizontal. Thus, the northerly direction of a magnetic needle supported at its center of gravity in the Tokyo area will be inclined to the horizontal at an angle of 49°. This angle between the direction of the north pole of a magnetic needle and horizontal plane is called the magnetic dip. A compass needle is generally supported at a point slightly towards its north pole from its center of gravity and therefore lies essentially horizontal.

Moreover, the direction indicated by a magnetic needle free to rotate in the horizontal plane is not the true north-south direction but one deviating partly to the east or to the west.

For example, within Japan the north pole of a magnetic needle points 5–9° westerly. This angle is called the declination. Since the declination in the vicinity of the earth's poles is very large, it is not possible to ascertain readily the north-south direction from a magnetic needle there.

If we know the horizontal component of the earth's magnetic field and the declination and inclination, then, since the magnetic field at any point is thereby completely determined, we call these the three main elements of terrestrial magnetism.

EXPLANATORY NOTES

(1) hette shimau

-te shimau means "ends up by ...ing", "finishes ...ing," thus indicating the finality of completeness of the action. The idea embodied in *-te shimau* is not always expressed in English.

(2) kuraku suru

"to darken" (cf. *kuraku naru,*" to become dark").

(3) tentō sezu

Negative of *tentō shi.*

(4) nanboku

Combinations of the four compass directions in Japanese are always given in the order 東西南北 *tō-zai-nan-boku* (East-West-North-South). Geographical names and locations follow the same order.

東 北 大 学　Tōhoku ("Northeastern") University
東南アジア　Southeast Asia
南北 戦 争　The U.S. Civil War
西 南 諸 島　Seinan Islands
都の西北に　in the northwest of Tōkyō

Note, however, that in giving wind directions, the English order is used: "northwest wind" 北西の風 *hokusei no kaze.*

(5) jūshin yori sukoshi N-kyoku-yori no hō

"slightly towards its north pole from its center of gravity."

The first *yori* is the particle meaning "from." The second *-yori* is a suffix used with compass directions and comes from the verb *yoru* (寄る) meaning "to approach, draw near."

E. g., "north by east" (the compass direction slightly east of north) is *higashi-yori no kita,* and *sukoshi minami-yori no tokoro ni* is "slightly to the south."

(6) (verb) + wake ni wa ikanai

"cannot". If the verb is negative, then the meaning is "can't help but..."or "must"; e.g. *Shiranai wake ni wa ikanai* "can't help but know," "has to know." These constructions occur frequently in Japanese.

CONSTRUCTION EXAMPLES

…に相当する

"to correspond to...," "to be equivalent to..."

1. アインシュタインの $E=mc^2$ という式によると，質量 m がエネルギー E に相当する。

2. 機械振動の変位，速度，質量は，それぞれ電気振動の電気量，電流，インダクタン

スに相当する。

必ずしも…ない   "not necessarily..."

1. 自由落下運動は，必ずしも直線運動でない。

2. 温度が上がると，液体の粘度は必ずしも減少しない。

…を意味する   "to signify..."

1. 水に硫酸を加えると発熱するということは，なんらかの化学反応が起こったことを
    意味するものである。

2. 通常単に転位といえば，結晶転位を意味する場合が多い。

なんらかの	nanra ka no	some kind of
通常	tsūjō	ordinarily
転位	ten'i	dislocation

…訳にはいかない   "cannot..."

1. 原子や分子の運動を解くのにニュートン力学を用いる訳にはいかない。

2. 熱力学第一法則だけによって化学変化の方向を定める訳にはいかない。

SUPPLEMENTARY READINGS

A. *Selections from Rikagaku Jiten*

1)	左回り	hidari-mawari	counter-clockwise
	右回り	migi-mawari	clockwise

時計の針と反対の回り方を左回りといい，時計の針と同じ回り方を右回りという。

2)	亜硫酸	a-ryūsan	sulfurous acid
	(二酸化)イオウ	(ni-sanka)iō	sulfur (dioxide)
	ただち	tadachi	immediately
	生成する	seisei suru	to be produced
	酸素	sanso	oxygen
	還元作用	kangen-sayō	reducing activity
	酸化作用	sanka-sayō	oxidizing activity
	弱い	yowai	weak
	自身	jishin	itself

亜 硫 酸 (2RJ 40)

二酸化イオウを水に溶かすとただちに生成する酸。水溶液だけが知られている。これの

水溶液は酸素をとって硫酸となる性質があるので還元作用をもつ。また弱い酸化作用も示し，自身はイオウになる。

3)

左手	hidari-te	left hand
座標系	zahyō-kei	coordinate system
親指	oya-yubi	thumb
人さし指	hitosashi-yubi	index finger
中指	naka-yubi	middle finger

左手座標系 (2RJ 1100)

直角座標系において *x-, y-, z-* 軸の正の向きがそれぞれ左手の親指，人さし指，中指の関係にあるようなもの。

4)

鉛 (化合物)	namari(kagō-butsu)	lead (compounds)
酸化鉛	sanka-namari	lead oxide
水酸化鉛	suisanka-namari	lead hydroxide
塩化鉛	enka-namari	lead chloride
硫化鉛	ryūka-namari	lead sulfide
硝酸鉛	shōsan-namari	lead nitrate
大部分	dai-bubun	majority
2価・4価	nika; yonka	bivalent; tetravalent
まれな	mare na	rare
鉛塩	namari-en	lead salts
さす	sasu	to call, designate

鉛化合物　(2RJ 985)

酸化鉛，水酸化鉛，塩化鉛，硫化鉛，硫酸鉛，硝酸鉛などがある。これらの大部分にはそれぞれ2価および4価の化合物があるが，4価の方がまれなので，単に鉛塩といえば鉛(II)塩をさす。

5)

熱電対	netsuden-tsui	thermocouple
熱起電力	netsu-kiden-ryoku	thermoelectromotive force
2種の	nishu no	two kinds of
両種	ryōshu	both kinds of
接続部	setsuzoku-bu	contact
接合部	setsugō-bu	junction
既知の	kichi no	known
未知の	michi no	unknown
銅—コンスタンタン	dō-konsutantan	copper-constantan
白金	hakkin	platinum

ロジウム	rojiumu	rhodium

熱 電 対 (2RJ 1021)

　　熱起電力を利用するための2種の金属の組み合わせ。熱起電力は両種金属の種類と両接続部の温度とによって定まる。熱電対は温度測定に利用され，一方の接合部を既知の温度に保ち，他方の接合部を未知の温度とし，その間に生ずる熱起電力を測定して，温度差を知る装置で，銅—コンスタンタン，白金—白金ロジウムなどの組み合わせがよく用いられる。

6)	陰極線	inkyoku-sen	cathode rays
	数千—数万	sūsen naishi sūman	several thousand to several ten thousand
	電子ボルト	denshi-boruto	electron volts
	電子線	denshi-sen	electron ray
	熱電子	netsu-denshi	thermoelectron
	冷陰極放出	rei-inkyoku-hōshutsu	cold (cathode) emission
	二次電子	niji-denshi	secondary electron
	放電	hōden	discharge
	衝撃する	shōgeki suru	to bombard, strike against
	ルミネセンス	ruminesensu	luminescence
	注目する	chūmoku suru	to observe
	…と命名する	…to meimei suru	to call…
	わん曲	wankyoku	bending
	帯びる	obiru	to carry
	微粒子	bi-ryūshi	corpuscle
	確認する	kakunin suru	to confirm

陰 極 線 (3RJ 303)

　　数千—数万電子ボルト(eV)の電子線で，熱電子または冷陰極放出，二次電子放出などでつくられた自由電子を高電圧の電場で加速して得られるもの。 10^{-2}〜10^{-4} Torr の真空放電で，陽イオンが陰極を衝撃するときに二次電子放出がおこり，電極間で加速されてガラス壁に陰極線ルミネセンスを生ずるのを1859年 J. Plücker が注目し，1876年 E. Goldstein が陰極線と命名した。のち電場および磁場によるわん曲を測定して，負の電荷を帯びた微粒子の流れであることが J.J. Thomson(1897)によって確認され，これによって電子の存在がはじめて知られた。

7)	希薄	kihaku	dilute
	ヘンリーの	Henrii no	Henry's

ラウールの	Raūru no	Raoult's
ファント・ホッフの	Fanto Hoffu no	van't Hoff's
浸透圧	shintō-atsu	osmotic pressure

希薄溶液　(3RJ 303)

溶質の濃度が十分に小さい溶液をいう。希薄溶液ではヘンリーの法則，ラウールの法則，ファント・ホッフの浸透圧の法則などが成立する。

8)	偏向	henkō	deflection
	コイル	koiru	coil
	進路	shinro	path
	ブラウン管	Buraun-kan	Braun tube

偏向コイル　(3RJ 1243)

荷電粒子線の進行方向に対して横向きの磁場をつくり，進路を曲げるために用いられるコイル。ブラウン管ではふつう2個のコイルを向かいあわせたものに電流を流し，その間の磁場を利用する。

9)	電磁…	denji...	electromagnetic...
	閉じる	tojiru	to close
	一次・二次	ichiji; niji	primary; secondary
	もともと	moto-moto	originally

電磁誘導　(3RJ 911)

1つの閉じた回路（二次回路）の近くで，電流の流れている他の回路（一次回路）または磁石を動かせば二次回路に電流が流れる。また，もともと電流が流れていればその強さが変わる。一次回路を固定したままその電流を変えたり，あるいは二次回路の方を動かしたりするときも同様のことがおこる。

B.	X線	X-sen	X-rays
	かつ	katsu	moreover, also
	透過力	tōka-ryoku	penetrating power
	電磁波	denji-ha	electromagnetic wave
	発生	hassei	generation, production
	現在	genzai	presently, now
	X線発生用の	X-sen-hassei-yō no	(used) for the production of X-rays
	X線管	X-senkan	X-ray tube
	大体	daitai	generally

対陰極	tai-inkyoku	target
材質	zaishitsu	nature of the material
強度	kyōdo	strength, intensity
同程度	dō-teido	same degree, measure
規則正しい	kisoku-tadashii	orderly
配列する	hairetsu suru	to be arrayed, arranged
回折格子	kaisetsu-gōshi	diffraction grating
…の役をする	…no yaku o suru	to act as…, serve as…
波動光学	hadō-kōgaku	wave optics
理論	riron	theory
微細構造	bisai-kōzō	microscopic structure
活用する	katsuyō suru	to put (knowledge, etc.) to practical use
散乱する	sanran suru	to disperse
回折波	kaisetsu-ha	diffraction wave
重なり合う	kasanari-au	to overlap one another
交角	kōkaku	angle of intersection
隣接	rinsetsu	adjacent, contiguous
行路差	kōro-sa	path-difference
整数倍	seisū-bai	integral multiple
満たす	mitasu	to satisfy
一致する	itchi suru	to agree

X線および電子回折　(BN 267–268)

　高速度の電子流を金属表面に当てると，X線とよばれる極めて波長の短い，かつ物質に対して透過力の強い電磁波が発生する。現在使われているX線発生用の真空管，すなわちX線管では電子の加速電圧は目的によって異なるが大体30—100kV，またX線の波長は電圧および陽極—X線管の場合には対陰極とよばれる—の材質によるが，大体 0.5—10Å 程度である。同じ対陰極を用いる場合には加速電圧が高いほど，得られるX線の強度が大きく，波長が短く，かつ透過力が強くなる。一般に物質内の原子間隔はX線の波長と同程度であるから，原子（または分子）が規則正しく配列している結晶体はX線に対して回折格子の役をする。この現象は波動光学の理論を用いてくわしく研究されており，現在でも物質の微細構造を調べる方法として盛んに活用されている。

　いま図に示すような格子面 AA′ にP方向からX線が入射すると，各原子によって散乱された二次X線（回折波）は Huygens の原理にしたがってQ方向に一つの反

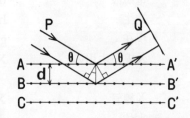

射波を構成する。同様なことが BB′, CC′ 面についても起り，その結果多数の（平行格子面の数に等しい）反射波がQ方向に重なり合う。入射線と格子面との交角を θ，各格子面の間隔を d, 隣接格子面によって反射される二次X線の行路差を δ で表わすと，図から明らかなように δ＝2d sin θで，このδがX線の波長λの整数倍の場合，すなわち，2d sin θ＝nλ（n＝1, 2, 3...）という条件が満たされたときに，これらの反射波は位相が一致して互いに強め合うことになる。これをBraggの反射条件という。

FINAL TRANSLATION TEST

　大気中で針金などがさびるのは日常よく見られる現象である。これは同一金属の表面でも細かく見れば物理的，化学的に異なった状態の所が交じっているために，電極電位が異なっていることに基づく。希硫酸の中に銅と亜鉛を入れると亜鉛がとけてイオンとなり，この際に生成した電子は，銅の表面に引きつけられて水素イオンと結合して水素となるように，電位の低い部分は電位の高い部分に電子を与えながら液中に溶けて行く。すなわち，金属表面のしめりと，電極電位の異なった部分とによって，陰陽二つの電極をもった電池が形成されたわけである。この状態が続く限り，さびは進行する。大気中には常に水分があり，亜硫酸ガスなどの化学成分がこれに溶解して電解質を形成し，また手でさわったりすれば，水分その他の化学物質が与えられる。

　金属は何によってさびるかということは非常に重要な問題であるので多くの研究がなされたが，最近は電子顕微鏡の使用によって，多くの事実が解明された。これは，光学顕微鏡において電燈などの光源を使用するのに対して，電子の生成，加速装置を用い，ガラスのレンズのかわりに，電界，磁界を用いて電子線を偏向させるもので，サンプルを通ってくる光で見るか，反射光で見るか，明るい所で見るか，暗い所で見るかなどによって種々の形式がある。加速電圧が高い程すぐれているわけで，最近のものでは 3×10^6 ボルトの加速電圧を用いて金属結晶の内部構造や，生物を生きたまま観察することができるようになっている。

LESSON 16
第十六課

KANJI

核	232b	KAKU		在	613	ZAI
	2254				1055	
元	68	GEN GAN		天	119	TEN
	275	moto			16	ame
炭	274	TAN		混	787	KON
	1418	sumi			2604	{ma(zeru) {ma(zaru)
窒	242a	CHITSU		述	809	JUTSU
	3325				4675	no(beru)
倍	694	BAI		類	534	RUI
	483				5138	
番	306	BAN		記	180	KI
	4811				4318	
号	215	GŌ		書	92	SHO
	882				3719	ka(ku)
然	450	ZEN NEN		集	243	SHŪ
	2770				5031	{atsu(meru) {atsu(maru)
塩	354	EN		粒	242b	RYŪ
	1125	shio			3471	tsubu
析	217b	SEKI		含	208a	GAN
	2194				402	fuku(mu)

原子核	genshi-kaku	atomic nucleus
大部分	dai-bubun	the greater part
占める	shimeru	to take up, include
だいたい（大体）	daitai	approximately
原子量	genshi-ryō	atomic weight
炭素	tanso	carbon
窒素	chisso	nitrogen
酸素	sanso	oxygen
陽子	yōshi	proton

整数倍	seisū-bai	integral multiple
質量数	shitsuryō-sū	mass number
負電気を帯びる	fu-denki o obiru	to carry a negative charge
中性の	chūsei no	neutral
原子番号	genshi-bangō	atomic number
周期(律)表	shūki(ritsu)hyō	periodic table
順番	junban	order
…に属する	…ni zoku suru	to belong to…
…もとになる	…moto ni naru	(which) serves as the basis for…
しかしながら（＝しかし）	shikashi nagara	however, but
自然	shizen	nature
塩素	enso	chlorine
中途半ぱ	chūto-hanpa	in-between, halfway
まじる	majiru	to be mixed
差異	sai	difference
分析法	bunseki-hō	analytical method
分ける	wakeru	to separate
…による	…ni yoru	to rely on…, depend on…
はぎ取る	hagi-toru	to strip off, take off
電界	denkai	electrical field
磁界	jikai	magnetic field
走らせる	hashiraseru	to let run, make run
曲げられにくい	magerare-nikui	difficult to be deflected
同位体	dōi-tai	isotope
同位核	dōi-kaku	isotope (nuclear physics)
重水素	jū-suiso	heavy hydrogen
天然の	tennen no	natural
混合したもの	kongō shita mono	mixture
述べる	noberu	to tell, state
記号	kigō	symbol
慣用	kan'yō	ordinary usage, common use
添える	soeru	to affix, attach
集まり	atsumari	collection
つごうがよい	tsugō ga yoi	to favor
粒子	ryūshi	particle
含む	fukumu	to contain
中性子	chūsei-shi	neutron

原子核の質量と電荷　(B 342–345)

　原子核の質量は，原子の質量の大部分を占めるので，だいたいその元素の原子量に比例することになる。したがって，水素原子核の質量を単位として測れば，他の原子核の質量はほとんどその原子量に等しい値になる。

　たとえば炭素(C)，窒素(N)，酸素(O)の原子核の質量は，この単位でほぼ 12, 14, 16 である。水素原子核のことを陽子とよぶ。原子核の質量はだいたい陽子の質量の整数倍になる。この原子量に近い整数 A を質量数という。

　また，電子は $-e$ の負電気を帯びているから，Z 個の電子をもっている中性原子の核は $+Ze$ の正電気を帯びている。$Z=1, 2, 3, \cdots$ に相当する [1] 原子は水素(H)，ヘリウム(He)，リチウム(Li)，$\cdots$ で，Z を原子番号といい，ちょうど元素の周期律表の順番に Z が増している。原子の光学的・化学的性質はこれに属する電子の数で決まるので，Z は原子の性質を決定するもとになる重要な数である。

　しかしながら，自然には塩素(Cl)の原子量 35.5 のように中途半ばのものもある。これは質量数の異なった二つ以上の原子がまじっているためである [2]。これらの Z が等しい原子からなる物質は A は異なるが，化学的性質にはほとんど差異がないから，ふつうの化学分析法では分けられない。これを分けるには，物理的な方法による。その方法は原子から電子をいくつかはぎ取って正のイオンとして，電界または磁界の中を走らせたとき，質量が大きいものほど [3] 曲げられにくい [4] ことを利用する。このような方法により [5]，たとえば Cl の元素には $A=35, 37$ の2種の質量数の原子がまじっていることがわかる。

　Z が等しく，A の異なる原子を同位体（同位核）という。水素もふつうの $A=1$ なるもののほかに，$A=2$ の水素，いわゆる重水素が存在する。天然の水素は，これら2種の同位体の混合したものである。

　以上述べたように，原子核の種類は二つの整数，質量数 A，原子番号 Z により [5] 定まる。これを記号で表わすときには慣用の化学記号に Z, A を添えて書く。たとえば $^{14}_{7}N$ は $A=14$，$Z=7$ の窒素を示す。この記号によれば塩素の二つの同位体は $^{35}_{17}Cl$, $^{37}_{17}Cl$ である。

　原子核の質量がだいたい陽子の質量の整数倍であることは，原子核が陽子の集まりと考えられればつごうがよい [6]。そうすれば $Z=A$ となるはずである。実際は，Z は A より小で [7]，多くはその半分以下である。したがって原子核には，質量がだいたい陽子に等しく，電荷をもたない粒子が含まれていると考えられる。この粒子を中性子という。たとえば $^{16}_{8}O$ の酸素原子核は，8個の陽子と8個の中性子とからできている。

GENSHI-KAKU NO SHITSURYŌ TO DENKA

Genshi-kaku no shitsuryō wa, genshi no shitsuryō no dai-bubun o shimeru no de, daitai sono genso no genshi-ryō ni hirei suru koto ni naru. Shitagatte, suiso-genshi-kaku no shitsuryō o tan'i to shite hakareba, ta no genshi-kaku no shitsuryō wa hotondo sono genshi-ryō ni hitoshii atai ni naru.

Tatoeba tanso (C), chisso (N), sanso (O) no genshi-kaku no shitsuryō wa, kono tan'i de hobo 12, 14, 16 de aru. Suiso-genshi-kaku no koto o yōshi to yobu. Genshi-kaku no shitsuryō wa daitai yōshi no shitsuryō no seisū-bai ni naru. Kono genshi-ryō ni chikai seisū A o shitsuryō-sū to iu.

Mata, denshi wa $-e$ no fu-denki o obite iru kara, Z ko no denshi o motte iru chūsei-genshi no kaku wa $+Ze$ no sei-denki o obite iru. $Z=1, 2, 3$, ni sōtō suru [1] genshi wa suiso (H), heriumu (He), richiumu (Li), ...de, Z o genshi-bangō to ii, chōdo genso no shūki-ritsu-hyō no junban ni Z ga mashite iru. Genshi no kōgaku-teki, kagaku-teki seishitsu wa kore ni zoku suru denshi no kazu de kimaru no de, Z wa genshi no seishitsu o kettei suru moto ni naru jūyō na kazu de aru.

Shikashinagara, shizen ni wa enso (Cl) no genshi-ryō 35.5 no yō ni chūto-hanpa no mono mo aru. Kore wa shitsuryō-sū no kotonatta futatsu ijō no genshi ga majitte iru tame de aru. [2] Korera no Z ga hitoshii genshi kara naru busshitsu wa A wa kotonaru ga, kagaku-teki seishitsu ni wa hotondo sa ga nai kara, futsū no kagaku-bunseki-hō de wa wakerarenai. Kore o wakeru ni wa, butsuri-teki na hōhō ni yoru. Sono hōhō wa genshi kara denshi o ikutsu ka hagi-totte sei no ion to shite, denkai mata wa jikai no naka o hashiraseta toki, shitsuryō ga ōkii mono hodo [3] magerare-nikui [4] koto o riyō suru. Kono yō na hōhō ni yori, [5] tatoeba Cl no genso ni wa $A=35, 37$ no nishu no shitsuryō-sū no genshi ga majitte iru koto ga wakaru.

Z ga hitoshiku, A no kotonaru genshi o dōi-tai (dōi-kaku) to iu. Suiso mo futsū no $A=1$ naru mono no hoka ni, $A=2$ no suiso, iwayuru jū-suiso ga sonzai suru. Tennen no suiso wa korera nishu no dōi-tai no kongō shita mono de aru.

Ijō nobeta yō ni, genshi-kaku no shurui wa futatsu no seisū, shitsuryō-sū A, genshi-bangō Z ni yori [5] sadamaru. Kore o kigō de arawasu toki ni wa kan'yō no kagaku-kigō ni Z, A o soete kaku. Tatoeba $^{14}_{7}$N wa $A=14$, $Z=7$ no chisso o shimesu. Kono kigō ni yoreba enso no futatsu no dōi-tai wa $^{35}_{17}$Cl, $^{37}_{17}$Cl de aru.

Genshi-kaku no shitsuryō ga daitai yōshi no shitsuryō no seisū-bai de aru koto wa genshi-kaku ga yōshi no atsumari to kangaerarereba tsugō ga yoi. [6] Sō sureba $Z=A$ to naru hazu de aru. Jissai wa Z wa A yori shō de, [7] ōku wa sono hanbun-ika de aru. Shitagatte genshi-kaku ni wa, shitsuryō ga daitai yōshi ni hitoshiku, denka o motanai ryūshi ga fukumarete iru to kangaerareru. Kono ryūshi o chūsei-shi to iu. Tatoeba $^{16}_{8}$O no sanso-genshi-kaku wa, hakko no yōshi to hakko no chūsei-shi to kara dekite iru.

THE MASS AND CHARGE OF ATOMIC NUCLEI

Since a large proportion of the mass of an atom is taken up by the nucleus, the mass of the atomic nucleus is approximately proportional to the atomic weight of that element. Consequently, if we adopt the mass of the hydrogen nucleus as the mass unit and measure the masses of other atomic nuclei, they will have values almost equal to their atomic weights.

For example, the masses of the nuclei of carbon (C), nitrogen (N), and oxygen (O) are around 12, 14, and 16 in terms of this unit. The nucleus of the hydrogen atom is called the proton. The mass of an atomic nucleus is approximately an integral multiple of the mass of a proton. The integer A closest to the atomic weight is called the mass number.

Moreover, since electrons carry a negative charge $-e$, the nucleus of a neutral atom which possesses Z electrons will carry a positive charge of $+Ze$. The atoms which correspond to $Z=1$, 2, 3, ...are hydrogen (H), helium (He), lithium (Li), ...and Z, which is called the atomic number, increases with the order of the elements in the periodic table. Since the optical and chemical properties of an atom are determined by the number of electrons belonging to it, Z is an important number, fundamental to establishing the properties of atoms.

In nature, however, there are also in-between cases such as chlorine (Cl) which has an atomic weight of 35.5. This is because two or more atoms with different mass numbers are mixed together. These substances composed of atoms with equal values of Z have different values of A, but they cannot be separated by the usual methods of chemical analysis because there are practically no differences in their chemical properties.

Their separation depends upon a physical method. This technique utilizes the fact that the larger masses are more difficult to deflect when the atoms, stripped of some of their electrons, are made to stream through electrical and magnetic fields as positive ions. With this method, for example, we have learned that there are two kinds of atoms with mass numbers $A=35$, 37 in elementary Cl.

Atoms which have equal values of Z but different values of A are called isotopes. Hydrogen too, in addition to the usual $A=1$ form, exists as so-called heavy hydrogen, $A=2$. Natural hydrogen is a mixture of these two isotopes.

As we have said above, the type of atomic nucleus is fixed by two integral numbers, the mass numer A and the atomic number Z. To express these symbolically, the Z and A numbers are affixed to the usual chemical symbol. For example, $^{14}_{7}N$ indicates nitrogen with $A=14$ and $Z=7$. The two isotopes of chlorine, in this notation, are $^{37}_{17}Cl$ and $^{35}_{17}Cl$.

The fact that the mass of an atomic nucleus is approximately an integral multiple of the mass of a proton favors considering the nucleus as a collection

of protons. If that were the case, Z should equal A. In actuality Z is less than A and frequently less than half its value. Therefore, we believe that the atomic nucleus contains additional particles whose mass is almost equal to the proton and which carry no electrical charge. These particles are called neutrons. For example, the oxygen nucleus $^{16}_{8}O$ consists of 8 protons and 8 neutrons.

EXPLANATORY NOTES

(1) ...ni sōtō suru

Here this expression means "corresponds to...." In technical words "corresponding" or "correspondence" is almost always translated by *taiō* (対応).

taiō-jōtai (対応状態)   corresponding states (in thermodynamics)

taiō-genri (対応原理)   correspondence principle (in quantum mechanics)

taiō-kaku (対応角)   corresponding angles (in mathematics)

Note the following uses of *sōtō*:

"Meson" ni sōtō suru Nihon-go wa nan desu ka?   What is the Japanese equivalent of "meson"?

Ichi-inchi wa 2.54 senchi ni sōtō suru.   One inch is equivalent to 2.54 centimeters.

Tetsu wa sōtō ichijirushiku bōchō suru.   Iron exhibits a rather noticeable expansion.

(2) (verb) + tame de aru

"This is because..." or "The reason for this is that...". This construction is used to give further explanation for something in the preceding sentence. The phrase (verb) + *kara de aru* may also be used.

(3) hodo

See Construction Examples in Lesson 2. Here "the larger... the more difficult to deflect...".

(4) -nikui, -yasui

Useful endings indicating "difficult to...," "easy to...". The phrase in which *-nikui* appears could be rephrased as: *shitsuryō ga chiisai mono hodo magerare-yasui hodo.*

(5) ...ni yori

Same as *...ni yotte*. See Construction Examples in Chapter 9.

(6) tsugō ga yoi

Often this expression is used with the meaning "it is convenient." For examples: *Kono hōteishiki de wa x no kawari ni y to oku hō ga tsugō ga yoi.* "It is more convenient to replace x by y in this equation."

(7) shō de

Same as *chiisakute* (小さくて); similarly *dai de* (大で) can de used in lieu of *ōkikute* (大きくて). The use

of these *ON*-forms for 大 and 小 in written Japanese is not uncommon.

CONSTRUCTION EXAMPLES

| …に属する | "to belong to…" |

1. 原子がこれに属する電子を何個か失^{うしな}うとイオンになる。
2. フッ素，塩素，臭^{しゅう}素，ヨウ素は周期表の第Ⅶ族^{だいぞく}aに属する。

フッ素	fusso	fluorine
臭素	shūso	bromine
ヨウ素	yōso	iodine

もと（本）にする	"to base something on"
もと（本）になる	"to serve as the basis for"
もと（下）で	"under", "at"
もと（下）に	"under", "in (the presence of)"

1. 質量分析器は原子の質量数の相違をもとにして元素を分折する装置である。
2. 量子力学は近代^{だい}物理学のもとになる重要な学問である。
3. 水は1気圧のもとで100°Cで沸騰^{ふっとう}する。
4. 白金^{はっきん}存在のもとにアンモニアと空気の混合気体を約800°Cに熱すると一酸化窒素 (NO) ができる。

質量分析器	shitsuryō-bunseki-ki	mass spectrometer
近代の	kindai no	modern
白金	hakkin	platinum

| (verb) ＋ ためである | 1. "is because"   2. "is for the sake of" |

1. 水に硫酸を加えると発熱するのは水と硫酸とが反応するためである。
2. 軸受けに油をさすのは摩擦を減少するためである。

軸受け	jiku-uke	bearing

SUPPLEMENTARY READINGS

A. 1)

有機化合物	yūki-kagō-butsu	organic compound
元素分析	genso-bunseki	ultimate analysis, elementary analysis
検出する	kenshutsu suru	to detect
定性分析	teisei-bunseki	qualitative analysis

含有量	gan'yū-ryō	content
定量分析	teiryō-bunseki	quantitative analysis
分解する	bunkai suru	to decompose
成分	seibun	component
簡単な	kantan na	simple
無機化合物	muki-kagō-butsu	inorganic compound
定量する	teiryō suru	to determine quantitatively
リービヒ	Riibihi	Liebig
炭水素	tansui-so	elementary carbon and hydrogen
ケルダール	Kerudāru	Kjeldahl
カリウス	Kariusu	Carius
直接に	chokusetsu ni	directly
百分率	hyakubun-ritsu	hundred per cent
総和	sōwa	sum total

元素分析　(3RJ 422)

　有機化合物を構成する元素に関する化学分析をいう。元素をそれぞれ検出する定性分析と各元素の含有量を求める定量分析がある。有機化合物を高温に加熱して分解し，その成分元素をそれぞれ簡単な無機化合物に変えて検出または定量するのがふつうである（リービヒの炭水素定量法，ケルダールの窒素定量法，カリウス法）。酸素を直接に分析することもできるが，定量分析ではふつうは他のすべての元素の百分率の総和と 100 との差を酸素の含有量とする。

2)	決定する	kettei suru	to determine
	構造模型	kōzō-mokei	structural model
	もっぱら	moppara	exclusively
	分類表	bunrui-hyō	table of classification
	順位	jun'i	order
	配置する	haichi suru	to arrange
	順	jun	order
	一部の例外を除き	ichibu no reigai o nozoki	aside from certain exceptions
	ならべる	naraberu	to arrange in order
	散乱	sanran	scattering
	意義・意味	igi; imi	meaning
	特性…	tokusei...	characteristic...
	明確な	meikaku na	clear and accurate

原子番号　(3RJ 418)

　原子の種類，したがって化学元素の種類を決定する数値をいい，原子構造模型によって示される原子核の外にある電子の数に等しい。これはまた原子核の中にある陽子の数Zにも等しく，原子番号の記号はZで表わされる。原子の質量は，核の中の陽子の数と中性子の数Nとの和（質量数という）によって定められるが，原子の化学的性質はもっぱら核の外の電子の数，すなわち原子番号で定められる。したがって原子の化学的性質による元素の分類表，すなわち周期表においては，各元素は原子番号の順位に配置される。原子番号ははじめ単に元素を原子量の順に（一部の例外を除き）ならべた番号として考えられていたが，E. Rutherford (1911) の実験（ラザフォード散乱）によって物理的意義が明らかになり，また H. G. J. Moseley (1913) の原子の特性 X 線スペクトルについての研究（モーズリーの法則）によって，物理的，化学的現象において原子番号のもつ意味の重要性が初めて明確になった。

3)	天然に	tennen ni	naturally
	地中から	chichū kara	from within the earth
	産出する	sanshutsu suru	to produce
	メタン	metan	methane
	二酸化炭素	ni-sanka-tanso	carbon dioxide
	産する（＝産出する）	san-suru	to produce
	地方	chihō	locality, region
	噴出する	funshutsu suru	to gush, spout
	地帯	chitai	area, region
	主成分	shu-seibun	principal component
	なお	nao	further, more still
	気状	kijō	gaseous (state)
	液状	ekijō	liquid (state)
	メタン列	metan-retsu	methane series
	炭化水素	tanka-suiso	hydrocarbons
	エチレン	echiren	ethylene
	プロピレン	puropiren	propylene
	ブチレン	buchiren	butylene
	(不)飽和	(fu)hōwa	(un)saturated
	所によっては	tokoro ni yotte wa	in some places

天然ガス　(2RJ 935)

　天然に地中から産出するメタン，二酸化炭素，または窒素などのようなガスを広く天然ガスというが，普通は石油の産する地方に噴出するガスをいう。このガスの成分は噴出地

帯によって違うが，通常メタンを主成分とし，なお気状（CH$_4$〜C$_4$H$_{10}$），液状（C$_5$H$_{12}$〜C$_8$H$_{18}$）のメタン列炭化水素，およびエチレン，プロピレン，ブチレンなどの不飽和炭化水素や，窒素，所によっては水素なども含む。

4)	核反応	kaku-hannō	nuclear reactions
	総称	sōshō	generic name
	転換	tenkan	transformation
	ともなう	tomonau	to accompany
	限定する	gentei suru	to limit
	標的核	hyōteki-kaku	target nucleus
	入射粒子	nyūsha-ryūshi	incident particle
	残留核	zanryū-kaku	residual nucleus
	放出粒子	hōshutsu-ryūshi	emission particles

核 反 応 （3RJ 232）

原子核反応ともいう。原子核とほかの粒子との衝突によって起こる現象の総称であるが，原子核の転換をともなう場合に限定することが多い。原子核 X（標的核）に粒子 a（入射粒子）が衝突し，原子核 Y（残留核）と粒子 b$_1$, ..., b$_n$（放出粒子）ができる反応を

$$X+a \rightarrow Y+b_1+\cdots+b_n,$$

$$X(a, b_1, ..., b_n) \, Y$$

などと書く。

5)	混晶	konshō	mixed crystal
	均一	kin'itsu	homogeneous
	溶相	yōsō	solution (phase)
	固溶体	ko-yōtai	solid solution
	同形の	dōkei no	isomorphic
	塩	en	salts
	ミョウバン類	myōban-rui	alums
	あらゆる	arayuru	every possible
	条件	jōken	condition
	類似	ruiji	similarity, likeness
	挙げる	ageru	to raise, propose

混　　晶　（3RJ 480）

2種またはそれ以上の物質が混合し，均一な溶相となった結晶をつくるとき，その結晶を混晶という。一種の固溶体である。同形の塩は混晶をつくる（たとえば各種のミョウバン類）。金属においても，たとえば金と銀，あるいは金と銅とはあらゆる割合に混晶をつ

くる。混晶をつくるのに必要な条件としては，結晶格子の類似，原子半径があまり違わないことなどが挙げられる。

6)	塩析	enseki	salting out
	可溶性の	kayō-sei no	soluble
	塩類	enrui	salts
	析出する	sekishutsu suru	to separate
	タンパク質	tanpaku-shitsu	proteins
	石けん	sekken	soap
	製造	seizō	manufacturing
	食塩	shokuen	table salt

塩　　析　(3RJ 176)

ある物質（主として有機物質）の溶液に可溶性塩類を加えてその溶質を析出させること。タンパク質の塩析効果のほか，石けんの製造において食塩を加えて石けんを析出させるなどの例がある。

7)	倍数比例	baisū-hirei	multiple proportions
	カッコ	kakko	parentheses
	亜酸化窒素	a-sanka-chisso	nitrous oxide
	酸化窒素	sanka-chisso	nitric oxide
	三二酸化窒素	san-ni-sanka-chisso	nitrogen sesquioxide
	二酸化窒素	ni-sanka-chisso	nitrogen dioxide
	五二酸化窒素	go-ni-sanka-chisso	nitrogen pentoxide

倍数比例の法則　(2RJ 1036)

元素 A, B が化合して2種以上の化合物ができることがある。このとき各化合物における A の一定量に対する B の量は簡単な整数の比になっている。例えば窒素と酸素との化合物については次のような化合物が存在し，その成分元素の比は窒素14に対しカッコの中に与えられてある：亜酸化窒素 N_2O $(14:8\times1)$，酸化窒素 NO $(14:8\times2)$，三二酸化窒素 N_2O_3 $(14:8\times3)$，二酸化窒素 NO_2 $(14:8\times4)$，五二酸化窒素 N_2O_5 $(14:8\times5)$ など。

B.	比較する	hikaku suru	to compare
	知識	chisiki	knowledge
	技術	gijutsu	technique
	沸点	futten	boiling point
	融点	yūten	melting point
	かたさ	katasa	hardness
	吸収率	kyūshū-ritsu	absorption coefficient

磁力	jiryoku	magnetization
精密に	seimitsu ni	accurately, precisely
組成	sosei	composition
はっきり	hakkiri	clearly, distinctly
紫外線	shigai-sen	ultraviolet rays
X線	X-sen	X-rays
必要	hitsuyō	necessary, essential
化学者	kagaku-sha	chemist
取り入れる	tori-ireru	to introduce, adopt
影響を受ける	eikyō o ukeru	to be influenced by
物理化学	butsuri-kagaku	physical chemistry
化学理論	kagaku-riron	chemical theory
部門	bumon	branch, division
…のなかだちが あって	…no nakadachi ga atte	through the medium (agency) of…
種類	shurui	kind, species, type
鋼	kō	steel
ゴム	gomu	rubber
まるで	maru de	utterly, completely
一応	ichiō	in a way
取り扱う	tori-atsukau	to treat
化学物理	kagaku-butsuri	chemical physics
出す	dasu	to give out, put out
構造	kōzō	structure
うかがう	ukagau	to inquire, ask about
てがかり	tegakari	clue
理解する	rikai suru	to understand
化学結合	kagaku-ketsugō	chemical bond
機構	kikō	mechanism
進歩する	shimpo suru	to progress
ますます	masu-masu	more and more, increasingly
本質	honshitsu	essential nature
きわめる	kiwameru	to investigate
共通の	kyōtsū no	common
分野	bunya	field

化学と物理学　(1K 378–379)

化学では物質の性質を研究するが物質の性質を比較(かく)するのに，物理学の知識(しき)を使い，物

理学の研究技術を応用することによって，その沸点・融点・密度・かたさ・強さ・電気伝導度・屈折率・光の吸収率・磁力などを精密に測定することができて，物質の化学的組成とその性質との関係がたいへんはっきりわかった。

また，化学変化についても高圧・高温・低温などで実験したり，また，電気分解を行なったり，紫外線やX線に当てたりするようになって，物理学の知識が必要となった。また，化学者が物理学の知識を取り入れて研究するようになったので，化学変化が熱・電気・光でどのように影響を受けるかというようなことが明らかになった。

物理化学というのは物理学や数学を取り入れて化学理論を研究する化学の部門である。

力・熱・光・電気・磁気などの現象は物質のなかだちがあって現われる。しかも，物質の種類によってその現われ方が違っている。例えば鋼とゴムは弾性がまるで違うし，金属は電気を導くが非金属は導かない。鉄やニッケルは磁石に引きつけられるが，銅や亜鉛は引きつけられない。物理学はこれらの現象を物質との関係から一応離れて一般的に取り扱うが，これを物質の種類と関係させて研究しようとすれば，化学が必要となる。化学を取り入れて研究する物理学の部門を化学物理という。

原子の出すスペクトル線を測定し研究することによって，原子の構造をうかがうてがかりが得られた。このようにして明らかにされた原子の構造をもとにして，元素の周期律も理解され，化学結合の機構も明らかにされるようになった。そして化学が進歩して物質の成分や構造が知られるにつれて，物質的現象の現われ方はますますはっきりと理解されるようになった。このように，化学と物理学とは物質の本質をきわめるという点で，共通の研究分野をもつことになった。

FINAL TRANSLATION TEST

地球を取り巻く大気は，その大部分が窒素と酸素であるが，常に少量の水蒸気や二酸化炭素も含まれている。このような天然の組成に加えて，種々の酸化物の微粒子，一酸化炭素，窒素酸化物，硫酸塩，塩化物等が微量ではあるが混在して，多くの問題を引き起こしている。特に，天気がよくて空気の動きの少ない時には，大気の逆転を生じ，光化学スモッグが発生しやすい。現在では大気中にうかぶ光化学スモッグの原因となる微粒子及び一酸化炭素の量は，規制されて減少したが，そのかわりに窒素酸化物，その他アクロレイン等いままで空気中に見られなかったような物質が現われはじめた。例えば，自動車のエンジンでは効率を高め，一酸化炭素の生成量を少なくするために，元来使用温度を高めるという方向をたどって来た。このために，エンジンにすいこまれた空気中の窒素が酸化されて，窒素酸化物が生成されるようになった。これは，エンジンの使用温度が低かった時には問題にならなかった事である。さらに，自動車のエンジンでは，ノッキングをふせぐた

めに，ガソリンに種々の物質を混入するが，これらのものが大気中に放出されて，光化学反応を受けて後，微粒子としてうかび，これを核としてスモッグを生じると考えられている。これらの物質は，1,000,000 分の1程度の極微量であっても，生物にとっては，異物として作用するもので，在来の方法では，その分析はむずかしかったが，最近はクロマトグラフィーによって，正確に分析されるようになった。大気のポリューション（汚染）の問題は，物理学，化学，気象学等，多くの方面にまたがっているため，各方面の研究者を集めて研究が進められているが，まだ解決されていない問題が多く，書物には記述されていないような種類の化学反応が起こっているものと考えられている。また，地上の汚染源に一々番号をつけて，どの番号の汚染源によってどれだけの大気汚染が生じたかということを明確にすることが出来ない事も，問題のむずかしさを倍加している。

LESSON 17
第十七課

KANJI

造	662	ZŌ	吸	203a	KYŪ	
	4701			885	su(u)	
型	595	KEI	収	631	SHŪ	
	1077	kata		860	{osa(meru) / osa(maru)	
年	126	NEN	検	771	KEN	
	188			2304		
割	246a	KATSU	層	261b	SŌ	
	703	{wa(ru) / wa(reru)		1402		
者	235	SHA	命	519	MEI / MYŌ	
	3685			430		
系	765	KEI	日	11	NICHI, JITSU	
	195			2097	hi / -ka	
似	625	JI	人	30	NIN / JIN	
	376	ni(ru)		339	hito	
星	264	SEI	工	71	KŌ / KU	
	2121	hoshi		1451		
道	122	DŌ	消	429	SHŌ	
	4724	michi		2574	{ke(su) / ki(eru)	
求	583	KYŪ	不	500	FU	
	137	{moto(meru) / moto(maru)		17		

READING SELECTIONS

構造	kōzō	structure
模型	mokei	model
すでに	sude ni	already, previously
放出する	hōshutsu suru	to emit, release
構成要素	kōsei-yōso	constituent element
ラザフォード	Razafōdo	Rutherford
α線	arufa-sen	alpha rays
ぶつける	butsukeru	to throw, hurl
		(here: to bombard)

分布	bunpu	distribution
4倍	yonbai	four times
割合に	wariai ni	relatively
範囲	han'i	extent, range
広がる	hirogaru	to spread, reach, extend
α粒子	arufa-ryūshi	alpha particle
偏向角	henkō-kaku	angle of deflection
狭い	semai	small, limited, narrow
機会	kikai	opportunity, chance
正しい	tadashii	correct
みいだす（見出す）	mi-idasu	to discover
閉じこめる	toji-komeru	to confine, shut in
ところで	tokoro de	now, further
集まる	atsumaru	to come together
そこで	soko de	now, further
いくつかの	ikutsu ka no	several
太陽系	taiyō-kei	solar system
…に似る	…ni niru	to resemble…
万有引力	banyū-inryoku	universal gravitation
…と同じく	…to onajiku	is the same as…and
惑星	wakusei	planet
量子（力学）	ryōshi(rikigaku)	quantum(mechanics)
とびとびである	tobi-tobi de aru	to be discrete, incremental
軌道	kidō	orbit
かってな	katte na	arbitrary
許す	yurusu	to permit, allow
仮定する	katei suru	to adopt a hypothesis, suppose, postulate

求める	motomeru	to seek, search for
ちょうど	chōdo	exactly
バルマー	Barumā	Balmer
公式	kōshiki	formula
推測する	suisoku suru	to deduce
…と一致する	…to itchi suru	to agree with…
理論	riron	theory
基底状態	kitei-jōtai	ground state
ボーア	Bōa	Bohr
飛び移る	tobi-utsuru	to jump
吸収	kyūshū	absorption

原子の構造とその模型 （B 337–339）

すでに学んだように，原子からは，いろいろの方法によって負の電気を帯びた電子が放出されるから，原子は電子をその構成要素として含んでいると考えられる。ところが原子は全体として中性であるから，正電気をもったもの[1]が原子の中になければならない。

1911年ラザフォードは原子にα線をぶつける実験をして，原子の中での正電荷の分布を調べた。α線は正の電荷 $2e$（$-e$ は電子の電荷）をもち，水素原子の約4倍の質量をもった粒子[1]の流れである。原子の中に正電荷が割合広い範囲に広がっていれば，これに衝突して曲げられるα粒子の数は多いが，その偏向角は小さいはずである。これに反して，狭い範囲にあれば衝突する機会は少ないが，そのかわり大きな角で曲げられるものがある[2]（図 1）。

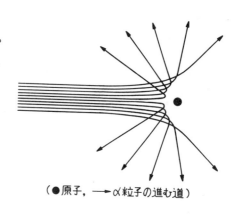

（●原子，——α粒子の進む道）

ラザフォードの実験の結果，後者のほうが正しいことが見出された[3]。すなわち，正電荷は半径 10^{-12} cm 程度の球の中に閉じこめられていることがわかった。これに対して，原子の半径は X 線の実験からもわかるように，だいたい 10^{-8} cm すなわち 1Å の程度である。ところで電子の質量は水素原子の質量の約 $\frac{1}{1840}$ であるから，原子の質量はほとんどこの正電気の部分に集まっている。この原子の中心にある小さくて重い正電気をもった粒子[1,4]を原子核とよんでいる。

そこで，原子の模型としては，中心に重い原子核があって，そのまわりにいくつかの電子が回っている[5]太陽系に似たもの[1]が考えられている。特に水素原子では，電子は1個だけあると考えられる。正負電荷の間の引力は，万有引力と同じく，距離の2乗に反比例するから，電子の運動は太陽系の惑星の運動と同じようになる。量子力学によると，原子のエネルギーはとびとびであるから，水素原子の中の電子の軌道は，かってな半径の円であることは許されないと仮定し，この仮定から電子のエネルギーの値を求めると，ちょうど，

$$E_n = -hc\, R\left(\frac{1}{n^2}\right)$$

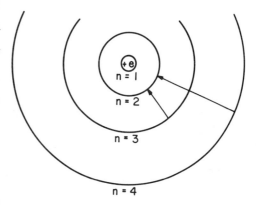

となる。これはバルマーの公式から推測されるものと一致する。この理論によれば，エネルギ

ー E_n に対する電子の軌道半径 r は，n^2a で表わされる。

ここに，$a=h^2/(4\pi^2me^2)=0.529\text{Å}$ は基底状態[6] のエネルギーに対する軌道の大きさでボーア半径とよばれる。この模型では，光は，電子が一つの軌道から他の軌道に飛び移るときに放出，または吸収されると考えられる。

宇宙線	uchū-sen	cosmic rays
中間子	chūkan-shi	meson
はく検電器	haku-kenden-ki	leaf electrometer
十分（＝充分）	jūbun	sufficiently
はくが 閉じる	haku ga tojiru	the leaves close
電離する	denri suru	to ionize
透過力	tōka-ryoku	penetrating power, power to penetrate
放射線	hōsha-sen	radiation
上層	jōsō	upper layers
降り注ぐ	furi-sosogu	to pour down
起源	kigen	source
破壊する	hakai suru	to break down
作り出す	tsukuri-dasu	to produce
π中間子	pai-chūkan-shi	π-meson
寿命	jumyō	life, life-time
μ中間子	myū-chūkan-shi	μ-meson
光子	kōshi	photon
陽電子	yō-denshi	positron
湯川秀樹	Yukawa Hideki	Japanese nuclear physicist and Nobel Laureate
核子	kakushi	nucleon
総称した	sōshō shita	generically named
核力	kakuryoku	nuclear force
予言する	yogen suru	to predict
今日では	konnichi de wa	at the present time
高エネルギー	kō-enerugii	high energy
加速装置	kasoku-sōchi	accelerator
人工的な	jinkō-teki na	artificial, man-made
生成する	seisei suru	to create
自然界	shizen-kai	the natural world
素粒子	so-ryūshi	elementary particle
容易に	yōi ni	easily, readily
消滅する	shōmetsu suru	to disappear, vanish
あらたに	arata ni	again, anew

かつて	katsute	at one time
不変な	fuhen na	invariable, permanent
相互に	sōgo ni	mutually
移り変わる	utsuri-kawaru	to change, shift
統一する	tōitsu suru	to unify
ひとまとめに	hito-matome ni	as one group
取り扱う	tori-atsukau	to treat, deal with
つくる	tsukuru	to make
現代物理学	gendai butsuri-gaku	modern physics
解決する	kaiketsu suru	to solve
課題	kadai	question, problem
教授	kyōju	professor
ノーベル賞	Nōberu-shō	Nobel Prize
受賞する	jushō suru	to receive a prize, award
日本人	Nihon-jin	Japanese
初めての	hajimete no	the first
これに続いて	kore ni tsuzuite	following this
同窓	dōsō	classmate
朝永振一郎	Tomonaga Shin'ichirō	Japanese Nobel Laureate in the field of quantum electrodynamics
理論物理学者	riron-butsuri-gakusha	theoretical physicist
2人目	futari-me	the second
受賞者	jushō-sha	prize winner

宇宙線と中間子　(B 355–356)

　はく検電器に電気を与えて，十分絶縁しておいても，長い間にははくが閉じる。これは空気を電離する作用をもち透過力の強い放射線が，大気の上層から絶えず地上に降り注いでいるためで，この放射線を宇宙線とよぶ。その起源は太陽系の外の宇宙のどこかにあると考えられる。宇宙線を構成する非常に高速度の原子核，主として陽子は，大気中の原子と衝突して，原子核を破壊し，同時に電子の約300倍の質量をもった π 中間子という粒子を作り出す。π 中間子は 10^{-8} 秒ぐらいの寿命[7]をもち，μ 中間子または光子に変わる。μ 中間子は電子の質量の約200倍の質量をもち，10^{-6} 秒ほどの寿命で，電子または陽電子に変わる。地上の宇宙線は主として μ 中間子と電子とである。

　π 中間子は湯川秀樹*が1935年に核子（陽子，中性子を総称したもの）の間にはたらく

---

*　湯川教授はその中間子理論によって1949年ノーベル賞を受賞した。日本人としては初めての受賞である。これに続いて湯川教授と同窓で同じく理論物理学者の朝永教授が日本人として2人目のノーベル賞受賞者となった。

核力の研究において，その存在を予言したものである。今日では高エネルギーの加速装置により，人工的に中間子を生成することができる。

　電子・光子・核子・中間子のような自然界における基本的の粒子を素粒子という。このうち，光子は容易に消滅したり，新たに発生したりするが，核子や電子は原子を構成する要素で，かつては変化しないものと思われていた。しかし，β線が出るときには中性子は陽子に変わり，電子が核の中から生まれてくる。また，電子と陽電子はγ線を原子核に当てることにより同時に作り出され，それはまたγ線を出して同時に消滅する。中間子がπ→μ→電子の変化をするほか，陽子が正電気を帯びた中間子π⁺を出して中性子に変わり，また，中性子がπ⁻を出して陽子に変わることも知られている。このように素粒子といっても不変なものではなく，相互に移り変わるものである。ただその変化に際しても，エネルギーや運動量の保存の法則が常に成り立っているのは重要なことである。このような互いに変化する素粒子を統一して，ひとまとめに取り扱う理論をつくることは，現代物理学のまだ解決されていない大きな課題である。

GENSHI NO KŌZŌ TO SONO MOKEI

Sude ni mananda yō ni, genshi kara wa, iroiro no hōhō ni yotte fu no denki o obita denshi ga hōshutsu sareru kara, genshi wa denshi o sono kōsei-yōso to shite fukunde iru to kangaerareru. Tokoro ga genshi wa zentai to shite chūsei de aru kara, sei-denki o motta mono[1] ga genshi no naka ni nakereba naranai.

1911-nen Razafōdo wa genshi ni arufa-sen o butsukeru jikken o shite, genshi no naka de no sei-denka no bunpu o shirabeta. Arufa-sen wa sei no denka $2e$ (-e wa denshi no denka) o mochi, suiso-genshi no yaku yonbai no shitsuryō o motta ryūshi[1] no nagare de aru. Genshi no naka ni sei-denka ga wariai hiroi han'i ni hirogatte ireba, kore ni shōtotsu shite magerareru arufa-ryūshi no kazu wa ōi ga, sono henkō-kaku wa chiisai hazu de aru. Kore ni han-shite, semai han'i ni areba shōtotsu suru kikai wa sukunai ga, sono kawari ōki na kaku de magerareru mono ga aru[2] (Zu-ichi).

Razafōdo no jikken no kekka, kōsha no hō ga tadashii koto ga mi-idasareta.[3] Sunawachi, sei-denka wa hankei $10^{-12} cm$ teido no kyū no naka ni toji-komerarete iru koto ga wakatta. Kore ni taishite, genshi no hankei wa X-sen no jikken kara mo wakaru yō ni daitai $10^{-8} cm$ sunawachi ichi-ongusutorōmu no teido de aru. Tokoro de, denshi no shitsuryō wa suiso-genshi no shitsuryō no yaku sen-happyaku-yonjū-bun no ichi de aru kara, genshi no shitsuryō wa, hotondo kono sei-denki no bubun ni atsumatte iru. Kono genshi no chūshin ni aru chiisakute omoi sei-denki o motta ryūshi[1,4] o genshi-kaku to yonde iru.

Soko de, genshi no mokei to shite wa, chūshin ni omoi genshi-kaku ga atte, sono mawari ni ikutsu ka no denshi ga mawatte iru[5] taiyō-kei ni nita mono[1] ga

kangaerarete iru. Toku ni suiso-genshi de wa, denshi wa ikko dake aru to kang-aerareru. Sei-fu-denka no aida no inryoku wa banyū-inryoku to onajiku, kyori no ni-jō ni hanpirei suru kara, denshi no undō wa taiyō-kei no wakusei no undō to onaji yō ni naru.

Ryōshi-rikigaku ni yoru to, genshi no enerugii wa tobi-tobi de aru kara, suiso-genshi no naka no denshi[1] no kidō wa, katte na hankei no en de aru koto wa yurusarenai to katei shita.

Kono katei kara denshi no enerugii no atai o motomeru to, chōdo,

$$E_n = -hcR \times 1/n^2$$

to naru. Kore wa Barumā no kōshiki kara suisoku sareru mono to itchi suru. Kono riron ni yoreba, enerugii E_n ni tai-suru denshi no kidō-hankei r wa, n^2a de arawasareru.

Koko ni, $a = h^2/(4\pi^2me^2) = 0.529$ Å wa, kitei-jōtai[6] no enerugii ni tai-suru kidō no ōkisa de, Bōa-hankei to yobareru.

Kono mokei de wa, hikari wa, denshi ga hitotsu no kidō kara ta no kidō ni tobi-utsuru toki ni hōshutsu, mata wa kyūshū sareru to kangaerareru.

UCHŪ-SEN TO CHŪKAN-SHI

Haku-kenden-ki ni denki o ataete, jūbun zetsuen shite oite mo, nagai aida ni wa haku ga tojiru. Kore wa kūki o denri suru sayō o mochi tōka-ryoku no tsuyoi hōsha-sen ga taiki no jōsō kara taezu chijō ni furi-sosoide iru tame de, kono hōsha-sen o uchū-sen to yobu. Sono kigen wa taiyō-kei no soto no uchū no doko ka ni aru to kangaerareru. Uchū-sen o kōsei suru hijō ni kō-sokudo no genshi-kaku, shu to shite yōshi wa, taiki-chū no genshi to shōtotsu shite, genshi-kaku o hakai shi, dōji ni denshi no yaku 300-bai no shitsuryō o motta pai-chūkan-shi to iu ryūshi o tsukuri-dasu. Pai-chūkan-shi wa 10^{-8}byō gurai no jumyō[7] o mochi, myū-chūkan-shi mata wa kōshi ni kawaru. Myū-chūkan-shi wa denshi no shitsuryō no yaku 200-bai no shitsuryō o mochi, 10^{-6} byō hodo no jumyō de, denshi mata wa yō-denshi ni kawaru. Chijō no uchū-sen wa shu to shite myū-chūkan-shi to denshi to de aru.

Pai-chūkan-shi wa Yukawa Hideki* ga, 1935-nen ni kakushi (yōshi, chūsei-shi o sōshō shita mono) no aida ni hataraku kakuryoku no kenkyū ni oite, sono sonzai o yogen shita mono de aru. Konnichi de wa kō-enerugii no kasoku-sōchi ni yori, jinkō-teki ni chūkan-shi o seisei suru koto ga dekiru.

Denshi, kōshi, kakushi, chūkan-shi no yō na shizen-kai ni okeru kihon-teki no ryūshi o so-ryūshi to iu. Kono uchi, kōshi wa yōi ni shōmetsu shitari, arata ni hassei shitari suru ga, kakushi ya denshi wa genshi o kōsei suru yōso de, katsute

---

* Yukawa-kyōju wa sono chūkan-shi-riron ni yotte 1949-nen Nōberu-shō o jushō shita. Nihon-jin to shite wa hajimete no jushō de aru. Kore ni tsuzuite Yukawa-kyōju to dōsō de onajiku riron-butsuri-gakusha no Tomonaga-kyōju ga Nihon-jin to shite futarime no Nōberu-shō-jushō-sha to natta.

wa henka shinai mono to omowarete ita. Shikashi, bēta-sen ga deru toki ni wa chūsei-shi wa yōshi ni kawari, denshi ga kaku no naka kara umarete kuru. Mata, denshi to yō-denshi wa ganma-sen o genshi-kaku ni ateru koto ni yori dōji ni tsukuri-dasare, sore wa mata ganma-sen o dashite dōji ni shōmetsu suru. Chūkanshi ga pai→myū→denshi no henka o suru hoka, yōshi ga sei-denki o obita chūkanshi pai-purasu o dashite chūsei-shi ni kawari, mata, chūsei-shi ga pai-mainasu o dashite yōshi ni kawaru koto mo shirarete iru. Kono yō ni soryūshi to itte mo, fuhen na mono de wa naku, sōgo ni utsuri-kawaru mono de aru. Tada sono henka ni saishite mo, enerugii ya undō-ryō no hozon no hōsoku ga tsune ni nari-tatte iru no wa jūyō na koto de aru. Kono yō na tagai ni henka suru so-ryūshi o tōitsu shite, hito-matome ni tori-atsukau riron o tsukuru koto wa, gendai-butsuri-gaku no mada kaiketsu sarete inai ōki na kadai de aru.

ATOMIC STRUCTURE AND ATOMIC MODEL

As you have already learned, the atom is thought to contain electrons as constituent elements because electrons carrying negative charges are emitted from atoms in various ways. However, since the atom as a whole is neutral, there must also be positively charged constituents in the atom. In 1911 Rutherford performed an experiment in which he bombarded the atom with alpha rays in order to investigate the distribution of positive charges within the atom. Alpha rays are streams of particles which have a positive charge of $2e$ ($-e$ is the charge on an electron) and a mass about four times that of the hydrogen atom. If the positive charge were spread out over a relatively broad region in the atom, then the number of alpha particles which encounter it and are deflected would be large but their angles of deflection small. In contrast, if the region were restricted, the chances for collision would be small but, instead of the above, some alpha particles would be deflected through a large angle (Fig. 1).

From the results of Rutherford's experiments the latter view was found to be correct. That is, it was discovered that the positive charge was confined within a sphere of about 10^{-12}cm radius. In contrast to this, we know from X-ray experiments that the radius of the atom is about 10^{-8}cm, that is about 1Å. Now since the mass of the electron is about 1/1840 of the mass of the hydrogen atom, the mass of the atom is almost all collected in the positive electrical part. This small heavy kernel at the center of the atom containing positive electricity is called the atomic nucleus.

Now, in the atomic model, the atom is regarded as being something like the solar system, with a heavy atomic nucleus at the center and electrons revolving around it. For the hydrogen atom in particular, we imagine there is but one electron.

Since the attractive force between negative and positive electricities, like the force of gravitation, is inversely proportional to the square of the distance, the

movement of the electrons is the same as that of the planets in the solar system.

Since, according to quantum mechanics, atomic energies are discrete, we adopt the hypothesis that the orbits of the electrons in the hydrogen atom are not permitted to be circles of any arbitrary radius.

If we seek the energy values of the electron starting from this hypothesis, then we obtain exactly

$$E_n = -hcR \times 1/n^2,$$

which agrees with that deduced from the Balmer formula. According to this theory, the radius of the electron orbit for energy E_n is given by n^2a.

Here the value $a = h^2/(4\pi^2me^2) = 0.529\text{Å}$ gives the size of the orbit corresponding to the ground state energy and is called the Bohr radius.

In this model, the emission and absorption of light are believed to occur when the electron jumps from one orbit to another.

COSMIC RAYS AND MESONS

The leaves of a charged electrometer will eventually close even though the electrometer is adequately insulated. This is because there are radiations of strong penetrating power, called cosmic rays, which continually pour down upon the earth from the upper layers of the atmosphere and ionize the air. Their source is believed to lie outside of the solar system somewhere in the cosmos. The extremely high velocity atomic nuclei which constitute cosmic rays, mainly protons, collide with the atoms in the atomsphere, breaking down their nuclei and simultaneously creating π-mesons, particles with masses about 300 times that of the electron. π-mesons have a life of about 10^{-8} seconds and then change into μ-mesons or photons. μ-mesons with a mass of about 200 times that of the electron have a life of about 10^{-6} seconds and then change into electrons or positrons. Cosmic rays on earth are principally μ-meson and electrons.

The existence of π-mesons was predicted by Hideki Yukawa* in 1935 during his research on the nuclear forces acting among nucleons (the generic name for protons and neutrons). At the present time it is possible to create mesons artificially with high-energy accelerators.

The fundamental particles of the natural world such as electrons, photons, nucleons and mesons are called elementary particles. Among them the photon readily disappears and reappears, but nucleons and electrons which are the constituent elements of atoms were at one time thought to be permanent. However, when beta rays emerge, neutrons are changing into protons, and electrons are being generated from within the nucleus. Moreover, electrons and positrons are simul-

---

* Professor Yukawa received the Nobel Prize in 1949 for his meson theory, the first Japanese to receive the prize. Following this, Professor Tomonaga, a classmate of Professor Yukawa and similarly a theoretical physicist, became the second Japanese to became a Nobel prize winner.

taneously produced by gamma rays striking the atomic nucleus, and they in turn are annihilated simultaneously with the production of gamma rays. In addition to mesons changing into electrons, $\pi \rightarrow \mu \rightarrow$electrons, we also know that protons change into neutrons by giving off positively charged π^+-mesons, and neutrons change into protons by giving off π^-mesons. Thus, though we speak of elementary particles, they are not invariant but mutually transformable. Nonetheless it is important that, even with these changes, the laws of energy and momentum conservation are always valid. The creation of a theory in which these mutually changing elementary particles can be unified and treated as a single group is one of the great but yet unsolved problems of modern physics.

EXPLANATORY NOTES

(1) sei-denki o motta mo-no; 4-bai no shitsuryō o motta ryūshi; sei-denki o motta ryūshi; taiyō-kei ni nita mono

The *-ta* forms here all have the same meaning as the corresponding *-te iru* forms, and are translated by the present tense in English

(2) mono ga aru

"There are cases for which..." Hence *some* (but not all) alpha particles are deflected through large angles.

(3) mi-idasu

出す is read *dasu*, but the frequently encountered 見出す is read *mi-idasu*. (The reading *idasu* is not included in the current *Tōyō kanji* tabulation.)

(4) Kono... ryūshi

Ryūshi is modified by *kono*, *genshi no chūshin ni aru*, *chiisakute omoi*, and *sei-denki o motta*.

(5) chūshin... iru

This phrase modifies *taiyō-kei ni nita mono*. Literally: "a solar-system-like thing, in which..."

(6) kitei-jōtai

"Ground state." For "excited state" the term is 励起状態 *reiki-jōtai*.

(7) jumyō

"Life, lifetime." The term for "half-life" is 半減期 *hangen-ki*.

SUPPLEMENTARY READINGS

A. 1) 電波天文学   denpa-tenmon-gaku   radio astronomy

一分野	ichi-bunya	a field
宇宙電波	uchū-denpa	cosmic radio emission
電波星	denpa-sei	radio star
銀河電波	ginga-denpa	galactic radio (frequency) radiation
熱放射	netsu-hōsha	thermal radiation
連続スペクトル	renzoku-supekutoru	continuous spectrum

線スペクトル	sen-supekutoru	line spectrum
シンクロトロン	shinkurotoron	synchrotron
電波望遠鏡	denpa-bōen-kyō	radio telescope
星間物質	seikan-busshitsu	interstellar matter
知見	chiken	information, knowledge
レーダー	rēdā	radar
流星	ryūsei	meteor
精密な	seimitsu na	precise

電波天文学   (3RJ 918)

電波を用いる天文学の一分野。天体から放射される電波には，太陽電波や，月，惑星など太陽系内の電波源からのもののほかに宇宙電波があり，後者には電波星を電波源とするものと，銀河電波とがある。熱放射による連続スペクトル，線スペクトル（21cm 波）のほかに，銀河電波などにはシンクロトロン放射によるものも含まれる。測定には電波望遠鏡が用いられ，各種の電波源や銀河系の構造とくに星間物質などについて，光学的測定では求められない知見が得られている。ほかにレーダーを用いて流星，月，惑星などからの反射を研究する分野があり，距離，軌道などの精密な測定に利用されている。

2)	理学部	rigaku-bu	Faculty of Science
	物理学科	butsuri-gakka	Department of Physics
	卒業	sotsugyō	graduation
	理化学研究所	Rikagaku Kenkyūjo	(see Lesson 11)
	仁科研究室	Nishina Kenkyū-shitsu	Nishina Laboratory

(a very famous laboratory established by Nishina, one of the most prominent nuclear physicists in Japan.)

東京文理科大学	Tōkyō Bunrika Daigaku	Tokyo University of Literature and Science
現…	gen…	presently…
東京教育大学	Tōkyō Kyōiku Daigaku	Tokyo University of Education
定年	teinen	the age of retirement
退職する	taishoku suru	to retire
留学	ryūgaku	to study abroad
日本学術会議	Nihon Gakujutsu Kaigi	The Science Council of Japan
会長	kaichō	chairman
日本学士院	Nihon Gakushi-in	The Japan Academy
会員	kaiin	member

相対論的場	sōtai-ron-teki-ba	relativistic fields
定式化する	teishiki-ka suru	to formalize
超多時間理論	chō-tajikan-riron	super-many-time-theory
発表	happyō	publication
くりこみ理論	kurikomi-riron	renormalization theory
完成する	kansei suru	to perfect, complete
戦時	senji	war-time
極超短波	kyokuchō-tanpa	microwave
…に従う	...ni shitagau	to engage in...
マグネトロン	magunetoron	magnetron
発振理論	hasshin-riron	oscillation theory
小谷正雄	Kotani Masao	Famous Japanese physicist; President of Tōkyō University of Science (1971–)
日本学士院賞	Nihon Gakushi-inShō	The Japan Academy Prize
文化勲章	Bunka Kunshō	The Order of Cultural Merit
量子電気力学	ryōshi-denki-rikigaku	quantum electrodynamics
業績	gyōseki	achievements, contributions

朝永振一郎　(3RJ 946)

1906年3月31日生まれ，理論物理学者。1929年京都大学理学部物理学科卒業後，1932年理化学研究所仁科研究室にはいり，1941年東京文理科大学（現東京教育大学）教授となる。1969年定年退職。1937—39年には Leipzig 大学の W. K. Heisenberg のもとに留学，1963—68年日本学術会議会長。日本学士院会員。1943年相対論的場の量子論を定式化した超多時間理論を発表，1967年，これを発展させてくりこみ理論を完成した。1943—45年戦時研究として極超短波の研究に従い，マグネトロンの発振理論を完成し，これに対して小谷正雄とともに1948年日本学士院賞，1952年文化勲章を受けた。1965年に J. S. Schwinger, R. P. Feynman とともに量子電気力学を発展させた業績によってノーベル物理学賞を受けた。

3) | 二光子吸収 | ni-kōshi kyushū | two photon absorption |
多光子遷移	ta-kōshi-sen'i	multiple photon transition
パリティ	pariti	parity
許容（禁制）遷移	kyoyō (kinsei) sen'i	allowed (forbidden) transition
遷移確率	sen'i-kakuritsu	transition probability
共鳴	kyōmei	resonance

レーザー	rēzā	laser
光領域	kō-ryōiki	optical domain
分光学	bunkō-gaku	spectroscopy

二光子吸収　(3RJ 972)

　2個の光子を同時に吸収する多光子遷移をいう。一光子吸収はパリティの異なる状態の間を結びつけるが，二光子吸収ではパリティの同じ状態の間が許容遷移となる。遷移確率は一般にエネルギーが大きい程小さく，また2つの光子密度の積に比例する。 1950年 D. E. Hughes と Grabner とが分子線磁気共鳴で初めて二光子吸収を観測したが，レーザー光が使えるようになってから光領域でも観測され，特にレーザー光とふつうの光源からの光の組み合わせの二光子吸収は種々の物質の分光学的研究に利用されている。

4) 坂田昌一	Sakata Shōichi	Japanese physicist
提出する	teishutsu suru	to present
探究する	tankyū suru	to investigate
統一的に扱う	tōitsu-teki ni atsukau	to treat in a unified way
基本粒子	kihon-ryūshi	fundamental particle
複合粒子	fukugō-ryūshi	composite particle
バリオン	barion	baryon
多重項	tajū-kō	multiplet term
群論	gunron	group theory
分類学	bunrui-gaku	taxonomy
基礎	kiso	fundamentals
導入する	dōnyū suru	to introduce
展開	tenkai	development
一時代を開く	ichi-jidai o hiraku	to open an era
階層	kaisō	class
ストレンジネス	sutorenjinesu	strangeness
着想	chakusō	conception, idea
類推	ruisui	analogy
励起状態	reiki-jōtai	excited state
予測	yosoku	prediction
池田，小川，大貫	Ikeda, Ogawa, Ōnuki	Japanese physicists
近似	kinji	approximation
対称性	taishō-sei	symmetry
世界的流行	sekai-teki-ryūko	worldwide trend
…年頃	...nen goro	about the year...
ハドロン	hadoron	hadron
発見する	hakken suru	discover

八重項	hachijū-kō	octet

坂田模型　(3RJ 943–494)

坂田昌一（1956）の提出した素粒子の内部構造を探究する基本的な理論で，各種の素粒子を統一的に扱い，まず基本粒子と複合粒子とに分け，バリオンや中間子がいくつかで多重項をなすとみて，群論的取り扱いをなし得る分類学の基礎を導入し，素粒子論の展開に一時代を開いた。自然は分子→原子→原子核→素粒子→基本粒子→…という階層構造をもつという考えから出ている。ストレンジネス保存則と電荷の保存則をλ粒子の数と陽子の数の保存則によって表わすという着想を核構造の類推から導入し，バリオンや中間子に基底状態だけでなく，励起状態が多数存在し得ることを予測した。池田―小川―大貫（1959）は第0近似として基本粒子を同等とみた場合に成立する素粒子の対称性を論じ，初めて荷電・ストレンジネス多重項による素粒子の分類を導入した。これはその後の群論的研究の世界的流行を開いたものであった。1960年頃からハドロン共鳴状態が多数実験によって発見され，ハドロンおよびその共鳴状態が八重項や十重項などを作っていることがたしかめられた。

5) 遊離基	yūri-ki	free radical
とどまる	todomaru	to stay in, continue in
平均	heikin	average
指数関数	shisū-kansū	exponential function
（部分）崩壊（定数）	(bubun) hōkai (teisū)	(partial) decay (constant)
存在	sonzai	existence
確率	kakuritsu	probability
経過する	keika suru	to elapse
…ごとに	...goto ni	each time that...
チャンネル	channeru	channel
注目する…	chūmoku suru...	the...under consideration
再結合	sai-ketsugō	recombination
消える	kieru	to disappear
便宜的に	bengi-teki ni	conventionally

寿命　(3RJ 626)

素粒子，原子，分子，イオン，遊離基などがある不安定な状態にとどまっている時間をいうが，これらの粒子一つ一つについてはその時間は一定でないので，一般には平均寿命で表わされる。

[1] 放射性原子や素粒子の数は，ふつう時間とともに指数関数的に減少する。その場合，平均寿命は崩壊定数λの逆数に等しい。存在確率は，平均寿命が経過するごとに$1/e$（eは

自然対数の底） の割合で減少する。いくつかの崩壊チャンネルがあるときは，注目するチャンネルに関する崩壊定数（これを部分崩壊定数という）を λ_i として，$1/\lambda_i$ を部分平均寿命という。

[2] 化学反応において平均寿命が正確に定義できるのは，ある不安定な状態にあるものの数が時間 t の指数関数 $\exp(-kt)$（k は定数）で表わされる場合（一次反応）である。この場合の平均寿命 τ は $\tau = 1/k$ で表わされる。そのほかの場合，例えば遊離基が再結合反応で消えて行くような場合（二次反応）には上のような平均寿命は定義しにくいことが多いので，指数関数でなく，数（または濃度）が半分になるまでの時間をもって便宜的に寿命ということがある。

6) 人工衛星	jinkō-eisei	artificial satellite
周囲	shūi	circumference
公転	kōten	revolution
ソ連	Soren	Soviet Union
打ち上げる	uchi-ageru	to send off, launch
…に成功する	…ni seikō suru	to succeed in…
米ソ両国	Bei-So-ryōkoku	both the U.S. and the U.S.S.R.
…の手で	…no te de	by (the effort of)…
数個ずつ	sūko-zutsu	several by each (country)
自身	jishin	itself
上層	jōsō	upper layers
大気	taiki	atmosphere
検証	kenshō	inspection, verification
装備	sōbi	equipment
微粒子流	bi-ryūshi-ryū	stream of microscopic particles
流星じん	ryūsei-jin	meteoric dust
熱輻射	netsu-fukusha	thermal radiation

人工衛星　(2RJ 1504)

地球の周囲を公転する人工の物体をいう。1957年10月4日，ソ連がはじめて打ち上げに成功し，その後米ソ両国の手で数個ずつ打ち上げられている。人工衛星の目的は，人工衛星自身の軌道の変化によっては，地球上層大気密度，地球の形と大きさの決定，地球の内部構造の検証などがあり，人工衛星に装備された測定装置によっては，太陽の紫外線およびX線，宇宙線，太陽からの微粒子流，流星じん，地球磁場，地球上層大気の組成，地球の熱輻射などを測定する。これらはいずれも地上にあっては観測できないもので，その科

学的意義は非常に大きい。

B. 振動子　　　　　　　shindō-shi　　　　　　oscillator
　一歩を進める　　　　ippo o susumeru　　　to go one step further
　伝播する　　　　　　denpa suru　　　　　to propagate
　光量子　　　　　　　kō-ryōshi　　　　　light quantum
　光電効果　　　　　　kōden-kōka　　　　photo-electric effect
　確立する　　　　　　kakuritsu suru　　to establish
　解明する　　　　　　kaimei suru　　　to elucidate
　量子論　　　　　　　ryōshi-ron　　　quantum theory
　もはや…ない　　　　mohaya...nai　　no longer
　疑いを容れる　　　　utagai o ireru　to have doubts, doubt
　長岡　　　　　　　　Nagaoka　　　famous Japanese physicist
　周囲　　　　　　　　shūi　　　surrounding(s)
　軽い　　　　　　　　karui　　light (weight)
　提出する　　　　　　teishutsu suru　to propose
　説　　　　　　　　　setsu　　theory, view, opinion
　小孔　　　　　　　　shōkō　　small hole
　鉛板　　　　　　　　enban　　lead plate
　ビーム　　　　　　　biimu　　beam
　うすい…はく　　　　usui...haku　thin...foil
　通りぬける　　　　　tōri-nukeru　to pass through
　硫化亜鉛　　　　　　ryūka-aen　zinc sulfide
　ぬる　　　　　　　　nuru　　to paint
　発光する　　　　　　hakkō suru　to become luminescent, emit light

　シンチレーション　　shinchirēshon　scintillation
　カウンター　　　　　kauntā　　counter
　検出　　　　　　　　kenshutsu　detection
　素通りする　　　　　sudōri suru　to pass without stopping
　斥力　　　　　　　　sekiryoku　repulsive force
　逆二乗　　　　　　　gyaku-nijō　inverse square
　結論する　　　　　　ketsuron suru　to conclude
　正面衝突　　　　　　shōmen-shōtotsu　head-on collision
　静止する　　　　　　seishi suru　to be stationary
　…わけにはゆかず　　...wake ni wa yukazu　cannot...
　(＝わけにはいかないで)　　　　(see Construction Examples for Lesson 15)

　古典…　　　　　　　koten...　classical...
　失う　　　　　　　　ushinau　to lose

次第に	shidai ni	gradually
縮小する	shukushō suru	to contract
ついに	tsui ni	finally, eventually
矛盾	mujun	contradiction
公準	kōjun	postulate
定常状態	teijō-jōtai	stationary state
エネルギー準位	enerugii-jun'i	energy level
採用する	saiyō suru	to employ, utilize
終りの	owari no	final
逆過程	gyaku-katei	inverse process
相容れない	ai-irenai	incompatible
常態	jōtai	the usual state
励起状態	reiki-jōtai	excited state
励起する	reiki suru	to be excited

Bohr の原子模型　(BN 280–282)

　Planck は光を放射し吸収する振動子のエネルギーが振動数 ν に比例し hν の整数倍であると仮定したが，1905年 Stark および Einstein はさらに一歩を進め，振動数 ν の光が伝播する際には hν のエネルギーをもつ粒子すなわち光量子（あるいは光子）として進むこと，およびその進行方向に hν/c（c は真空中の光速度）の運動量をもつことを仮定して光電効果その他の説明に成功した。これらの成果に基づいて Bohr は原子模型を確立し水素スペクトルを解明した（1913）ので量子論はもはや疑いを容れないものとなった。

　1903年に長岡は，原子は太陽系のように中心部に小さな重い核があり，その周囲に軽い電子が円運動をしているという考えを提出した。この説は Rutherford が1910—1911年に行なった α 粒子の実験で確かめられたので，これを長岡—Rutherford の原子模型という。

　Rutherford の実験。図1において S は天然放射性物質で，これから 10^7m/sec 程度の高速の α 粒子（後述）が飛び出す。これが小孔をあけた2枚の鉛板 D_1，D_2 を通って細いビームとなり，うすい金属はく（金，銀，銅など）に当たる。はくを通りぬけた α 粒子が硫化亜鉛をぬった板 P に当たれば，そこが瞬間的に発光する。これをシンチレーションという。

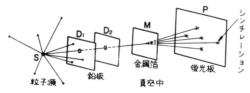

これにより α 粒子が M で曲げられた方向と数とを知ることができる。この方法は現在で

もシンチレーション・カウンターとして放射線の検出に使われている。実験の結果によれば，α粒子の大部分は曲げられずに M を素通りし，ごく少数のもののみが90°以上の大きな角度で曲げられた。Rutherford は α粒子と M を構成する原子の核との間にクーロンの斥力が働くものとして，曲げられる角度と数とを計算し，実験とくらべた結果，粒子が核に10⁻¹²cm程度に近づくまで逆二乗の法則が成り立つことを確かめ，核の大きさが10^{-12}cm程度であると結論した。図1 (p. 239) は長岡の模型に対する α粒子の曲がり方を示す。電子は非常に軽いから，α粒子は電子に衝突してもほとんど曲がらない。重い核に正面衝突に近い衝突をしたものだけ大きく曲げられるのである。

Bohr の水素原子理論. Rutherford の実験により，原子は極めて小さい正電荷の核とその周囲にある負電荷の電子とから構成されることが分ったが，電子が核から一定の距離を保つためには，電子は静止しているわけにはゆかず，核のまわりに回転していると考えなければならない。しかし，回転している電子は常に中心に向う加速度を持つから，古典電磁気学によれば，電子はその回転数に等しい振動数の電磁波を発射し，それにつれて運動エネルギーを失う。したがってその軌道は次第に縮小して回転数も変り，連続的に振動数の変化する光を出しながらついに核に落ち込んで静止するはずである。しかし，実験事実は原子が極めて安定であること，および不連続的な一定振動数の光だけを発することを示している。この矛盾を解決するために，Bohr は原子には古典電磁気学は適用できないと考え，次の二つの公準を立てて水素スペクトルの説明に成功した。

(1) 原子内の電子はある特別な軌道だけを回転できる。この軌道を回る間は光を放出しない。この状態を定常状態といい，各状態のエネルギーをエネルギー準位という。

(2) 電子は一つの軌道から他の低いエネルギー準位の軌道に飛び移ることがある。このとき一個の光量子が放出されて発光する。この光量子のエネルギーは両軌道のエネルギーの差に等しく，その振動数 ν は $h\nu = W_1 - W_2$ で与えられる。W_1, W_2 はそれぞれ初めと終りの軌道のエネルギーである（発光の逆過程が光の吸収である）。

この二つの公準はいずれも古典物理学とは相容れないのであって，(1) の仮定には Planck の量子仮説を採用し，電子の角運動量が $h/2\pi$ の n 倍である軌道だけが許されるとする。(2) の仮定は Einstein の光量子の仮説に対応するものである。$n=1$ の軌道はエネルギーが最低であって基底状態とよばれる。これが最も安定で電子は常態ではこの軌道の上にあるが，放電管の中の速い電子などが原子に衝突すれば，原子内の電子はエネルギーを得てエネルギーの高い外側の軌道に移る。この状態を励起状態という。励起された電子がエネルギーの低い軌道へ移ればエネルギーの差が光量子として放出される。

FINAL TRANSLATION TEST　　(SN 108–116)

　1947年にはアメリカで中間子を人工的に発生し得る最初の大加速器が出来た。それ以後今日まで，加速器はますます大型となり，宇宙線中で発見された新粒子はすべて人工的に作り出された。特に最近は，共鳴準位 (resonance level) とよばれる，極度に寿命の短い粒子が何十種類も検出された。元来物理学者は，自然はその本質において割合に単純であると考えて，自然の法則，自然を理解する道を求めて来た。その物理学者が現在直面しているのは，素粒子の世界の多種多様性である。

　電子の運動が太陽系の惑星の運動との類推を手がかりとしたように，中間子論は最初，電磁場の理論との類推を手がかりとした。しかし，核力の場と電磁場，従ってまた中間子と光子の間には，いちじるしい違いがあり，例えば，核力は電磁気的な力のように遠方までとどかないかわり，近い所では電磁気的な力よりはるかに強い。そして，そうであればこそ，少量の物質から大きな原子力が取り出せるのである。ところが，近距離での強い力を正確に表わすには，電磁力の場合と同じ計算法では近似がよくない。このために新しく中間結合の方法が考え出され，核力の研究は多くの成果を収め，核子自身の構造を問題にし得るようになっている。

　ところが一方，素粒子の種類は増加する一方で，それらの大多数の間には強い力がはたらくこともわかって来た。そこで素粒子間の強い相互作用をもっと一般的に考究するにはどうしたらよいかということが問題になって来た。これに対して，現在多くの学者たち，特に若い階層の人々によって使われているのは，アメリカのチュウ (Chu) によって代表される S 行列 (S Matrix) の方法である。この方法は，一口にいえば，素粒子間で衝突が起こってさまざまな反応を起こす際，衝突の細かい機構に立ち入ることをやめて，衝突の前に素粒子が遠く離れていた状態と，衝突がすんでしまって出来た素粒子がふたたび互いに遠く離れてしまった状態とを，確率的に結び付ける S 行列の形を決めることだけを問題にする。この方法は複素関数論 (theory of functions of a complex variable) を用いて，相当な成果を収めて来た。しかしここで問題となるのは，この方法が果して素粒子を本当に理解したいという要求をみたしているかどうかである。

　2400年前に，デモクリトスが考えた物質系では，定まった形をもった多くの原子が何もない空間を，互いに衝突しながら飛び回り続けていたのである。20世紀になって物理学者たちが，数多くの実験的事実の上に立って考え出した原子あるいは素粒子は，デモクリトスのイメージとは色々の点で違っていた。重要な相違点の一つは，素粒子が形や大きさをもたない点だと考えられたことであった。しかし，それぞれの素粒子に固有な有限の質量，従ってそれに相当するエネルギーを一点に集中させようとすると，どうしても，どこかに

矛循がのこる。その後，素粒子の種類が増加するに従って，ひろがりを考えるべき理由が
ますます強くなって来たようにおもわれる。形も大きさもない点が，どうして数多くの違
った種類の素粒子として個性をもち得るか，ひろがりをもった素粒子の間の相互作用をど
う考えるかということが最大の課題で，この問題の解決は，従来の考え方では不可能に
近く，新しいアイデアが必要であろう。結局は，時空構造そのものまで問題にしなけれ
ばならなくなるだろう。

　多くの新発見，新事実を吸収消化した後，全く違った局面で解かねばならないのであ
る。

LESSON 18
第十八課

KANJI

沸	218b	FUTSU
	2524	wa(kasu) wa(ku)
凝	270a	GYŌ
	652	
媒	247a	BAI
	1241	
糖	271b	TŌ
	3485	
純	810	JUN
	3509	
浸	233b	SHIN
	2572	hita(su) hita(ru)
透	236a	TŌ
	4699	
沈	210b	CHIN
	2508	shizu(meru) shizu(mu)
殿	257a	DEN
	242	
焼	434	SHŌ
	2772	ya(ku) ya(keru)

膜	263b	MAKU
	3803	
融	272a	YŪ
	5274	
操	271a	SŌ
	2015	
毛	142	MŌ
	2473	ke
軽	387	KEI
	4620	karu(i)
試	416	SHI
	4361	kokoro(miru)
注	277	CHŪ
	2531	soso(gu)
意	155	I
	5113	
弱	236	JAKU yowa(i)
	650	yowa(meru) yowa(maru)
火	13	KA
	2743	hi

READING SELECTIONS

希薄	kihaku	dilute
沸点	futten	boiling point
凝固点	gyōko-ten	freezing point
(不)揮発性	(fu)kihatsu-sei	(non)-volatile
溶質	yōshitsu	solute
溶媒	yōbai	solvent
ラウール	Raūru	Raoult
発見する	hakken suru	to discover
(非)電解質	(hi)denkai-shitsu	(non)-electrolyte

薄い	usui	dilute
溶ける	tokeru	to be dissolved
上昇度	jōshō-do	degree of elevation
かつ	katsu	moreover
降下度	kōka-do	degree of depression
ショ糖	shotō	sucrose
溶かす	tokasu	to dissolve
ブドウ糖	budō-tō	grape sugar, dextrose
純粋な	junsui na	pure
モル沸点上昇	moru-futten-jōshō	molar boiling point elevation
モル凝固点降下	moru-gyōko-ten-kōka	molar freezing point depression
浸透圧	shintō-atsu	osmotic pressure
ドイツの	Doitsu no	German
植物学者	shokubutsu-gakusha	botanist
プェッファー	Peffā	Pfeffer
フェロシアン化銅	feroshian-ka-dō	copper ferrocyanide
沈殿	chinden	precipitate
目をふさぐ	me o fusagu	to clog the pores
素焼き	suyaki	unglazed pottery
通す	tōsu	to let pass through
膜	maku	membrane
半透膜	hantō-maku	semi-permeable **membrane**
浸入する	shinnyū suru	to enter into
オランダの	Oranda no	Dutch
化学者	kagaku-shə	chemist
ファントホッフ	Fanto Hoffu	van't Hoff
あてはまる	atehamaru	to be applicable to, apply to
グラム分子	guramu-bunshi	gram molecule
書きなおす	kaki-naosu	to rewrite
融点	yūten	melting point
ガラス細工	garasu-zaiku	glass blowing
練習する	renshū suru	to practice
操作	sōsa	operation, process
毛細管	mōsai-kan	capillary tube
バーナー	bānā	burner
引きのばす	hiki-nobasu	to draw out
内径	naikei	internal diameter
閉じる	tojiru	to close

ショウノウ	shōnō	camphor
乳ばち	nyūbachi	mortar
砕く	kudaku	to grind, break up
開く	hiraku	to open
すくう	sukuu	to scoop up
机	tsukue	desk
軽くたたく	karuku tataku	to tap lightly
数回	sūkai	several times
くり返す	kuri-kaesu	to repeat
つめる	tsumeru	to pack in, fill
中ほど	naka-hodo	the middle
封管	fūkan	sealed tube
アセトアニリド	aseto-anirido	acetanilide
試験管	shiken-kan	test tube
昇華する	shōka suru	to sublimate
注意する	chūi suru	to be careful
弱い火	yowai hi	low flame
融解する	yūkai suru	to melt
時計ざら	tokei-zara	watch glass
蒸発ざら	jōhatsu-zara	evaporating dish
うつす	utsusu	to transfer
固まる	katamaru	to harden
混ぜ合わせる	maze-awaseru	to mix together
グリセリン	guriserin	glycerine
切る	kiru	to cut
はめる	hameru	to pull on
つく	tsuku	to reach
とめる	tomeru	to fasten, fix in place
すみやかに	sumiyaka ni	rapidly
じか火	jikabi	direct heat, flame
徐々に	jojo ni	slowly

希薄溶液の沸点と凝固点　(3K 57–58)

　不揮発性の溶質の溶液の沸点は溶媒よりも高く，その凝固点は溶媒よりも低い。ラウールは1886年，次の法則を発見した。非電解質のうすい溶液では，その溶媒の一定量に溶けている溶質の分子数が等しければ，溶質が何であっても [1]，その沸点の上昇度は等しく，かつ溶質の量に比例する。凝固点の降下度についても同様の法則が成り立つ。

　たとえば，1kgの水にショ糖0.1グラム分子を溶かした溶液も，ブドウ糖0.1グラム分

子を溶かした溶液も，沸点は互いに等しく，純粋な水よりも 0.052°C 高い。 もし 1kg の水に 0.2 グラム分子を溶かせば，何を溶かしても[1]，純粋な水の沸点よりも， 0.052×2＝0.104°C 高くなる。

溶媒 1kg に溶質 1 グラム分子を溶かしたときの沸点上昇度・凝固点降下度を，それぞれモル沸点上昇・モル凝固点降下という。これらの値を使って，溶質の分子量を知ることができる。

たとえば 1kg の水に 20g のアルコールを溶かした溶液は，凝固点が 0.80°C 下がる。いま，アルコールの分子量を x とすると，水のモル凝固点降下が 1.86°C であるから

$$20\,(g) : x\,(g) = 0.80° : 1.86°$$

という式が成り立ち，これから，

$$x = 46.5$$

が得られる。この値は，アルコールの分子量（$C_2H_6O = 46$）とほぼ等しい。

希薄溶液の浸透圧　（3K 58–60）

ドイツの植物学者プェッファーは，1874 年に浸透圧の研究を行なった。フェロシアン化銅の沈殿[2]で目をふさいだ素焼き[3]は，水を通すが水に溶けているショ糖の分子を通さない。このように，ある物質を通し，ある物質を通さない膜を半透膜という。溶質は通さないで溶媒だけを通す半透膜によって溶液と溶媒を分離すると，膜を通って，溶媒が溶液中に浸入しようとする圧力が，その溶液の浸透圧である。

1885 年，オランダの化学者ファントホッフは，プェッファーの実験の結果をしらべ，浸透圧には気体の法則 $pv=nRT$ と同じ形の式があてはまることを知った。すなわち，浸透圧を π 気圧，n グラム分子の溶質を溶かしている希薄溶液の体積を v リットル，絶対温度を T とすると，次の関係があることがわかった。

$$\pi v = nRT$$

これを書きなおす[4]と $\pi = \dfrac{n}{v}RT$，すなわち $\dfrac{n}{v}$ は溶液 1 リットルに溶けている溶質のモル数であるから，浸透圧は溶液 1 リットル中に溶けている溶質のモル数に比例することとなり，溶質がどんなものであっても[1]，モル数が等しければ，浸透圧は等しいことになる。

実験：凝固点降下度

目的 1.　凝固点降下度から分子量を計算する。

目的 2.　融点の測り方や，ガラス細工を練習する。

操作 1.　融点測定用のガラス毛細管をつくる。ガラス管をバーナーで熱して引きのばし，内径 1mm，長さ約 7cm のものを 2 本つくり，その一端を図 1 のようにバーナーで熱して閉じる。

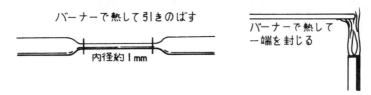

バーナーで熱して引きのばす

内径約 1mm

バーナーで熱して一端を封じる

（図1）ガラス毛細管のつくり方

操作 2. ショウノウを乳ばちでくだき，操作 1. の毛細管を 1 本とり，開いた端を乳ばちに入れてショウノウをすくい，閉じた端を下にして，机の上で軽く [5] たたく。これを数回くり返して，ショウノウの高さが約 3mm になるまでつめる。毛細管の中ほどをバーナーでとかし，封管とする。

操作 3. ショウノウ 1g にアセトアニリド 0.05g を混ぜたものを，かわいた試験管に入れ，ショウノウが昇華しないように注意しながら [6]，ごく弱い [5] 火で熱して融解する。とけたら，これを時計ざらまたは蒸発ざらに全部うつし，固まったものをガラス棒で砕いてよく混ぜ合わせる。操作 2. のショウノウと同様に毛細管につめて封じる。

操作 4. 太い試験管の下部にグリセリンを入れて融点測定装置とする。ゴム管を短く切って温度計にはめ，物質を入れた部分が，温度計の下部へつくように，操作 2. または 3. でつくった毛細管をとめる。試験管を 150℃ くらいまですみやかに熱し，それからは，小さなじか火で徐々に熱して，毛細管の中の固体がとける温度を測定せよ。

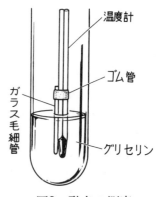

温度計

ゴム管

ガラス毛細管

グリセリン

図2　融点の測定

KIHAKU-YŌEKI NO FUTTEN TO GYŌKO-TEN

Fu-kihatsu-sei no yōshitsu no yōeki no futten wa yōbai yori mo takaku, sono gyōko-ten wa yōbai yori mo hikui. Raūru wa 1886-nen, tsugi no hōsoku o hakken shita. Hi-denkai-shitsu no usui yōeki de wa, sono yōbai no ittei-ryō ni tokete iru yōshitsu no bunshi-sū ga hitoshikereba, yōshitsu ga nan de atte mo, [1] sono futten no jōshō-do wa hitoshiku, katsu yōshitsu no ryō ni hirei suru. Gyōko-ten no kōka-do ni tsuite mo dōyō no hōsoku ga naritatsu.

Tatoeba, 1 kg no mizu ni shotō 0.1 guramu-bunshi o tokashita yōeki mo, budō-tō 0.1 guramu-bunshi o tokashita yōeki mo, [1] futten wa tagai ni hitoshiku, junsui na mizu yori mo, 0.052°C takai. Moshi, 1 kg no mizu ni 0.2 guramu-bunshi o tokaseba, nani o tokashite mo, junsui na mizu no futten yori mo 0.052×2＝0.104°C takaku naru.

Yōbai 1 kg ni yōshitsu 1 guramu-bunshi o tokashita toki no futten-jōshō-do, gyōko-ten-kōka-do o sorezore moru-futten-jōshō, moru-gyōko-ten-kōka to iu.

Korera no atai o tsukatte, yōshitsu no bunshi-ryō o shiru koto ga dekiru.

Tatoeba, 1 kg no mizu ni 20 g no arukōru o tokashita yōeki wa, gyōko-ten ga 0.80°C sagaru. Ima, arukōru no bunshiryō o x to suru to, mizu no moru-gyōko-ten-kōka ga 1.86°C de aru kara,

$$20(g) : x(g) = 0.80° : 1.86°$$

to iu shiki ga naritachi, kore kara

$$x = 46.5$$

ga erareru. Kono atai wa arukōru no bunshiryō $(C_2H_6O = 46)$ to hobo hitoshii.

KIHAKU-YŌEKI NO SHINTŌ-ATSU

Doitsu no shokubutsu-gakusha Peffā wa, 1874-nen ni shintō-atsu no kenkyū o okonatta. Feroshian-ka-dō no chinden [2] de me o fusaida suyaki [3] wa, mizu o tōsu ga mizu ni tokete iru shotō no bunshi o tōsanai. Kono yō ni, aru busshitsu o tōshi, aru busshitsu o tōsanai maku o hantō-maku to iu. Yōshitsu wa tōsanai de yōbai dake o tōsu hantō-maku ni yotte, yōeki to yōbai o bunri suru to, maku o tōtte, yōbai ga yōeki-chū ni shinnyū shiyō to suru atsuryoku ga, sono yōeki no shintō-atsu de aru.

1885-nen, Oranda no kagaku-sha Fanto Hoffu wa, Peffā no jikken no kekka o shirabe, shintō-atsu ni wa kitai no hōsoku $pv = nRT$ to onaji katachi no shiki ga atehamaru koto o shitta. Sunawachi, shintō-atsu o π kiatsu, n guramu-bunshi no yōshitsu o tokashite iru kihaku-yōeki no taiseki o v rittoru, zettai-ondo o T to suru to, tsugi no kankei ga aru koto ga wakatta.

$$\pi v = nRT$$

Kore o kaki-naosu [4] to $\pi = (n/v) RT$, sunawachi n/v wa yōeki ichi-rittoru ni tokete iru yōshitsu no moru-sū de aru kara, shintō-atsu wa yōeki ichi-rittoru-chū ni tokete iru yōshitsu no moru-sū ni hirei suru koto to nari, yōshitsu ga donna mono de atte mo, [1] moru-sū ga hitoshikereba, shintō-atsu wa hitoshii koto ni naru.

Jikken: Gyōko-ten-kōka-do

Mokuteki 1. Gyōko-ten-kōka-do kara, bunshi-ryō o keisan suru.

Mokuteki 2. Yūten no hakari-kata ya, garasu-zaiku o renshū suru.

Sōsa 1. Yūten-sokutei-yō no garasu-mōsai-kan o tsukuru. Garasukan o bānā de nesshite hiki-nobashi, naikei 1 mm, nagasa yaku 7 cm no mono o nihon tsukuri, sono ittan o zu-ichi no yō ni bānā de nesshite tojiru.

Sōsa 2. Shōnō o nyūbachi de kudaki, sōsa 1 no mōsai-kan o ippon tori, hiraita hashi o nyūbachi ni irete shōnō o sukui, tojita hashi o shita ni shite, tsukue no ue de karuku [5] tataku. Kore o sūkai kuri-kaeshite, shōnō no takasa ga yaku 3 mm ni naru made tsumeru. Mōsai-kan no naka-hodo o bānā de tokashi, fūkan to suru.

Sōsa 3. Shōnō 1 g ni asetoanirido 0.05 g o mazeta mono o, kawaita shiken-kan ni ire, shōnō ga shōka shinai yō ni chūi shinagara, [6] goku yowai [5] hi de nesshite

yūkai suru. Toketara, kore o tokei-zara mata wa jōhatsu-zara ni zembu utsushi, katamatta mono o garasu-bō de kudaite yoku maze-awaseru. Sōsa 2 no shōnō to dōyō ni mōsai-kan ni tsumete fūjiru.

Sosa 4. Futoi shiken-kan nc kabu ni guriserin o irete, yūten-sokutei-sōchi to suru. Gomu-kan o mijikaku kitte ondo-kei ni hame, busshitsu o ireta bubun ga, ondo-kei no kabu e tsuku yō ni, sōsa 2 mata wa 3 de tsukutta mōsai-kan o tomeru. Shiken-kan o 150°C kurai made sumiyaka ni nesshi, sore kara wa, chiisa na jikabi de jojo ni nesshite, mōsai-kan no naka no kotai ga tokeru ondo o sokutei se-yo.

THE BOILING AND FREEZING POINTS OF DILUTE SOLUTIONS

The boiling point of a solution containing a non-volatile solute is higher than that of the solvent, and its freezing point is lower. In 1886 Raoult discovered the following law. If the number of molecules of solute dissolved in a fixed amount of a certain solvent is the same for dilute solutions of nonelectrolytes, then the boiling point elevation is the same, no matter what the solute, and is proportional to the amount of solute. The same law holds for freezing point depressions as well.

For example, both a solution in which 0.1 gram molecule of sucrose is dissolved in 1 kg of water and a solution in which 0.1 gram molecule of dextrose is dissolved have the same boiling point, 0.052°C higher than that of pure water. If 0.2 gram molecules were dissolved in 1 kg of water then, no matter what is dissolved, the boiling point would be $0.052 \times 2 = 0.014$°C higher than that of pure water.

The boiling point elevation and the freezing point depression obtained when 1 gram molecule of solute is dissolved in 1 kg of solvent are called the molar boiling point elevation and the molar freezing point depression respectively. Molecular weights of solutes can be determined using these values.

For example, with a solution of 20 g of alcohol dissolved in 1 kg of water the freezing point is lowered 0.80°C. Since the molar freezing point depression of water is 1.86°C, we obtain the equation 20 (g) : x (g) $= 0.80° : 1.86°$, where x is the molecular weight of alcohol, from which

$$x = 46.5$$

This value is almost equal to the molecular weight of alcohol ($C_2H_6O = 46$).

THE OSMOTIC PRESSURE OF DILUTE SOLUTIONS

In 1874 the German botanist Pfeffer made studies of osomotic pressure. He found that unglazed pottery whose pores were clogged by copper ferrocyanide

precipitate would allow water to pass through but not the sucrose molecules dissolved in the water. Such a membrane which allows one substance to pass through but not another is called a semi-permeable membrane. If a solution and its solvent are separated by a semi-permeable membrane which permits only the solvent to pass through and not the solute, than the pressure arising from the solvent's tendency to enter the solution through the membrane is the osmotic pressure of the solution.

In 1885 the Dutch chemist van't Hoff studied the results of Pfeffer's experiments and found that an equation of the same form as the gas law $pv=nRT$ applies to osmotic pressure. That is to say he found that, taking the osmotic pressure π in atmospheres, the volume v of the dilute solution in liters, where n gram molecules of solute were dissolved at the absolute temperature T, the following relation exists.

$$\pi v = nRT$$

If this is rewritten as $\pi = (n/v)RT$ then, since n/v is the number of moles of solute dissolved in 1 liter of solution, the osmotic pressure becomes proportional to the number of moles of solute dissolved in one liter of solution and, whatever the solute may be, the osmotic pressure will be the same if the number of moles is equal.

Experiment: Freezing Point Depression

Objective 1. To calculate the molecular weight from the freezing point depression.

Objective 2. The measurement of melting points and practice in glass blowing.

Procedure 1. To make glass capillary tubes for use in melting point determinations. Heat a glass tube with the burner, draw it out to an internal diameter of 1 mm, make two tubes of about 7 cm length, and close one end by heating with the burner as shown in Figure 1.

Procedure 2. Break up some camphor in a mortar, take one of the capillary tubes prepared in Procedure 1 and scoop camphor into the open end from the mortar, then tapping the closed end gently on the desk. Repeat this procedure several times until the camphor is packed in to a height of about 3 mm. Now melt the capillary tube in the middle to form a closed tube.

Procedure 3. Mix 1 g of camphor with 0.05 g of acetanilide, place in a dry test tube and, being careful not to sublimate the camphor, melt the mixture by heating with a low flame. When it melts, transfer all of it to a watch glass or evaporating dish and pulverize the lumps with a glass rod and thoroughly mix. Fill and seal a capillary tube as was done with the camphor in Procedure 2.

Procedure 4. Fill the lower part of a large test tube with glycerine to serve as the melting point measurement apparatus. Cut off a short piece of

rubber tubing, slide onto the thermometer and attach the capillary tubes prepared in Procedures 2 and 3 such that the ends containing material reach to the lower part of the thermometer. Heat the test tube rapidly to about 150°C and then heat slowly with a small direct flame. Measure the temperatures at which the solids in the capillary tubes melt.

EXPLANATORY NOTES

(1) (interrogative) + te mo

Combinations like this are usually translated by "....ever"or "no matter what....".

nan de atte mo: whatever it is; no matter what it is.

nani o tokashite mo: whatever we dissolve; no matter what we dissolve.

donna mono de atte mo: whatever kind of material it is; no matter what kind of material it is.

(2) chinden

沈 is the character used for settling of fine particles. In the case of precipitates in chemical reactions, 沈殿 is used. In the more general case of sedimentations, 沈降 is used. Thus 沈降岩 is sedimentary rock.

(3) yaku

焼 is frequently used as a prefix in words concerning the heat treatment of metals, thus 焼入れ, 焼なまし, 焼もどし. Which of these words would you associate with annealing, tempering, quenching?

(4) kaki-naosu

The verb *naosu* means "to mend, to correct." When used as the second component of a verb it has the idea of "redoing something to put it in better form." Hence, *hōteishiki o kaki-naosu* means "to rewrite the equation" (putting it, for example, into a more useful form).

(5) karui, yowai

軽 and 弱 are frequently used as prefixes in contrast to 重 and 強. Compare, for example,

軽金属：重金属　　　　弱酸　　：強酸
軽合金：重合金　　　　弱塩基　：強塩基
軽油　：重油　　　　　弱電解質：強電解質

(6) -nagara

This suffix is used to indicate two simultaneous actions by the same person(s). Hence *shōnō ga shōka shinai yō ni chūi shinagara, nesshite yūkai suru* means "we supply heat and melt the camphor, while being careful that it doesn't sublime."

SUPPLEMENTARY READINGS

A.

氷点	hyōten	freezing point of water
準備	junbi	preparation
フラスコ	furasuko	flask
塩化カリウム	enka-kariumu	potassium chloride
かくはん器	kakuhan-ki	agitator
試料溶液	shiryō-yōeki	test solutions
拡大鏡	kakudai-kyō	magnifying lens
大要	taiyō	general outline
氷水	kōri-mizu	ice water
浸す	hitasu	to immerse
蒸留水	jōryū-sui	distilled water
図中に	zuchū ni	in the figure
綿フィルター	men-firutā	cotton filter
ピペット	pipetto	pipette
脱脂綿	dasshi-men	absorbent cotton
洗う	arau	to wash
清潔な	seiketsu na	clean
綿布	menpu	cotton cloth
包む	tsutsumu	to wrap
木づち	kizuchi	wooden mallet
約1/3程	yaku sanbun **no ichi hodo**	to the extent of about 1/3
浸る	hitaru	to be immersed
ふたをする	futa o suru	to cover
挿入する	sōnyū suru	to insert
はげしくかくはんする	hageshiku **kakuhan suru**	to shake vigorously
一定になったら	ittei ni nattara	when it has become constant
記録する	kiroku suru	to record
不純な	fujun na	impure
きれいな	kirei na	clean
使うこと	tsukau koto	be sure to use!
食塩	shokuen	table salt
寒剤	kanzai	freezing mixture
冷却する	reikyaku suru	to chill
ふたを取る	futa o toru	to uncover
静かに	shizuka ni	gently
流し去る	nagashi-saru	to pour off
注ぎ入れる	sosogi-ireru	to pour in

数分間	sūfun-kan	several minutes
A 付の B	A-tsuki no B	B to which A is attached
取り出す	tori-dasu	to remove
やめる	yameru	to stop, cease doing
外挿する	gaisō suru	to extrapolate (a curve)
大差	taisa	a large difference
電離度	denri-do	degree of dissociation
示すべき	shimesu-beki	which ought to express
既知である	kichi de aru	to be known
前述の	zenjutsu no	the previously described
簡単な	kantan na	simple
精度	seido	accuracy

氷点降下法による分子量の測定　(BKJ 108–109)

実験。種々の物質の水溶液を用いて氷点降下法により，その分子量を測定せよ。
準備。氷点降下測定装置(Dewar フラスコ，かくはん器, Beckmann 温度計)，ピペット (25 ml 4 本)，試料溶液 (ショ糖，ブドウ糖等非電解質及び塩化カリウム等電解質溶液)，拡大鏡。

第 1 図

　装置の大要を第 1 図に示す。約 0.3M の試料水溶液を作り，フラスコに入れ氷水中に浸しておく。 同様に 200〜300 ml の蒸留水も氷水中に浸しておく。 図中に示した綿フィルターは 3 組作っておく。これは 25ml ピペットの先に短いゴム管をはめ，この中に脱脂綿をつめたものである。 氷を蒸留水でよく洗い，清潔な綿布で包んで木づちでたたき細くくだく。Dewar フラスコに約 1/3 程氷をつめ，これが浸る位の量の蒸留水を加えてふたをし，Beckmann 温度計を挿入し， はげしくかくはんし，温度が一定になったら，その温度を記録する。 氷が不純であると一定にならないから，きれいな氷を使うこと。純粋な氷のないときは，不純な氷と食塩で寒剤を作り，これで蒸留水を冷却して作った氷を用いる。温度を記録したらふたを取り，静かに水を流し去り，先に作っておいて冷却しておいた試料溶液を注ぎ入れる。数分間かくはんして一定温度になったら温度を記録して，綿フィルター付のピペットを挿入し，試料溶液を取り出し， それと同量の冷

却しておいた蒸留水を加えて同じ操作を繰り返す。温度降下が初めの1/2になるまで行なってやめる。 取り出した試料溶液の密度を測定してその濃度を定める。このためには試料溶液について濃度と密度との関係を求めておく必要がある。

こうして氷―水系について測定した温度と氷―試料溶液系の測定温度の差を，試料溶液の各濃度について得ると，次式によってその分子量が求められる。

$$M = \frac{1853W}{W_0 \Delta T}$$

ここでMは分子量，Wは溶質の重量，W_0は水の重量，ΔTは測定した温度降下である。各濃度(W/W_0)について計算したMを，W/W_0に対してプロットして得られる直線を外挿して，濃度零におけるMの値を得る。この値と原子量から計算した分子量の値とを比較してみよ。試料溶質が電解質であるときには，この二つの値に大差がある。これは電離してイオンとなるためであって，電解質の試料の場合その電離度αは次式で表わされる。

$$\Delta T = \{1 + \alpha(n-1)\}\Delta T_0$$

ΔT_0は電離しないと仮定したときに示すべき温度降下，nは1個の分子から電離してできるイオンの数，ΔTは実測される温度降下である。それで試料の分子量が既知であれば，氷点降下を測定して，電離度を求めることができる。前述の方法は簡単で精度の高い方法であるが，非水溶液の場合には用いることができない。一般的な方法としてBeckmannの方法がある。

B. 困難な	konnan na	difficult
既知量	kichi-ryō	a known quantity
要点	yōten	the main points, essentials
過熱する	kanetsu suru	to superheat
…ことなしに	…koto nashi ni	without…
沸とうする	futtō suru	to boil
考案	kōan	design, scheme
要は	yō wa	the essentials are
冷却器	reikyaku-ki	condenser
側管	sokkan	side arm
ニクロム線	nikuromu-sen	nichrome wire
石綿	ishiwata	asbestos
白金	hakkin	platinum
…行なうか…行なう	…okonau ka …okonau	to do it by… or by…
陶土板	tōdo-ban	porcelain clay plate
破片	hahen	fragments
防ぐ	fusegu	to prevent
やはり	yahari	also

ガラス製	garasu-sei	made of glass
器具	kigu	utensil
上昇させる	jōshō saseru	to cause to rise, lift
注ぎかける	sosogi-kakeru	to pour onto
やや	yaya	somewhat, slightly
複雑な	fukuzatsu na	complicated
難点	nanten	difficulty
調節する	chōsetsu suru	to regulate, control

沸点上昇法による分子量の測定　(BKJ 111–113)

　一定圧力の下における純溶媒の沸点と，その溶媒に不揮発性の溶質を少量溶解したいわゆる希薄溶液の沸点との差を測定することにより，溶質分子の分子量を知る事ができる。物質の分子量を知るには普通，蒸気密度の測定，凝固点降下の測定，それにこの沸点上昇の三つの方法がある。沸点上昇法は，不揮発性，あるいは高温で分解して蒸気とすることができず，また低温では溶解度が小さくて凝固点降下の測定が困難なものに応用される。

　この方法は，Beckmann 温度計で純溶媒の沸点を測定し，その中に既知量の溶質を溶解し，その沸点を Beckmann 温度計でよみ，前との差，すなわち沸点上昇 ΔT を知り，それから次式で分子量 M を計算によって求める。

$$M = \frac{kW}{W_0 \Delta T}$$

ここに W は溶質の重量，W_0 は溶媒の重量，k は溶媒によって決まる定数である。

　この実験の要点は，溶液の沸とうを過熱することなしに行なうことと，Beckmann 温度計で，発生する蒸気の温度ではなく，沸とうしている溶液の温度を正しく測定することである。このため測定装置には，いろいろ考案があるが，要は純溶媒あるいは溶液を入れ，上部に冷却器をつけるための側管を持った大型の試験管，それからBeckmann温度計とからなり，加熱の方法にいろいろあるだけである。加熱には電熱を用いるものと，ガスのもの，それから溶媒蒸気によるものとがある。電熱を利用するには，試験管の外側にニクロム線を石綿で包んで行なうか，あるいは直接液中に白金のコイルを浸して行なう。後者の方が過熱のおそれが少ない。ガスの場合は底から熱するが，液中に陶土板の破片あるいは白金線を入れて過熱を防ぐ必要がある。Cottrell の方法は，加熱にはやはりガスを用いるが，温度計を以上の方法とは異なって液中に入れないでよむ。それには第1図のようなガラス製の器具を用いて，発生する蒸気で液体を上昇させ，温度計に注ぎかけるようになっている。溶媒蒸気を用いるもの（第2図）は，過熱を起こすおそれはないが，装置がやや複雑になる。これはまず電気，ガス等で純溶媒を加熱して，その時発生する蒸気を，測定する溶液中に導く。溶液内で蒸気が凝縮するときに放出される凝縮熱は，この溶液の温度

を上昇させる。こうして溶液の温度が上昇して沸とうになると，蒸気は溶液内で凝縮しなくなり，液体の温度上昇は止まる。この時の温度をよむわけである。この方法の難点は溶液中の溶媒重量を正確に知ることである。いずれの型のものでも加熱を調節するのに注意するとよい。

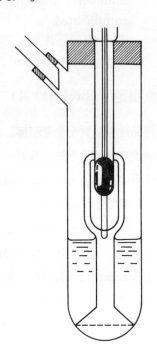

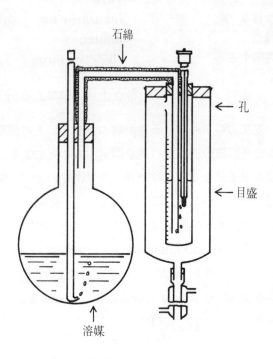

石綿

← 孔

← 目盛

↑
溶媒

C. | 活動度 | katsudō-do | activity |
|---|---|---|
| 消去する | shōkyo suru | to eliminate |
| 誤差 | gosa | error |
| 遅い | osoi | slow |
| 平衡に達する | heikō ni tassuru | to reach equilibrium |
| 指標 | shihyō | indicator |
| 積極的に | sekkyoku-teki ni | directly |
| 平衡点 | heikō-ten | equilibrium point |
| 開発する | kaihatsu suru | to develop |
| 気泡 | kihō | gas bubble |
| 押す | osu | to push |
| 光電管 | kōden-kan | photo-electric tube |
| 監視する | kanshi suru | to observe, watch closely |
| 特色 | tokushoku | special characteristic |
| よごれ | yogore | dirt |

意外に	igai ni	surprisingly, far more than expected
影響	eikyō	influence, effect
守る	mamoru	to abide by
熟練	jukuren	experience
あらい	arai	coarse
数万の	sūman no	to several 10 thousands
もれる	moreru	to leak through
図示する	zushi suru	to graph, plot
外挿する	gaisō suru	to extrapolate (a curve)
数平均分子量	sū-heikin-bunshi-ryō	number-average molecular weight
重量平均分子量	jūryō-heikin-bunshi-ryō	weight-average molecular weight
比較する	hikaku suru	to compare
…意味で	.... imi de	with regard to....
分布	bunpu	distribution
有用な	yūyō na	useful
…に従って（につれて）	.... ni shitagatte	See Construction Example, Lesson 12
会合する	kaigō suru	to associate
傾き	katamuki	slope
ビリアル	biriaru	virial
排除	haijo	excluded
球状の	kyūjō no	spherical
棒状の	bōjō no	needle-shaped
項	kō	term
無視できる	mushi dekiru	can be neglected

浸透圧　(BK 33–35)

溶液中の溶媒の活動度は溶質のモル濃度に比例して減少する。希薄溶液では浸透圧 π と溶媒の活動度 a_1 との間には次の関係がある。

$$\pi V_1 = -RT\ln a_1 \tag{1}$$

$$V_1: \text{溶媒のモル容積}$$

希薄溶液では活動度と溶媒と溶質のモル分率 N_1, N_2 との間には次の関係がある。

$$a_1 \doteqdot N_1 = (1 - N_2)$$

また、　　　　$\ln(1 - N_2) \doteqdot N_2$

であるから　　$\pi V_1 \doteqdot RTN_2 \tag{2}$

そこで溶媒の活動度を浸透圧から測定し，溶質の濃度を同時に知っていれば溶質の分子量を測定できる。

$$C_2/M_2 = m_2 \fallingdotseq N_2/V_1$$

C_2: 溶液 $1l$ 中の溶質の g 数，M_2: 溶質の分子量，m_2: 溶質のモル濃度。(1)，(2)式から V_1 を消去して

$$\pi/C_2 = RT/M_2 \qquad\qquad\qquad (3)$$

浸透圧 π を実験で求め C_2 と組み合わせて M_2 を求めることができる。

溶質の分子量が大きくなると，同じ濃度の溶液でも浸透圧が小さく誤差がはいりやすくなるのと，半透膜の両側に小さい圧力差が現われても溶媒の通る速度が非常に遅く平衡に達するまでの時間が長すぎるために実用されにくかった。最近半透膜を通るわずかな溶媒の流れを指標にして，膜の両側の圧力を積極的に変化させて速く平衡点を求める方法が開発され，浸透圧による分子量の測定が実用になるようになった。

溶媒の浸透圧によるわずかな流れを検出するには，毛細管の中に気泡を入れて溶媒に押されて動くところを光電管で監視したり，移動する溶媒で半透膜が押されてわずかに変位するのを電気容量の変化として検出したりする。それぞれの方式によって特色があるが，いずれの場合にもわずかな流れを問題にするので装置内部のよごれとか管の接続部分に残った小気泡などによって意外に大きな影響を生ずるので，使用法の注意を守るとともに相当の熟練を必要とする。半透膜の性質も重要である。目が細かすぎれば溶媒が通りにくいし，あらすぎれば数方の分子量のものがもれるようになる。

(3) 式で示される関係で分子量を求められるのは，溶液が非常に希薄な場合に限る。しかしあまり希薄な溶液では測定がむずかしい。そこで実際には測定のできる濃度の範囲で π を測定し，π/C_2 を C_2 に対して図示し，濃度 0 へ外挿して(3)式を使う。

溶質が分子量の一様でないものの混合物である場合に，浸透圧によって分子量を求めると数平均分子量が得られる。他の方法では多くの場合に重量平均分子量が得られるので，それと比較する意味で浸透圧で数平均分子量を求めることは分子量分布を知るためには有用である。

π/C_2 を C_2 に対して図示するとき，普通は C_2 が大きく なるに従って π/C_2 の値が増す。溶液が理想状態から遠くなるほど増し方も多い。ところがときには π/C_2 が C_2 の増加に従って減少するようなこともある。これは濃度が高くなると活動度が減ることを示すので，濃度が高くなると会合する分子の割合が増すような場合がこれに相当する。

π/C_2 と C_2 の関係の曲線の傾きの係数は第二ビリアル係数と呼ばれ，分子の排除体積に関係する量である。

$$\frac{\pi}{C_2}\ \frac{1}{RT}=\frac{1}{M_2}+\frac{B}{M_2}$$

$$B=b-(a/RT) \tag{3}$$

球状の分子では (2)式の *b* は分子の実際の容積の 4 倍である。$\left(b=4N_{\mathrm{A}}\cdot\dfrac{4}{3}\pi r^3\right)$。球状でない場合には分子が回転するために排除体積の実際の大きさに対する割合はずっと大きくなる。たとえば長さ *l*,　直径 *d* の棒状分子では, $b=N_{\mathrm{A}}\pi dl^2/4$ である。*a/RT* は分子相互の引力を表わす項であるが, 溶液の中では多くの場合無視できる。

FINAL TRANSLATION TEST

　分子量を実験的に決定することは，化学において重要な問題である。組成式と分子量がわかれば分子式が決定できる。有機化学でよく用いられる方法では，例えば Liebig の炭水素定量法のように，試料を燃焼させて，その燃焼生成物の定量から組成式を求め，これと分子量から分子式を定める。

　一般に気体や蒸気圧の高い物質の場合には，その気体あるいは蒸気の密度の測定によって分子量を定める。蒸気圧の低い物質の場合には溶媒をえらんで希薄溶液を作り，その蒸気圧降下あるいは沸点上昇，凝固点降下を測定する方法，あるいは固体の融点を測定する等の方法がふつう用いられている。ところが，高分子の分子量という場合には多少注意を必要とする。合成高分子はその大きさが一定でなく，分子の大きさに軽度の変化があっても性質はほとんど変わらない。生体高分子でも，多くの場合，分子の極小部分を切り取っても分子の性質は変わらないので，純物質として分け取ったものの中に必ず不ぞろいがあると考えられる。これらの現象のために，同じ物質の分子の大きさはすべて同じとは限らず，平均分子量しか求められない。

　このような多分散系 (polydisperse system) では，測定に用いた方法によって平均の仕方が異なるため，同一の物質について数種の方法で求めた分子量の値は必ずしも等しくならない。通常，溶液の浸透圧，光の散乱，拡散係数，沈降速度などを測定する方法が用いられるが，糖類例えばアミロースの分子量を浸透圧などで測定して数平均分子量を求めると 100,000 程度の値が得られるのに対して，光散乱を用いれば 2,000,000 位になる。これは分子量がひろいはんいにわたっているからで，ジメチルスルホキシドに溶かし，エタノールを加えて沈殿させる方法でたしかめられている。

　多分散系の分子量を浸透圧によって求めると数平均分子量が得られるが，他の方法では多くの場合, 重量平均分子量が得られる。分子量の分布を調べるのにはゲル口過 (gel filtration) クロマトグラフ法を用いるのがよく，分子の形の直接観察には電子顕微鏡が用いられる。この際試料を薄いプラスチック膜の上にのせるが，プラスチックも高分子であるか

ら，試料がこれと区別されるよう操作上注意を要する。生体高分子の構造を調べるために
はX線回折も用いられ，毛髪などに含まれるケラチンの構造はこの方法によって解析され
た。一般に生体高分子では，共有結合による一次構造のほかに，van der Waals 結合，
イオン結合，水素結合等の弱い結合もあって，その決定も重要な問題となる。例えば，タ
ンパク質を弱火で熱しても，場合によっては常温に放置するだけで変性するのは，これら
の弱い結合による高次構造がくずれるからである。

LESSON 19
第十九課
K A N J I

価	563	KA		付	502	FU
	422				363	tsu(keru) tsu(ku)
飽	260b	HŌ		炉	219a	RO
	5162				2750	
環	274a	KAN		留	733	RYŪ
	2970				3003	to(meru) to(maru)
配	299	HAI		燃	690	NEN
	4779				2808	mo(yasu) mo(eru)
芳	211b	HŌ		料	531	RYŌ
	3907				3468	
香	228b	KŌ		樹	271a	JU
	5188	ka			2377	
族	455	ZOKU		脂	235a	SHI
	2090				3766	
紙	85	SHI		製	648	SEI
	3510	kami			4249	
白	37	HAKU		滴	262b	TEKI
	3095	shiro shiro(i)			2674	
触	259a	SHOKU		指	226	SHI
	4305	fu(reru)			1904	yubi

READING SELECTIONS

炭化水素	tanka-suiso	hydrocarbon
パラフィン	parafin	paraffin
シクロパラフィン	shikuro-parafin	cyclo-paraffin
満たす	mitasu	to satisfy
二重結合	nijū-ketsugō	double bond
三重結合	sanjū-ketsugō	triple bond
(不)飽和	(fu)hōwa	(un)saturated
オレフィン	orefin	olefin
エチレン系	echiren-kei	ethylene series

アセチレン系	asechiren-kei	acetylene series
環状に	kanjō ni	in a ring
配列する	hairetsu suru	to be arrayed, arranged
一つおきに	hitotsu-oki ni	every other one
芳香族の環	hōkō-zoku no kan	aromatic ring
その例	sono rei	examples of these
単結合	tan-ketsugō	single bond
本来の	honrai no	proper, normal
しいていえば	shiite ieba	one might say
炭素間	tanso-kan	carbon to carbon
隣り合った	tonari-atta	adjacent
それにもかかわらず	sore ni mo kakawarazu	in spite of that, nevertheless
便宜上	bengi-jō	as a convention, conventionally
交互に	kōgo ni	alternately
しるす	shirusu	to write down
習慣となる	shūkan to naru	become customary
どの…てもよい	dono...te mo yoi	it does not matter which...
…に示したとおり	...ni shimeshita tōri	as shown in...
紙	kami	paper
一平面	ichi-heimen	single plane
四面体	shimen-tai	tetrahedron
頂点	chōten	vertex
白金	hakkin	platinum
触媒	shokubai	catalyst
水素を化合させる	suiso o kagō saseru	to hydrogenate
付加反応	fuka-hannō	addition reaction
エタン	etan	ethane
ポリエチレン	pori-echiren	polyethylene
重合	jūgō	polymerization
原子価	genshi-ka	atomic valence
互いに飽和し合う	tagai ni hōwa shi-au	to saturate each other
化合する	kagō suru	to combine
付加重合	fuka-jūgō	addition polymerization
一般式	ippan-shiki	general formula
分子式	bunshi-shiki	molecular formula
異性体	isei-tai	isomers
石油化学	sekiyu-kagaku	petrochemistry
重油	jūyu	heavy oil
軽油	keiyu	light oil

反応炉	hannō-ro	reactor
分解する	bunkai suru	to decompose
プロパン	puropan	propane
プロピレン	puropiren	propylene
ブタン	butan	butane
ブチレン	buchiren	butylene
分解蒸留	bunkai-jōryū	destructive distillation
接触分解	sesshoku-bunkai	catalytic cracking
ガソリン	gasorin	gasoline
自動車	jidō-sha	automobile
航空機	kōkū-ki	airplane
燃料	nenryō	fuel
有機合成	yūki-gōsei	organic synthesis
中間	chūkan	intermediate
原料	genryō	raw materials
樹脂	jushi	resin
耐圧容器	taiatsu-yōki	pressure vessel
家庭の	katei no	household, domestic
液化する	ekika suru	to liquefy
つめる	tsumeru	to fill, store
コールタール	kōru-tāru	coal tar
ベンゼン	benzen	benzene
トルエン	toruen	toluene
製造する	seizō suru	to manufacture
合成化学	gōsei-kagaku	synthetic chemistry
一酸化炭素	issanka-tanso	carbon monoxide
アンモニア	anmonia	ammonia
都市	toshi	city
オイルガス	oiru-gasu	oil gas

種々の炭化水素　(3K 236–240)

<u>炭化水素の例</u>。炭化水素には，パラフィン炭化水素・シクロパラフィン炭化水素のほか，炭素の四つの原子価が4個の他原子によって満たされないで，二重結合＞C＝C＜や，三重結合 ―C≡C― のある炭化水素がある。

　二重結合・三重結合を不飽和結合といい，これらを含む炭化水素を不飽和炭化水素という。二重結合が一つあるものをオレフィン炭化水素（エチレン系炭化水素）といい，三重結合の一つあるものをアセチレン系炭化水素という。構造式を次にあげる。

$$H_2C=CH_2$$
（エチレン）

（プロピレン）

$$H-C\equiv C-H$$
（アセチレン）

また，6原子の炭素が環状 [1] に配列し， 一つおきに [2] 二重結合があるような構造を芳香族の環といい，これを分子中にもつ炭化水素を芳香族炭化水素という。次に示すものは，その例である。

（ベンゼン）

（トルエン）

（ナフタリン）

芳香族の環では，二重結合と単結合の本来の性質はなく，しいていえば，それらの結合の中間の性質をもっている。たとえば，ベンゼンでは，どの炭素間の結合も全く同じ性質の結合であるし，隣り合った炭素原子間の距離がどれも同じである。それにもかかわらず，便宜上 [3]，二重結合と単結合とを交互にしるして，芳香族の環の結合をあらわす習慣となっている。このようなわけであるから， どの炭素と炭素の間の結合から二重結合をしるし始めてもよい。種々の炭化水素の分子の形は，図1に示したとおりである。

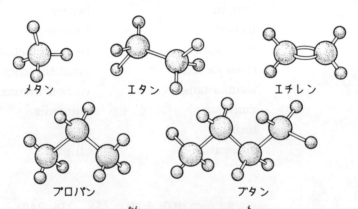

メタン　　　　エタン　　　　エチレン

プロパン　　　　　　ブタン

図1　簡単な炭化水素の分子模型

炭素原子から出る4個の結合の方向は，紙に書かれた構造式にあらわされているような一平面にあるのではなくて，四面体の中心からその頂点に向かって引いた直線の方向にある。 したがって， 二つの結合のなす角は109°28′である。

<u>飽和化合物と不飽和化合物</u>。二重結合や三重結合，すなわち，不飽和結合をもつ化合物を不飽和化合物という。エチレンやアセチレンに白金などを触媒として水素を化合させると，次のようにエタンができる。このように，不飽和化合物が他の分子と化合することを付加反応という。

これに対し，パラフィン炭化水素や，シクロパラフィン炭化水素は，不飽和結合を含まないので，飽和化合物という。エチレンは二重結合があるから，次のような付加反応もする。

（エチレン）　　　　　　　　　　　　　　　　　　　　　　　　　　　　　　（ポリエチレン）

一般に，同種の分子が2個以上互いに結合することを重合といい，同種の分子間で二重結合の原子価を互いに飽和し合い，多数の分子が化合することを付加重合という。

オレフィン炭化水素は C_nH_{2n} の一般式で示されるから，シクロパラフィン炭化水素と同じ分子式のものがある。たとえば，次に示すようなものである。

（シクロブタン）　　　　　　　　　　　（1-ブテン）

このように，違う物質が同じ分子式をもっているとき，これらの互いに違う物質を異性体という。

石油化学。重油・軽油などを，反応炉の中で高温で分解すると，ガソリン・水素や，分子の小さい炭化水素（メタン CH_4, エチレン C_2H_4, プロパン C_3H_8, プロピレン C_3H_6, ブタン C_4H_{10}, ブチレン C_4H_8 など）ができる。この方法を分解蒸留という。触媒を使ってこの反応を行なう方法を接触分解という。

ガソリンは自動車や航空機の燃料として使われ，これらの炭化水素からは，有機合成の中間原料や合成樹脂（たとえば，エチレンからポリエチレン）をつくる。プロパンとプロピレンは耐圧容器に液化してつめ，家庭燃料として使われる。ブタン・ブチレンも同様に使われる。これらを液化石油ガスという。コールタールから得られるベンゼン・トルエンなども，化学反応によって石油から製造できるようになった。一般に，石油を原料とする合成化学を石油化学という。

天然ガスや重油を酸素と高温で反応させると，水素と一酸化炭素が得られる。この水素をアンモニア合成に利用する。都市ガスに混ぜるために，重油を分解して製造するガスをオイルガスという。これは水素・メタン・エチレン・プロピレンなどを含んでいる。

塩基　　　　　　　　　　　　enki　　　　　　　　　　　　base

定量(分析)	teiryō (bunseki)	quantitative analysis
ピペット	pipetto	pipet (te)
うつす（移す）	utsusu	to transfer
滴下する	tekika suru	to titrate (but literally and in other contexts, to drip in, to add by drops)
中和する	chūwa suru	to neutralize
読みとる	yomi-toru	to take a reading
滴定	tekitei	titration
終点	shūten	end point
色素	shikiso	coloring matter
指示薬	shiji-yaku	indicator
容量分析	yōryō-bunseki	volumetric analysis
フェノールフタレイン	fenōru-futarein	phenolphthalein
メチルレッド	mechiru-reddo	methyl red

酸・塩基の定量　(3K 142)

　物質の存在量を測ることを定量という。酸の定量には，その酸の溶液の一定体積をピペットでとり，これを三角フラスコにうつし，これにビュレットから濃度のわかっている塩基の溶液を滴下し，ちょうど中和するまでに滴下した塩基の体積を読みとる。塩基の定量は，同じようにして酸の溶液を滴下して行なう。

　この方法を滴定という。滴定の終点，すなわち中和点を知るために，種々の色素溶液を用いる。これを指示薬という。滴定のように，体積を測る方法で定量することを容量分析という。

　酸が弱くて塩基が強いときには，指示薬にフェノールフタレインのアルコール溶液を用い，酸が強くて塩基が弱いときには，メチルレッド（またはメチルオレンジ）の水溶液を用いる。酸も塩基もともに強いときには，どちらの指示薬を用いてもよい[4]。

SHUJU NO TANKA-SUISO

Tanka-Suiso no Rei: Tanka-suiso ni wa parafin tanka-suiso, shikuro-parafin tanka-suiso no hoka, tanso no yottsu no genshi-ka ga yonko no ta-genshi ni yotte mitasarenai de, nijū-ketsugō >C=C< ya, sanjū-ketsugō −C≡C− no aru tanka-suiso ga aru.

　Nijū-ketsugō, sanjū-ketsugō o fu-hōwa-ketsugō to ii, korera o fukumu tanka-suiso o fu-hōwa-tanka-suiso to iu. Nijū-ketsugō ga hitotsu aru mono o orefin-tanka-suiso (echiren-kei-tanka-suiso) to ii, sanjū-ketsugō no hitotsu aru mono o asechiren-kei-tanka-suiso to iu. Kōzō-shiki o tsugi ni ageru.

$$H_2C=CH_2$$

(Echiren)

$$H_2C=CH-CH_3$$

(Puropiren)

$$H-C\equiv C-H$$

(Asechiren)

Mata, roku-genshi no tanso ga kanjō[1] ni hairetsu shi, hitotsu oki[2] ni nijū-ketsugō ga aru yō na kōzō o hōkō-zoku no kan to ii, kore o bunshi-chū ni motsu tanka-suiso o hōkō-zoku-tanka-suiso to iu. Tsugi ni shimesu mono wa sono rei de aru.

(Benzen)

(Toruen)

(Nafutarin)

Hōkō-zoku no kan de wa nijū-ketsugō to tan-ketsugō no honrai no seishitsu wa naku, shiite ieba, sorera no ketsugō no chūkan no seishitsu o motte iru. Tatoeba, benzen de wa, dono tanso-kan no ketsugō mo mattaku onaji seishitsu no ketsugō de aru shi, tonari-atta tanso-genshi-kan no kyori ga dore mo onaji de aru. Sore ni mo kakawarazu, bengi-jō,[3] nijū-ketsugō to tan-ketsugō to o kōgo ni shirushite, hōkō-zoku no kan no ketsugō o arawasu shūkan to natte iru. Kono yō na wake de aru kara, dono tanso to tanso no aida no ketsugō kara nijū-ketsugō o shirushi-hajimete mo yoi.

Shuju no tanka-suiso no bunshi no katachi wa zu-ichi ni shimeshita tōri de aru.

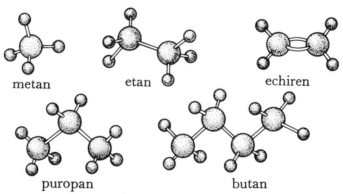

metan   etan   echiren

puropan   butan

Zu-1 *Kantan na Tanka-Suiso no Bunshi-Mokei.*

Tanso-genshi kara deru yon-ko no ketsugō no hōkō wa, kami ni kakareta kōzōshiki ni arawasarete iru yō na ichi-heimen ni aru no de wa nakute, shimen-tai no chūshin kara sono chōten ni mukatte hiita chokusen no hōkō ni aru. Shitagatte, futatsu no ketsugō no nasu kaku wa 109° 28' de aru.

Hōwa-kagōbutsu to Fu-hōwa-kagō-butsu: Nijū-ketsugō ya sanjū-ketsugō, sunawachi,

fu-hōwa-ketsugō o motsu kagō-butsu o fu-hōwa-kagō-butsu to iu. Echiren ya ase-chiren ni hakkin nado o shokubai to shite suiso o kagō saseru to, tsugi no yō ni etan ga dekiru. Kono yō ni, fu-hōwa-kagō-butsu ga ta no bunshi to kagō suru koto o fuka-hannō to iu.

$$\begin{array}{c}\text{H}\\ \text{H}\end{array}\!\!>\!\!\text{C}=\text{C}\!\!<\!\!\begin{array}{c}\text{H}\\ \text{H}\end{array}\ +\ \text{H}-\text{H} \longrightarrow \text{H}-\overset{\text{H}}{\underset{\text{H}}{\text{C}}}-\overset{\text{H}}{\underset{\text{H}}{\text{C}}}-\text{H} \longleftarrow \text{H}-\text{C}\equiv\text{C}-\text{H}\ +\ \begin{array}{c}\text{H}-\text{H}\\ \text{H}-\text{H}\end{array}$$

Kore ni taishi, parafin-tanka-suiso ya, shikuro-parafin-tanka-suiso wa, fu-hōwa-ketsugō o fukumanai no de, hōwa-kagō-butsu to iu.

Echiren wa nijū-ketsugō ga aru kara, tsugi no yō na fuka-hannō mo suru.

$$\begin{array}{c}\text{H}\\ \text{H}\end{array}\!\!>\!\!\text{C}=\text{C}\!\!<\!\!\begin{array}{c}\text{H}\\ \text{H}\end{array}\ +\ \begin{array}{c}\text{H}\\ \text{H}\end{array}\!\!>\!\!\text{C}=\text{C}\!\!<\!\!\begin{array}{c}\text{H}\\ \text{H}\end{array} \longrightarrow \left[-\overset{\text{H}}{\underset{\text{H}}{\text{C}}}-\overset{\text{H}}{\underset{\text{H}}{\text{C}}}-\ -\overset{\text{H}}{\underset{\text{H}}{\text{C}}}-\overset{\text{H}}{\underset{\text{H}}{\text{C}}}-\right] \longrightarrow \cdots-\overset{\text{H}}{\underset{\text{H}}{\text{C}}}-\overset{\text{H}}{\underset{\text{H}}{\text{C}}}-\overset{\text{H}}{\underset{\text{H}}{\text{C}}}-\overset{\text{H}}{\underset{\text{H}}{\text{C}}}-\cdots$$

(Echiren) (Pori-echiren)

Ippan ni, dōshu no bunshi ga niko-ijō tagai ni ketsugō suru koto o jūgō to ii, dōshu no bunshi-kan de nijū-ketsugō no genshi-ka o tagai ni hōwa shi-ai, tasū no bunshi ga kagō suru koto o fuka-jūgō to iu.

Orefin-tanka-suiso wa C_nH_{2n} no ippan-shiki de shimesareru kara, shikuro-parafin-tanka-suiso to onaji bunshi-shiki no mono ga aru. Tatoeba, tsugi ni shimesu yō na mono de aru.

$$\text{H}-\overset{\text{H}}{\underset{\underset{\text{H}}{|}}{\text{C}}}-\overset{\text{H}}{\underset{\text{H}}{\text{C}}}-\text{H}$$

(Shikuro-butan) (1-buten)

Kono yō ni, chigau busshitsu ga, onaji bunshi-shiki o motte iru toki, korera no tagai ni chigau busshitsu o isei-tai to iu.

Sekiyu Kagaku: Jūyu, keiyu nado o hannō-ro no naka de kōon de bunkai suru to, gasorin, suiso ya, bunshi no chiisai tanka-suiso (metan CH_4, echiren C_2H_4, puro-pan C_3H_8, puropiren C_3H_6, butan C_4H_{10}, buchiren C_4H_8 nado) ga dekiru. Kono hōhō o bunkai-jōryū to iu. Shokubai o tsukatte kono hannō o okonau hōhō o sesshoku-bunkai to iu. Gasorin wa jidōsha ya kōkū-ki no nenryō to shite tsuka-ware, korera no tanka-suiso kara wa, yūki-gōsei no chūkan-genryō ya gōsei-jushi (tatoeba, echiren kara pori-echiren) o tsukuru. Puropan to puropiren wa taiatsu-yōki ni ekika shite tsume, katei-nenryō to shite tsukawareru. Butan buchiren mo dōyō ni tsukawareru. Korera o ekika-sekiyu-gasu to iu.

Kōru-tāru kara erareru benzen, toruen nado mo, kagaku-hannō ni yotte, sekiyu kara seizō dekiru yō ni natta. Ippan ni, sekiyu o genryō to suru gōsei-kagaku o

sekiyu-kagaku to iu.

Tennen-gasu ya jūyu o sanso to kō-on de hannō saseru to, suiso to issanka-tanso ga erareru. Kono suiso o anmonia-gōsei ni riyō suru. Toshi-gasu ni mazeru tame ni, jūyu o bunkai shite seizō suru gasu o oiru-gasu to iu. Kore wa, suiso, metan, echiren, puropiren nado o fukunde iru.

SAN, ENKI NO TEIRYŌ

Busshitsu no sonzai-ryō o hakaru koto o teiryō to iu. San no teiryō ni wa, sono san no yōeki no ittei taiseki o pipetto de tori, kore o sankaku furasuko ni utsushi, kore ni byuretto kara nōdo no wakatte iru enki no yōeki o tekika shi, chōdo chūwa suru made ni tekika shita enki no taiseki o yomitoru. Enki no teiryō wa, onaji yō ni shite san no yōeki o tekika shite okonau.

Kono hōhō o tekitei to iu. Tekitei no shūten, sunawachi chūwa-ten o shiru tame ni, shuju no shikiso-yōeki o mochi-iru. Kore o shiji-yaku to iu. Tekitei no yō ni, taiseki o hakaru hōhō de teiryō suru koto o yōryō-bunseki to iu.

San ga yowakute enki ga tsuyoi toki ni wa, shiji-yaku ni fenōru-futarein no arukōru yōeki o mochi-i, san ga tsuyokute enki ga yowai toki ni wa, mechiru-reddo (mata wa mechiru-orenji) no sui-yōeki o mochi-iru. San mo enki mo tomo ni tsuyoi toki ni wa, dochira no shiji-yaku o mochi-ite mo yoi. [4]

THE VARIETIES OF HYDROCARBONS

Examples of Hydrocarbons: There are among the hydrocarbons, in addition to the paraffins and cyclo-paraffins, others which contain double bonds $>C=C<$ and triple bonds $-C\equiv C-$ in which the four valences of carbon atoms are not satisfied by four other atoms.

Double and triple bonds are called unsaturated bonds, and hydrocarbons which contain them are called unsaturated hydrocarbons. Those with a single double bond are called olefin hydrocarbons (the ethylene series), those with a single triple bond the acetylene series. Their structural formulas are given as follows.

(Ethylene)   (Propylene)   (Acetylene)

Moreover, the structure where 6 carbon-atoms are arranged in a ring with every other bond a double bond is called the aromatic ring, and hydrocarbons which carry this ring within their molecules are called aromatic hydrocarbons. The following are examples.

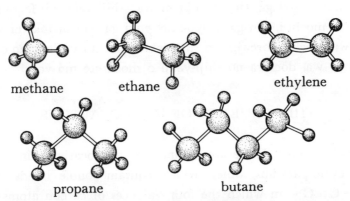

(Benzene)   (Toluene)   (Naphthalene)

The double and single bonds in the aromatic ring do not have their natural properties and we might say that their properties lie in between those of the two bonds. For example, all of the carbon to carbon bonds in benzene are bonds of completely similar characteristics, and the distances between adjacent carbon atoms are all the same. Nevertheless, as a convention, it has become customary to portray the bonds in an aromatic ring as alternating between single and double bonds. For this reason, it does not matter which carbon to carbon bond you initially designate as a double bond.

The shapes of various hydrocarbon molecules are as shown in Figure 1.

methane   ethane   ethylene

propane   butane

Figure 1 *Molecular Models of Simple Hydrocarbons.*

The directions of the four bonds which proceed from a carbon atom are not in a single plane as depicted by structural formulas written on paper. Rather they lie in the directions of the straight lines drawn from the center of a tetrahedron to its vertices. The angle between two bonds, therefore, is 109° 28′.

Saturated and Unsaturated Compounds: Compounds containing double and triple bonds, that is, unsaturated bonds, are called unsaturated compounds. If ethylene or acetylene are hydrogenated using platinum or some other catalyst, ethane is produced as shown below. Reactions in which unsaturated compounds combine with other molecules are called addition reactions.

In contrast, paraffin and cycloparaffin hydrocarbons, since they do not contain unsaturated bonds, are called saturated compounds.

Since ethylene has a double bond, it also performs the following addition reaction.

(Ethylene)   (Polyethylene)

In general, the mutual bonding of two or more molecules of the same kind is called polymerization, and the combining of many molecules such that the valences of their double bonds at the same molecular interval are mutually satisfied is called addition polymerization.

Since the olefin hydrocarbons are represented by the general equation C_nH_{2n} there are some which have the same molecular formula as cycloparaffin hydrocarbons. There is, for example, the following case.

(Cyclobutane)   (1-butene)

When different substances thus have the same molecular formula, these mutually differing substances are called isomers.

Petrochemistry: If substances such as heavy or light oils are decomposed in a reactor at high temperatures, gasoline, hydrogen and hydrocarbons with small molecules (methane CH_4, ethylene C_2H_4, propane C_3H_8, butane C_4H_{10}, butylene C_4H_8, for example) are produced. This method is called destructive distillation, and the method using a catalyst for the reaction is called catalytic cracking.

Gasolines are used as fuels for automobiles and airplanes, and from their hydrocarbons we produce intermediates for organic synthesis and synthetic resins (such as polyethylene from ethylene). Propane and propylene are liquefied and stored in pressure vessels for use as a domestic fuel. Butane and butylene are similarly used. These are called liquified petroleum gases.

Substances such as benzene and toluene which are obtained from coal tar can also now be produced from petroleum through chemical reactions. Synthetic chemistry using petroleum as raw material is called petrochemistry.

If natural gas or heavy oil is reacted with oxygen at high temperature, hydrogen and carbon monoxide are obtained. This hydrogen is employed in ammonia synthesis. Gas manufactured by decomposing heavy oil for mixing with city gas is

286 Comprehending Technical Japanese

called oil gas. It contains hydrogen, methane, ethylene, propylene and other hydro-carbons.

QUANTITATIVE ANALYSIS OF ACIDS AND BASES

Measuring amounts of substances present is called quantitative analysis. In the quantitative analysis of acids, a fixed volume of acid is taken by pipet and trans-ferred to an Erlenmeyer flask, to which an alkaline solution of known concentra-tion is added from a burette, and a reading taken of the volume of base titrated for exact neutralization. The quantitative analysis of a base is similarly conducted by titrating with an acid solution.

This procedure is called titration. In order to detect the end point of the titration, that is, the neutral point, various colored solutions called indicators are used. Quantitative analyses which, like titration, use volume measurements are called volumetric analyses.

With a weak acid and a strong base, an alcohol solution of phenolphthalein is used as indicator and, with a strong acid and a weak base, an aqueous solution of methyl red (or of methyl orange) is used. When both acid and base are strong, either indicator may be used.

EXPLANATORY NOTES

(1) kanjō   The suffix -jō (状) has the meaning of "-shaped", "having the form of", "-state".

kanjō no	環状の	ring-shaped
senjō no	線状の	linear
kyūjō no	球状の	globular
gomu-jō	ゴム状	rubbery state

(2) ...oki ni   Often oki ni is exactly equivalent to goto ni and is translated by "every."

jippun oki ni	every ten minutes
go-mētoru oki ni	every five meters
ichi-senchi oki ni	every centimeter

However with the number "one" oki ni, when applied to discrete rather than continuous systems, means "every other":

hitori oki ni	every other person
ichi-nichi oki ni	every other day
ichidai oki ni	every other vehicle

(3) bengi-jō   The suffix -jō (上) has the meaning of "from the view-point of," "as a (matter of)," "in".

Examples:

bengi-jō	便宜上	as a (matter of) convention
kagaku-jō	化学上	in chemistry
kōgyō-jō no	工業上の	in industrial problems
mondai ni	問題に	

(4) dochira no...mochi-ite mo yoi

"You may use either indicator." This should not be confused with the ... *te mo yoi* construction in Explanatory Note 4 of Lesson 11. Here the ... *te mo* is associated with the interrogative (Explanatory Note 1 of Lesson 18) and the meaning, therefore, is the same as ...*te yoi*, namely, "you may," without the nuance "if necessary" which is associated with ...*te mo yoi* without interrogative.

SUPPLEMENTARY READINGS

A. *Selections from Rikagaku Jiten*

ポリエステル	pori-esuteru	polyester
基	ki	radical
線状	senjō	linear
ビニル	biniru	vinyl
単量体	tanryō-tai	monomer
共重合	kyō-jūgō	copolymerization
熱硬化性	netsu-kōka-sei	thermo-setting
マレイン酸	marein-san	maleic acid
フマル酸	fumaru-san	fumaric acid
イタコン酸	itakon-san	itaconic acid
ジカルボン酸	ji-karubon-san	di-carboxylic acid
フタル酸	futaru-san	phthalic acid
アジピン酸	ajipin-san	adipic acid
ジオール	jiōru	diol
エチレングリコール	echiren-gurikōru	ethylene glycol
プロピレングリコール	puropiren-gurikōru	propylene glycol
スチレン	suchiren	styrene
フタル酸ジアリル	futaru-san-ji-ariru	diallyl phthalate
メタクリル酸メチル	metakuriru-san-mechiru	methyl methacrylate
黄色	ōshoku	yellow
禁止剤	kinshi-zai	inhibitor
開始剤	kaishi-zai	initiator
注型する	chūkei suru	to mold, pour into a mold
橋かけ反応	hashi-kake hannō	cross-linking reactions

不溶不融の	fuyō-fuyū no	insoluble and infusible
成形物	seikei-butsu	molding
成形する	seikei suru	to mold
利点	riten	advantage

不飽和ポリエステル樹脂　(3RJ 1163)

　不飽和基をもつ線状ポリエステルとビニル単量体との共重合によって得られる熱硬化性樹脂をいう。不飽和酸（マレイン酸，フマル酸，イタコン酸等）及びジカルボン酸（フタル酸，アジピン酸等）とジオール（エチレングリコール，プロピレングリコール等）とを100～200℃で反応させて不飽和基をもつポリエステルを作り，これにスチレン，フタル酸ジアリル，メタクリル酸メチル等の単量体を混合して溶液とする。これは一般に黄色粘性液体で，重合禁止剤を入れて保存した後，この樹脂に反応開始剤を加えて注型すると共重合橋かけ反応が起こり，不溶不融の成形物を得ることが出来る。低圧で成形できる利点をもつ。

芳香族化	hōkō-zoku-ka	aromatization
接触改質	sesshoku-kaishitsu	catalytic reforming
主体	shutai	primary substance, constituent
六員環	rokuin-kan	six membered ring
ナフテン	nafuten	naphthene
脱水素	dassuiso	dehydrogenation
五員環	goin-kan	five membered ring
環化	kanka	cyclization
諸反応	sho-hannō	various reactions
酸化モリブデン	sanka-moribuden	molybdenum oxide
促進する	sokushin suru	to accelerate

芳香族化反応　(3RJ 1258)

　各種炭化水素から芳香族炭化水素を生成する化学反応で，接触改質の主体をなす。六員環ナフテンの脱水素，五員環ナフテンの異性化と脱水素，パラフィンの脱水素，環化，および脱水素等の諸反応からなる。白金，酸化モリブデン等の触媒によって促進される。

高重合	kō-jūgō	high polymerization
低分子化合物	tei-bunshi-kagō-butsu	low molecular weight compound
脱離	datsuri	separation, coming off
重付加反応	jū-fuka-hannō	polyaddition reaction

付加重合　(3RJ 1426)

　高重合に同じ。高重合では低分子化合物の脱離を伴わずに反応が進行するので，その意味でこう呼ぶことがある。付加反応による重合（重付加）のことではない。

硫酸紙	ryūsan-shi	parchment paper
パーチメント紙	pāchimento-shi	parchment paper
羊皮	yōhi	sheepskin
模造品	mozō-hin	imitation
木材パルプ	mokuzai-parupu	wood pulp
綿ぼろ	wata-boro	waste cotton
濃硫酸	nō-ryūsan	concentrated sulfuric acid
膠化させる	kōka saseru	to gelatinize
水洗する	suisen suru	to wash with water
半透明	han-tōmei	translucent
耐水性	taisui-sei	waterproof
耐油性	taiyu-sei	oil-proof
バター	batā	butter
チーズ	chiizu	cheese
食品	shokuhin	foods
薬品	yakuhin	medicines, chemicals
包装	hōsō	packing, wrapping

硫　酸　紙　(3RJ 1139)

　パーチメント紙ともいう。羊皮紙すなわちパーチメントの模造品で，木材パルプから作った化学パルプ，あるいは綿ぼろパルプ等を原料として紙を作り，その紙を濃硫酸に浸して膠化させ，よく水洗する。半透明で耐水性，耐油性があるので，バター，チーズ等の食品，薬品包装に用いられる。

蒸留水	jōryū-sui	distilled water
脱塩	datsuen	removal of salts
精製する	seisei suru	to purify
比抵抗	hi-teikō	specific resistance
イオン交換	ion-kōkan	ion exchange
精密な	seimitsu na	precise
注射液	chūsha-eki	injection fluids
調製	chōsei	preparation, manufacture

蒸　留　水　(3RJ 646)

　蒸留によって脱塩精製した水。ふつうの蒸留で得た水は比抵抗 $2 \times 10^5 \Omega$cm 程度で，イ

オン交換樹脂により精製した純水の比抵抗 $10^6\Omega\mathrm{cm}$ より小さいが，特別の装置でくりかえし蒸留すれば $10^6\Omega\mathrm{cm}$ 程度になる。水溶液の電気伝導度の精密測定等にはこの程度の純水が必要なので，これを伝導水と呼ぶことがある。蒸留水は有機物等を含まないので，注射液，薬品の調製等に使用できる。

白金族	hakkin-zoku	platinum family
ルテニウム	ruteniumu	ruthenium
ロジウム	rojiumu	rhodium
パラジウム	parajiumu	palladium
オスミウム	osumiumu	osmium
イリジウム	irijiumu	iridium

白金族元素　(3RJ 1032)

周期表 VIII 族に属する元素のうち，ルテニウム Ru, ロジウム Rh, パラジウム Pd, オスミウム Os, イリジウム Ir, および白金 Pt の 6 元素をいう。

B.	原子炉	genshi-ro	nuclear reactor
	核分裂	kaku-bunretsu	fission
	連鎖	rensa	chain
	制御する	seigyo suru	to control
	Fermiら (＝Fermi 等)	Fermi-ra	Fermi et al.
	大学構内	daigaku-kōnai	university campus
	成功する	seikō suru	to succeed
	パイル	pairu	pile
	ウラン	uran	uranium
	プルトニウム	purutoniumu	plutonium
	濃縮ウラン	nōshuku uran	concentrated uranium
	ひきおこす	hiki-okosu	to cause, bring about
	どの…かに応じて	dono...ka ni ōjite	in accordance with the kind of...
	高速中性子	kōsoku-chūsei-shi	fast neutron
	熱中性子	netsu-chūsei-shi	thermal neutron
	減速材	gensoku-zai	a moderator
	一様な	ichiyō na	uniform
	(非)均質炉	(hi)kinshitsu-ro	(non) homogeneous reactor
	つまり	tsumari	in other words, that is
	炉心	roshin	reactor core
	逃げ出す	nige-dasu	to escape
	防ぐ	fusegu	to prevent
	グラファイト	gurafaito	graphite

ベリリウム	beririumu	beryllium
コンクリート	konkuriito	concrete
遮蔽	shahei	shield
運転制御	unten-seigyo	operation and control
停止	teishi	stopping
制御棒	seigyo-bō	control rods
冷却材	reikyaku-zai	coolant
動力源	dōryoku-gen	power sources
動力炉	dōryoku-ro	power reactor
…用	…yō	for use in…
材料	zairyō	materials
推進	suishin	propulsion, drive
生産	seisan	production
アイソトープ	aisotōpu	isotopes
医療	iryō	medical treatment
消費する	shōhi suru	to consume
新しい	atarashii	new
生み出す	umi-dasu	to produce
増殖炉	zōshoku-ro	breeder reactor

原 子 炉 (3RJ 419)

　核分裂連鎖反応を制御しながら続けさせることができるようにした装置。1942年12月2日，E. Fermi らによってアメリカのシカゴ大学構内で初めて成功した CP-1 が最初のものである。この構造から，初期にはパイルと呼ばれていた。原子炉の燃料として用いられる核分裂性物質には，ウラン，プルトニウムなどがある。ウランは天然ウランを用いることもあるし，濃縮ウランを用いることもある。核分裂の連鎖反応が主としてどのような運動エネルギーの中性子によってひきおこされるかに応じて，高速中性子炉，中速中性子炉，熱中性子炉に分けることができる。核分裂で生じた中性子は高速中性子であるから，熱中性子炉では減速材を配置して中性子の弾性衝突により熱エネルギーまで減速する。減速材と燃料との配置が一様であるかどうかによって，均質炉と非均質炉とに分けられる。燃料と減速材のある部分，つまり核分裂連鎖反応が実際に行なわれる部分を炉心とよぶ。多くの場合，炉心のまわりには，中性子が外に逃げ出すのを防ぐために，グラファイトまたベリリウムなどの反射体をおく。またその外側には，原子炉で発生する強い放射線を吸収させるために，コンクリートなどで作った厚い遮蔽の壁がある。原子炉の運転制御や停止は，ふつう制御棒によって行なわれる。原子炉を運転しているときは，核分裂によって多量のエネルギーが放出されるから，高出力で運転するには燃料のまわりに冷却材を通して熱を原

子炉の外に取り出す。その熱を動力源として用いるのが動力炉である。原子炉はその目的によって，研究用・原子炉試験用・材料試験用・発電用・推進機関用・プルトニウム生産用・アイソトープ生産用・医療用などに区別することができる。消費される燃料以上に新しく燃料が生み出される構造のものを増殖炉という。

FINAL TRANSLATION TEST

脂肪族，芳香族，高分子化合物などは，石油および天然ガスを原料とする，いわゆる石油化学製品である。日本の石油化学工業は，ナフサを最も基本的な原料とし，これを分解加熱炉で水蒸気とともに加熱して，エチレン，プロピレン等のオレフィン系不飽和炭化水素，メタン，エタン等のパラフィン系飽和炭化水素，ブタジエン等のジオレフィン系炭化水素等に分解する。分解されたガスは，凝縮，滴下，吸収，蒸発の過程をくりかえして，メタン，水素，プロパン，ブタン，エタンをとり，エチレンを取り出すが，ここまでのプロセスは，燃料としての石油を得るための石油精製工業である。

エチレンは，これを 1000 気圧以上まで圧縮して，管状炉内で 200-270°C の反応温度で重合させてポリエチレンを作り出す。この工程は付加価値が高く，企業にとって非常に有利なものとなっている。

エチレンはまた，ベンゾールを加えてスチレンモノマーとし，スチロール樹脂，ポリスチレン，SBR 等の原料とする。その他，空気酸化によって酸化エチレンとし，界面活性剤として用いられる。また，エチレンそのものも塩化ビニール用のエチレンジクロライド製造用や過酸化水素用に用いられる。

ナフサの分解油からペンタンをのぞき，接触分解や接触改質などによって，ベンゼン，トルエン，キシレン等の炭素環式化合物が製造され，このベンゾールが前述のエチレンからスチレンモノマーを製造する工程に使われる。このように，石油化学工業においては，製油所からおくられて来たナフサを分解し，それから作られた中間体が結集する工場間を結ぶパイプによって供給され，それぞれ別個の企業が，最終製品の製造を行なっている。このような石油化学集団は，通常石油化学コンビナートとよばれている。コンビナートは，多くの関連工場を近接して配置し，各工場をパイプによって連結するという利点がある反面，工場からの排出物による種々の問題をひき起こしている。多くの製紙工場や製鉄工場がかたまっている地方でも同種の問題が発生し，最近の白書に見られるように，その解決がなくては石油化学工業の発展がのぞまれないことが指摘されている。

LESSON 20
第二十課

KANJI

繊	274a	SEN	
	3607		
維	263a	I	
	3552		
械	360	KAI	
	2264		
薬	521	YAKU	
	4074	kusuri	
品	311	HIN	
	923		
虫	114	CHŪ	
	4115	mushi	
食	253	SHOKU	
	5154	ku(u) ta(beru)	
室	232	SHITSU	
	1300		
織	644	SHIKI, SHOKU	
	3613	o(ru)	
業	380	GYŌ	
	143		

材	403	ZAI	
	2189		
乳	213a	NYŪ	
	266	chichi	
黄	214	Ō KŌ	
	5399	ki	
乾	237a	KAN	
	784		
較	259b	KAKU	
	4623		
染	224b	SEN	
	2240	{so(meru) {so(maru)	
洗	225a	SEN	
	2551	ara(u)	
黒	80	KOKU	
	5403	kuro kuro(i)	
青	36	SHŌ, SEI	
	5076	ao ao(i)	
論	881	RON	
	4391		

READING SELECTION

合成繊維	gōsei-sen'i	synthetic fibers
ゴム	gomu	rubber
特徴	tokuchō	(distinctive) feature, characteristic
細長い	hoso-nagai	long and slender
機械的に	kikai-teki ni	mechanically
じょうぶな	jōbu na	strong, hardy
しわがよりにくい	shiwa ga yori-nikui	difficult to wrinkle
水を吸う	mizu o suu	to absorb water

かわきやすい	kawaki-yasui	easy to dry
薬品に強い	yakuhin ni tsuyoi	resistant to chemicals
虫に食われる	mushi ni kuwareru	to be eaten by insects
衣料	iryō	clothing
室内装飾	shitsunai-sōshoku	interior decorating
…用	…yō	for use in…
織物	orimono	woven fabrics
いすの上張り	isu no uwabari	chair coverings
工業資材	kōgyō-shizai	industrial materials
ろ布	rofu	cloth
漁網	gyomō	fishing net
ナイロン	nairon	Nylon
アジピン酸	ajipin-san	adipic acid
ヘキサメチレンジアミン	hekisa-mechiren-jiamin	hexamethylene diamine
(縮)重合	(shuku)jūgō	(condensation) polymerization
カプロラクタム	kapurorakutamu	caprolactam
テレフタル酸	terefutaru-san	terephthalic acid
グリコール	gurikōru	glycol
交互に	kōgo ni	alternately
エステル	esuteru	ester
つながる	tsunagaru	to be joined together
熱帯地方	nettai-chihō	the tropics
栽培する	saibai suru	to cultivate
パラゴムノキ	paragomu no ki	Hevea brasiliensis
樹液	jueki	sap
乳液	nyūeki	milky liquid
ラテックス	ratekkusu	latex
微粒子	bi-ryūshi	tiny particles
分散する	bunsan suru	to be dispersed
凝固する	gyōko suru	to coagulate
分かれる	wakareru	to separate
生ゴム	nama-gomu	raw rubber
黄かっ色	kō-kasshoku	yellow-brown
半透明な	han-tōmei na	translucent
かたい	katai	hard, tough
粘りけが出る	nebari-ke ga deru	to become viscous
徐々に	jojo ni	gradually
イオウ	iō	sulfur
練る	neru	to knead

伸び縮みする	nobi-chijimi suru	to be flexible
弾性がつく	dansei ga tsuku	becomes elastic
橋	hashi	bridge
すべり合う	suberi-au	to slide past one another
加硫	karyū	vulcanization
促進する	sokushin suru	to accelerate, promote
製品	seihin	manufactured objects
エボナイト	ebonaito	ebonite, hard rubber
乾留	kanryū	dry distillation
イソプレン	isopuren	isoprene
放置する	hōchi suru	to leave alone
まねる	maneru	to imitate
比較的（たやすく）	hikaku-teki(tayasuku)	relatively (easily)
ブタジエン	butajien	butadiene
クロロプレン	kuroropuren	chloroprene
今日では	konnichi de wa	today
スチレン	suchiren	styrene
アクリロニトリル	akuriro-nitoriru	acrylonitrile
いっしょに	issho ni	together
耐油性	taiyu-sei	oil resistant property
耐摩耗性	tai-mamō-sei	abrasion resistant property
天然品	tennen-hin	natural products
すぐれた	sugureta	superior, outstanding
自由な	jiyū na	voluntary, optional
染めてない	somete nai	undyed
もちよる	mochi-yoru	to collect together
ヨウ素	yōso	iodine
ヨウ化カリウム	yōka-kariumu	potassium iodide
鑑別する	kanbetsu suru	to discriminate, distinguish
抜く	nuku	remove
四塩化炭素	shi-enka-tanso	carbon tetrachloride
新しい	atarashii	new, fresh
かわかす	kawakasu	to dry
溶かす	tokasu	to dissolve
ビーカー	biikā	beaker
洗う	arau	to wash
ビニロン	biniron	Vinylon
ビスコースレーヨン	bisukōsu-rēyon	viscose rayon
銅アンモニアレーヨン	dō-anmonia-rēyon	cupro-ammonium rayon

羊毛	yōmō	wool
アセテート	asetēto	acetate
補充	hojū	supplementary
結論	ketsuron	conclusion
高分子	kō-bunshi	macromolecule
多種多様の	tashu-tayō no	wide variety
日常生浩において	nichijō-seikatsu ni oite	in every day life
プラスチック(ス)	purasuchikku(su)	plastic, plastics
加工する	kakō suru	to process
経験	keiken	experience
長年にわたって	naganen ni watatte	over many years
開発する	kaihatsu suru	to develop
生産過程	seisan-katei	production processes
理論的に	riron-teki ni	theoretically
解明する	kaimei suru	to elucidate
充分（＝十分）な	jūbun na	sufficient
成果	seika	result
収める	osameru	to obtain, harvest, achieve
適用する	tekiyō suru	to apply
溶融高分子	yōyū-kō-bunshi	polymer melt
粘弾性	nendan-sei	viscoelastic
発展	hatten	development
高度に	kōdo ni	extensively

合成繊維と合成ゴム　(3K 281–285)

<u>合成繊維の特徴</u>。合成樹脂のうち，細長い分子から成るものは，糸に引いて，合成繊維としても利用される。合成繊維は，一般に機械的にじょうぶで，しわがよりにくく，水を吸わなくてかわきやすいものが多く，薬品[1]にも強い。また，虫に食われることもない。衣料のほかに，室内装飾用[2]織物，いすの上張り，化学工場などの工業資材（たとえばろ布）や漁網などに使われる。

<u>合成繊維の例</u>。ナイロン66は，アジピン酸 $HOOC \cdot (CH_2)_4 \cdot COOH$ とヘキサメチレンジアミン $H_2N(CH_2)_6NH_2$ とを縮重合させたもので，次の構造をもっている。

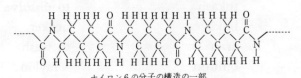

ナイロン6の分子の構造の一部

ナイロン6はカプロラクタムの重合ででき，次の構造をもち，ナイロン66と似ている。

ナイロン66の分子の構造の一部

ポリテレフタル酸エチレンはテレフタル酸 HOOC·C₆H₄·COOH とエチレングリコール HOCH₂·CH₂OH とが，交互にエステルをつくって長くつながったもので，次の構造をもっている。

ポリテレフタル酸エチレン分子の構造の一部

天然ゴム。熱帯地方で栽培されているパラゴムノキの樹液からとった乳液をラテックスという。これは，ゴム炭化水素(C₅H₈)n の微粒子が水に分散しているものである[3]。

　ラテックスに酸を加えると，ゴム質の微粒子は集まって凝固し[4]，液から分かれる。これが生ゴムである。これは，黄かっ色半透明で，低温ではかたく，温度が高いと粘りけが出る。空気中の酸素によって徐々に酸化される。

ゴムの分子の構造の一部

　生ゴムにイオウ3〜10% を混ぜてよく練り，140°C ぐらいに熱すると，性質が変わってよく伸び縮みする弾性がつき，また，化学的にも機械的にも強くなる。イオウの原子がゴム分子に化合して，長いゴム分子とゴム分子との間に橋をかけたような構造をつくるために，外から力が加わっても，分子が自由にすべり合わなくなり[5]，動くことがなくなる[5]からであると考えられている[6]。ゴムにイオウを化合させる操作を加硫という。この加硫を促進させたり，製品の強さを増したりするために[7]，種々の物質を加える。ゴムにイオウを40%ほど加えて熱すると，エボナイトができる。これは，かたくて薬品にも強く，電気絶縁性がよい。

合成ゴム。天然ゴムを乾留[8]するとイソプレンができ，逆にイソプレンを放置するとゴムのような物質に変化する。この変化をまねてゴムの合成が研究された。イソプレンに似た

構造をもち，比較的たやすくつくられるブタジエンやクロロプレンを原料として付加重合させて合成ゴムをつくる。

今日では，ブタジエンにスチレン $C_6H_5 \cdot CH = CH_2$ やアクリロニトリル $CH_2 = CH \cdot C \equiv N$ などを加えて，いっしょに付加重合させる。このようにして，耐油性[9]・耐熱性・耐摩耗性などの点で，天然品よりもすぐれた合成ゴムもつくられるようになった。また，イソプレンからも合成ゴムがつくられている。

自由研究。染めてない[10]繊維をもちより，ヨウ素ヨウ化カリウム溶液によって鑑別しよう。初めに，次のように繊維から油を抜いておく。繊維0.1gほどを四塩化炭素20ccに浸して，室温で約2時間放置し，ときどきかき混ぜる。次に新しい四塩化炭素に約30分浸した後，空気中でかわかす。

ヨウ化カリウムの飽和水溶液10ccにヨウ素2gを溶かしてヨウ素ヨウ化カリウム溶液をつくれ。この溶液に油を抜いた繊維を1分間浸して取り出し，ビーカーに入れた水に浸し，約6分間かき混ぜてよく洗う。繊維を取り出して，空気中でかわかす。種々の繊維は，次のような色に染まる。

　　　黒…ナイロン66, ナイロン6, ポリアクリロニトリル繊維

　　　青…ビニロン，ビスコースレーヨン，銅アンモニアレーヨン

　　　黄…羊毛，絹，アセテート繊維

　　　染まらないもの…その他の繊維

結論。高分子材料は多種多様の化学的，機械的および電気的性質をもったものがあるので，工業的にも，また日常生活においても重要な材料である。これら高分子物質あるいはプラスチックを加工する方法は，実際の経験によって長年にわたって開発されてきたが，生産過程における高分子物質の流れを理論的に解明することについては，まだ充分な成果が収められていない。これは，高分子溶液や溶融高分子が非ニュートン流体であるからである。粘弾性流体の力学に関する理論は最近急速に発展したが，これを工業上の問題に適用しょうとすると，高速計算機を高度に使用することが必要になってくるのである。

GŌSEI-SEN'I TO GŌSEI-GOMU

Gōsei-sen'i no Tokuchō: Gōsei-jushi no uchi, hoso-nagai bunshi kara naru mono wa, ito ni hiite, gōsei-sen'i to shite mo riyō sareru.

　Gōsei-sen'i wa, ippan ni kikai-teki ni jōbu de, shiwa ga yori-nikuku, mizu o suwanakute kawaki-yasui mono ga ōku, yakuhin[1] ni mo tsuyoi. Mata, mushi ni kuwareru koto mo nai. Iryō no hoka ni shitsunai sōshoku-yō[2] orimono, isu no uwabari, kagaku-kōjō nado no kōgyō-shizai (tatoeba rofu) ya gyomō nado ni tsukawareru.

Gōsei-sen'i no Rei: Nairon rokujū-roku wa, ajipin-san $HOOC \cdot (CH_2)_4 \cdot COOH$ to

hekisa-mechiren-jiamin $H_2N(CH_2)_6NH_2$ to o shuku-jūgō saseta mono de, tsugi no kōzō o motte iru.

(Nairon 66 no bunshi no kōzō no ichibu)

Nairon roku wa kapurorakutamu no jūgō de deki, tsugi no kōzō o mochi, nairon rokujū-roku to nite iru.

(Nairon-roku no bunshi no kōzō no ichibu)

Pori-terefutaru-san-echiren wa terefutaru-san $HOOC \cdot C_6H_4 \cdot COOH$ to echiren-gurikōru $HOCH_2 \cdot CH_2OH$ to ga, kōgo ni esuteru o tsukutte nagaku tsunagatta mono de, tsugi no kōzō o motte iru.

(Pori-terefutaru-san-echiren bunshi no kōzō no ichibu)

Tennen-gomu: Nettai-chihō de saibai sarete iru paragomu-no-ki no jueki kara totta nyūeki o ratekkusu to iu. Kore wa, gomu-tanka-suiso $(C_5H_8)_n$ no bi-ryūshi ga mizu ni bunsan shite iru mono de aru. [3]

Ratekkusu ni san o kuwaeru to, gomu-shitsu no bi-ryūshi wa atsumatte gyōko shi, [4] eki kara wakareru. Kore ga nama-gomu de aru. Kore wa, kō-kasshoku han-tōmei de, teion de wa kataku, ondo ga takai to nebari-ke ga deru. Kūki-chū no sanso ni yotte jojo ni sanka sareru.

(Gomu no bunshi no kōzō no ichibu)

Nama-gomu ni iō san kara jū-pāsento (san naishi jū-pāsento) o mazete yoku neri, hyaku-yonjū-do gurai ni nessuru to, seishitsu ga kawatte yoku nobi-chijimi suru dansei ga tsuki, mata, kagaku-teki ni mo kikai-teki ni mo tsuyoku naru. Iō

no genshi ga gomu-bunshi ni kagō shite, nagai gomu-bunshi to gomu-bunshi to no aida ni hashi o kaketa yō na kōzō o tsukuru tame ni, soto kara chikara ga kuwawatte mo, bunshi ga jiyū ni suberi-awanaku nari, [5] ugoku koto ga naku naru [5] kara de aru to kangaerarete iru. [6] Gomu ni iō o kagō saseru sōsa o karyū to iu. Kono karyū o sokushin sasetari, seihin no tsuyosa o mashitari suru tame ni, [7] shuju no busshitsu o kuwaeru. Gomu ni iō o yonjū-pāsento hodo kuwaete nessuru to, ebonaito ga dekiru. Kore wa, katakute yakuhin ni mo tsuyoku, denki-zetsuen-sei ga yoi.

Gōsei-gomu: Tennen-gomu o kanryū [8] suru to isopuren ga deki, gyaku ni isopuren o hōchi suru to gomu no yō na busshitsu ni henka suru. Kono henka o manete gomu no gōsei ga kenkyū sareta.

Isopuren ni nita kōzō o mochi, hikaku-teki tayasuku tsukurareru butajien ya kuroropuren o genryō to shite fuka-jūgō sasete gōsei gomu o tsukuru.

Konnichi de wa, butajien ni suchiren $C_6H_5 \cdot CH=CH_2$ ya akurironitoriru $CH_2=CH \cdot C \equiv N$ nado o kuwaete, issho ni fuka-jūgō saseru. Kono yō ni shite, taiyu-sei, [9] tainetsu-sei, tai-mamō-sei nado no ten de, tennen-hin yori mo sugureta gōsei-gomu mo tsukurareru yō ni natta. Mata isopuren kara mo gōsei-gomu ga tsukurarete iru.

Jiyū Kenkyū: Somete nai [10] sen'i o mochi-yori, yōso yōka-kariumu yōeki ni yotte kanbetsu shiyō.

Hajime ni, tsugi no yō ni sen'i kara abura o nuite oku. Sen'i rei-ten-ichi guramu hodo o shi-enka-tanso nijū-shii-shii ni hitashite, shitsuon de yaku ni-jikan hōchi shi, tokidoki kakimazeru. Tsugi ni, atarashii shi-enka-tanso ni yaku sanjippun hitashita nochi, kūki-chū de kawakasu.

Yōka kariumu no hōwa-sui-yōeki jū-shii-shii ni yōso ni-guramu o tokashite yōso-yōka-kariumu yōeki o tsukure. Kono yōeki ni abura o nuita sen'i o ippun-kan hitashite tori-dashi, biikā ni ireta mizu ni hitashi, yaku roppun-kan kaki-mazete yoku arau. Sen'i o tori-dashite, kūki-chū de kawakasu. Shuju no sen'i wa, tsugi no yō na iro ni somaru.

      Kuro......nairon rokujū-roku, nairon roku, pori-akuriro-nitoriru sen'i

      Ao......biniron, bisukōsu-rēyon, dō-anmonia-rēyon

      Ki......yōmō, kinu, asetēto sen'i

      Somaranai mono......sono ta no sen'i

Ketsuron: Kō-bunshi-zairyō wa tashu-tayō no kagaku-teki, kikai-teki, oyobi denki-teki seishitsu o motta mono ga aru no de, kōgyō-teki ni mo, mata nichijō–seikatsu ni oite mo jūyō na zairyō de aru. Korera kō-bunshi-busshitsu aruiwa purasuchikku o kakō suru hōhō wa, jissai no keiken ni yotte naganen ni watatte kaihatsu sarete kita ga, seisan-katei ni okeru kō-bunshi-busshitsu no nagare o riron-teki ni kaimei suru koto ni tsuite wa mada jūbun na seika ga osamerarete inai. Kore wa, kō-bunshi yōeki ya yōyū-kō-bunshi ga hi-Nyūton ryūtai de aru kara de aru.

Nendan-sei ryūtai no rikigaku ni kansuru riron wa saikin kyūsoku ni hatten shita ga, kore o kōgyō-jō no mondai ni tekiyō shiyō to suru to, kōsoku-keisan-ki o kōdo ni shiyō suru koto ga hitsuyō ni natte kuru no de aru.

SYNTHETIC FIBERS AND SYNTHETIC RUBBER

Characteristics of Synthetic Fibers: Some synthetic resins are made of long slender molecules which may be drawn out into threads and used as synthetic fibers. Synthetic fibers generally exhibit good mechanical strength, resist wrinkling, and dry readily since they do not absorb water. They are also resistant to chemicals and are not attacked by insects. They are used not only for clothing but also for woven fabrics in interior decorating, for chair coverings, as industrial materials in chemical and other factories (cloth, for example), in fishing nets, and in other ways.

Examples of Synthetic Fibers: Nylon 66, a synthetic made by the condensation polymerization of adipic acid and hexamethylene diamine, has the following structure:

(A Portion of the Structure of a Nylon 66 Molecule)

Nylon 6 is made by the polymerization of caprolactam; it resembles Nylon 66 and has the following structure:

(A Portion of the Structure of a Nylon 6 Molecule)

Polyethylene terephthalate is a long-chain substance formed by the alternating esterification of terephthalic acid and ethylene glycol and has the following structure:

(A Portion of the Structure of a Polyethylene Terephthalate Molecule)

Natural Rubber:

$$CH_3 \quad H \qquad\qquad CH_3 \quad H$$
$$H \; H \quad C=C \quad H\,H \quad H\,H \quad C=C \quad H\,H \quad H\,H$$
$$C-C \qquad C-C \qquad C-C \qquad C-\!-\!-$$
$$-\!-\!-\!/ \quad H\,H \quad H\,H \quad C=C \quad H\,H \quad H\,H \quad C=C$$
$$CH_3 \quad H \qquad\qquad CH_3 \quad H$$

(A Portion of the Structure of a Rubber Molecule)

The liquid obtained from the sap of the rubber tree (Hevea brasiliensis), which is cultivated in the tropics, is called latex. It is an aqueous dispersion of tiny particles of the rubber hydrocarbon $(C_5H_8)\,n$.

If we acidify the latex, the particles of rubbery material coagulate and separate from the liquid. This is raw rubber. It is yellowish brown and translucent, hard at low temperatures, and viscous at high temperatures. It is gradually oxidized by the oxygen in the air.

If we mix 3—10 % of sulfur with the raw rubber, knead it well, and then heat it to 140°C, its properties change. It becomes a highly flexible elastic material, which is also mechanically strong and chemically resistant. It is thought that this comes about because the sulfur atoms combine with the rubber molecules to form a bridge-like structure between the long rubber molecules, so that the molecules no longer slide freely over one another and are immobilized, even when external forces are applied. The operation which chemically combines sulfur and rubber is called vulcanization. Various materials are added to accelerate the vulcanization and to increase the strength of the fabricated products. If as much as 40% sulfur is added to the rubber and (the resulting mixture) heated, then ebonite is obtained. This is a strong substance, resistant to chemicals, and a good electrical insulator.

Synthetic Rubber: If natural rubber is dry-distilled, isoprene is obtained; conversely, if isoprene is allowed to stand, it changes into a material akin to rubber. By following the example of this (chemical) change, the synthesis of rubber was investigated.

Synthetic rubbers are prepared by addition polymerization using starting materials, such as butadiene and chloroprene, which have structures similar to isoprene and are relatively easy to prepare.

At present, addition polymerization is carried out by adding substances like styrene and acrylonitrile to butadiene. In this way synthetic rubbers are now made which are superior to natural rubbers in their oil, heat, and abrasion resistance. Synthetic rubber is also made from isoprene.

Optional Research: Collect some undyed fibers and try to distinguish among them by means of an iodine-potassium iodide solution.

First, remove the oil from the fiber in the following way. Immerse about 0.1g of fiber in 20cc of CCl_4 and leave it for about 2 hours at room temperature, stirring occasionally. Then, after soaking the fiber in fresh CCl_4 for about thirty minutes, dry it in air.

Prepare a solution of iodine and potassium iodide by dissolving 2g of iodine in 10cc of a saturated aqueous solution of potassium iodide. Soak the oil-free fibers in this solution for 1 miunte, remove them and wash them by putting them into a beaker of water and stirring for about 6 minutes. Then take them out and dry them in the air. The various fibers will then be dyed with the following colors:

> Black......Nylon 66, Nylon 6, and Polyacrylonitrile Fibers
> Blue......Vinylon, Viscose and Copper-Ammonium Rayons
> Yellow......Wool, Silk, and Acetate Fibers

Other fibers will not be dyed.

Conclusion: Macromolecular materials are important in industry and daily life because they have a wide variety of chemical, mechanical, and electrical properties. Methods of processing polymers and plastics have been developed by practical experience over many years, but theoretical treatments of the flow of polymers in industrial systems have not yet been very successful. This is because polymer solutions and polymer melts are non – Newtonian fluids. Theories for viscoelastic fluid mechanics have developed rapidly in recent years, but their application to industrial problems requires the extensive use of high speed computers.

EXPLANATORY NOTES

(1) yakuhin	In this context *yakuhin* means "chemicals" in general. Usually, however, *yakuhin* is used in the narrower sense of "drugs" or "medicines."
(2) shitsunai-sōshoku-yō	The suffix *-yō* means "for use in..." Some examples: *katei-yō* 家庭用 for household use *kagaku-bunseki-yō-shiji-yaku* 化学分析用指示薬 an indicator for use in chemical analysis *shashin-firumu-yō-shikiso* 写真フィルム用色素 pigment for photographic film
(3) Kore wa...de aru	Literally: "This is a material (for which) the tiny particles of hydrocarbon rubber are dispersed in water."
(4) Gyōko shi	Note that *gyōko suru* may mean either to coagulate or to solidify or freeze (e.g. *gyōko-ten*) depending on

the context.

(5) suberi-awanaku naru; ugoku koto ga naku naru

To understand these constructions note how they may be built up:

suberi-au	to slide past one another
suberi-awanai	not to slide past one another
suberi-awanaku naru	to get into a state of not being able to slide past one another.

Similarly:

ugoku koto ga aru	they sometimes move
ugoku koto ga nai	they never move
ugoku koto ga naku naru	they get into a state of never moving (i.e., they become immobilized)

(6) ...kara de aru to kangaerarete iru

Literally: "It is thought that it is because..." A somewhat smoother translation might be: "It is thought that this comes about because..."

(7) tame ni

Here *tame ni* means "for the sake of" whereas two sentences earlier *tame ni* meant "because" or "owing to the fact that."

(8) kanryū

"Dry distillation". Some other separation processes are:

(水蒸気)蒸留	(sui-jōki) jōryū	(steam) distillation
抽 出	chūshutsu	extraction
浸 出	shinshutsu	leaching
乾 燥	kansō	drying
ロ 過	roka	filtration

(9) taiyu-sei
tainetsu-sei
tai-mamō-sei

The prefix *tai-* (耐) means "resistant to..." Other examples are:

tai-yakuhin-sei	耐薬品性	chemical resistance
taikō-sei no	耐光性の	light fast, sunproof
taika-butsu	耐火物	refractories
tai-arukōru-sei	耐アルコール性	alcohol resistance

(10) somete nai

Somete nai is the negative counterpart of *somete aru* (for the *-te aru* construction see Explanatory Note No. 4 in Lesson 12.)

somete iru	we are dyeing
somete inai	we are not dyeing
somete aru	it is dyed
somete nai	it is not dyed

CONSTRUCTION EXAMPLES

| …ために | "for the sake of…", "because of…" |

1. ゴムの弾性を増し，化学的機械的性質を向上するために加硫する。

2. 高分子化合物は，その極めて大きな分子量のために，溶媒に溶けにくく，溶けたものはコロイド状態になる。

向上する	kōjō suru	to improve

| …なくなる | See Explanatory Note No. 4. |

1. 多くのタンパク質の溶液は，熱すると凝固して，ふたたび溶かすことができなくなる。

2. 炭素のコロイド溶液にニカワを加えると，電解質を加えても凝析しなくなる。

タンパク質	tanpaku-shitsu	protein
ニカワ	nikawa	glue
凝析する	gyōseki suru	to coagulate

| …からである | See Explanatory Note No. 5. |

1. デンプンに希酸を加えて熱するとヨウ素デンプン反応を示さなくなるのは，デンプンが加水分解されてブドウ糖になるからである。

2. 塩化ビニルが付加重合をしやすいのは，二重結合を含み，不飽和性があるからである。

デンプン	denpun	starch

SUPPLEMENTARY READINGS

A.	染料	senryō	dye (stuff)
	適当な	tekitō na	suitable
	染着する	senchaku suru	to dye
	有色の	yūshoku no	colored
	昔の	mukashi no	ancient, in olden times
	植物	shokubutsu	plant(s)
	鉱物	kōbutsu	mineral(s)
	色素	shikiso	pigment
	有機合成品	yūki-gōsei-hin	organic synthetic materials
	歴史	rekishi	history

トルイジン	toruijin	toluidine
不純の	fujun no	impure
アニリン	anirin	aniline
モーヴ	mōvu	mauve
紫色	murasaki-iro	purple (color)
ドイツやスイス	Doitsu ya Suisu	German, Swiss, etc.
発達する	hattatsu suru	to develop, advance
およぶ	oyobu	to mount up to, reach
実用	jitsuyō	practical use
数百	sūhyaku	several hundred
色別に	iro-betsu ni	for each individual color
消費	shōhi	consumption
黒〜灰	kuro kara hai	from black to gray
青, 赤, 紫, 黄	ao, aka, murasaki, ki	blue, red, purple, yellow
用途	yōto	use, service
紡織	bōshoku	spinning and weaving
染色	senshoku	dyeing
塗料	toryō	paint (s)
製造	seizō	manufacture, production
雑貨	zakka	merchandise, goods
着色	chakushoku	coloration, coloring
油脂	yushi	oils and fats
皮革	hikaku	hides and skins; leather
化粧品	keshō-hin	cosmetics
食品	shokuhin	food stuffs
指示薬	shiji-yaku	indicator
組織染色	soshiki-senshoku	tissue-staining
医療	iryō	medical treatment
わたる	wataru	to range, extend

染　料　(2RJ 764–765)

適当な方法で繊維に染着する有色の化合物を染料という。昔の染料は動物, 植物, 鉱物などに含まれる天然色素であったが, 現在ではすべて有機合成品である。合成染料の歴史は1856年 Perkin がトルイジンを含む不純のアニリンを酸化して, モーヴという紫色の染料を得たのに始まる。そののち, ドイツやスイスで合成染料工業が発達し, コールタール製品から約4000種におよぶ染料が作られたが, そのうち実用されているのは数百種である。色別に消費量を見ると, 黒〜灰が50—60%, 青が20—25%, そのほかが赤, 紫, 黄などとなっている。染料の用途は紡織繊維の染色を第一として, 塗料, インキなどの製造, 紙,

セルロイドなどの雑貨の着色，油脂，皮革，化粧品，食品などの着色，写真フィルムやフィルター用色素，化学分析用指示薬，生物実験における組織染色および医療用などきわめて広い範囲にわたる。

B.

殺虫剤	satchū-zai	insecticide
害虫	gaichū	harmful insect
駆除	kujo	extermination
殺す	korosu	to kill
窒息	chissoku	suffocation
食毒	shokudoku	poison (in food)
石油乳剤	sekiyu-nyūzai	petroleum emulsion
ヒ酸鉛	hisan-namari	lead arsenate
亜ヒ酸亜鉛	a-hisan-aen	zinc arsenite
硫酸ニコチン	ryūsan-nikochin	nicotine sulfate

殺虫剤　(2RJ 512)

害虫を駆除するための化学薬品を殺虫剤という。虫体に接触して殺すもの，窒息させるもの，食毒など種々ある。石油乳剤，ヒ酸鉛，亜ヒ酸亜鉛，硫酸ニコチンなどがふつう使われる。

C.

合成洗剤	gōsei-senzai	synthetic detergent
油脂	yushi	oils and fat
乳濁(液)	nyūdaku(eki)	emulsion
ぬらす	nurasu	to wet
布	nuno	cloth
あか	aka	filth
しみ通る	shimi-tōru	to penetrate
汚物	obutsu	filth, dirt
洗い出す	arai-dasu	to wash out
洗浄	senjō	washing, cleansing
親和力	shinwa-ryoku	affinity
原子団	genshi-dan	atomic group
脂肪酸の塩	shibō-san no en	salt of a fatty acid
加水分解	kasui-bunkai	hydrolysis
アルカリ性	arukari-sei	alkaline properties
遊離する	yūri suru	to liberate
硬水・海水	kōsui; kaisui	hard water; sea water
不溶(解)性の	fu-yō(kai)sei no	insoluble
酸性硫酸エステル	sansei-ryūsan-esuteru	acidic sulfuric ester
スルホン酸の塩	surufon-san no en	salt of a sulfonic acid

中性	chūsei	neutral
溶解度	yōkai-do	solubility
沈殿	chinden	precipitation
失う	ushinau	to lose
いためる	itameru	to injure

セッケンと合成洗剤　(3K 291–292)

　セッケンは油脂を乳濁させ，微細な固体の粒子を水中に分散させる力があり，また，物体の表面をぬらすから，布の繊維やあかの中にしみ通り，汚物は細かい粒子に分散されて洗い出される。セッケンの洗浄作用は，その分子の中に，油脂に親和力のある原子団と水に親和力のある原子団とがあるためである。

　セッケンは脂肪酸の塩であるから，セッケン水は加水分解のために弱いアルカリ性を示す。酸を加えると，脂肪酸が遊離し，これが水に溶けにくいから分かれてくる。セッケン水に硬水を加えると，カルシウムやマグネシウムのイオンが脂肪酸イオンと結合して，不溶解性の塩をつくる。

　合成洗剤は酸性硫酸エステルやスルホン酸の塩であるから，それは加水分解を受けず，溶液は中性である。また，それらの酸自身もカルシウムやマグネシウムの塩も，溶解度が大きいから沈殿しない。合成洗剤は，硬水や海水でも，酸性の水でも，洗浄作用を失わず，また，水溶液がアルカリ性を示さないから布をいためない。

D. (粉)粒体	(fun)ryūtai	particles
粒度	ryūdo	grain size
機械的分離	kikai-teki-bunri	mechanical separation
因子	inshi	factor
単位操作	tan'i-sōsa	unit operations (of chemical engineering)
…に先だって	…ni sakidatte	…before
予備知識	yobi-chishiki	background knowledge
表示法	hyōji-hō	method of expressing
解説する	kaisetsu suru	to explain, comment on
沈降	chinkō	sedimentation
ロ過	roka	filtration
基礎	kiso	basis, foundation

粉粒体の粒度　(KKT 1)

　機械的分離の場合はもちろん化学的反応においても固体の大きさ，すなわち粒度は重要な因子である。したがって，まずおのおのの単位操作をのべるに先だって，予備知識とし

て粉粒体の粒度測定法について解説しよう。この測定理論はまたそのまま機械的分離法の沈降やロ過の基礎となっている。

E.	材料	zairyō	materials
	…より見ると	…yori miru to	if we regard from the viewpoint of…
	鎖状	sajō	chain (see Note 1, Lesson 19)
	熱(可)塑性	netsu(ka)sosei	thermoplastic
	ついで	tsuide	then, subsequently
	配向	haikō	orientation
	いかす	ikasu	to make good use of
	二次元	ni-jigen	two dimensional
	延伸法	enshin-hō	stretching technique
	架橋する	kakyō suru	to form a bridge, cross-linkages
	石材	sekizai	stone (materials)
	木材	mokuzai	wood (materials)
	硬質	kōshitsu	hardness
	粘弾性	nendan-sei	viscoelastic
	…らしい	…rashii	to be like…
	ずれ弾性率	zure-dansei-ritsu	shearing modulus
	低下	teika	lowering
	比較的	hikaku-teki	comparatively
	溶融粘度	yōyū-nendo	melt viscosity
	流し込む	nagashi-komu	to pour into
	成形	seikei	molding
	加工	kakō	processing
	耐食性	taishoku-sei	corrosion resistant property
	接着性	setchaku-sei	adhesive property

高分子材料の特徴 (KB 412–413)

　高分子物の特徴は分子構造より見ると第一に鎖状の高分子では熱可塑性，すなわち温度上昇とともにミクロ・ブラウン運動が自由になり，ついでマクロ・ブラウン運動も自由になることであり，また分子配向により著しく物性が変化することである。合成繊維やフィルムの製造に際してはこの特徴がいかされ，最近はフィルムやパイプの製造に二次元延伸法が利用されている。

　第二に，ゴム状の高分子では天然ゴムと同様にミクロ・ブラウン運動は自由になってい

るが，マクロ・ブラウン運動は生じないように架橋されていて，エントロピー弾性を示す。この性質は，石材，木材，金属などにはない性質である。

　第三に三次元架橋した硬質プラスチックスは固化したセメントに似ていて，必ずしも高分子物特有な構造あるいは特有な性質ではない。しかし粘弾性やその温度変化は高分子物らしく，温度上昇とともにずれ弾性率の低下が比較的著しい。また架橋する前の低い溶融粘度，低い溶液粘度で流し込め，成形が容易である点はセメントと異なる。

　材料的な特徴については，(1) 成形と加工が容易　(2) 電気絶縁性，熱絶縁性　(3) 耐食性　(4) 軽量　(5) 着色容易　(6) 透明性　(7) 接着性，があげられている。

F.　網目(構造)	amime (kōzō)	network (structure)
体系	taikei	system, structure
挙動	kyodō	behavior
数十〜数千	sūjū naishi sūsen	from several tens to several thousands
ポアズ	poazu	poise
顕著な	kencho na	striking
緩和	kanwa	relaxation
箱型	hakogata	box-shaped
曳糸性 (＝糸を引くことができる性質)	eishi-sei	spinnability
興味ある	kyōmi aru	interesting
…ら	…ra	…*et al.*
ゆるす	yurusu	to permit
ゆるせなくなってしまう	yurusenaku natte shimau	(See Notes, this lesson and Note 1, Lesson 15)
一本一本の	ippon-ippon no	singly
からまる	karamaru	to get twisted around
分子集合体	bunshi-shūgō-tai	molecular aggregate
扱う	atsukau	to deal with, treat
オーソドックスに	ōsodokkusu ni	in an orthodox way, manner
困難な	konnan na	troublesome, difficult
物性論	bussei-ron	molecular theory of matter
ゴム状	gomu-jō	rubbery state
高分子鎖	kō-bunshi-sa	macromolecular chains
永久的な	eikyū-teki na	permanent
要素	yōso	constituent; element
単なる	tan naru	simple
生成消滅	seisei-shōmetsu	formation and destruction

散逸機構	san'itsu-kikō	dissipation mechanism
発現する	hatsugen suru	to manifest itself
山本三三三	Yamamoto Misazō	(Japanese phsysicist)
林静男	Hayashi Shizuo	(Japanese physicist)
展開する	tenkai suru	to develop, unfold
元来	ganrai	originally
くさび型	kusabi-gata	wedge-shaped
説明	setsumei	explanation
成功する	seikō suru	to succeed
上限	jōgen	maximum
3.4乗	san-ten-yon-jō	the 3.4 power
依存性	izon-sei	reliability
…べきである	…beki de aru	ought to…
確立しておらず…	kakuritsu shite orazu…	is not established and…
（＝確立していないで…）		
意味	imi	meaning
域	iki	region, limits
寄与	kiyo	contribution, service

網目構造の粘弾性　（KB 214–215）

<u>弱い網目構造</u>。高分子系の濃度が高くなってくると，高分子間の相互作用が問題となってくるが，このような体系においては，すでにのべられているように，高分子濃度が希薄な場合とは相当に異なった挙動を示すようになる。すなわち，その粘度が高く数十〜数千ポアズとなり，顕著な非ニュートン流動を示し，また粘弾性の緩和スペクトルが長緩和時間側に伸びていわゆる箱型のスペクトルを示すばかりでなく，曳糸性，ワイセンベルグ (Weissenberg) 効果，バラス(Barus)効果などの興味ある現象を示すようになる。

　そしてこのような系に対しては Debye, Kirkwood のような取り扱いはまったくゆるせなくなってしまう。すなわち，このような場合には一本一本の高分子の挙動よりも，高分子がたがいにからまり合った分子集合体を系全体として扱わなければならなくなってくる。このような体系をオーソドックスに取り扱うことは非常に困難であるが，分子がからみ合って全体として網目構造をつくると考えると，高分子物性論のはじまりともなったゴム状弾性論の網目理論がそのまま用いられると思われる。ただし，ゴム状弾性論では高分子鎖の結合は永久的な化学結合によるが，ここでは各要素の間に働くファン・デル・ワールス力や，単なるからみ合いによるもので，高分子鎖のブラウン運動によって生成消滅するものと考える必要がある。このため体系の散逸機構が発現することになるのである。このような弱い網目構造の理論は Green-Tobolsky, Scott-Stein, 山本, Lodge, 林などによ

り展開された。元来このような体系の理論としては，Rouse-Zimm の理論がくさび型緩和スペクトルの説明に成功したのに対応して，箱型スペクトルの説明，とくに上限緩和時間の分子量 3.4 乗の依存性が導き出されるべきである。しかし現在では林のすぐれた研究があるが，まだこの方向の理論が確立しておらず，その意味では網目構造の理論は現象論の域に止っているといえるであろう。しかし，この理論はワイセンベルグ効果などの現象の説明に成功しているので，その方面での寄与は大きいものである。

G. 乾燥	kansō	drying
定義	teigi	definition
湿る	shimeru	to be wet
周囲の	shūi no	surrounding
外気	gaiki	(surrounding, ambient) air
水分	suibun	moisture, humidity
揮発する	kihatsu suru	to evaporate
取り除く	tori-nozoku	to remove
減湿	genshitsu	dehumidification
充分に（十分にis more common）	jūbun ni	sufficiently
乾く	kawaku	to be dry, dry up
湿度	shitsudo	humidity
風速	fūsoku	wind velocity
準備期間	junbi-kikan	preliminary period
恒率・減率	kōritsu; genritsu	constant rate; falling rate
出来る（＝できる）	dekiru	to be able
おそい	osoi	slow

乾　燥　(KKT 125)

定義。一般に湿った物体から周囲の外気へ水分を揮発させて取り除く操作を乾燥というが，固体からとは限らず液体や気体から水分を除くことも乾燥ということがある。しかし気体からの場合は減湿という方がよい。

　物体の表面は充分に湿っているときには表面の温度に相当した飽和水蒸気分圧 P_w を示し，周囲の外気は一般にそれよりも低い水蒸気分圧をもっているので，その差によって水分が揮発して物体が乾いてゆく。このように物体が充分湿っているときには乾燥条件（外気の温度，湿度および風速等）が一定であれば，乾燥準備期間がすぎると表面温度は一定となり，したがって乾燥速度も一定となる。この期間を恒率乾燥という。さらに乾燥をつづけてゆくと，表面が部分的に乾燥した状態となって，全体としては一定速度で揮発が出来なくなる。このだんだんに乾き方がおそくなってゆくときを減率乾燥という。

FINAL TRANSLATION TEST

化学繊維　(KS 13–19, 103–105)

　　合成繊維が最初に発表されたのは1938年である。この年にドイツでペー・ツェー (PC) 繊維，アメリカからビニヨン，そしてナイロンが発表された。合成繊維がこんなにおそくまで発明されなかったのはなぜだろう。そして，一度発明されると，次から次へとどんどん発明されて来たのはなぜだろう。この質問にこたえるのはむずかしくない。すなわち，繊維を形成するということの本質が1934～5年ごろ初めて確かめられたからである。繊維が何であるかということを知らないで繊維を作り上げることは出来なかったのである。繊維が従来考えられていたような形ではなくて，非常に細長い形をしたものであると考え始めたのはフライブルグ大学のシュタウジンガー (Staudinger) である。シュタウジンガーは，初めから天然の繊維をあつかわず，小さい分子，少しだけ大きくした分子，もう少しのばした分子，よほど長くした分子，…という工合に，形の小さいもの，大きいものを自分で作って進んで行った。自分で作ったものであるから，大きさも確かにわかっている。そして，それらの性質を比較してみると，繊維の性質は，最も大きい分子の性質とよく似ていたのである。しかし，大きい分子ということが合成繊維だけで問題になったのではない。ゴムがそうであったし，プラスチックスがそうである。食物がすべてそうである。われわれが生きて行く上に直接に関係のあるもの，特に何かの材料となり得るものは大部分が大きい分子である。かりに，われわれのまわりに小さい分子から出来ているものを見つけ出そうとしても，空気，水，薬品類，油等位のものであり，あまりない。着るもの，食べるもの，紙等すべて大きい分子である。このように，全体として，大きい分子という本質が理論的に解明されて来たため，繊維の問題もまたその一部分として理解されるようになったのである。1932年カローザス (Carothers) はデュポン (Dupont) の実験室で，火にかけて熔融された高分子物質の中にガラス棒をつけ，これを引き上げると，この物質は細長くのびてきれないことを見出した。この物質は後にデュポンで発明されたナイロンの色々の特性に比べると，はるかに単純であって，すぐれた糸としては使えないものであったが，このようにして合成繊維が作られ得るという重要な事実が確かめられたのである。

　　ナイロンは，その機械的性質において天然繊維よりはるかにまさっていて，引っ張り強度，折り曲げ強度，特に織物にした場合に必要な摩擦強度等すべて比較にならない程大きい。軽くて吸水性がなく，水で洗っても風乾してすぐに使用できる状態になる。長く使用している間には多少黄色に変色するが，これはナイロンが光や熱により酸素や水分と反応して，いくらか分解するためである。一般に合成繊維は染色しにくいが，天然繊維と同様に

染めやすいものも出来ている。ナイロンは，石炭酸（フェノール）から，あるいはベンゼンから直接に製造される。ブタジェンを出発点として，塩素と青酸ソーダとを使っても合成される。また，石油特に天然ガスからアセチレンを製造する工業がアメリカで盛んであるが，それからも合成される。製造されたナイロン塩は，水に溶けた形のままで繊維工場に運ばれて来る。これを熱して水をとばして後，圧力と熱をかけて構成単位を一列の長い分子に仕上げてしまう。同時に 220–230°C 位に温度を上げるので，出来たナイロンは融けてしまっている。これを，あなからおし出してベルト状に巻き，フレーキ状にする。このフレークをもう一度水素中で融かして乳状とし，細いあなからおし出して巻き取るとナイロン繊維が出来上がるのである。

LESSON 21

第二十一課

KANJI

粉	507	FUN		臭	227a	SHŪ	
	3469	kona ko			3841	kusa(i)	
濃	271a	NŌ		剤	229b	ZAI	
	2711	ko(i)			2524		
灰	205a	KAI		無	723	MU	
	820	hai			2773	na(i)	
緑	532	RYOKU		硝	250b	SHŌ	
	3564	midori			3192		
刺	214a	SHI		名	140	MEI	
	682	sa(su)			1170	na	
激	271a	GEKI		皮	307	HI	
	2712	hage(shii)			3109	kawa	
衡	272b	KŌ		酵	264b	KŌ	
	1641				4787		
残	409	ZAN		胞	227a	HŌ	
	2445	{noko(su) {noko(ru)			3749		
菌	243b	KIN		呼	214b	KO	
	3976				914	yo(bu)	
植	435	SHOKU		芽	358	GA	
	2303	{u(eru) {u(waru)			3920	me	

READING SELECTIONS

塩素	enso	chlorine
ハロゲン	harogen	halogen
製法	seihō	method of producing
工業的に	kōgyō-teki ni	industrially
塩化ナトリウム	enka-natoriumu	sodium chloride
実験室	jikken-shitsu	laboratory
サラシ粉	sarashi-ko	bleaching powder
濃塩酸	nō-ensan	concentrated HCl
注ぐ	sosogu	to pour

水酸化カルシウム	suisanka-karushiumu	calcium hydroxide
消石灰	shō-sekkai	slaked lime
AにBを吸わせる	A ni B o suwaseru	to have A absorb B
主成分	shu-seibun	main constituent
発生する	hassei suru	to be generated
二酸化マンガン	ni-sanka-mangan	manganese dioxide
塩化マンガン	enka-mangan	manganese chloride
緑色を帯びた	midori-iro o obita	tinged with green
淡黄色	tankō-shoku	straw color
刺激性のにおい	shigeki-sei no nioi	irritating odor
粘膜	nenmaku	mucous membrane
おかす	okasu	to attack, affect
湿ったリトマス紙	shimetta ritomasu-shi	moist litmus paper
漂白する	hyōhaku suru	to bleach
ヨウ化カリウムデンプン紙	yōka-kariumu-denpun-shi	potassium iodide starch paper
日光	nikkō	sunlight
直射する	chokusha suru	to shine directly on
爆発的に	bakuhatsu teki ni	explosively
日かげで	hikage de	in the shade
徐々に	jojo ni	slowly, gradually
塩化水素	enka-suiso	hydrogen-chloride
燃やす	moyasu	to burn
大気中で	taiki-chū de	in the atmosphere
燃焼	nenshō	combustion
塩素水	enso-sui	chlorine water
次亜塩素酸	jia-enso-san	hypochlorous acid
両方	ryōhō	both
平衡	heikō	equilibrium
酸化する	sanka suru	to oxidize
残る	nokoru	to remain
作用する	sayō suru	to react
呈する	tei-suru	to exhibit, present
殺菌	sakkin	sterilizing, disinfecting
除く	nozoku	to remove
フッ素	fusso	fluorine
臭素	shūso	bromine
ヨー素	yōso	iodine
総称する	sōshō suru	to name generically
(非)金属	(hi)kinzoku	(non)metal

順	jun	order
それゆえ	sore yue	therefore
酸化剤	sanka-zai	oxidizing agent
アルコール	arukōru	alcohol
ヨードチンキ	yōdo-chinki	tincture of iodine
医薬	iyaku	medicine
臭化水素	shūka-suiso	hydrogen bromide
…と同じく（=…と同じように）		
無色の	mushoku no	colorless
発煙性の	hatsuen-sei no	fuming
きわめて	kiwamete	exceedingly, very
沸騰	futtō	boiling
二酸化ケイ素	ni-sanka-keiso	silicon dioxide

塩素とハロゲン元素　(3K 75–79)

　塩素の製法。塩素 Cl_2 は，工業的には塩化ナトリウム溶液の電気分解でつくるが，実験室では次の二つの方法が用いられる。

　（1）　サラシ粉に濃塩酸を注ぐ。サラシ粉は，水酸化カルシウム（消石灰）$Ca(OH)_2$ に塩素を吸わせて得たもので，その主成分は，$CaCl(ClO)\cdot H_2O$ であらわされる結晶性の物質である。

$$Ca(OH)_2 + Cl_2 \longrightarrow CaCl(ClO)\cdot H_2O$$

これに塩酸を注ぐと，次のように塩素が発生する。

$$CaCl(ClO)\cdot H_2O + 2HCl \longrightarrow CaCl_2 + Cl_2 + 2H_2O$$

　（2）　二酸化マンガンに塩酸を加えて熱する。この場合には，二酸化マンガンが，次のように塩酸を酸化して塩素とする。

$$MnO_2 + 4HCl \longrightarrow Cl_2 + MnCl_2 + 2H_2O$$
$$\text{塩化マンガン}$$

　塩素の性質。　塩素 Cl_2 は緑色を帯びた淡黄色の重い気体で，刺激性のにおいがあり，粘膜をおかして有毒である。塩素は湿ったリトマス紙を赤くした後漂白し，ヨウ化カリウムデンプン紙を青くした後漂白する。塩素と水素の混合気体に日光を直射すると，爆発的に化合する。この混合気体は日かげでも徐々に化合し，次のように塩化水素ができる。

$$H_2 + Cl_2 \longrightarrow 2HCl$$

　水素を塩素の中で燃やすこともできるし，塩素を水素の中で燃やすこともできる。これらのときも，塩化水素ができる。大気中の燃焼は酸素との化合[1]であるが，塩素中の燃焼は塩素との化合である。

　塩素水。塩素を水に溶かしたものを塩素水という。塩素と水とは次のように反応して塩

化水素 HCl と次亜塩素酸 [2] HClO となる。

$$Cl_2 + H_2O \longrightarrow HCl + HClO \tag{1}$$

こうして塩化水素と次亜塩素酸ができると，これらが次のように反応して塩素と水とを生じる。

$$HCl + HClO \longrightarrow Cl_2 + H_2O \tag{2}$$

そこでこの水溶液中では，(1) の反応と (2) の反応との両方が起こっているが，ちょうどつり合いがとれて，塩素・水・塩化水素・次亜塩素酸の4物質が，増しもしなければ減りもしない [3]，すなわち，どちらの反応も止まっているようにみえる状態にある。この状態を化学平衡の状態といい，次のような化学反応式であらわされる。

$$Cl_2 + H_2O \rightleftharpoons HCl + HClO$$

塩素水中では，これらの4物質が化学平衡の状態にある。

次亜塩素酸 HClO は，次の式の示すように酸素を与えて，他の物質を酸化することができる。

$$HClO \longrightarrow HCl + (O)$$

次亜塩素酸がなくなれば，上の平衡が右へ移動し，残っている塩素が水と作用してまた次亜塩素酸となる。このように，湿った塩素が漂白の作用を呈する。

サラシ粉も，塩素と同じように漂白，殺菌に用いられるが，塩酸などを注いで酸性にしたとき，その作用が強くあらわれる。塩素やサラシ粉は，動物性の物質をおかす。植物性の物質でも漂白したあとで，残っている塩素をよく除いておかなければならない。

ハロゲン元素。フッ素・塩素・臭素・ヨウ素は互いによく似ていてハロゲン元素と総称される。このうち，塩素・臭素・ヨウ素は特によく似ている。一般に，非金属と金属とはよく化合する。ハロゲン元素も金属や水素とよく化合するが，その化合力は次の順に小さくなっている。

$$フッ素 > 塩素 > 臭素 > ヨウ素$$

それゆえ，次のような反応が起こる。

$$2NaBr + Cl_2 \longrightarrow 2NaCl + Br_2$$

$$2KI + Cl_2 \longrightarrow 2KCl + I_2$$

この方法で，臭素やヨウ素をつくることができる。

臭素は塩素と同じように，酸化剤として用いられる。ヨウ素は水にほとんど溶けないがヨウ化物の水溶液やアルコールには溶ける。ヨウ素をヨウ化カリウムの水溶液に溶かしたものが実験室で使うヨウ素溶液である。ヨードチンキは医薬に用いられる。

臭化水素 HBr・ヨウ化水素 HI は，塩化水素 HCl と同じく無色・発煙性・刺激性の気体で，きわめて水に溶けやすく，水溶液は強い酸性を示す。フッ化水素 HF は，$19.5°C$

で沸騰する液体で，水溶液は弱い酸性を示し，他のハロゲン化水素と違い，ガラスをおかす。ガラスの成分の二酸化ケイ素 SiO_2 が次のようにフッ化ケイ素 SiF_4（気体）となるからである。

$$SiO_2 + 4HF \longrightarrow SiF_4 + 2H_2O$$

（濃）硝酸	(nō) shōsan	(concentrated) nitric acid
市販の	shihan no	commercial, on the market
名づける	na-zukeru	to name, call
市販する	shihan suru	to market
分解する	bunkai suru	to decompose
二酸化窒素	ni-sanka-chisso	nitrogen dioxide
刺激臭（＝刺激性のにおい）	shigeki-shū	irritating odor
有毒な	yūdoku na	poisonous
溶かし込む	tokashi-komu	to dissolve into
皮膚	hifu	skin
羊毛	yōmō	wool
タンパク質	tanpaku-shitsu	protein
キサントプロテイン反応	kisanto-purotein-hannō	xanthoprotein-reaction
白金	hakkin	platinum
王水	ōsui	aqua regia
塩化金酸	enka-kinsan	chloroauric acid
塩化白金酸	enka-hakkin-san	chloroplatinic acid
暗赤色	anseki-shoku	dark red
湿りやすい	shimeri-yasui	hygroscopic

(A more technical word is 吸湿性の kyūshitsu-sei no)

硝酸の性質　(3K 108–109)

市販の硝酸は，硝酸 HNO_3 と名づける無色・発煙性の液体（比重1.52, 沸点86°C)の水溶液であり，濃度が大きくなるにつれて，比重が大きくなる。硝酸は種々の濃度のものが市販されていて，いずれも濃硝酸といわれている。硝酸は光が当たると黄かっ色を帯びる。これは光のために硝酸が一部分次のように分解し，二酸化窒素 NO_2 というかっ色の刺激臭のある有毒な気体ができて，それが溶けているからである。

$$4HNO_3 \underset{暗}{\overset{明}{\rightleftharpoons}} 4NO_2 + 2H_2O + O_2$$

濃硝酸に二酸化窒素を溶かし込んだものを，発煙硝酸という。硝酸が皮膚や羊毛などのタンパク質に作用すると，黄色の物質ができる。これをキサントプロテイン反応という。

金や白金は塩酸にも硝酸にもおかされないが，塩酸と硝酸の混合溶液である王水には溶

ける。この溶液を蒸発させると，それぞれ，塩化金酸 $HAuCl_4 \cdot 4H_2O$（黄色）および塩化白金酸 $H_2PtCl_6 \cdot 6H_2O$（暗赤色）が得られる。これはどちらも湿^{しめ}りやすい結晶である。

酵素	kōso	enzyme
発酵	hakkō	fermentation
腐敗	fuhai	decomposition, putrefaction
微生物	bi-seibutsu	micro-organism
触媒	shokubai	catalyst
細胞	saihō; saibō	cell (in biology)
消化酵素	shōka-kōso	digestive enzyme
呼吸酵素	kokyū-kōso	respiratory enzyme
促す	unagasu	to accelerate
範囲	han'i	range
…で影響を受ける	…de eikyō o ukeru	to be affected by…
無機塩類	muki-enrui	inorganic salts
だ液	daeki	saliva
アミラーゼ	amirāze	amylase
マルターゼ	marutāze	maltase
麦芽糖	bakuga-tō	maltose
加水分解	kasui-bunkai	hydrolysis
インベルターゼ	inberutāze	invertase

酵　　素　(3K 308)

発酵や腐敗^{ふはい}には微生物が関係する。これは微生物の体内でできる酵素が触媒となって化学変化を起こすのである。一般に，細胞の中でつくられる触媒作用のある物質を酵素という。酵素には，消化酵素や呼吸酵素などいろいろな種類のものがあって，生物体内で種々の化学変化を促^{うなが}す。酵素はタンパク質としての性質[4]をもっていて，たいてい 35～55°C の範囲^{はんい}で最も作用が強い。　また，酵素のはたらきは，溶液の酸性・アルカリ性の強さの程度 (pH) で影響^{えいきょう}を受けるし，種々の無機塩類の存在でも影響^{えいきょう}を受ける。たとえば，だ液アミラーゼの作用には，塩素イオンの存在が必要である。一方，銅や水銀などの重金属の塩類の存在は，酵素の作用を止めるものである[5]。一つの酵素は，特定の物質の特定の反応に対してだけ作用する。たとえば，マルターゼは麦芽糖^{ばく}を加水分解するが，ショ糖，その他を加水分解することはできない。インベルターゼは，ショ糖を加水分解するが，麦芽糖その他を加水分解することはできない。

ENSO TO HAROGEN GENSO

Enso no Seihō: Enso Cl_2 wa, kōgyō-teki ni wa enka-natoriumu yōeki no denki-bunkai de tsukuru ga, jikken-shitsu de wa tsugi no futatsu no hōhō ga mochi-

irareru.

(1) Sarashi-ko ni nō-ensan o sosogu. Sarashi-ko wa, suisanka-karushiumu (shō-sekkai) Ca(OH)₂ ni enso o suwasete eta mono de, sono shu-seibun wa, CaCl(ClO)·H₂O de arawasareru kesshō-sei no busshitsu de aru.

$$Ca(OH)_2 + Cl_2 \longrightarrow CaCl(ClO) \cdot H_2O$$

Kore ni ensan o sosogu to, tsugi no yō ni enso ga hassei suru.

$$CaCl(ClO) \cdot H_2O + 2HCl \longrightarrow CaCl_2 + Cl_2 + 2H_2O$$

(2) Ni-sanka-mangan ni ensan o kuwaete nessuru. Kono baai ni wa, ni-sanka-mangan ga, tsugi no yō ni ensan o sanka shite enso to suru.

$$MnO_2 + 4HCl \longrightarrow Cl_2 + MnCl_2 + 2H_2O$$
Enka-mangan

Enso no Seishitsu: Enso Cl₂ wa midori-iro o obita tankō-shoku no omoi kitai de, shigeki-sei no nioi ga ari, nenmaku o okashite yūdoku de aru. Enso wa shimetta ritomasu-shi o akaku shita nochi hyōhaku shi, yōka-kariumu-denpun-shi o aoku shita nochi hyōhaku suru. Enso to suiso no kongō-kitai ni nikkō o chokusha suru to, bakuhatsu-teki ni kagō suru. Kono kongō-kitai wa hikage de mo jojo ni kagō shi, tsugi no yō ni enka-suiso ga dekiru.

$$H_2 + Cl_2 \longrightarrow 2HCl$$

Suiso o enso no naka de moyasu koto mo dekiru shi, enso o suiso no naka de moyasu koto mo dekiru. Korera no toki mo, enka-suiso ga dekiru. Taiki-chū no nenshō wa sanso to no kagō [1] de aru ga, enso-chū no nenshō wa enso to no ka-gō de aru.

Enso-sui: Enso o mizu ni tokashita mono o enso-sui to iu. Enso to mizu to wa, tsugi no yō ni hannō shite enka-suiso HCl to jia-enso-san HClO to naru.

$$Cl_2 + H_2O \longrightarrow HCl + HClO \qquad (1)$$

Kō shite enka-suiso to jia-enso-san [2] ga dekiru to, korera ga tsugi no yō ni hannō shite enso to mizu to o shōjiru.

$$HCl + HClO \longrightarrow Cl_2 + H_2O \qquad (2)$$

Soko de kono sui-yōeki-chū de wa, (1) no hannō to (2) no hannō to no ryōhō ga okotte iru ga, chōdo tsuri-ai ga torete, enso, mizu, enka-suiso, jia-enso-san no yon-busshitsu ga, mashi mo shinakereba heri mo shinai, [3] sunawachi, dochira no hannō mo tomatte iru yō ni mieru jōtai ni aru. Kono jōtai o kagaku-heikō no jōtai to ii, tsugi no yō na kagaku-hannō-shiki de arawasareru.

$$Cl_2 + H_2O \rightleftharpoons HCl + HClO$$

Enso-sui-chū de wa, korera no yon-busshitsu ga kagaku-heikō no jōtai ni aru.

Jia-enso-san HClO wa, tsugi no shiki no shimesu yō ni sanso o ataete, ta no busshitsu o sanka suru koto ga dekiru.

$$HClO \longrightarrow HCl + (O)$$

Jia-enso-san ga naku nareba, ue no heikō ga migi e idō shi, nokotte iru enso ga mizu to sayō shite mata jia-enso-san to naru. Kono yō ni, shimetta enso ga

hyōhaku no sayō o tei-suru.

Sarashi-ko mo, enso to onaji yō ni hyōhaku, sakkin ni mochi-irareru ga, ensan nado o sosoide sansei ni shita toki, sono sayō ga tsuyoku arawareru.

Enso ya sarashi-ko wa, dō-bussei no busshitsu o okasu. Shoku-bussei no busshitsu de mo hyōhaku shita ato de, nokotte iru enso o yoku nozoite okanakereba nara-nai.

Harogen-genso: Fusso, enso, shūso, yōso wa tagai ni yoku nite ite harogen-genso to sōshō sareru. Kono uchi, enso, shūso, yōso wa toku ni yoku nite iru.

Ippan ni, hi-kinzoku to kinzoku to wa yoku kagō suru. Harogen-genso mo kin-zoku ya suiso to yoku kagō suru ga, sono kagō-ryoku wa tsugi no jun ni chiisaku natte iru.

$$\text{Fusso} > \text{Enso} > \text{Shūso} > \text{Yōso}$$

Sore yue, tsugi no yō na hannō ga okoru.

$$2NaBr + Cl_2 \longrightarrow 2NaCl + Br_2$$
$$2KI + Cl_2 \longrightarrow 2KCl + I_2$$

Kono hōhō de, shūso ya yōso o tsukuru koto ga dekiru.

Shūso wa, enso to onaji yō ni, sanka-zai to shite mochi-irareru. Yōso wa mizu ni hotondo tokenai ga, yōka-butsu no suiyōeki ya arukōru ni wa tokeru. Yōso o yōka-kariumu no sui-yōeki ni tokashita mono ga jikken-shitsu de tsukau yōso-yōeki de aru. Yōdo-chinki wa, iyaku ni mochi-irareru.

Shūka-suiso HBr, yōka suiso HI wa, enka-suiso HCl to onajiku mushoku, hatsuen-sei, shigeki-sei no kitai de, kiwamete mizu ni toke-yasuku, sui-yōeki wa tsuyoi sansei o shimesu. Fukka-suiso HF wa, sesshi-jūkyū-ten-go-do de futtō suru ekitai de, sui-yōeki wa yowai sansei o shimeshi, ta no harogenka-suiso to chigai, garasu o okasu. Garasu no seibun no ni-sanka-keiso SiO_2 ga tsugi no yō ni fukka-keiso SiF_4 (kitai) to naru kara de aru.

$$SiO_2 + 4HF \longrightarrow SiF_4 + 2H_2O$$

SHŌSAN NO SEISHITSU

Shihan no shōsan wa, shōsan HNO_3 to na-zukeru mushoku, hatsuen-sei no ekitai (hijū ichi-ten-go-ni, futten sesshi-hachijū-roku-do) no sui-yōeki de ari, nōdo ga ōkiku naru ni tsurete, hijū ga ōkiku naru. Shōsan wa shuju no nōdo no mono ga shihan sarete ite, izure mo nō-shōsan to iwarete iru.

Shōsan wa, hikari ga ataru to kō-kasshoku o obiru. Kore wa hikari no tame ni shōsan ga ichi-bubun tsugi no yō ni bunkai shi, ni-sanka-chisso NO_2 to iu kasshoku no shigeki-shū no aru yūdoku na kitai ga dekite, sore ga tokete iru kara de aru.

$$4HNO_3 \overset{mei}{\underset{an}{\rightleftharpoons}} 4NO_2 + 2H_2O + O_2$$

Nō-shōsan ni ni-sanka-chisso o tokashi-konda mono o, hatsuen-shōsan to iu.

Shōsan ga hifu ya yōmō nado no tanpaku-shitsu ni sayō suru to, ki-iro no busshitsu ga dekiru. Kore o kisanto-purotein-hannō to iu.

Kin ya hakkin wa, ensan ni mo shōsan ni mo okasarenai ga, ensan to shōsan no kongō-yōeki de aru ōsui ni wa tokeru. Kono yōeki o jōhatsu saseru to, sorezore, enka-kinsan $HAuCl_4 \cdot 4H_2O$ (ki-iro) oyobi enka-hakkin-san $H_2PtCl_6 \cdot 6H_2O$ (anseki-shoku) ga erareru. Kore wa dochira mo shimeri-yasui kesshō de aru.

KŌSO

Hakkō ya fuhai ni wa bi-seibutsu ga kankei suru. Kore wa bi-seibutsu no tainai de dekiru kōso ga shokubai to natte, kagaku-henka o okosu no de aru. Ippan ni, saihō no naka de tsukurareru shokubai-sayō no aru busshitsu o kōso to iu.

Kōso ni wa, shōka-kōso ya kokyū-kōso nado iroiro na shurui no mono ga atte, seibutsu-tainai de shuju no kagaku-henka o unagasu. Kōso wa tanpaku-shitsu to shite no seishitsu [4] o motte ite, taitei sesshi-sanjū-go-do naishi gojū-go-do no han'i de mottomo sayō ga tsuyoi. Mata, kōso no hataraki wa, yōeki no sansei, arukari-sei no tsuyosa no teido (pH) de eikyō o ukeru shi, shuju no muki-enrui no sonzai de mo eikyō o ukeru. Tatoeba, daeki-amirāze no sayō ni wa, enso-ion no sonzai ga hitsuyō de aru. Ippō, dō ya suigin nado no jū-kinzoku no enrui no sonzai wa, kōso no sayō o tomeru mono de aru. [5]

Hitotsu no kōso wa, tokutei no busshitsu no tokutei no hannō ni taishite dake sayō suru. Tatoeba, marutāze wa, bakuga-tō o kasui-bunkai suru ga, shotō sono ta o kasui-bunkai suru koto wa dekinai. Inberutāze wa, shotō o kasui-bunkai suru ga, bakuga-tō, sono ta o kasui-bunkai suru koto wa dekinai.

CHLORINE AND THE HALOGENS

Methods of Preparing Chlorine: Chlorine Cl_2 is made industrially by electrolysis of sodium chloride solutions; but in the laboratory the following two methods are used:

(1) Concentrated HCl is poured on bleaching powder. Bleaching powder is obtained by having calcium hydroxide (slaked lime) absorb chlorine, and its principal constituent is a crystalline material represented by $CaCl(ClO) \cdot H_2O$.

$$Ca(OH)_2 + Cl_2 \longrightarrow CaCl(ClO) \cdot H_2O$$

Upon the addition of HCl, chlorine is generated as follows:

$$CaCl(ClO) \cdot H_2O + 2HCl \longrightarrow CaCl_2 + Cl_2 + 2H_2O$$

(2) HCl is added to MnO_2 and heated. In this case MnO_2 oxidizes the HCl to give Cl_2 as follows:

$$MnO_2 + 4HCl \longrightarrow Cl_2 + MnCl_2 + 2H_2O$$

Properties of Cl_2: Chlorine is a greenish-yellow, heavy gas with an irritating odor, which attacks the mucous membranes and is poisonous. Chlorine bleaches moist litmus paper after turning it red, and also bleaches potassium iodide starch

paper after turning it blue.

When sun light is directed into a gaseous mixture of chlorine and hydrogen, they combine explosively. Even in the shade this gaseous mixture will react slowly to produce hydrogen chloride as follows:

$$H_2 + Cl_2 \longrightarrow 2HCl$$

It is possible both to burn hydrogen in chlorine, and chlorine in hydrogen. In both cases HCl is produced. Atmospheric combustion is a combination with oxygen, but combustion in a chlorine atmosphere is a combination with chlorine.

Chlorine Water: Water in which chlorine has been dissolved is called chlorine water. Chlorine and water react as follows and produce HCl and HClO.

$$Cl_2 + H_2O \longrightarrow HCl + HClO \qquad (1)$$

When HCl and HClO arise in this way, they react as follows and produce Cl_2 and H_2O:

$$HCl + HClO \longrightarrow Cl_2 + H_2O \qquad (2)$$

Accordingly, both reactions (1) and (2) are occurring in this aqueous solution, and an exact equilibrium is attained in which the four substances Cl_2, H_2O, HCl and HClO neither increase nor decrease, that is, a state in which both reactions appear to have stopped. This condition is called a state of chemical equilibrium, and it is indicated by the following chemical (reaction) equation.

$$Cl_2 + H_2O \rightleftharpoons HCl + HClO$$

These four substances are in a state of chemical equilibrium in chlorine water.

Hypochlorous acid HClO, as the following equation shows, can give off oxygen, and thereby oxidize other substances:

$$HClO \longrightarrow HCl + (O)$$

When hypochlorous acid disappears, the above equilibrium shifts to the right, the remaining chlorine reacting with water to give more hypochlorous acid. In this way wet chlorine exhibits a bleaching action.

Bleaching powder is also used as a bleach and disinfectant in the same way as chlorine; and its action is enhanced by acidification with hydrochloric or other acids.

Agents like chlorine and bleaching powder attack animal tissue. After bleaching plant substances, any residual chlorine must be thoroughly removed.

The Halogens: Fluorine, chlorine, bromine, and iodine are quite similar to one another and are called halogens. Among them chlorine, bromine, and iodine are particularly similar.

Non-metals and metals generally combine readily. Halogens thus combine with metals and hydrogen, their chemical reactivities decreasing in the following order:

$$\text{Fluorine} > \text{Chlorine} > \text{Bromine} > \text{Iodine}$$

The following kinds of reactions therefore occur:

$$2NaBr+Cl_2 \longrightarrow 2NaCl+Br_2$$
$$2KI+Cl_2 \longrightarrow 2KCl+I_2$$

Bromine and iodine can be prepared in this way.

Bromine like chlorine is used as an oxidizing agent. Iodine is almost insoluble in water but does dissolve in alcohol and in aqueous solutions of iodides. The iodine solution used in the laboratory consists of iodine dissolved in an aqueous solution of potassium iodide. Tincture of iodine is used in medicine.

Hydrogen bromide HBr and hydrogen iodide HI like hydrogen chloride HCl are colorless, fuming, pungent gases, quite soluble in water, their aqueous solutions exhibiting strong acidity. Hydrogen fluoride HF is a liquid, boiling at $19.5°C$, whose aqueous solutions exhibit weak acidity; HF differs from the other hydrogen halides in that it attacks glass. This is because the silicon dioxide component of glass, SiO_2, goes to silicon fluoride SiF_4 (gas) as follows:

$$SiO_2+4HF \longrightarrow SiF_4+2H_2O$$

THE PROPERTIES OF NITRIC ACID

Commercial nitric acid is an aqueous solution of a colorless, fuming liquid, called nitric acid HNO_3, which has a specific gravity of 1.52 and a boiling point of $86°C$; its specific gravity increases with concentration. Various concentrations of nitric acid are marketed, all of which are called concentrated nitric acid.

When light falls on nitric acid it becomes yellowish-brown. This is because the nitric acid is partially decomposed by the light as follows:

$$4HNO_3 \underset{\text{darkness}}{\overset{\text{light}}{\rightleftarrows}} 4NO_2+2H_2O+O_2$$

to form the brown, pungent, poisonous gas nitrogen dioxide NO_2 which then goes into solution.

A solution of nitrogen dioxide in concentrated nitric acid is called fuming nitric acid.

When nitric acid reacts with protein materials, such as skin and wool, yellowish substances are produced. This is called the xanthoprotein reaction.

Gold and platinum are not attacked by either hydrochloric acid or nitric acid, but they will dissolve in aqua regia, a mixture of hydrochloric acid and nitric acid solutions. Upon evaporating such solutions, we obtain chloroauric acid (yellow) and chloro-platinic acid (dark red) respectively. Both are hygroscopic crystals.

ENZYMES

Micro-organisms are related to such processes as fermentation and putrefaction, because enzymes which are the catalysts causing such chemical changes are produced in the bodies of micro-organisms. Substances with catalytic activity

which are produced in cells are generally called enzymes. There are various kinds of enzymes, such as digestive enzymes and respiratory enzymes, and these accelerate a variety of chemical changes within the bodies of living beings. Since enzymes have the properties of proteins, they are generally most active in the range 35—55°C. Furthermore, the action of enzymes is affected by the degree of acidity or alkalinity (pH) of the solution as well as by the presence of various inorganic salts. For example the presence of chlorine ion is necessary for the action of amylase in saliva. On the other hand, the presence of the salts of copper, mercury, and other heavy metals stops enzyme activity.

An enzyme acts only with regard to one specific reaction of one specific substance. For example, maltase can hydrolyze maltose but not sucrose or other sugars. Invertase can hydrolyze sucrose, but not maltose or other sugars.

EXPLANATORY NOTES

(1) sanso to no kagō — "Combination with oxygen" (See Explanatory Note No. 3 of Lesson 11).

(2) jia-enso-san — The prefix *a-* (亜) corresponds to the suffixes "-ous" and "-ite".

The prefix *ji-* (次) corresponds to "hypo-" in English.

リン酸	rinsan	phosphoric acid
亜リン酸	a-rinsan	phosphorous acid
リン酸ナトリウム	rinsan-natoriumu	sodium phosphate
亜リン酸ナトリウム	a-rinsan-natoriumu	sodium phosphite
次亜リン酸ナトリウム	jia-rinsan-natoriumu	sodium hypophosphite

Note further that the sound *jia*, written in *kana*, frequently occurs in organic nomenclature, with a totally different meaning of course:

ジアゾ化合物	jiazo-kagō-butsu	diazo compound
ジアミン	jiamin	diamine

(3) mashi mo shinakere-ba heri mo shinai — "Neither increase nor decrease." This kind of construction is not uncommon. As another example we cite:

atsuku mo naranakereba — neither becomes hotter nor
tsumetaku mo naranai — colder

(4) tanpaku-shitsu to shite no seishitsu — "Properties as proteins." This construction implies that enzymes fulfill several roles, one of them being proteins.

As an added illustration, consider a man who is simultaneously 工学部長 *kōgaku-buchō* "dean of the engineering college" and 化学工学科の教授 *kagaku-*

kōgaku-ka no kyōju "professor of chemical engineering."

The expression 部長としての意見 *buchō to shite no iken* means his "opinion as dean".

(5) ...mono de aru   This phrase, appended to a statement means "it happens that..." or "it is characteristic that..." or "typically..." It is often omitted in translation.

SUPPLEMENTARY READINGS

A. | 残存 | zanson | relic |
植物地理学	shokubutsu-chiri-gaku	plant geography
用語	yōgo	technical term
かつて	katsute	formerly
広い	hiroi	broad
分布圏	bunpu-ken	area of distribution
狭い	semai	narrow
地域	chi-iki	region
生育する	sei-iku suru	to grow, be born and bred

残　　存　(SJ 397)

植物地理学の用語。かつて広い分布圏をもっていた植物が環境条件の変化などによって分布圏を移動縮小し，現在限られた狭い地域にのみ生育する現象。

B. | 発芽 | hatsuga | germination |
芽	me	bud
休止する	kyūshi suru	to be dormant, resting
生長する	seichō suru	to grow
胞子	hōshi	spore
花粉	kafun	pollen
植物体	shokubutsu-tai	plant body
発生	hassei	embryo
種子	shushi	seed
受精卵	jusei-ran	fertilized egg
幼芽	yōga	plumule
幼根	yōkon	radicle
子葉	shiyō	cotyledon
形生する	keisei suru	to form
機構	kikō	mechanism
適温	tekion	suitable temperature
光発芽種子	kō-hatsuga-shushi	light germinator

| 吸水 | kyūsui | absorbent water |
| 不可欠 | fukaketsu | indispensable |

発　芽　(SJ 802)

一般的に芽，特に休止していた芽が生長を始めること。さらに胞子・花粉などからの植物体の発生が始まることをもいう。種子植物では受精卵は分裂して幼芽，幼根，子葉を形成する。発芽の機構はまだよくわかっていないが，適温・酸素あるいは光発芽種子のように光を必要とし，特に吸水は不可欠の条件である。

C.	非平衡	hi-heikō	non-equilibrium
	死んでしばらくたつ	shinde shibaraku tatsu	a short while after dying
	局部的に	kyokubu-teki ni	in certain parts, partially
	少なくとも	sukunakutomo	at least
	20年余	nijū-nen-yo	more than 20 years
	経過する	keika suru	to elapse
	開く	hiraku	to open
	しか…ない	shika...nai	only

非平衡状態の熱力学　(BK 157–158)

生物に関係のある現象では，生物の生きている間に平衡状態ができるものはほとんどなく，死んでしばらくたって，初めて局部的には平衡のところができる。完全に平衡になるには全体が分解してしまわなければならない。したがって生きている状態を問題にする限り，熱力学は不要のようにみえる。しかしそうではない。平衡でない場合にも状態を表わすすべての変数は，平衡状態へ近づくように変化するから，どこに平衡状態があるかを知ることによって，少なくとも変化の方向は知ることができる。平衡状態でない場合について，定量的な考察をするために非平衡状態の熱力学というものが作られてから20年余が経過，少しずつ応用の道が開かれつつある。非平衡状態を扱うといっても，平衡状態からわずかにずれた状態をしか扱うことができない。

D.	肥料	hiryō	fertilizer
	石灰窒素	sekkai-chisso	lime nitrogen
	黒鉛	kokuen	graphite (black lead)
	チリ硝石	chiri-shōseki	Chile saltpeter
	尿素	nyōso	urea
	マメ科	mame-ka	bean family
	植物	shokubutsu	plant
	根	ne	root
	寄生する	kisei suru	to live on, be parasitic on

根粒細菌	konryū-saikin	root-nodule bacteria
栽培する	saibai suru	to cultivate
緑肥	ryokuhi	green manure (fertilizer made from green plants)
リン酸	rinsan	phosphoric acid
黄リン	ōrin	yellow phosphorous
血液	ketsueki	blood
尿	nyō	urine
役にたつ	yaku ni tatsu	to help
骨粉	koppun	bone meal (dust)
骨灰	kotsubai	bone ashes
米ぬか	kome-nuka	rice bran
カリ肥料	kari-hiryō	potash fertilizers
灰	hai	ash
わが国	waga-kuni	our country (i. e., Japan)
ドイツ・フランス	Doitsu, Furansu	Germany; France
鉱床	kōshō	ore deposits
輸入する	yunyū suru	to import
石灰石	sekkai-seki	limestone
粉	kona	powder
畑	hatake	field
まく	maku	to spread
栄養	eiyō	nutrition
長年	naganen	a long time, for many years
土	tsuchi	earth, ground

肥　料　(3K 220–221)

窒素肥料

　窒素肥料としては，硫酸アンモニウム $(NH_4)_2SO_4$ を多く使うが，そのほか，石灰窒素（カルシウムシアナミド $CaCN_2$ と黒鉛 C との混合物）・チリ硝石 $NaNO_3$・硝酸アンモニウム NH_4NO_3・塩化アンモニウム NH_4Cl・尿素 $CO(NH_2)_2$ も用いられている。

　マメ科の植物は，その根に寄生する根粒細菌が空気中の窒素を取り入れて化合物にするはたらきがあるから，窒素肥料を特に与える必要はない。マメ科を栽培して緑肥をつくるのは，根粒細菌の固定した窒素を肥料に利用するためである。

リン酸肥料

　黄リンは有毒なものであるが，リンの化合物は植物にも動物にも必要である。骨の主成

分はリン酸カルシウムであり，細胞や血液の中にも尿の中にもリン酸化合物がある。

　尿や有機質肥料も，リン酸肥料としていくらか役にたつ。しかし，特にリン酸を多く与えるには，骨粉・骨灰・米ぬかなどを用いる。

カリ肥料

　植物の灰は炭酸カリウム K_2CO_3 などを含むのでカリ肥料となる。わが国ではドイツ・フランスなどで天然に鉱床をつくっている硫酸カリウム K_2SO_4 や塩化カリウムを多量に輸入して用いている。

カルシウム化合物

　消石灰や石灰石の粉を畑にまくことがある。これは，植物の栄養としてではない。硫酸アンモニウムなどの肥料を長年与えると，しだいに土が酸性となるからその酸性を中和するためである。

E.	除草剤	josō-zai	herbicide
	雑草	zassō	weeds
	枯死する	koshi suru	to wither, die
	薬剤	yakuzai	chemical
	生長ホルモン	seichō-horumon	growth hormone
	適当な	tekitō na	suitable
	散布する	sanpu suru	to scatter
	(異常)発育	(ijō) hatsuiku	(abnormal) growth
	刺激する	shigeki suru	to stimulate
	貯蔵	chozō	storage
	消費する	shōhi suru	to consume
	(verb stem)＋つくす	(verb stem)＋tsukusu	to exhaust completely
	根部	konbu	the roots
	乳濁液	nyūdaku-eki	emulsion

除草剤　(2RJ 656)

　雑草を枯死させる作用のある薬剤を除草剤という。植物生長ホルモンを適当な濃度に散布するとある種の植物の異常発育を刺激し，貯蔵物質を消費しつくして根部から枯死し，除草剤としていちじるしい効果があることが見出された。

　2, 4−D という除草剤は重要で，無色の結晶で，融点139°C，水にわずかしか溶けないから乳濁液として使用される。

F.	乳酸	nyūsan	lactic acid

| 酢酸（菌） | sakusan (kin) | acetic acid (bacteria) |
| 悪臭 | akushū | bad odor |

発酵と腐敗 (S 105)

　微生物のはたらきで有機物質が分解する現象をふつう発酵といっているが，そのなかには，アルコール発酵や乳酸発酵と違って酸素を必要とする場合も少なくない。たとえば，酢酸発酵は酢酸菌がエチルアルコールから酢酸をつくるはたらきであるが，これは酸化反応である。

$$C_2H_5OH + O_2 \longrightarrow CH_3COOH + H_2O + 115 \text{ kcal}$$

　微生物が有機物質を分解するとき，その生成物が有毒であったり，悪臭を発したりする場合は，これを腐敗という。腐敗のとき，材料となる物質はたんぱく質である場合が多い。

G.	呼吸器管	kokyū-kikan	respiratory organs
	交換	kōkan	exchange
	アメーバ	amēba	amoeba
	クラゲ	kurage	jellyfish
	ミミズ	mimizu	earthworm
	下等動物	katō-dōbutsu	lower animals
	菌類	kinrui	fungi
	藻類	sōrui	algae
	さまざまな (＝いろいろな)	samazama na	various
	備える	sonaeru	to be equipped with

呼吸器管の構造とはたらき (S 105)

　体内で発生する二酸化炭素と外界からとり入れる酸素との交換は，アメーバ・クラゲ・ミミズなどの下等動物や，細菌類・菌類・藻類などの下等植物では，からだの表面で行なわれ，特別な呼吸器管をもたない。しかし，多くの動物ではさまざな構造の呼吸器官を備えていて，ガスの交換を行なっている。

FINAL TRANSLATION TEST

酵　素 (SS 78, 72–75)

　酵素と酵母の役割を区別することはむずかしい問題であった。酵母は植物性の微生物であって，単細胞の菌類の一群の名前である。d-グルコースを水に溶かすと，そこに微生物がいなければ，いつまでたっても変化は起こらない。ところが，そこに酵母を入れると，

d-グルコースはすぐにエタノールと二酸化炭素に分解する。いわゆるアルコール発酵を行なう。このアルコール発酵と呼ばれる生体化学反応を行なわせるものは，酵母という生物の中にある物質であって，それが酵素なのである。ブドウからブドウ酒ができるのは，ブドウの果皮に酵母がついているからであり，この酵母のもっている酵素によってアルコール発酵が起こるのである。さらにこれを放置すると，刺激臭を生じてすっぱくなるのは，酢酸菌による酢酸発酵が起こったからである。牛乳を長期間保存するためには，濃縮，脱水して粉状とするのは酵母が活動するのをふせぐためである。

　酵素の発見は，デンプン質のものからのアルコール製造の機構を研究する目的でなされた実験の過程においてであった。アーヴィン，キルヒホフらは，発芽している大麦がデンプンを発酵性の糖にするという研究をしていたが，ジュブランフォーは麦芽を温湯中に浸し，透明な液を取り出してそれをデンプンに作用させ，麦芽を直接作用させた場合と同じ液化および糖化が行なわれることを知った。このようにして生体反応が，生命力がなくても生命なき物質（酵素）によって行なわれることが，だんだん明らかになって来た。ところが，それ以後発見された酵素は，いずれも加水分解反応をうながすトリプシン，リパーゼなどの酵素に限られていたので，まだ生命力論が残存していたが，ビュヒナーの研究によって酵素の存在は確立された。

　生体を分析するとその大部分は水であるが，残りの約半分は炭素で，極めて微量の灰分のほかは酸素，窒素，水素が占めている。すなわち，炭素化合物が生物の基本的物質になっている。実験室で有機化学者が炭素化合物の合成を行なう場合には，種々の有機溶剤，塩酸，硝酸，硫酸のような強酸，カ性ソーダのような強塩基，高温，高圧などのかなり激しい条件を用いることが多いのに反し，生体内では37—38℃以下の温度で，水を主体としたほとんど中性の環境で合成を行なっている。緑色植物は二酸化炭素と水から有機物を光合成し，またこの有機物を直接間接に酸化または分解してエネルギーを出す。これらの反応はすべて生物が生きている穏和な条件の下で行なわれる。これができるのは，種々の酵素が生細胞の中に配置されているからである。酵素の種類は非常に多くて，現在700種以上発見されているが，いずれも生体反応の反応速度は変えるが，平衡状態には無関係で，一種の触媒である。

LESSON 22

第二十二課

KANJI

海	55	KAI		安	153	AN
	2553	umi			1283	yasu(i)
味	516	MI		硬	250b	KŌ
	913	aji			3193	
精	647	SEI		肪	219b	BŌ
	3480				3734	
換	248a	KAN		第	273	DAI
	1964	ka(eru)			3385	
代	463	DAI		別	508	BETSU
	364	ka(wari)			674	
毒	686	DOKU		活	174	KATSU
	2468				2552	
適	679	TEKI		失	418	SHITSU
	4738				178	ushina(u)
鉱	610	KŌ		炎	219a	EN
	4843				2751	hono-o
煮	250a	SHA		酢	253b	SAKU
	2771	ni(ru)			4783	su
殖	249b	SHOKU		着	276	CHAKU
	2448				3665	tsu(ku)

READING SELECTIONS

海水	kaisui	sea water
析出する	sekishutsu suru	to separate
除く	nozoku	to remove
食塩	shokuen	table salt
(苦い)味	(nigai) aji	(bitter) taste
精製	seisei	purification
イオン交換樹脂	ion-kōkan-jushi	ion-exchange resin
脱塩	datsuen	desalting
層	sō	beds, layers

つかまる	tsukamaru	to be held
不純物	fujun-butsu	impurity
ろ過する	roka suru	to filter
ろ紙の目	roshi no me	pores of the filter paper
ミョウバン	myōban	alum
たやすく	tayasuku	easily
飲料水	inryō-sui	drinking water
濁った	nigotta	turbid, muddy
澄んだ	sunda	clear
いやな	iya na	unpleasant, disagreeable
有毒な	yūdoku na	poisonous
有害な	yūgai na	injurious, harmful
細菌	saikin	bacteria
病原菌	byōgen-kin	pathogenic bacteria
…に適する	…ni tekisuru	to be suitable for…
…かどうか	…ka dō ka	whether or not…
純粋の	junsui no	pure
気のぬけた	ki no nuketa	flat (tasting)
(不)愉快な	(fu)yukai na	(un)pleasant
鉱物質	kō-busshitsu	minerals
湯ざまし	yuzamashi	boiled water (which has been cooled)
追い出す	oi-dasu	to expel, drive out
殺す	korosu	to kill
煮沸する	shafutsu suru	to boil
ためす（＝試す）	tamesu	to test
検査	kensa	test
判定	hantei	judgment
繁殖	hanshoku	breeding, propagation
助ける	tasukeru	to help
安全な	anzen na	safe
亜硝酸塩	a-shōsan-en	nitrites
硬水	kōsui	hard water
軟水	nansui	soft water
セッケン（石けん）	sekken	soap
あわのできにくい水	awa no dekinikui mizu	water which forms suds with difficulty
脂肪酸	shibō-san	fatty acid

天 然 水 （3K 204, 209–211）

<u>海水</u>。海水 1kg 中に含まれるイオンの量は約 35g で，ほぼ表 1 のとおりである。

　海水から水分を蒸発させていくと，まずカルシウムイオン Ca^{2+} と硫酸イオン SO_4^{2-} とが 2 分子の水と結合して，硫酸カルシウム $CaSO_4 \cdot 2H_2O$ となって析出する。それを除いて，さらに水分を蒸発させると，ナトリウムイオン Na^+ と塩素イオン Cl^- とが結合して塩化ナトリウム（食塩）$NaCl$ となって析出する。この塩化ナトリウムを除いた残りの液は，マグネシウムイオン Mg^{2+} を含んでいるために，苦い味がする。[1] この液からはマグネシウム塩・カリウム塩・臭素を製造する。

表 1：海水 1kg に含まれるイオンの量（g）

陽イオン	記　号	重量 g	陰イオン	記　号	重量 g
ナトリウムイオン	Na^+	10.56	塩素イオン	Cl^-	18.98
マグネシウムイオン	Mg^{2+}	1.27	硫酸イオン	SO_4^{2-}	2.65
カルシウムイオン	Ca^{2+}	0.40	炭酸水素イオン	HCO_3^-	0.14
カリウムイオン	K^+	0.38	臭素イオン	Br^-	0.065

<u>水の精製</u>。天然水にはいろいろの塩類が溶けている。これを精製するには，蒸留するか，イオン交換樹脂で脱塩する。水を陽イオン交換樹脂と陰イオン交換樹脂の層を通すと，Na^+, Ca^{2+}, や Mg^{2+} のような陽イオンはすべて陽イオン交換樹脂につかまり，その代わりに水素イオン H^+ が樹脂から出てくる。Cl^- や SO_4^{2-} のような陰イオンはすべて陰イオン交換樹脂につかまって，その代わりに水酸イオン OH^- が樹脂から出てくる。水素イオンと水酸イオンとは結合して水分子となってしまうので，水の中の陽イオンも陰イオンもみな除かれる。ただし，この方法では，イオンにならない不純物を除くことはできない。

　水に混じっている固体を除くには，ろ過すればよい。しかし，ろ紙の目を通過するような細かい固体があるときは，水に硫酸アルミニウム，またはミョウバンの水溶液を加えておくと，これらの粒子が集まって大きな粒子となり，たやすく除かれる。

<u>飲料水</u>。濁った水はもちろん，澄んだ水でも，いやな味やにおいがあったり[1]，有毒な物質が溶けていたり，有害な細菌（病原菌）を含んでいたりするものは，飲料に適しない。

　蒸留水はほとんど純粋の水であるが，気のぬけたような不愉快な味がある。それで飲料水としては少量の鉱物質や空気の溶け込んでいる水がよい。湯や[2]湯ざましがおいしくないのは，水の中に溶けていた空気が追い出されているからである。水に含まれている病原菌を殺すには，水を 5 分間ほど煮沸すればよい。しかし多量の水の場合には，サラシ粉または塩素で殺菌する。

天然水が飲料に適するかどうかをためすには，細菌学的検査を行なって，細菌の多少をしらべなければならないが，それをしなくても，薬品で化学的検査をすれば，ある程度判定ができる。

有機物は細菌の繁殖を助けるから，有機物の少ない水が安全である。また，タンパク質が腐敗すると，アンモニウム塩や亜硝酸塩ができるから，これらを含まない水が安全である。

硬水と軟水。セッケンを加えたときに濁りができて，あわのできにくい水を硬水といい，セッケンをよく溶かし，あわのよくたつ水を軟水という。天然の硬水は，ふつう，カルシウムイオン Ca^{2+} やマグネシウムイオン Mg^{2+} を含んでいる。セッケンは脂肪酸のナトリウム塩であって，水に溶けるが，脂肪酸のカルシウム塩やマグネシウム塩は水に溶けない。硬水の中では，セッケンがカルシウム塩やマグネシウム塩に変わって濁るのである。

元素	genso	element
周期律表	shūki-ritsu-hyō	periodic table
形式	keishiki	form
横 (縦) の配列	yoko (tate) no hairetsu	row (column); horizontal (vertical) arrangement
周期	shūki	period
族	zoku	group
同族元素	dōzoku-genso	elements belonging to the same group
順番	junban	order
くり返す	kuri-kaesu	to repeat
区別する	kubetsu suru	to distinguish
典型元素	tenkei-genso	typical (pattern) elements
遷移元素	sen'i-genso	transition elements
別に	betsu ni	separately
取り出す	tori-dasu	to take out
不活性ガス	fu-kassei-gasu	inert gas
何物とも…ない	nanimono to mo...nai	with no other substances
活性の大きい	kassei no ōkii	highly active
1 価の陽イオン	ikka no yō-ion	monovalent cation
アルカリ土類金属	arukari-dorui-kinzoku	alkaline earth metal
いずれも＝どれも		
分類する	bunrui suru	to classify
容易に	yōi ni	easily
失う	ushinau	to lose
陽性	yōsei	cationic properties
陰性	insei	anionic properties

橋渡しとなる	hashi-watashi to naru	to form a bridge
原子価	genshi-ka	valence

元素の周期律表　(3K 82, 84)

　元素の周期律表には，いろいろな形式のものがあるが，どれでも横の配列を周期といい，縦の配列を族といい，同じ一つの元素がどの族のどの周期に属するかは定まっている。同じ族の元素を同族元素といい，性質が互いに似ている。族の順番は0から VIII までになっているが，第4周期から後は，第 I 族から第 VII 族までが2回くり返されている。それで，これを A, B として区別し，A と第0族の元素を典型元素，B と第 VIII 族の元素を遷移元素という。第6周期と第7周期には B の第 III 族に属する元素がたくさんあって，周期律表に書き込むことができないので，これを別に取り出して示してある。

　周期律表の第0族には，不活性ガスが集まっている。これらの元素はふつう何物とも化合せず，陽イオンにも陰イオンにもならない。第 I 族 A には，変化を起こしやすい，すなわち化学的に活性の大きいアルカリ金属がある。これらは1価の陽イオンとなりやすい。第 II 族 A には，アルカリ土類金属のように，2価の陽イオンとなる金属がある。第 VII 族 A に集まっているハロゲン元素は，化学的に活性の大きい非金属元素で，いずれも1価の陰イオンとなるものである。他の族でも，同じ族の元素は似た性質を示す。したがって，周期律の族によって元素を分類することができる。

　次に同じ周期に属する元素を見ると，その初めにある第 I 族 A の元素が最も容易に電子を失って陽イオンになりやすい。すなわち，最も陽性が強い。原子番号が増すにつれて，少しずつ性質が変わり，第 VII 族 A で最も陰性が強くなる。すなわち，電子を得て陰イオンになりやすい。その次の第0族の元素は陽性も陰性もなく，次の周期への橋渡しとなっている。周期律表の A の元素と B の元素とは，族の番号が同じならば原子価は似た点がある。たとえば，第 VII 族では最高7価の原子価を示す。しかし，A の塩素は，陰イオン Cl^- とはなるが陽イオンとはならないし，B のマンガンは，陽イオン Mn^{2+} とはなるが，陰イオンとはならない。

エーテル	ēteru	ether
悪臭	akushū	bad odor
耐圧容器	taiatsu-yōki	pressure vessel
アセトン	aseton	acetone
特殊の吹管	tokushu no suikan	special blow torch
吹き出す	fuki-dasu	to blow forth
酸素アセチレン炎	sanso-asechiren-en	oxy-acetylene flame
炎	hono-o	flame
鉄材	tetsuzai	iron (materials)

切る	kiru	to cut
つなぐ	tsunagu	to join
酢酸	sakusan	acetic acid
アセトアルデヒド	aseto-arudehido	acetaldehyde
塩化ビニル	enka-biniru	vinyl chloride
不飽和性がある	fu-hōwa-sei ga aru	to be unsaturated
ポリ酢酸ビニル	pori-sakusan-biniru	polyvinyl acetate
接着剤	setchaku-zai	adhesive (material)
ホルマリン	horumarin	formalin
…と…をはたらかせる	…to…o hatarakaseru	to cause…to react with…
特有の	tokuyū no	characteristic
含量	ganryō	content
凍る	kōru	to freeze
氷酢酸	hyō-sakusan	glacial acetic acid
合成酢	gōsei-su	(artificial) vinegar
カルボキシル基	karubokishiru-ki	carboxyl group
無水酢酸	musui-sakusan	acetic anhydride
酸無水物	san-musui-butsu	acid anhydride

アセチレン　(3K 259–261)

アセチレン C_2H_2 は，炭化カルシウムに水を注いでつくる。

$$CaC_2 + 2H_2O \longrightarrow C_2H_2 + Ca(OH)_2$$

アセチレンは，無色・有毒な気体であり，エーテルのようなかおりのものであるが，ふつうは不純物のために悪臭がある。圧力をかけて耐圧容器中のアセトンに溶かし込み，特殊の吹管から酸素とともに吹き出させて，酸素アセチレン炎 [3] をつくる。この炎は非常に温度が高いから，鉄材を切ったりつないだりするのに使う。

アセチレンは三重結合があるから，付加反応をすることができる。すなわち，水銀塩を触媒として，アセチレンに水・塩化水素・酢酸を付加させ，それぞれアセトアルデヒド・塩化ビニル・酢酸ビニルを製造する。

塩化ビニルや酢酸ビニルは，二重結合を含み，不飽和性があるので，付加重合をしやすい。

ポリ酢酸ビニルは接着剤や塗料などに使われるもので，これからポリビニルアルコールが得られる。これを糸に引き，ホルマリンをはたらかせて水に溶けないものにしたのがビニロンという繊維である。

アセトアルデヒド $CH_3 \cdot CHO$ は，特有の刺激臭があり水によく溶ける。工業では，マンガン塩を触媒としてアセトアルデヒドを酸素で酸化して酢酸をつくる。

酢酸 CH₃・COOH （融点 17°C，沸点 119°C）は，強い刺激臭がある。水の含量が 1 ％
以下のものは凍りやすく，氷酢酸という。酢酸は，溶媒，合成酢の製造などに用いられる
ほか，化学工業上 [4] 重要な原料である。

酢酸は，水溶液中でカルボキシル基の水素が少し電離して平衡を保つから弱い酸性を示
す。

2 分子の酢酸から水のとれたものは無色の液体であって，無水酢酸という。このように，
酸から水のとれた化合物を酸無水物という。

TENNEN-SUI

Kaisui: Kaisui ichi-kiro-chū ni fukumareru ion no ryō wa yaku sanjū-go-guramu
de, hobo hyō-ichi no tōri de aru.

　Kaisui kara suibun o jōhatsu sasete iku to, mazu, karushiumu-ion Ca^{2+} to ryū-
san-ion $SO_4{}^{2-}$ to ga ni-bunshi no mizu to ketsugō shite, ryūsan karushiumu $CaSO_4\cdot$
$2H_2O$ to natte sekishutsu suru. Sore o nozoite, sara ni suibun o jōhatsu saseru to,
natoriumu-ion Na^+ to enso-ion Cl^- to ga ketsugō shite, enka-natoriumu (shokuen)
NaCl to natte sekishutsu suru. Kono enka-natoriumu o nozoita nokori no eki
wa, maguneshiumu-ion Mg^{2+} o fukunde iru tame ni, nigai aji ga suru. Kono eki
kara wa maguneshiumu-en, kariumu-en, shūso o seizō suru.

Mizu no Seisei: Tennen-sui ni wa iroiro no enrui ga tokete iru. Kore o seisei suru
ni wa, jōryū suru ka, ion-kōkan-jushi de datsuen suru. Mizu o yō-ion-kōkan-jushi
to in-ion-kōkan-jushi no sō o tōsu to, Na^+, Ca^{2+}, ya Mg^{2+} no yō na yō-ion
subete yō-ion-kōkan-jushi ni tsukamari, sono kawari ni suiso-ion H^+ ga jushi
kara dete kuru. Cl^- ya $SO_4{}^{2-}$ no yō na in-ion wa subete in-ion-kōkan-jushi ni
tsukamatte, sono kawari ni suisan-ion OH^- ga jushi kara dete kuru. Suiso-ion to
suisan-ion to wa, ketsugō shite mizu-bunshi to natte shimau no de, mizu no naka
no yō-ion mo in-ion mo mina nozokareru. Tadashi, kono hōhō de wa, ion ni
naranai fujun-butsu o nozoku koto wa dekinai. Mizu ni majitte iru kotai o nozoku ni wa, roka sureba yoi. Shikashi, roshi no me o tsūka suru yō na komakai
kotai ga aru toki wa, mizu ni ryūsan aruminiumu mata wa myōban no sui-yōeki
o kuwaete oku to, korera no ryūshi ga atsumatte ōki na ryūshi to nari, tayasuku
nozokareru.

Inryō-sui: Nigotta mizu wa mochiron, sunda mizu de mo, iya na aji ya nioi ga
attari, [1] yūdoku na busshitsu ga tokete itari, yūgai na saikin (byōgen-kin) o fukunde itari suru mono wa, inryō ni teki shinai.

　Jōryū-sui wa hotondo junsui no mizu de aru ga, ki no nuketa yō na fu-yukai
na aji ga aru. Sore de, inryō-sui to shite wa shōryō no kō-busshitsu ya kūki no
toke-konde iru mizu ga yoi. Yu ya [2] yuzamashi ga oishiku nai no wa, mizu no
naka ni tokete ita kūki ga oi-dasarete iru kara de aru. Mizu ni fukumarete iru

byōgen-kin o korosu ni wa, mizu o gofun-kan hodo shafutsu sureba yoi. Shika-shi, taryō no mizu no baai ni wa, sarashi-ko mata wa enso de sakkin suru.

Tennen-sui ga inryō ni teki-suru ka dō ka o tamesu ni wa, saikin-gaku-teki-kensa o okonatte, saikin no tashō o shirabenakereba naranai ga, sore o shinakute mo, yakuhin de kagaku-teki-kensa o sureba, aru teido hantei ga dekiru

Yūki-butsu wa saikin no hanshoku o tasukeru kara, yūki-butsu no sukunai mizu ga anzen de aru. Mata, tanpaku-shitsu ga fuhai suru to, anmoniumu-en ya a-shō-san-en ga dekiru kara, korera o fukumanai mizu ga anzen de aru.

Kōsui to Nansui: Sekken o kuwaeta toki ni nigori ga dekite, awa no deki-nikui mizu o kōsui to ii, sekken o yoku tokashi, awa no yoku tatsu mizu o nansui to iu. Tennen no kōsui wa, futsū, karushiumu-ion Ca^{2+} ya maguneshiumu ion Mg^{2+} o fukunde iru. Sekken wa, shibō-san no natoriumu-en de atte, mizu ni tokeru ga, shibō-san no karushiumu-en ya maguneshiumu-en wa mizu ni tokenai. Kōsui no naka de wa, sekken ga karushiumu-en ya maguneshiumu-en ni kawatte nigoru no de aru.

GENSO NO SHŪKI-RITSU-HYŌ

Genso no shūki-ritsu-hyō ni wa, iroiro na keishiki no mono ga aru ga, dore de mo yoko no hairetsu o shūki to ii, tate no hairetsu o zoku to ii, onaji hitotsu no genso ga dono zoku no dono shūki ni zoku suru ka wa sadamatte iru. Onaji zoku no genso o dōzoku-genso to ii, seishitsu ga tagai ni nite iru. Zoku no junban wa rei kara hachi made ni natte iru ga, daiyon-shūki kara ato wa, dai-ichi zoku kara dainana-zoku made ga nikai kuri-kaesarete iru. Sore de, kore o A, B to shite ku-betsu shi, A to dairei-zoku no genso o tenkei-genso, B to daihachi-zoku no genso o sen'i-genso to iu. Dairoku-shūki to dainana-shūki ni wa B no daisan-zoku ni zoku suru genso ga takusan atte, shūki-ritsu-hyō ni kaki-komu koto ga dekinai no de, kore o betsu ni tori-dashite shimeshite aru.

Shūki-ritsu-hyō no dairei-zoku ni wa, fu-kassei-gasu ga atsumatte iru. Korera no genso wa, futsū nanimono to mo kagō sezu, yō-ion ni mo in-ion ni mo naranai. Daiichi-zoku A ni wa, henka o okoshi-yasui, sunawachi kagaku-teki ni kassei no ōkii, arukari-kinzoku ga aru. Korera wa ikka no yō-ion to nari-yasui. Daini-zoku A ni wa, arukari-dorui-kinzoku no yō ni, nika no yō-ion to naru kinzoku ga aru. Dainana-zoku A ni atsumatte iru harogen genso wa, kagaku-teki ni kassei no ōkii hi-kinzoku-genso de, izure mo ikka no in-ion to naru mono de aru. Ta no zoku de mo, onaji zoku no genso wa nita seishitsu o shimesu. Shitagatte, shūki-ritsu no zoku ni yotte genso o bunrui suru koto ga dekiru.

Tsugi ni onaji shūki ni zoku suru genso o miru to, sono hajime ni aru daiichi-zoku A no genso ga mottomo yōi ni denshi o ushinatte yō-ion ni nari-yasui. Su-nawachi, mottomo yōsei ga tsuyoi. Genshi-bangō ga masu ni tsurete, sukoshi-zutsu seishitsu ga kawari, dainana-zoku A de mottomo insei ga tsuyoku naru. Sunawachi, denshi o ete in-ion ni nari-yasui. Sono tsugi no dairei-zoku no genso wa yōsei mo

insei mo naku, tsugi no shūki e no hashiwatashi to natte iru. Shūki-ritsu-hyō no A no genso to B no genso to wa, zoku no bangō ga onaji naraba, genshi-ka wa nita ten ga aru. Tatoeba, dainana-zoku de wa, saikō nanaka no genshi-ka o shimesu. Shikashi, A no enso wa, in-ion Cl^- to wa naru ga yō-ion to wa naranai shi, B no mangan wa, yō-ion Mn^{2+} to wa naru ga, in-ion to wa naranai.

ASECHIREN

Asechiren C_2H_2 wa, tanka-karushiumu ni mizu o sosoide tsukuru.

$$CaC_2 + 2H_2O \longrightarrow C_2H_2 + Ca(OH)_2$$

Asechiren wa, mushoku, yūdoku na kitai de ari, ēteru no yō na kaori no mono de aru ga, futsū wa fujun-butsu no tame ni akushū ga aru. Atsuryoku o kakete taiatsu-yōki-chū no aseton ni tokashi-komi, tokushu no suikan kara sanso to to-mo ni fuki-dasasete, sanso-asechiren-en [3] o tsukuru. Kono hono-o wa hijō ni ondo ga takai kara, tetsuzai o kittari tsunaidari suru no ni tsukau.

Asechiren wa sanjū-ketsugō ga aru kara, fuka-hannō o suru koto ga dekiru. Sunawachi, suigin-en o shokubai to shite, asechiren ni mizu, enka-suiso, sakusan o fuka sase, sorezore aseto-arudehido, enka-biniru, sakusan-biniru o seizō suru.

Enka-biniru ya sakusan-biniru wa, nijū-ketsugō o fukumi, fu-hōwasei ga aru no de, fuka-jūgō o shi-yasui.

Pori-sakusan-biniru wa setchaku-zai ya toryō nado ni tsukawareru mono de, kore kara pori-biniru-arukōru ga erareru. Kore o ito ni hiki, horumarin o hata-rakasete mizu ni tokenai mono ni shita no ga, biniron to iu sen'i de aru.

Aseto-arudehido CH_3CHO wa, tokuyū no shigeki-shū ga ari mizu ni yoku to-keru. Kōgyō de wa, mangan-en o shokubai to shite, aseto-arudehido o sanso de sanka shite, sakusan o tsukuru.

Sakusan CH_3COOH (yūten sesshi-jūnana-do, futten sesshi hyaku-jūkyū-do) wa, tsuyoi shigeki-shū ga aru. Mizu no ganryō ga ichi pāsento ika no mono wa, kō-ri-yasuku, hyō-sakusan to iu. Sakusan wa, yōbai, gōsei-su no seizō nado ni mochi-irareru hoka, kagaku-kōgyō-jō [4] jūyō na genryō de aru.

Sakusan wa, sui-yōeki-chū de karubokishiru-ki no suiso ga sukoshi denri shite heikō o tamotsu kara yowai sansei o shimesu.

Ni-bunshi no sakusan kara mizu no toreta mono wa mushoku no ekitai de atte, musui-sakusan to iu. Kono yō ni, san kara mizu no toreta kagō-butsu o san-musui-butsu to iu.

NATURAL WATER

Sea Water: The quantities of ions contained in 1 kg of sea water are essentially those given in Table 1, totaling approximately 35 g.

As we proceed to evaporate sea water, first of all, calcium Ca^{2+} and sulfate SO_4^{2-} ions combine with 2 molecules of water to form $CaSO_4 \cdot 2H_2O$ and precipi-

tate out. Upon their removal and further evaporation, the sodium Na^+ and Cl^- ions will combine to form NaCl which then precipitates out. The liquid which remains when this sodium chloride is removed has a bitter taste due to the magnesium ion Mg^{2+} content. Magnesium and potassium salts plus bromine are produced from this liquor.

Water Purification: Various salts are dissolved in natural waters, and they are purified either by distillation or by desalting with ion exchange resins. If water is passed through beds of cation and anion exchange resins, all of the cations such as Na^+, Ca^{2+}, and Mg^{2+} will be captured by the cation exchange resin and replaced by hydrogen ions H^+ coming from this resin, and all of the anions such as Cl^- and SO_4^{2-} will be captured by the anion exchange resin and replaced by hydroxyl ions OH^- coming from that resin. Since the hydrogen and hydroxyl ions combine completely into water molecules, all cations and anions in the water are removed. It is not possible by this method, however, to remove impurities which do not ionize.

Filtration is best for removing the solids suspended in water. When minute solids are present which pass through the pores of filter paper, however, the addition of aqueous solutions of either aluminum sulfate or alum leads to the coagulation of these particles into large particles which are easily removed.

Drinking Water: Turbid water, of course, is not suitable for drinking, but neither is clear water which has a disagreeable taste and smell or which contains dissolved poisonous substances or harmful (pathogenic) bacteria.

Distilled water is practically pure water but has a disagreeable flat taste. Thus, the best drinking water is water containing dissolved minerals and air. The reason that hot or boiled water does not taste right is because the dissolved air has been driven off. To kill pathogenic bacteria present in water, it is best to boil the water for 5 minutes. For large quantities of water, however, bleaching powder or chlorine are used for killing germs.

To judge whether or not some natural water is suitable for drinking, a bacteriological test must be made to establish the bacterial count, but even without it judgment to some degree is possible by chemical testing with chemical reagents.

Since organic substances favor bacterial propagation, water low in organic matter is safer. Moreover, since the putrefaction of proteins produces ammonium chloride and nitrites, water without them is safest.

Hard and Soft Water: Water which becomes turbid upon the addition of soap and forms suds with difficulty is called hard water; water which dissolves soap and suds easily is called soft water. Natural hard waters usually contain such ions as calcium Ca^{2+} and magnesium Mg^{2+}. Soap is a sodium salt of fatty acids and is soluble in water, but the calcium and magnesium salts of fatty acids are insoluble in water. In hard water soap changes into its calcium and magnesium salts, which

cause turbidity.

THE PERIODIC TABLE OF THE ELEMENTS

There are various forms for the periodic table of the elements, but in every case the rows are called periods, the columns groups, and the period and the column to which a given element belongs are the same. The group numbers go from 0 to *VIII* but, from the 4th period on, the groups *I* through *VII* are repeated twice. These are distinguished by *A* and *B*, the elements in *A* and in group 0 being called "typical elements", those in the *B* groups and in Group *VIII* being called "transition elements". Since the elements belonging to the Group *III B* in the 6th and 7th periods are very large in number and cannot be written into the periodic table, they are presented separately,

The inert gases are collected together in Group 0. These elements usually do not combine with any substance nor do they form cations or anions. In Group *IA* are the alkali metals which readily cause chemical change: that is, they have pronounced chemical activity. They easily form monovalent cations. In the Group *IIA* are the metals which form bivalent cations such as the alkaline earth metals. The halogen elements gathered in Group *VII A* are chemically very active and in every case form monovalent anions. Atoms in other groups show similar properties as well. Thus, elements can be classified according to their group in the periodic table.

Considering now the elements which belong to the same period, the initial element is in Group *IA* and readily loses an electron to form a cation. That is, it has strong cationic properties. As the atomic number increases, the properties change little by little until the Group *VII A* element with the strongest anionic properties. That is, it readily accepts electrons and forms anions. The elements in the next group, the zeroeth group, neither form cations nor anions and act as a bridge to the next period. *A* elements and *B* elements in the periodic table have similar valence characteristics if their group numbers are the same. For example, in group *VII*, they show a maximum atomic valence of 7. However, the chlorine in *A* turns into the anion Cl^- but not into a cation, and the manganese in *B* turns into the cation Mn^{2+} but not into an anion.

ACETYLENE

Acetylene C_2H_2 is produced by pouring water on calcium carbide.

$$CaC_2 + 2H_2O \longrightarrow C_2H_2 + Ca(OH)_2$$

Acetylene is a colorless poisonous gas with an ether-like fragrance, although due to impurities it usually has a bad odor. By dissolving acetylene in acetone in a pressure vessel and blowing it forth together with oxygen from a special blow torch, the oxy-acetylene flame is produced. Since this flame has an exceedingly

high temperature, it is used to cut and join iron materials.

Since acetylene has a triple bond, addition reactions are possible. For example, water, hydrogen chloride and acetic acid may be added to acetylene with mercury salts as catalysts to produce acetaldehyde, vinyl chloride, and vinyl acetate respectively.

Vinyl chloride and vinyl acetate, because they have double bonds and are unsaturated, readily engage in addition polymerization.

Polyvinyl acetate is used in adhesives and paints, and polyvinyl alcohol is derived from it. Nylon fiber is obtained by drawing this material into threads and making it insoluble in water by reacting it with formalin.

Acetaldehyde has a uniquely pungent odor and is soluble in water. Acetaldehyde is oxidized with oxygen industrially using a manganese catalyst to produce acetic acid.

Acetic acid $CH_3 \cdot COOH$ (melting point 17°C, boiling point 119°C) has a strong pungent odor. With less than 1% of water it freezes easily and is called glacial acetic acid. In addition to being used as a solvent and in the manufacture of vinegar, acetic acid is also an important raw material in chemical industries.

In aqueous solution acetic acid is weakly acidic because the hydrogens in the carboxyl groups dissociate slightly and maintain an equilibrium.

Removing water from two molecules of acetic acid gives a colorless liquid called acetic anhydride. Compounds formed in this way by removing water from acids are called acid anhydrides.

Explanatory Notes

(1) nigai aji ga suru	"Has a bitter taste." A similar idiom is *warui nioi ga suru* "it has a bad smell." Later on in the text we also find *iya na aji ga aru* "has an unpleasant taste."
(2) mizu; yu	Note that the Japanese have two words for water: *mizu* water; cold water *yu* hot water The word *mizu* can be used for "water" in general or to imply "cold water" as in *mizu no shawā* "a cold shower (bath)".
(3) hono-o	Not *honō*! The second "o" is distinctly pronounced. (In *kana* 炎 is transcribed as ほのお rather than ほのう.)
(4) kagaku-kōgyō-jō	"In chemical industry." See Note 3, Lesson 19.

SUPPLEMENTARY READINGS

A.	木炭	mokutan	charcoal

然える	moeru	to burn
ろうそく	rōsoku	candle
いったん気体となって から	ittan kitai to natte kara	after once becoming a gas
やはり	yahari	also
燃やす	moyasu	to burn (something)
バーナー	bānā	(Bunsen) burner
空気孔	kūki-kō	air hole
外炎	gai-en	outer flame
内炎	nai-en	inner flame
さかいめ	sakai-me	boundary, border

燃焼と炎　 (3K 26–27)

　木炭などの固体が，液体や気体にならないで固体のまま燃えるときには炎ができない。気体が燃えるときには炎ができ，その炎の表面で燃焼が行なわれる。石油・ろうそくなどもいったん気体となってから燃えるので，やはり炎ができる。バーナーでガスを燃やして空気孔を開くと，ほとんど色のない外炎と青い色の内炎との重なった炎ができる。ガスはおもに内炎の表面，すなわち外炎とのさかいめで燃焼する。外炎は，主として高温の二酸化炭素と水蒸気である。

B.　アルデヒド	arudehido	aldehyde
ケトン	keton	ketone
カルボン酸	karubon-san	carboxylic acid
略記する	ryakki suru	to abbreviate
原子団	genshi-dan	atomic group
アルデヒド基	arudehido-ki	the aldehyde group
アンモニア性硝酸銀 溶液	anmonia-sei-shōsan-gin- yōeki	ammoniacal silver nitrate solution
鎖状炭化水素	sajō-tanka-suiso	chain hydrocarbons
…で置き換える	...de oki-kaeru	to be replaced by...
カルボニル基	karuboniru-ki	carbonyl group
代表的な	daihyō-teki na	representative

アルデヒドとケトンおよびカルボン酸　 (3K 243)

　一般に， $-C\underset{H}{\overset{O}{\diagup}}$（−CHOと略記する）のような原子団をもつ化合物をアルデヒドといい，この原子団をアルデヒド基という。アルデヒド基は酸化されやすく，したがって，アンモニア性硝酸銀溶液から銀を析出する。アルデヒド基が酸化されると，カルボキシル基 $-C\underset{O-H}{\overset{O}{\diagup}}$（−COOHと略記する）に変わる。カルボキシル基をもつ化合物は酸性を示

し，これをカルボン酸という。

　鎖状炭化水素の水素原子1個をカルボキシル基で置き換えた構造のカルボン酸を脂肪酸といい，酢酸もその一つである。アルデヒド基やカルボキシル基の中にある $\diagup$C=O という原子団をカルボニル基という。このCが二つの別のCに結合しているものをケトンという。アセトン CH_3COCH_3 は代表的なケトンで溶媒として用いられ，水と混ざる無色の液体である。

C.	生殖	seishoku	reproduction
	絶える	taeru	to become extinct
	個体	kotai	an individual
	いくつもの	ikutsu mo no	many, several
	種族	shuzoku	species
	生殖細胞	seishoku-saihō	reproductive cell, germ cell
	配偶子	haigū-shi	gamete
	胞子	hōshi	spore
	体細胞	tai-saihō	somatic cell
	ふえる	fueru	to multiply
	無性生殖	musei-seishoku	asexual reproduction
	有性生殖	yūsei-seishoku	sexual reproduction
	合一する	gōitsu suru	to unite (in one body)
	同形配偶子	dōkei-haigū-shi	isogametes
	異形配偶子	ikei-haigū-shi	anisogametes, heterogametes
	雌性	shisei	female
	雄性	yūsei	male
	卵	ran	egg
	精子	seishi	sperm
	…にあたる	…ni ataru	to correspond to…
	接合	setsugō	conjugation
	接合子	setsugō-shi	zygote
	受精	jusei	fertilization
	受精された	jusei sareta	fertilized
	受精卵	jusei-ran	fertilized egg

生　殖　(S 214-215)

　地球上に各種の生物が絶えないのは，一つの個体が生きている間にいくつもの新しい個体をつくり，その種族を残していくからである。生物が新しい個体をつくることを生殖という。生殖のための特別な細胞を生殖細胞といい，これには配偶子と胞子とがある。

　生殖には，からだの一部または体細胞や胞子によりふえる方法（無性生殖）と配偶子に

よりふえる方法（有性生殖）とがある。有性生殖ではふつう２個の配偶子が合一して新し
い個体をつくる。２個の配偶子が同じ形をしている場合を同形配偶子，いちじるしく異な
っている場合を異形配偶子という。異形配偶子のうち，大きくて運動力のないほうを雌性，
小さくて運動力のあるほうを雄性とし，雌性配偶子を卵，雄性配偶子を精子という。ただ
し，高等植物の雄性配偶子にあたるものは運動力をもたないのがふつうである。また，同
形配偶子が合一することを接合，その合一したものを接合子という。これに対し異形配偶
子が合一することを受精といい，受精された雌性配偶子を受精卵という。

D.

臭覚	shūkaku	sense of smell
味覚	mikaku	sense of taste
鼻腔	bikō	nasal cavity
粘膜	nenmaku	mucous membrane
おおう	ōu	to cover
におい	nioi	odor
臭細胞	shū-saihō	olfactory cell
刺激する	shigeki suru	to stimulate
野性の	yasei no	wild
感覚	kankaku	sensation
食物を取り入れるべき	shokumotsu o tori-ireru-beki	food they ought to gather (See Explanatory Note 2, Lesson 23 for -*beki*)
なかまどうし	nakama-dōshi	fellow family (or pack) members
認識する	ninshiki suru	to recognize
敵を避ける	teki o sakeru	to avoid enemies
配偶者	haigū-sha	spouse
舌	shita	tongue
触れる	fureru	to touch, come in contact
乳頭	nyūtō	papilla
突起	tokki	protuberance
味覚芽	mikaku-ga	taste bud
だ液	daeki	saliva
あまい	amai	sweet
からい	karai	salty
すっぱい	suppai	sour
にがい	nigai	bitter

臭覚と味覚　(S 176–177)

<u>臭覚</u>。臭覚をおこさせる物質は，空気を吸いこむときに，それにまじって分子の形で鼻腔

にはいってくる。鼻腔の上部の表面は粘膜におおわれ，その粘膜には，においを感ずる臭細胞がある。においの原因となる分子はこの細胞を刺激して，においをおこさせる。

　一般に野生の動物は，においの感覚によって，まず第一に食物を取り入れるべきかどうかを決定する。さらに，なかまどうしを認識したり，敵を避け，配偶者を見いだしたりするものも多い。

味覚。味の感覚は，舌に触れてみて，はじめておこる。舌の表面には味覚乳頭という小さい突起が並んでおり，それぞれの乳頭の側面にある味覚芽で，だ液に溶けた物質の分子またはイオンの刺激を感ずるのである。味はあまい・からい・すっぱい・にがいの4種類がもととなっている。

E.	活性中心	kassei-chūshin	activity center
	特異的な	tokui-teki na	singular, unique, specific
	部位	bui	region
	チクトクロム	chikutokuromu	cytochrome
	補欠分子族	hoketsu-bunshi-zoku	prosthetic group
	いとなむ	itonamu	to perform
	阻害因子	sogai-inshi	inhibitor
	停止する	teishi suru	to stop
	トリプシン	toripushin	trypsin
	ミオシン	mioshin	myosine
	切断する	setsudan suru	to cut, sever
	想定する	sōtei suru	to imagine, conjecture, suppose
	リゾチーム	rizochiimu	lysozyme
	基質アナログ	kishitsu-anarogu	substrate analog
	N-アセチルグルコサミン	N-asechiru-gurokosamin	N-acetylglucosamine
	オリゴマー	origomā	oligomer
	アミノ酸	amino-san	amino acids
	同定する	dōtei suru	to identify
	基質の特異的吸着	kishitsu no tokui-teki kyūchaku	substrate specific adsorption
	切り出す	kiri-dasu	to cut away
	断片	danpen	fragment

酵素の活性中心　(3RJ 444)

　酵素のもつ特異的な触媒作用は分子の特定の部分で行なわれると考えられる。この部分を活性中心，または活性部位とよぶ。チクトクロムcのように分子中に補欠分子族をもちこれがその作用をいとなむ場合の他にも，阻害因子となりうる低分子がただ1個酵素分子

に結合するだけで酵素活性を停止させることができるとか，トリプシンやミオシンのように酵素の一部をタンパク質分解酵素で切断しても活性が失われないものがあるなどの事実から活性中心の存在が想定された。 D.C.Phillips はリゾチームと基質アナログである N-アセチルグルコサミンオリゴマーとの結合様式を X 線回折によって明らかにした。活性中心に関係しているアミノ酸が同定されている場合もある。活性中心には基質の特異的吸着を行なう場所である吸着中心と，触媒作用を行なう場所である触媒中心とが含まれていると考えられる。酵素分子から切り出され活性中心を含む断片のことを活性フラグメントという。

F.	マグネシア	maguneshia	magnesia
	処理する	shori suru	to treat
	焼成する	shōsei suru	to calcine
	マグネサイト	magunesaito	magnesite
	耐火物	taika-butsu	refractories

海水マグネシア　(3RJ 208)

　海水を水酸化カルシウムで処理して製造した水酸化マグネシウム $Mg(OH)_2$ およびそれを焼成したマグネシア MgO をいう。マグネサイトのない日本では，耐火物原料として重要である。

G.	触媒毒	shokubai-doku	catalytic poison (ing)
	異物質	i-busshitsu	foreign substance
	ヒ素化合物	hiso-kagōbutsu	arsenic compounds
	(永久)被毒	(eikyū)hidoku	(permanent) poisoning
	一時的に	ichiji-teki ni	temporarily
	回復できる	kaifuku dekiru	can be regenerated
	主反応	shu-hannō	main reaction
	阻害する	sogai suru	to inhibit
	副反応	fuku-hannō	side reaction
	保護毒	hogo-doku	protective poison

触　媒　毒　(3RJ 647)

　触媒反応において，微量の異物質が触媒作用を著しく減少させるかまたは全く失わせるとき，その異物質を触媒毒という。接触法による硫酸製造におけるヒ素化合物はこの例である。触媒が触媒毒の作用を受けることを被毒といい，被毒によって触媒作用が永久的に失われる場合を永久被毒，一度は失われるが適当な方法で回復できる場合を一時的被毒という。ある種の触媒毒を適当に用いれば，主反応を阻害せずに副反応を止めることができ，そのため主反応の生成物の収量がふえるので，このようなものは保護毒とよばれる。

H. 含有量	gan'yū-ryō	content
炭酸水素塩	tansan-suiso-en	bicarbonates
一時硬水	ichiji-kōsui	temporary hard water
軟化する	nanka suru	to soften
し難い（＝しにくい）	shigatai	difficult to do
ニトリロ酢酸	nitoriro-sakusan	nitrilo-acetic acid
エチレンジアミン	echiren-jiamin-tetora-	ethylene diamine tetra-
テトラ酢酸	sakusan	acetic acid
キレート	kirēto	chelates
軟化しうる（＝軟化し得る）	nanka shiuru	can be softened

硬　水　(3RJ 436)

　カルシウム塩類およびマグネシウム塩類などの鉱物質を比較的多量に溶かしている天然水を硬水といい，それらの塩類の含有量の少ない水を軟水という。水の中のカルシウムおよびマグネシウムのイオンは主として硫酸塩と炭酸水素塩から来る。炭酸水素塩として存在するものは煮沸して炭酸塩として沈殿させ，軟水とすることができるから，一時硬水といい，硫酸塩として存在するものは煮沸しても軟化し難いから，永久硬水という。ただし永久硬水もイオン交換により，またはニトリロ酢酸，エチレンジアミンテトラ酢酸などを加えてキレートを作らせれば軟化しうる。水中のカルシウム塩およびマグネシウム塩の含有量によってその水の硬度を表わす。　日本では水 100cc 中に酸化カルシウムとして 1mg を含むとき 1 度とし，マグネシウムは $1.4MgO＝1CaO$ の関係で酸化カルシウムに換算する。通常 20 度以上のものを硬水，10 度以下のものを軟水という。

I. 代数学	daisū-gaku	algebra
文字	moji	letters
算法	sanpō	calculation methods
解法を行なう	kaihō o okonau	to solve
群	gun	groups
環	kan	rings
体	tai	fields
抽象	chūshō	abstract

代　数　学　(3RJ 794)

　代数なる語は数の代わりに文字を用いる意味で，algebra という。数を一般的な記号で代表させ，それらの記号の間に，数の間の算法と同じ法則にしたがって算法を行ない，それによって方程式の解法を行なうのが初期の代数学であった。今日の代数学は群，環，体

などのような代数系の理論であって初期の代数学と区別するため，これを抽象代数学という。

FINAL TRANSLATION TEST

　水は人類のみならず，すべての生物にとって無くてはならないものである。生物体がほとんど水分からできているのを見てもわかるように，水なくして生物は生きて行けない。人間の生活にとって用水は重要である。

　現代のように工業化が進む前には，細菌の有無が飲用に適するかどうかの条件であった。しかし，もし細菌が多くても煮沸さえすればよかったのである。工業用水としては，マグネシウムイオン及びカルシウムイオンの含有量を表わす硬度によって，用水の水質が表わせたのである。ところが次第に工業化が進むとともに新しい問題が現われた。まず，鉱毒の問題である。鉱山の排水は多くの重金属を含んでいる。これは，もちろん生物にとって有毒にならない程度にまで重金属イオンを取りのぞいてから出すのであるけれども，重金属イオンの中には，水中に生活する魚貝類の体内にたまって排出されないものがある。例えば有機水銀で，これは魚貝類の体内にたまるので，水中の含有量は低いものであっても，魚貝類の体内では有毒な程度にまで濃縮されているので，これを食べた者は中毒するのである。工場から排出された時には無機水銀の形であっても，水中で有機水銀に変換されるものもある。また，工場排水の処理法としてよく用いられる活性汚泥法などでは，微生物の作用によって排水を浄化しているので，排水中に重金属イオンの量が多いとその活性が失われる。工場排水の水質が規制されていても完全に安全であるとはいい得ないのである。

　さらに，主として湖水などについて富養化の問題がある。これは，窒素化合物，燐酸塩などが湖に流れこみ，藻類などの生物を繁殖させ，有機物質がふえ，その腐敗のため酸素を多量に消費することになる。精確にいえば，生物学的酸素要求量（BOD）が増加するのである。このために，水中に溶存する酸素量が減少し，ついには失われて，他の生物がすめなくなり，生態学的に大きな変化をもたらすのである。また，海においても問題が起こっている。海は，いわゆる海水の自浄作用によって，どんなものがはいって来てもこれを消化してしまう力があった。特別な規制の必要はなかったのである。ところが最近は石油が大量に海上を運ばれるため，石油という名前で一般的に呼ばれている脂肪族及び芳香族の炭化水素が海中へ流出する。火炎を用いて焼いたり，吸着剤その他の化学薬品を用いて取りのぞくが，このような海からとれる魚貝類は油が付着していたり，油の味やにおいがして有毒であるから，煮ても焼いても酢の物にしても，食用にはならない。さらに石油類の混入量が多くなれば，生物はすむことができなくなる。

　工業材料界では，次第にプラスチックが金属の代わりに使われるようになって来た。プラスチックは海中においても金属のように形を失って細かく分解しないので，これをどうして取りのぞくかが大きな問題になっている。

　一方において，工業用水に対する要求はますます増加し，その確保は次第にむずかしくなって来た。これらの点を考えあわせると，次の時代には，用廃水に一つの循環過程を作らせて途中で失われることのないように考えなければならなくなるといわれている。

LESSON 23
第二十三課

K A N J I

卵	207b	RAN	参	616	SAN	
	199	tamago		850		
裂	252a	RETSU	照	433	SHŌ	
	4233	sa(ku) sa(keru)		2785		
開	171	KAI	神	257	SHIN	
	4950	hira(ku)		3245		
育	347	IKU	経	596	KEI	
	296	soda(teru) soda(tsu)		3523		
幼	199b	YŌ	遺	739	I	
	1495	osana(i)		4745		
胚	......*	HAI	雌	260b	SHI	
	3748			2435	mesu, me	
官	364	KAN	雄	254a	YU	
	1295			5030	osu, o	
偶	237b	GŪ	説	654	SETSU	
	508			4373		
顕	276b	KEN	因	548	IN	
	5137			1026		
葉	327	YŌ	再	788	SAI	
	4001	ha		35	futata(bi)	

READING SELECTIONS

発生	hassei	development
卵	tamago	egg
受精する	jusei suru	to fertilize
刺激を受ける	shigeki o ukeru	to receive a stimulus
分裂	bunretsu	division, fission
開始する	kaishi suru	to begin, commence
しだいに（次第に）	shidai ni	gradually
細胞	saihō	cell

---

*Not one of the *tōyō kanji*.

育つ	sodatsu	to develop
成体	seitai	adult
幼生	yōsei	larva
…にいたる	...ni itaru	to reach...
胚	hai	embryo
卵割	rankatsu	cleavage
初期	shoki	initial stage
嬢細胞	jō-saihō	sister cell
割球	kakkyū	blastomere
しくみ（仕組）	shikumi	design, plan
器官	kikan	organ
偶然に	gūzen ni	by chance
必然性	hitsuzen-sei	necessity
予定域	yotei-iki	presumptive region
過程	katei	process
逆にたどる	gyaku ni tadoru	to trace backwards
胞胚	hōhai	blastula
…にあたる（当たる）	... ni ataru	to correspond to...
イモリ	imori	a newt
カエル	kaeru	frog
生体染色	seitai-senshoku	vital staining
なりゆき（成り行き）	nari-yuki	progress, course
ついに	tsui ni	finally
つきとめる（突き留める）	tsuki-tomeru	to identify
表皮	hyōhi	epidermis
神経管	shinkei-kan	neural tubes
内胚葉	nai-haiyō	endoderm, entoderm
中胚葉	chū-haiyō	mesoderm
原基分布図	genki-bunpu-zu	presumptive map
参照	sanshō	reference
囊胚	nōhai	gastrula
神経系	shinkei-kei	nervous system
交換する	kōkan suru	to interchange
手術	shujutsu	operation
見分ける	mi-wakeru	to distinguish
将来	shōrai	(in the) future
移植する	ishoku suru	to graft
組織	soshiki	tissue
影響される	eikyō sareru	to be influenced, affected
後期	kōki	later stage

こんど	kondo	this time
まったく（全く）	mattaku	completely
やはり	yahari	also
もはや	mohaya	already
つまり	tsumari	that is to say, in other words
完成される	kansei sareru	to be completely developed
途中で	tochū de	on the way

動物の発生　(S 233, 241–243)

　卵は受精されたり，外から刺激を受けたりすると分裂を開始し，しだいに多数の細胞になる。卵から育ち，まだ成体あるいは幼生の形をとるにいたらない発生の時代を胚という。
胚の初期発生。発生の初期に見られる細胞分裂を卵割という。卵割はふつうの細胞分裂とは異なり，分裂が急速に行なわれるが，その間，嬢細胞の成長を伴わない。したがって，分裂が進むにつれて細胞の大きさは$\frac{1}{2}$，$\frac{1}{4}$…というようにしだいに小さくなっていく。卵割によって生ずる嬢細胞を割球という。
発生のしくみ。どの生物を見ても，決まった位置には決まった器官がある。これは偶然そう[1]なったと考えるよりも必然性があったと見るべき[2]であろう。
胚の予定域。各器官が形成される過程を逆にたどると，それぞれの器官が胞胚ではどの部分にあたるかを決めることができるはずである。フォークト W. Vogt (1888—1941)は，実際にイモリやカエルの胞胚の表面を部分的に生体染色をして，そのなりゆきを顕微鏡下で観察し，ついに胞胚の表面の各部分が，のちに何になるかということをつきとめて図に示した（例えば，表皮，神経管，内胚葉，中胚葉など）。（イモリの原基分布図参照）
決定の問題。ドイツの動物学者シュペーマン H. Spemann (1869—1941)は，体色の違う2種のイモリの嚢胚初期を用い，それぞれ神経系と表皮になるべき[2]部分を交換する手術を行なった。交換した部分は色が違うので，発生が進んでからでもそれを見分けられる。その結果は，将来，神経系になるはず[3]であった部分が表皮に，表皮になるはずであった部分が神経系になった。このようなことから，嚢胚初期の時期には各部分がそれぞれ何になるか，まだ決定していないので，移植された場所の組織に強く影響されてしまうことがわかった。嚢胚後期に同じ手術をすると，こんどはまったく違った結果になる。すなわち，神経系になるべき[3]部分は移植された場所の組織にはほとんど影響されずに神経系となり，表皮になるべき部分はやはり表皮になった。そこでイモリの場合には，嚢胚後期では，各部分が何になるか，もはや決定していることになる。つまり，神経系や表皮は，嚢胚が完成される途中で決定されることになる。

遺伝	iden	heredity
親	oya	parents
顔	kao	face
性格	seikaku	temperament
伝わる	tsutawaru	to be transmitted
形質	keishitsu	character
先人たち	senjin-tachi	ancestors
個体	kotai	individual
子孫	shison	descendants
近縁関係	kin'en-kankei	close relations
多少	tashō	to some extent
…うえで	…ue de	in order to…, for the sake of…
注目される	chūmoku sareru	to receive attention
古くから	furuku kara	for a long time
雌雄	shiyū	male and female
かけあわせ	kake-awase	hybridization, crossing
統計的に	tōkei-teki ni	statistically
巧みに	takumi ni	with ingenuity
処理する	shori suru	to conduct, treat
法則性	hōsoku-sei	order
染色体	senshoku-tai	chromosome
減数分裂	gensū-bunretsu	meiosis
当時	tōji	that time, era
発現	hatsugen	manifestation
因子	inshi	factor
遺伝子	iden-shi	gene
予想する	yosō suru	to predict
遺伝学	iden-gaku	genetics
創始者	sōshi-sha	founder
うずもれる	uzumoreru	to be buried in obscurity
再発見	sai-hakken	rediscovery
…を契機に	…o keiki ni	on the occasion of…
急激に	kyūgeki ni	suddenly, abruptly
進歩する	shinpo suru	to progress

遺 伝 (S 253)

親のもついろいろな性質，たとえば顔かたちや性格などが親から子に伝わる現象を遺伝といい，これらの性質を形質とよぶ。先人たちは，個体の子孫や近縁関係の形質のあらわ

れかたをいろいろな方法で研究してきた。親から子に伝わるといっても，親とは多少異な
る形質が子にあらわれる場合もある。これらを含め，今日生命現象を理解するうえで，細
胞の研究などとともに，遺伝の研究はきわめて注目されている。

　古くから，多くの人々が雌雄のかけあわせを行なった結果について観察していたが，こ
のような実験を統計的にしかも巧みに処理して，そこに法則性を見いだしたのはメンデル
G.J. Mendel(1822—1884)が最初であった。染色体の存在や，減数分裂のしくみなどが知
られていなかった当時において，メンデルは親から子に伝えられて形質発現のもとになる
ものとして因子を仮定し，それによってこの法則を説明した。この因子こそ[4]，今日でい
う遺伝子であって，この遺伝子の存在を予想したことにより，メンデルは遺伝学の創始者
とよばれている。メンデルの研究は長い期間うずもれていたが，1900年の再発見[5]を契機
に遺伝学は急激に進歩した。

DŌBUTSU NO HASSEI

Tamago wa jusei saretari, soto kara shigeki o uketari suru to bunretsu o kaishi
shi, shidai ni tasū no saihō ni naru. Tamago kara sodachi, mada seitai arui wa
yōsei no katachi o toru ni itaranai hassei no jidai o hai to iu.

Hai no Shoki-Hassei: Hassei no shoki ni mirareru saihō-bunretsu o rankatsu to iu.
Rankatsu wa futsū no saihō-bunretsu to wa kotonari, bunretsu ga kyūsoku ni
okonawareru ga, sono aida, jō-saihō no seichō o tomonawanai. Shitagatte,
bunretsu ga susumu ni tsurete saihō no ōkisa wa nibun-no-ichi, yonbun-no-ichi,...
to iu yō ni shidai ni chiisaku natte iku. Rankatsu ni yotte, shōzuru jō-saihō o
kakkyū to iu.

Hassei no Shikumi: Dono seibutsu o mite mo, kimatta ichi ni wa kimatta kikan
ga aru. Kore wa gūzen sō[1] natta to kangaeru yori mo hitsuzen-sei ga atta to
miru-beki de arō.

Hai no Yotei-iki: Kaku-kikan ga keisei sareru katei o gyaku ni tadoru to, sorezore
no kikan ga hōhai de wa dono bubun ni ataru ka o kimeru koto ga dekiru hazu
de aru.

　Fōkuto (1888–1941) wa, jissai ni imori ya kaeru no hōhai no hyōmen o bubun-
teki ni seitai-senshoku o shite, sono nari-yuki o kenbi-kyō-ka de kansatsu shi, tsui
ni, hōhai no hyōmen no kaku-bubun ga, nochi ni nani ni naru ka to iu koto o
tsuki-tomete, zu ni shimeshita (tatoeba, hyōhi, shinkei-kan, nai-haiyō, chū-haiyō
nado). (Imori no genki-bunpu-zu sanshō).

Kettei no Mondai: Doitsu no dōbutsu-gakusha Shupēman (1869–1941) wa, taishoku
no chigau nishu no imori no nōhai-shoki o mochi-i, sorezore shinkei-kei to hyōhi
ni naru-beki[2] bubun o kōkan suru shujutsu o okonatta. Kōkan shita bubun wa
iro ga chigau no de, hassei ga susunde kara de mo sore o miwakerareru.

Sono kekka wa, shōrai, shinkei-kei ni naru hazu[3] de atta bubun ga hyōhi ni, hyōhi ni naru hazu de atta bubun ga shinkei-kei ni natta. Kono yō na koto kara, nōhai-shoki no jiki ni wa kaku-bubun ga sorezore nani ni naru ka, mada kettei shite inai no de, ishoku sareta basho no soshiki ni tsuyoku eikyō sarete shimau koto ga wakatta.

Nōhai-kōki ni onaji shujutsu o suru to, kondo wa mattaku chigatta kekka ni naru. Sunawachi, shinkei-kei ni naru-beki[3] bubun wa ishoku sareta basho no soshiki ni hotondo eikyō sarezu ni shinkei-kei to nari, hyōhi ni naru-beki bubun wa yahari hyōhi ni natta. Soko de imori no baai ni wa, nōhai-kōki de wa, kaku-bubun ga nani ni naru ka, mohaya kettei shite iru koto ni naru. Tsumari, shinkei-kei ya hyōhi wa nōhai ga kansei sareru tochū de kettei sareru koto ni naru.

IDEN

Oya no motsu iroiro na seishitsu, tatoeba kao-katachi ya seikaku nado ga oya kara ko ni tsutawaru genshō o iden to ii, korera no seishitsu o keishitsu to yobu. Senjin-tachi wa kotai no shison ya kin'en-kankei no keishitsu no araware-kata o, iroiro na hōhō de kenkyū shite kita. Oya kara ko ni tsutawaru to itte mo, oya to wa tashō kotonaru keishitsu ga ko ni arawareru baai ga aru. Korera o fukume, konnichi seimei-genshō o rikai suru ue de, saihō no kenkyū nado to tomo ni, iden no kenkyū wa kiwamete chūmoku sarete iru.

Furuku kara, ōku no hito-bito ga shiyū no kake-awase o okonatta kekka ni tsuite kansatsu shite ita ga, kono yō na jikken o tōkei-teki ni shikamo takumi ni shori shite, soko ni hōsoku-sei o mi-idashita no wa Menderu (1822–1884) ga saisho de atta. Senshoku-tai no sonzai ya, gensū-bunretsu no shikumi nado ga shirarete inakatta tōji ni oite, Menderu wa oya kara ko ni tsutaerareta keishitsu-hatsugen no moto ni naru mono to shite inshi o katei shi, sore ni yotte kono hōsoku o setsumei shita. Kono inshi koso,[4] konnichi de iu iden-shi de atte, kono iden-shi no sonzai o yosō shita koto ni yori, Menderu wa iden-gaku no sōshi-sha to yobarete iru. Menderu no kenkyū wa nagai kikan uzumorete ita ga, 1900-nen no sai-hakken[5] o keiki ni, iden-gaku wa kyūgeki ni shinpo shita.

ANIMAL DEVELOPMENT

When an egg is fertilized or receives an external stimulus, it begins to fission and gradually forms many cells. The stage of development during which the growth from the egg has not yet reached the point of the adult or larval form is called the embryo.

Initial Development of the Embryo: The cell division seen in the initial stage of development is called cleavage. Cleavage differs from the usual division of cells in that it occurs very rapidly and there is no accompanying growth of the sister

cells during the interval. As division progresses, therefore, the cellular size gradually decreases as in the series 1/2, 1/4, ... The sister cells produced by cleavage are called blastomeres.

Design in Development: In every living thing, a given organ will be in a fixed place. This should not be considered a chance outcome but should rather be looked upon as evidence of necessity.

The Presumptive Regions in the Embryo: If we were to trace back the process by which the individual organs are formed, we should be able to determine which part of the blastula corresponds to each of the respective organs. W. Vogt (1888–1941) actually stained portions of the blastula surfaces of newts and frogs and observed with a microscope their development. He finally identified the subsequent development of every part of the blastula surface and showed them on a diagram (the neural tubes, epidermis, endoderm, and mesoderm, for example). (See the Presumptive Map for a Newt)

The Problem of Determination: The German zoologist H. Spemann (1869–1941) used the gastrula of newts with two different body colors to perform an operation in which he interchanged the parts which were supposed to develop respectively into the nervous system and the epidermis. Since the interchanged parts were of a different color, they were distinguishable even after progressing in development.

The outcome was that those parts which should have become the nervous system became epidermis, and those which should have become the epidermis became nervous system tissue. He realized from facts such as these that the subsequent development of each part is not yet determined at the beginning of the gastrula stage and that each part is strongly influenced by the tissue at the location into which it was grafted.

When he performed the same operation at the later gastrula stage, the outcome was now completely different. The part which was supposed to develop into the nervous system was practically unaffected by the tissue into which it was grafted and did become nervous system tissue, and the part that was supposed to become epidermis also became epidermis. Thus, in the case of a newt, the subsequent development of each part is already determined at the later gastrula stage. In other words, the nervous system and the epidermis are determined intermediary to the completion of the gastrula.

GENETICS

The various characteristics of parents transmitted from parent to child, such as the shape of the face and temperament, for example, are called "heredity," and these characteristics are called "characters." The ways in which ancestors are manifest in the characters of descendants and close relations have been studied by various methods. Although we speak of transmittal from parent to child,

there are also cases in which characters somewhat different from the parent arise in the child. In order to incorporate these facts into our present understanding of the phenomena of life, genetic research is receiving considerable attention along with cellular research and other studies.

For a long time many people observed the results of crossing males and females, but G.J. Mendel (1822–1884) was the first to treat such experiments statistically and, moreover, with ingenuity, and to discover their orderliness. Mendel, in that era when the existence of chromosomes and the mechanism of meiosis, for example, were not known, assumed the existence of factors as the fundamental cause for the manifestation of characters transmitted from parent to child and in that way explained these laws. These very factors are what we call genes today, and it is due to his prediction of the existence of genes that Mendel is called the founder of genetics. Mendel's research was buried in obscurity for a long time but, on the occasion of its rediscovery in 1900, genetics made very sudden progress.

Explanatory Notes

(1) sō

This *sō* means "in that way" and is not the suffix *-sō* meaning "appearance".

(2) -beki (de aru)

This suffix, meaning "must," "ought to," "is (supposed) to" may be attached to the affirmative present tense of a verb.

miru-beki de aru	must see
kaku-beki de atta	should have written
sokutei su-beki	ought not to have (been)
de nakatta	measured
kangaeru-beki de arō	probably ought to consider

Note that *su-beki* is preferred over *suru-beki*. Sometimes *-beki* is used without *de aru*.

(3) ...ni naru hazu de atta; ...ni naru-beki

The phrase containing *hazu* means "should have become" ...i.e., "was expected to become (but didn't)". The phrase containing *beki* means "ought to become" ...i. e., "it was supposed to become (and did)."

(4) koso

This particle emphasizes the word which precedes it. Suitable English equivalents are "this very...", "...in particular," "...indeed", "...itself".

Examples are:

Kono keisan koso machigai no moto de atta. (This very calculation is the source of the error.)

Kono sokutei koso shintō-atsu no hakken ni michibiita mono

de aru. (It was this measurement in particular which led to the discovery of osmotic pressure.)

Kono jikken de wa mazeru koto koso seikō no hitsuyō-jōken de aru. (In this experiment the mixing itself is a necessary condition for success.)

(5) sai-hakken   The prefix *sai-* (再) means "again," or "re-":

再生ゴム	saisei-gomu	reclaimed rubber
再蒸留	sai-jōryū	redistillation
再結晶	sai-kesshō	recrystallization
再結合	sai-ketsugō	recombination

CONSTRUCTION EXAMPLES

| … はずである | See Explanatory Note (3) |
| … べき (である) | See Explanatory Note (2) |

1. ヒトはヒトを生むはずであり，イヌがネコを生むはずはない。

2. イモリの発生を研究すれば，カエルの発生もわかるはずである。

3. 部長が来るはずであったが，用事のため，部長代理が来た。

4. 遺伝現象の解析は，まずその原因をになう細胞の構造から始めるべきである。

5. エタノールを用いるべきであったのにメタノールを用いたので実験はうまく行かなかった。

6. サッカローズの水溶液に酸を加えると，その加水分解はいちじるしくさかんになるが，酸そのものは少しも変化を受けないから，酸はこの場合触媒と考えるべきである。

部長(代理)	buchō(dairi)	(the representative of the) dean
用事	yōji	engagement, business
になう	ninau	to carry
うまく	umaku	well
酸そのもの	san sono mono	the acid itself

| (verb)＋うえで | "in order to...", "for the sake of..." |

1. 生化学は，生物現象を理解するうえで非常に必要である。

2. 顕微鏡は，生物学の研究をするうえで，なくてはならないものである。

3. メンデルの法則は，遺伝を調べるうえで，ぜひ知っておかねばならぬものである。

4. ホウレンソウが炭酸同化を行なううえで日光はぜひ必要である。

| ぜひ | zehi | by all means |

おかねばならぬ＝おかなければならない

ホウレンソウ　hōrensō　　　　　　　　spinach

SUPPLEMENTARY READINGS

A. | ウニ | uni | a sea urchin |
|---|---|---|
| 等黄卵 | tō-ō-ran | homolecithal egg |
| 8 細胞期 | hachi saihō-ki | eight celled stage |
| 動物極 | dōbutsu-kyoku | animal pole |
| 植物極 | shokubutsu-kyoku | vegetative pole |
| にかたよる | ni katayoru | to tend towards |
| ひきつづく | hiki-tsuzuku | to continue in succession |
| 卵割腔 | rankatsu-kō | blastocoele |
| 陥入する | kannyū suru | to sink into |
| 袋状 | fukuro-jō | bag-shaped |
| 胚葉 | haiyō | germ layer |
| 外胚葉 | gai-haiyō | ectoderm |

ウニの卵割　(S 235)

　ウニは等黄卵であるから，縦2回，横1回の分裂によって各割球の大きさの等しい8細胞期をむかえる。つぎの第4回目の分裂は，動物極側の4割球では縦に，植物極側の4割球では植物極にかたよって水平に行なわれて16細胞期になる。ひきつづく分裂によって卵は胞胚となる。この時期になると，大きな卵割腔が中央にできて，各割球は外界と接する面に1層に並ぶようになる。まもなく植物極側の細胞層は内側に陥入し，結局，内外2層の壁からなる袋状の嚢胚になる。嚢胚をつくっている壁を胚葉といい，外層は外胚葉，内層は内胚葉とよばれる。このころ，内胚葉と外胚葉との間には，別の細胞のかたまりが分化してくる。これが中胚葉である。

B. | 多細胞 | ta-saihō | multi-cellular |
|---|---|---|
| 分化 | bunka | differentiation |
| 発育する | hatsuiku suru | to grow, develop |
| 生殖 | seishoku | reproduction |
| 花を開く | hana o hiraku | to open (their) flowers |
| 種子を生じる | shushi o shōjiru | to produce seeds |
| 遺伝する | iden suru | to be inherited, transmitted |
| 種族 | shuzoku | species |
| 維持する | iji suru | to preserve, maintain |
| 自己 | jiko | one's self |
| ふやす | fuyasu | to multiply, increase |

発生・成長・生殖・遺伝　(S 41)

発生・成長。生物体は細胞からできており，発生や成長の現象が見られる。多細胞生物も
はじめは1個の細胞であるが，細胞の分裂と分化とにより，発育して形が大きくなるとと
もに，複雑な個体になる。
生殖・遺伝。植物が花を開いて種子を生じ，また，動物が子を生むように，生物には子孫
を残す生殖のはたらきがある。この場合，いろいろな形質が親から子に遺伝し，生物のそ
れぞれの種族が維持される。すなわち，生物には自己と同じものをふやすはたらきがある。

C.	調節	chōsetsu	regulation, control
	限界値	genkai-chi	threshold value
	感覚細胞	kankaku-saihō	sensory cells
	分泌する	bunpitsu suru	to secrete
	ホルモン	horumon	hormone
	…と相伴う	…to aitomonau	together with…
	さまざま＝いろいろ		

反応調節　(S 41)

生物にはいろいろな変化を感じ，それに対し，さまざまな反応を示す性質がある。生物
に影響を与えるような外界の変化を刺激といい，反応に必要な最小の刺激の大きさを限界
値とよぶ。動物で感覚細胞の受けた刺激を，反応をおこす器官や組織に伝える特別な構造
を神経系という。神経系は動物・植物の器官から分泌されるホルモンと相伴って生物体の
さまざまな機能を調節している。

D.	単細胞の	tan-saihō no	unicellular
	胞子	hōshi	spore
	卵細胞	ran-saihō	egg cell
	過程をへる	katei o heru	to undergo a process
	終わる	owaru	to finish, complete

発　生　(S 231)

単細胞の生物は，一つの細胞がそのまま分かれて新しい個体となるが，多細胞の生物で
は，胞子や受精した卵細胞などのような1個の細胞が個体に育つまでには，複雑な過程を
へなければならない。一般には，受精卵が胚の形成を終わるまでの過程を発生という。

E.	ころ	koro	time
	神経胚	shinkei-hai	neurula
	成長曲線	seichō-kyokusen	growth curve

衰える	otoroeru	to decline
字状	jijō	shape (of a letter)
形態	keitai	form

成　長　(S 248)

　カエルの卵の初期発生のころには，その全体の大きさに変化が見られない。しかし，神経胚が完成されるころから，全体として大きくなりはじめ，これはその後，成体になるまでつづく。生物のからだが大きくなることが成長である。

成長曲線。一般に成長は最初のうちは盛んでないが，やがて盛んになり，その後しだいに衰えて，ついには停止してしまう。そこで，一定の時間をおいて，体長・体重などを測定し，それを縦軸に，時間を横軸にとってグラフを描いてみると，S字状の曲線となる。これを成長曲線という。

成長と形態。成長の速さは，からだの部分によって一様ではない。各部分の成長の速さを比較するためには，相対成長を用いる。相対成長とは，ある部分の成長の速さの，全体の成長の速さに対する割合である。

F.	変態	hentai	metamorphosis
	海産の	kaisan no	marine
	寄生虫	kisei-chū	parasites
	顕著な	kencho na	remarkable, notable
	魚形	gyokei	fish
	えら	era	gills
	はい上がる	hai-agaru	to crawl up
	陸上	riku-jō	on land
	肺	hai	lungs
	コン虫類	konchū-rui	insects
	チョウ	chō	butterfly
	ガ	ga	moth
	さなぎ	sanagi	pupa
	コン虫の系統	konchū no keitō	insect strain

変　態　(S 249)

　生物によっては，成長の間にいちじるしくその形を変えるものがある。これを変態といい，とくに海産動物や寄生虫の場合が顕著である。

　カエルの幼生は水中で生活するため，魚形で，しかもえらで呼吸し，おもに植物性の食物をとって成長する。陸上にはい上がるころになるとえらがなくなって，からだの中には肺ができ，食物も動物性のものに限られるようになる。このように，変態するときには，

幼生になかった器官が新たに生じたり，逆に幼生にあった器官（幼生器官）がなくなった
りする。

　コン虫類もいちじるしい変態をする。チョウやガなどでは，幼生がいったんさなぎになっ
てから成体になる。さなぎの時期には，運動もせず食物もとらないがその程度はコン虫
の系統と密接な関係がある。変態中には，内部の組織に大きな変化がおこり，幼生のから
だから成体のからだに変わる。

G.	再生	saisei	regeneration
	オタマジャクシ	otamajakushi	tadpole
	尾を切る	o o kiru	to cut off the tail
	跡	ato	remains
	再び	futatabi	again
	…とみなす	…to minasu	to look upon as…

再　生　(S 251)

　オタマジャクシの尾を切っておくと，やがて，その跡に新しい尾ができてくる。このよ
うに，失われた部分が再びつくられることを再生という。再生は特別な条件のもとでおこ
る発生や成長とみなすことができる。

H.	遺伝物質	iden-busshitsu	genetic substance
	配偶子	haigū-shi	gamete
	秘められている	himerarete iru	to be hidden
	細胞質	saihō-shitsu	cytoplasm
	父方	chichi-kata	the father's side, the male line
	母方	haha-kata	the mother's side, female line
	伝達する	dentatsu suru	to transmit
	優性の	yūsei no	dominant
	目印にとる	me-jirushi ni toru	to take as a mark
	正逆交雑	seigyaku-kōzatsu	reciprocal cross
	雄	osu	male
	劣性の	ressei no	recessive
	雌	mesu	female
	交雑する	kōzatsu suru	to cross
	担う	ninau	to carry
	推測する	suisoku suru	to infer
	興味ある	kyōmi aru	interesting
	指摘する	shiteki suru	to point out, indicate

| つかさどる | tsukasadoru | to govern, rule |
| 後章 | kōshō | a later chapter |

遺伝物質　(IG 12–13)

親と子をむすぶ実体は配偶子だけである。したがって，子が親に似ているとしたら，その原因はすべてこの配偶子，すなわち精子と卵との二つの細胞のなかに秘められているはずである。

精子と卵とはその構造を異にしている。卵は核と多量の細胞質をもっているが，精子は分化の途中でほとんどの細胞質を失って核だけを完全に残している。このように精子と卵とではその構造がかなり違っているが，それにもかかわらず，遺伝形質の多くは父方からも母方からも同じように子に伝えられていく。すなわち，精子も卵も子孫へ同じように遺伝形質を支配する要素を伝達しているのである。いま，一つの優性の遺伝形質を目印にとって雌雄の個体のあいだでいわゆる正逆交雑をしてみよう。すなわち，一つの優性の遺伝形質をもつ雄を劣性の雌と交雑し，つぎに，この優性の形質をもつ雌を劣性の雄と交雑してみるのである。すると，多くの遺伝形質はどちらの場合にも同じように子孫につたえられていく，すなわち，遺伝形質はその多くが子孫に母方からも父方からも同じように伝えられていくことがわかる。この事実は遺伝形質を支配する要素を担っている部分が細胞のなかで，卵と精子とが共にもっている部分であることを推測させる。それは細胞質体ではなくて核である。

核の構造をみると，その分裂のときには，たいてい，染色体がそのなかにあらわれる。そして染色体は細胞の分裂にともなって非常に興味ある動きをする。

W. S. Sutton はこの染色体の動きと遺伝現象とのあいだに密接な関係があることを指摘して，遺伝形質を支配する要素は染色体のうえにあろうと推測した。この推測はのちに T. H. Morgan や C. B. Bridges らによって実験的に証明された。そして，染色体上にあって一つの遺伝形質をつかさどる要素は，一つの単位として遺伝子とよばれた。遺伝子ということばは現在ではもっとも複雑に定義されている。これについては後章で説明する。

I.	基礎	kiso	basis
	もしも…とすれば	moshimo ...to sureba	if we believe that...
	間接的な	kansetsu-teki na	indirect
	直接的な	chokusetsu-teki na	direct
	代謝活性	daisha-kassei	metabolic activity
	確実に	kakujitsu ni	for certain
	おそらく	osoraku	probably, in all likelihood

推定する	suitei suru	to infer
照射する	shōsha suru	to apply (a light, X-ray)
突然	totsuzen	sudden, abrupt
突然変異体	totsuzen-hen'i-tai	mutant
突然変異	totsuzen-hen'i	mutation

DNA と蛋白質　(IG 13–14)

　遺伝子を担っている染色体は DNA と塩基性の蛋白質とからなっている。どちらも高分子の物質でその構造は複雑である。遺伝形質を支配する要素にもしも物質的基礎があるとすれば，この遺伝物質は染色体を構成している DNA か塩基性蛋白質かのいずれかということになろう。

　現在得られている結論からいえば，遺伝物質は DNA であるとされている。このことを証明する間接的あるいは直接的な実験事実はたくさん知られている。

　たとえば，放射性の同位元素をつかって DNA と蛋白質との代謝活性の度合をしらべてみると，蛋白質が不安定なのにくらべて DNA は安定であることがわかる。遺伝物質は親から子へと確実にその形質を遺伝していかなければならず，その性質からみても安定な物質でなくてはならないであろう。したがって，遺伝物質はおそらく蛋白質ではなくて，DNA であろうと推定される。細菌などに紫外線を照射すると，その子孫に突然変異体とよばれる親とは異なる形質をもつ個体があらわれてくることが知られている。これは紫外線の照射によって，細胞のもつ遺伝物質の分子の構成に一部分変異がおこったためであると考えられている。この突然変異を発生させるのに最も有効な紫外線の波長はおよそ2,600Å である。これは蛋白質ではなくて DNA によって吸収される波長である。このように，DNA が遺伝物質であることを，間接的にしめしている事実はたくさんある。

FINAL TRANSLATION TEST

遺伝物質　(IG 47–48)

　Mendel に始まった遺伝研究は，1900 年 Mendel の研究が再発見されて以来急激に進歩した。ヒトを初めとして多くの高等な生物の体を見ると，それはたくさんの細胞からなる一つの集合体として出来上っている。上皮組織，結合組織，筋組織，神経組織ならびに多くの器官系は，それぞれ分化しているが，これはもともとは一つの受精卵から発生して来たものである。ヒトがヒト以外のものを作らず，子が親に似ていたり，あるいは多少異なっていたりするとすれば，その原因はすべてこの一つの受精卵，換言すれば，父方と母方とから来た二つの配偶子，精子と卵とにまでさかのぼることができる。遺伝現象の原因

はすべてこれらの細胞の中に含まれているということができる。

　生殖細胞では，一つの細胞が引き続く２回の分裂によって四つの配偶子細胞に分けられるのであるが，配偶子形成の過程は雄と雌との間で異なっている。すなわち，雄では一つの精母細胞から分裂してできた四つの精細胞は，それぞれ成育して四つの精子となるが，一方雌では一つの卵母細胞から分裂してできた四つの細胞の内，三つは退化して残った一つだけが卵となる。その際，分裂は不平等に起こり，退化する三つの細胞はごくわずかしか細胞質をもたないので，残った卵細胞だけが大部分の細胞質と卵黄とをもつことになる。このように，分裂の結果，細胞質と卵黄との量が減ることをふせぎ，残った卵がより多くの細胞質と卵黄とをもつようになることは，卵が受精されて胚となり，植物では子葉・幼芽・胚軸・幼根の四つの部分に，動物では卵割へと分化を続けて行くのに必要なことである。遺伝現象の原因が配偶子の中の染色体にあることがわかってからは，遺伝物質をつきとめるために多くの研究がなされたが，これがDNAであることを直接的に証明したのは，バクテリオファージの増殖機構の電子顕微鏡的研究であった。遺伝の問題には二つの基本的な問題がある。一つはどのようにして遺伝物質が自己を複製するかということであり，もう一つは，いかにして遺伝物質が形質の発現に関与するのかということである。このような遺伝物質の機能は，その化学構造を調べることによって明らかになった。この分野での研究は，WatsonとCrickによるDNAモデルの出現によって道が開かれた。この説の詳細については参考書を参照されたいが，ここでは，DNAがどのようにして形質の発現，すなわち蛋白質の合成に関与しているかということに触れておく。

　DNAはほとんどが細胞の核のなかに存在している。したがって，DNAが直接に蛋白質の合成に関与しているとすれば，可能性として蛋白質合成は核のなかでおこなわれていると考えることができる。しかし，しらべてみると蛋白質合成は核の中ではなく細胞質体でおこなわれている。たとえば，アメーバAmoeba proteusを二つに切ってほぼ等しい有核と無核との部分にわけ，ラベルされたアミノ酸をつかって，それがそれぞれのアメーバの細胞片の中にどのくらいとりこまれるかをしらべてみる。すると，一時的にではあるが，無核の細胞片も相当量のアミノ酸をとりこんで蛋白質の合成をおこなうことがわかる。もちろん，無核の細胞片はやがて細胞の交代能がおとろえて死んでしまう。しかし，この事実は蛋白質の合成が細胞質体でおこなわれていることを明らかにしめしている。

　蛋白質の合成が細胞質体の中でおこなわれていることは，アメーバの細胞だけではなく，いろいろな生物体の細胞についてもしらべられており同じ結果がえられている。

　細胞質体のなかで蛋白質の合成がおこなわれているものとすれば，DNAはそれに直接関与するためには核からでて細胞質体に移行しなくてはならないであろう。しかし，実際にはこのようなことをしめす事実はない。DNAは核のなかにとどまっていて細胞質体に

はでないのである。

　これらの結果は，DNA は蛋白質の合成にたずさわってはいるが，直接的にではなく間接的に，おそらく何かの仲介物質をつかって蛋白質の合成に関与しているのではないかと推測させる。

　T. Caspersson や J. Brachet らは以前から蛋白質合成と RNA との密接な関係を指摘してきた。それによると，蛋白質合成のさかんな細胞には必ず多量の RNA がみられるという。

　RNA は DNA と非常によく似た化学構造をもっていて，しかも DNA とちがって細胞質体の中にも核の中にも存在している。RNA は自由に核から細胞質体へと移行することもわかっている。こうした事実は，RNA が DNA と蛋白質との仲介物質として働いているのではないかと推測させるのに充分である。この推測が正しいことは放射性物質をつかっての実験でやがて証明された。

LESSON 24
第二十四課
KANJI

臓	276b	ZŌ		節	446	SETSU
	3828				3402	fushi
達	465	TATSU		泌	218b	HITSU
	4721				2522	
血	389	KETSU		脳	243a	NŌ
	4205	chi			3774	
腸	676	CHŌ		感	176	KAN
	3798				1731	
送	268	SŌ		覚	363	KAKU
	4683	oku(ru)			4288	obo(eru)
尿	209a	NYŌ		頭	294	TŌ ZU
	1382				4469	atama
排	228b	HAI		走	105	SŌ
	1948				4539	hashi(ru)
複	865	FUKU		筋	251a	KIN
	4255				3395	suji
雑	615	ZATSU		肉	297	NIKU
	5032				3724	
境	761	KYŌ		骨	237b	KOTSU
	1135	sakai			5236	hone

READING SELECTIONS

肝臓	kanzō	liver
腹腔	fukkō	peritoneal (abdominal) cavity
…に達する	...ni tassuru	to reach..., come up to...
右上部	migi-jōbu	upper right part
血液	ketsueki	blood
暗赤色	anseki-shoku	dark red
活発な	kappatsu na	vigorous
全身	zenshin	the whole body

炭水化物	tansui-kabutsu	carbohydrates
豊富に	hōfu ni	plentifully
交代	kōtai	interchange
…にわたって	…ni watatte	extending through…, throughout…
役割	yakuwari	role
貯臓	chozō	storage
一時的に	ichiji-teki ni	temporarily
小腸	shōchō	small intestine
グリコーゲン	gurikōgen	glycogen
たくわえる	takuwaeru	to store
送り出す	okuri-dasu	to send out
供給する	kyōkyū suru	to supply
解毒	gedoku	detoxication
グルクロン酸	gurukuron-san	glucuronic acid
尿素	nyōso	urea
腎臓	jinzō	kidney
…を通して	…o tōshite	through…, via…
排出する	haishutsu suru	to discharge
オルニシン回路	orunishin-kairo	ornithine cycle
呼吸	kokyū	respiration
シトルリン	shitorurin	citrulline
アルギニン	aruginin	arginine
複雑な	fukuzatsu na	complicated, complex
環境	kankyō	surroundings, environment
アデノシン二リン酸(ADP)	adenoshin-ni-rinsan	adenosine diphosphate
アデノシン三リン酸(ATP)	adenoshin-san-rinsan	adenosine triphosphate

肝臓のはたらき (S 131–132)

　肝臓は腹腔の右上部にある大きな器管で，その重さはヒトでは体重の3〜4％に達し，血液を多く含んでいて暗赤色である。肝臓のはたらきはたいへん活発で，全身で発生するエネルギーのうち，およそ12％は肝臓で生ずる。また，肝臓には炭水化物・脂肪・たんぱく質・核酸などの合成および分解にはたらく酵素が，他の器管にくらべて非常に豊富に含まれている。そのほか，いままでにわかっている酵素の大部分は肝臓に存在することが知られている。

　これらの事実から，肝臓は物質およびエネルギー交代のすべてにわたって重要な役割をしているものと考えられているが，まだわかっていない点も少なくない。おもなはたらきは，つぎのようである。

<u>物質の貯蔵</u>。肝臓は炭水化物の一時的な貯蔵場所になっている。すなわち，小腸で吸収されたぶどう糖の一部は，肝臓の中でグリコーゲンとなってたくわえられ，必要に応じて，再びぶどう糖に変わって血液中に送り出され，全身に供給される。同じように，脂肪も肝臓で一時的にたくわえられる。

<u>解毒</u>。有毒な物質が食物[1]とともに体内にはいったり，あるいは腸の中で細菌のはたらきによって生じたりすると，それらを含んだ血液が肝臓を通るとき，毒物が無毒のものに変えられる。この場合に，毒物が分解されて無毒となることもあり，また硫酸やグルクロン酸と結合して毒性のなくなることもある。

<u>尿素の生成</u>。たんぱく質が分解して生ずるアンモニアは，細胞に有毒な物質である。ヒトではアンモニアの大部分は肝臓の中で二酸化炭素と結合して無毒の尿素となり，腎臓を通して排出される。尿素はオルニシン回路で生ずる。

　肝臓には，オルニシンという物質が含まれている。アンモニアと呼吸の結果生じた二酸化炭素とは，オルニシンと結合してシトルリンを生ずる。つぎにシトルリンは，もう1分子のアンモニアと結合してアルギニンとなる。

　最後に，アルギニンは加水分解されて尿素とオルニシンとになる。ここに生じたオルニシンはまた同じ反応をくりかえす。以上の反応はもっと複雑であるが，その大要は図1のようになる。排出物質の種類は，環境からの水の供給と関係があると考えられている。

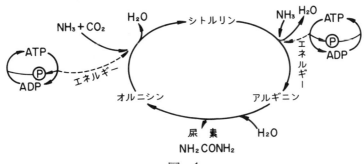

図　1

ホルモン	horumon	hormones
調節	chōsetsu	regulation, control
分泌する	bunpitsu suru	to secrete
ビタミン	bitamin	vitamin
およぼす	oyobosu	to exert
組成	sosei	composition
ポリペプチド	pori-pepuchido	polypeptide
アミノ酸	amino-san	amino acids
ステロイド	steroido	steroid
内分泌腺	nai-bunpitsu-sen	endocrine glands

腺	sen	gland
分泌物	bunpitsu-butsu	secretion
送りこむ	okuri-komu	to send into
血管	kekkan	blood vessels
脊椎動物	sekitsui-dōbutsu	vertebrate
脳下垂体	nōka-suitai	pituitary body
甲状腺	kōjō-sen	thyroid gland
副甲状腺	fuku-kōjō-sen	parathyroid
副腎	fukujin	adrenal
すい臓	suizō	pancreas
精巣	seisō	testes
卵巣	ransō	ovary
恒常性	kōjō-sei	homeostasis
維持	iji	maintenance
…にあずかる	…ni azukaru	to take part in…, share in…

ホルモンによる調節　(S 160–162)

　神経のほかに，からだ全体の調節を保つものにホルモンがある。ホルモンはからだの特定の部分でつくられ，体液中に分泌され，ビタミンや酵素のように，ごく微量でからだの特定の部分のはたらきに大きな影響をおよぼす物質である。ホルモンの化学的組成はさまざまであって，あるものはたんぱく質・ポリペプチド・アミノ酸，あるものはステロイドであり，さらにこれ以外のものや，化学構造のはっきりわかっていないものもある。

内分泌腺。ホルモンを分泌する器官（腺）には，管がなく，内分泌腺といわれ，分泌物は血管内に送りこまれる[2]。脊椎動物では，脳下垂体・甲状腺・副甲状腺[3]・副腎・すい臓・精巣・卵巣などから，それぞれ異なったホルモンが分泌されており，これらが互いにつりあいを保つことによって，からだの恒常性の維持にあずかっている。

感覚	kankaku	senses, sensation
発達	hattatsu	development
生活様式	seikatsu-yōshiki	way of life
本質的な	honshitsu-teki na	essential
中枢神経	chūsū-shinkei	central nerves
感覚中枢	kankaku-chūsū	sensory center
自律神経	jiritsu-shinkei	autonomic nerves
興奮	kōfun	excitation
何らかの…	nanra ka no…	some… (or other)

感　覚　(S 168)

　外界の刺激を受け入れるために，動物では特別の器官（感覚器官）が発達している。その発達は，動物の生活様式に応じていちじるしく異なっているが，その最も本質的なことは，どのような刺激を受け入れるしくみができているかということである。感覚器官で受けとられた外界の刺激は，ここに分布する感覚神経によって中枢神経に伝えられ，その刺激に対応する感覚中枢でそれぞれの刺激に応じた感覚がおこされる。さらに，中枢神経からはからだのそれぞれの器官に興奮が伝えられ，いろいろな反応がおこされるが，これとともに，自律神経によっても何らかの反応を生ずることが多い。

アメーバ運動	amēba-undō	amoeboid movement
アメーバ	amēba	amoeba
擬足	gisoku	pseudopodium
原形質	genkei-shitsu	protoplasm
突起	tokki	protrusion
原形質流動	genkei-shitsu-ryūdō	protoplasm streaming
変形菌	henkei-kin	myxomycetes, slime molds
白血球	hakkekkyū	leucocyte, white blood cells
べん毛(繊毛)運動	benmō (senmō) undō	flagellar (ciliary) movement
ゾウリムシ	zōri-mushi	paramecium
おおう	ōu	to cover
繊毛	senmō	cilia
気管	kikan	trachea
粘液	nen'eki	mucus
こう頭	kōtō	larynx
ミドリムシ	midori-mushi	euglenophyta algae
遊走子	yūsō-shi	zoospore
べん毛	benmō	flagella
遊泳する	yūei suru	to swim
筋肉	kinniku	muscle
ヘン形動物	henkei-dōbutsu	flatworms
ミミズ	mimizu	earthworm
消化管	shōka-kan	alimentary canal
縦走筋	jūsō-kin	longitudinal muscle
環状筋	kanjō-kin	circular muscle
ぜん動	zendō	peristalsis
収縮する	shūshuku suru	to contract
剛毛	gōmō	bristle, seta
ささえる	sasaeru	to support

骨	hone	bone
エビ	ebi	prawn
外骨格	gai-kokkaku	external skeleton, exoskeleton
関節	kansetsu	articulation, joint
横紋筋	ōmon-kin	striated muscle
骨格筋	kokkaku-kin	skeletal muscle
はさむ	hasamu	to lie (between two things)
てこ	teko	lever
対抗的に	taikō-teki ni	in opposition
拮抗筋	kikkō-kin	antagonistic muscles

動物の運動　(S 145–147)

アメーバ運動。アメーバは，擬足という原形質の突起を出し，それがのびる方向に移動する。これはアメーバ運動といわれ，原形質流動と密接な関係をもっているものとみなされている。植物の変形菌も動物の白血球も同様な運動をする。

繊毛運動・べん毛運動。ゾウリムシ[4]は全身をおおっている繊毛を動かして泳ぐ。ヒトの気管内にも繊毛があり，その運動で粘液をこう頭に送る。ミドリムシや遊走子などは，べん毛により水中を遊泳する。

筋肉運動。ヘン形動物より高等[5]な動物は，一般に筋肉によって運動をする。ミミズのからだや，ヒトの消化管の壁には，縦走筋と環状筋とがあり，これらの筋肉のはたらきによって，いわゆるぜん動運動を行なう。

　ミミズのぜん動運動では，体壁の縦走筋が収縮すると，その部分がちぢみ，環状筋が収縮するとその部分はのびる。また，からだの一部を地につけて剛毛でささえ，ぜん動運動を交互に行ない，からだを移動させる。

筋肉と骨との関係。エビやコン虫などは，外骨格をもっていて，互いに動くことができるような関節になっている。ここには，内部から筋肉がついており，この収縮によって外骨格を動かすことができる。

　脊椎動物では，横紋筋を骨格筋ともいい，これが骨についている。一つの筋肉は関節をはさんで別々の骨につき，その収縮によって，てこの原理で骨を動かす。たいてい一つの関節には，曲げる筋肉とのばす筋肉とがあって，互いに対抗的にはたらきあっている。このような筋肉を拮抗筋という。

KANZŌ NO HATARAKI

Kanzō wa fukukō no migi-jōbu ni aru ōki na kikan de, sono omosa wa hito

de wa taijū no san naishi yon-pāsento ni tasshi, ketsu-eki o ōku fukunde ite anseki-shoku de aru. Kanzō no hataraki wa taihen kappatsu de, zenshin de hassei suru enerugii no uchi, oyoso jūni-pāsento wa kanzō de shōzuru. Mata, kanzō ni wa, tansui-kabutsu, shibō, tanpaku-shitsu, kakusan nado no gōsei oyobi bunkai ni hataraku kōso ga, ta no kikan ni kurabete hijō ni hōfu ni fukumarete iru. Sono hoka, ima made ni wakatte iru kōso no dai-bubun wa kanzō ni sonzai suru koto ga shirarete iru.

Korera no jijitsu kara, kanzō wa busshitsu oyobi enerugii kōtai no subete ni watatte jūyō na yakuwari o shite iru mono to kangaerarete iru ga, mada wakatte inai ten mo sukunaku nai. Omo na hataraki wa, tsugi no yō de aru.

Busshitsu no Chozō: Kanzō wa tansui-kabutsu no ichiji-teki na chozō basho ni natte iru. Sunawachi, shōchō de kyūshū sareta budō-tō no ichibu wa kanzō no naka de gurikōgen to natte takuwaerare, hitsuyō ni ōjite, futatabi budō-tō ni kawatte ketsu-eki-chū ni okuridasare, zenshin ni kyōkyū sareru. Onaji yō ni, shibō mo kanzō de ichiji-teki ni takuwaerareru.

Gedoku: Yūdoku na busshitsu ga shokumotsu [1] to tomo ni tainai ni haittari, arui wa chō no naka de saikin no hataraki ni yotte shōjitari suru to, sorera o fukunda ketsueki ga kanzō o tōru toki, dokubutsu ga mudoku no mono ni kaerareru. Kono baai ni, dokubutsu ga bunkai sarete mudoku to naru koto mo ari, mata ryūsan ya gurukuron-san to ketsugō shite dokusei no naku naru koto mo aru.

Nyōso nado no Seisei: Tanpaku-shitsu ga bunkai shite shōzuru anmonia wa, saihō ni yūdoku na busshitsu de aru. Hito de wa anmonia no dai-bubun wa, kanzō no naka de ni-sanka-tanso to ketsugō shite, mudoku no nyōso to nari, jinzō o tōshite haishutsu sareru. Nyōso wa orunishin-kairo de shōzuru.

Kanzō ni wa, orunishin to iu busshitsu ga fukumarete iru. Anmonia to kokyū no kekka shōjita ni-sanka-tanso to wa, orunishin to ketsugō shite, shitorurin o shōzuru. Tsugi ni shitorurin wa mō ichi-bunshi no anmonia to ketsugō shite aruginin to naru.

Saigo ni, aruginin wa kasui-bunkai sarete nyōso to orunishin to ni naru. Koko ni shōjita orunishin wa mata onaji hannō o kurikaesu. Ijō no hannō wa motto fukuzatsu de aru ga, sono taiyō wa zu-ichi no yō ni naru.

Haishutsu-busshitsu no shurui wa kankyō kara no mizu no kyōkyū to kankei ga aru to kangaerarete iru.

HORUMON NI YORU CHŌSETSU

Shinkei no hoka ni, karada zentai no chōsetsu o tamotsu mono ni horumon ga aru. Horumon wa karada no tokutei no bubun de tsukurare, taieki-chū ni bunpitsu sare, bitamin ya kōso no yō ni, goku biryō de karada no tokutei no bubun no hataraki ni ōki na eikyō o oyobosu busshitsu de aru.

Horumon no kagaku-teki sosei wa samazama de atte, aru mono wa tanpaku-

shitsu, pori-pepuchido, amino-san, aru mono wa suteroido de ari, sara ni kore igai no mono ya, kagaku-kōzō no hakkiri wakatte inai mono mo aru.

Nai-bunpitsu-sen: Horumon o bunpitsu suru kikan(sen) ni wa, kan ga naku, nai-bunpitsu-sen to iware, bunpitsu-butsu wa kekkan-nai ni okuri-komareru. [2]

Sekitsui-dōbutsu de wa, nōka-suitai, kōjō-sen, fuku-kōjō-sen [3] fukujin, suizō, seisō, ransō nado kara, sorezore kotonatta horumon ga bunpitsu sarete ori, korera ga tagai ni tsuriai o tamotsu koto ni yotte, karada no kōjō-sei no iji ni azukatte iru.

KANKAKU

Gaikai no shigeki o uke-ireru tame ni, dōbutsu de wa tokubetsu no kikan (kankaku-kikan) ga hattatsu shite iru. Sono hattatsu wa dōbutsu no seikatsu-yōshiki ni ōjite ichijirushiku kotonatte iru ga, sono mottomo honshitsu-teki na koto wa, dono yō na shigeki o uke-ireru shikumi ga dekite iru ka to iu koto de aru. Kankaku-kikan de uke-torareta gaikai no shigeki wa, koko ni bunpu suru kankaku-shinkei ni yotte chūsū-shinkei ni tsutaerare, sono shigeki ni taiō suru kankaku-chūsū de sorezore no shigeki ni ōjita kankaku ga okosareru. Sara ni, chūsū-shinkei kara wa karada no sorezore no kikan ni kōfun ga tsutaerare, iroiro na hannō ga okosareru ga, kore to tomo ni, jiritsu-shinkei ni yotte mo nanra ka no hannō o shōzuru koto ga ōi.

DŌBUTSU NO UNDŌ

Amēba-undō: Amēba wa gisoku to iu genkei-shitsu no tokki o dashi, sore ga nobiru hōkō ni idō suru. Kore wa amēba-undō to iware, genkei-shitsu-ryūdō to missetsu na kankei o motte iru mono to minasarete iru. Shokubutsu no hen'i-kin mo dōbutsu no hakkekkyū mo dōyō na undō o suru.

Senmō-undō, Benmō-undō: Zōri-mushi [4] wa zenshin o ōtte iru senmō o ugokashite oyogu. Hito no kikan-nai ni mo senmō ga ari, sono undō de nen'eki o kōtō ni okuru. Midori-mushi ya yūsō-shi nado wa, benmō ni yori suichū o yūei suru.

Kinniku-undō: Henkei-dōbutsu yori kōtō [5] na dōbutsu wa, ippan ni kinniku ni yotte undō o suru. Mimizu no karada ya, hito no shōka-kan no kabe ni wa, jūsō-kin to kanjō-kin to ga ari, korera no kinniku no hataraki ni yotte, iwayuru zendō-undō o okonau.

Mimizu no zendō-undō de wa, taiheki no jūsō-kin ga shūshuku suru to, sono bubun ga chijimi, kanjō-kin ga shūshuku suru to, sono bubun wa nobiru. Mata, karada no ichibu o chi ni tsukete gōmō de sasae, zendō-undō o kōgo ni okonai, karada o idō saseru.

Kinniku to Hone to no Kankei: Ebi ya konchū nado wa, gai-kokkaku o motte ite, tagai ni ugoku koto ga dekiru yō na kansetsu ni natte iru. Koko ni wa, naibu kara kinniku ga tsuite ori, kono shūshuku ni yotte gai-kokkaku o ugokasu koto ga dekiru.

Sekitsui-dōbutsu de wa, ōmon-kin o kokkaku-kin to mo ii, kore ga hone ni tsuite iru. Hitotsu no kinniku wa kansetsu o hasande betsu-betsu no hone ni tsuki, sono shūshuku ni yotte, teko no genri de hone o ugokasu. Taitei hitotsu no kansetsu ni wa, mageru kinniku to nobasu kinniku ga atte, tagai ni taikō-teki ni hataraki-atte iru. Kono yō na kinniku o kikkō-kin to iu.

THE FUNCTIONS OF THE LIVER

The liver, located in the upper right portion of the peritoneal cavity, is a large organ, with a weight which in man reaches 3—4% of body weight, and is dark red with the large quantity of blood it contains. The functioning of the liver is very vigorous and, of the energy produced in the entire body, about 12% is generated in the liver. Moreover, the enzymes which act to synthesize and decompose substances like carbohydrates, fats, proteins, and nucleic acids are present in far greater abundance in the liver than in other organs. In addition, a major portion of the enzymes thus far identified are known to be present in the liver.

From these facts we are led to believe that the liver plays an important role throughout all material and energy interchanges, but there are more than a few points not yet understood. The main functions are the following.

The Storage of Substances: The liver is the location where carbohydrates are temporarily stored. For example, part of the dextrose absorbed by the small intestine is changed to glycogen and stored within the liver, becoming dextrose again as need arises, being sent out into the blood and supplied to the whole body. In the same way fats are temporarily stored in the liver.

Detoxication: When poisonous substances enter the body in foods or arise from the activity of bacteria in the intestines, they are rendered non-toxic when the blood containing them passes through the liver. In such cases, the poisons may become detoxified by decomposition, or they may lose their toxicity by combining with acids such as sulfuric and glucuronic.

The Production of Urea: The ammonia produced in the decomposition of proteins is a substance toxic to cells. In man, the great portion of the ammonia reacts with carbon dioxide in the liver to form non-toxic urea and is discharged through the kidneys.

Urea is produced in the ornithine cycle. The substance ornithine is contained in the liver. Ammonia and the carbon dioxide resulting from respiration combine with ornithine to produce citrulline. The citrulline then combines with one more molecule of ammonia to become arginine.

Finally, the arginine hydrolyzes into urea and ornithine, and the ornithine thus produced will again repeat the same reactions. The above reactions are more complicated, but their general outline is as given in Figure 1. The type of

substance discharged is thought to be related to the supply of water from the surroundings.

REGULATION BY HORMONES

Among the things which regulate the body as a whole, there are, in addition to the nerves, hormones. Hormones are produced by particular parts of the body and secreted into the body fluids. They are substances which, like vitamins and enzymes, exert a great influence on the activity of specific parts of the body in extremely small quantities.

Hormones have a variety of chemical compositions, some being proteins, poly-peptides or amino acids, and others steriods. There are compositions other than these and even some whose chemical structure is not clearly understood.

Endocrine Glands: Among the organs (glands) which secrete hormones, those called endocrine glands have no tubes, their secretions being sent into the blood vessels. Distinctive hormones are secreted from such parts of vertebrate animals as the pituitary body, thyroid gland, parathyroid, adrenal, pancreas, testes, and ovary; by keeping mutually balanced, they share in maintaining bodily homeostasis.

SENSATION

Special organs (sensory organs) have developed in animals for the sake of receiving stimuli from the outside world. These developments differ markedly according to the animal's way of life, and the most essential feature is the kind of stimulus which the mechanism is designed to receive. An external stimulus received by a sensory organ is transmitted to central nerves by the sensory nerves distributed within the organ, and sensations arise in those sensory centers corre-sponding to that stimulus in proportion to their respective stimulations. Further-more, excitations are sent from the central nerves to the respective bodily organs and cause various responses. These are frequently accompanied by some response or other arising from the autonomic nerves as well.

ANIMAL MOVEMENTS

Amoeboid Movement: The amoeba puts forth protoplasmic protrusions called pseu-dopodia and moves in the direction of these extensions. This is called amoeboid movement and is considered to have a very close relation to protoplasm streaming. Both plant slime molds and white blood cells make similar movements.

Ciliary and Flagellar Movements: The paramecium swims by moving the cilia which cover its entire body. There are also cilia in man's trachea which send mucus to the larynx by their movements. Algae in the division euglenophyta and zoospores swim in the water by means of flagella.

Muscular Movements: Animals in higher classes than flatworms generally move by

means of muscles. The actions of longitudinal and circular muscles in the body of an earthworm and in the human alimentary canal perform the movement called peristalsis.

In earthworm peristalsis, a part of the body will shrink when the longitudinal muscles in its body wall contract, and it will elongate when the circular muscles contract. Furthermore, the alternation of these movements in peristalsis will move the body when a part of the body is attached to the earth with the support of the bristles.

The Relation between Muscles and Bones: Prawns, insects, and the like have an external skeleton which is so articulated that mutual movements are possible. In these cases, muscles are attached from within, and the exoskeleton can be moved by means of their contractions.

In vertebrates, the striated muscles (also called skeletal muscles) are connected to the bones. A single muscle is attached to each of the bones between which there is a joint and will move the bones by contraction on the principle of the lever. At any single joint there are usually bending muscles and straightening muscles which act in opposition to each other. Such muscles are called antagonistic muscles.

EXPLANATORY NOTES

(1) shokumotsu   "Food". Note that that this is written 食物, whereas *tabemeno* is written 食べ物。

(2) okuri-komu   In those compounds verbs having -*komu* as the second element, the -*komu* gives the idea of "into." Examples are:

nagare-komu	to flow into
kaki-komu	to write in
iri-komu	to enter

(3) fuku-   The prefix *fuku-* (副) usually connotes "assistant," "associate," "secondary," "sub-," "supplementary." Examples:

副業	fukugyō	subsidiary business
副社長	fuku-shachō	vice-president (of a company)
副産物	fuku-sanbutsu	by-product
副原子価力	fuku-genshi-karyoku	secondary valence force

There is another prefix *fuku-* (複), which occurs in the compound *fukuzatsu* (複雑) in this lesson, which means "composite," "complexity," "multiple," "repeating." Some examples of this prefix are:

複屈折	fuku-kussetsu	double refraction

複素平面	fukuso-heimen	complex plane (in mathematics)
複素環式化合物	fukuso-kanshiki-kagō-butsu	heterocyclic compound
複合顕微鏡	fukugō-kenbi-kyō	compound microscope

(4) *zōri-mushi*   To a Westerner the paramecium is shoeshaped, but to a Japanese it is *zōri*-shaped. *Zōri* are Japanese sandals held on the foot by a thong between the big toe and the second toe.

(5) *kōtō*   In earlier readings 等 was encountered with various meanings:

等しい	*hitoshii*	equal
等速度	*tō-sokudo*	constant velocity
金属等	*kinzoku nado*	metals and the like
山本等	*Yamamoto-ra*	Yamamoto *et al.*

Here we find the same character in the meaning of "class" or "rank." Hence 高等 *kōtō* is "high class", and 一等 *ittō* is "first class".

(Note: The readings *nado* and *ra* are not *Tōyō* readings, but they are frequently encountered in the technical literature.)

| …にわたって | "throughout…," "extending through…" |

1. 血管は動物のからだ全体にわたってひろがっている。
2. メンデルはエンドウの多くの世代にわたって交雑の実験を行なった。
3. ヒトが音として感じ得る音波は，振動数が毎秒16回から20,000回位のひろい範囲にわたっている。

| …を通して | "through"… "via…" |

1. 動物が食べた食物は，食道を通して胃に送られる。
2. 細胞への物質の出入は原形質を通して行なわれる。
3. 感覚器官で受けとられた外界の刺激は，感覚神経を通して中枢神経に伝えられる。

A.	物質交代	busshitsu-kōtai	metabolism
	同化	dōka	assimilation
	異化	ika	catabolism

有用な	yūyō na	useful, of use
炭酸同化	tansan-dōka	carbon dioxide assimilation
養分	yōbun	nutrient
体物質	tai-busshitsu	body substance
能力	nōryoku	ability
はるかに	haruka ni	by far
入れかわる	ire-kawaru	to change into
消費する	shōhi suru	to consume

物質交代 (S 58–59)

物質交代は同化と異化とに分けられ，すべて酵素のはたらきによって行なわれる。

同化：生物が体内にとり入れた物質をその生物にとって有用な物質につくり変えるはたらきが同化で，化学的にはおもに合成反応である。植物には，炭酸同化・窒素同化などがあり，簡単な無機物質から複雑な有機物質がつくられる。動物でも食物としてとり入れた植物性または動物性のたんぱく質やその他の養分を原料として，核酸やそれぞれの動物の種類と器官とに特有な体物質をつくるはたらきが行なわれている。一般に，植物は動物にくらべて同化の能力がはるかに大きく，このことが植物と動物との大きな違いのもとになっている。

異化：同化された体物質は，分解してエネルギーを供給し，また新しい体物質と入れかわって，消費されていく。このように，体物質が分解される過程を異化という。

B.	消化	shōka	digestion
	消化管	shōka-kan	digestive tract
	付属器	fuzoku-ki	appended organs
	食性	shokusei	food habits
	肉食性の	niku-shokusei no	carnivorous
	ホ乳類	honyū-rui	mammals
	犬歯	kenshi	canine teeth
	草食性の	sō-shokusei no	herbivorous
	うす歯	usuba	molars
	平滑筋	heikatsu-kin	smooth muscles

消化器官の構造と機能 (S 90)

消化器官には口と腸だけからなる簡単なものから，複雑に分化した消化管や付属器をもっているものまであってさまざまである。多くは食性に応じて発達した特徴をもっていて，肉食性のホ乳類では犬歯が発達し，体長にくらべて腸が短いが，草食性のホ乳類ではうす歯が発達して腸が長い。消化管には消化液を分泌する消化腺が発達し，消化運動にあ

ずかる平滑筋がある。

C.   保生臓器   hosei-zōki   living organs (preserved)

保生臓器	hosei-zōki	living organs (preserved)
輸血	yuketsu	blood transfusion
存否	sonpi	existence, presence
全摘出	zen-tekishutsu	complete extraction, removal
イヌ	inu	dog
認められる程の	mitomerareru hodo no	detectable
損傷	sonshō	damage
…にすぎない	…ni suginai	no more than…
切片	seppen	fragment
消失する	shōshitsu suru	to disappear
乾燥量	kansō-ryō	dry weight

尿素合成   (SK 49–50)

体内のどこで尿素ができるか，の問題は保生臓器についての輸血実験できめられた。腎臓，肝臓，筋などに入る血液中に炭酸アンモニウムを入れておき，それから出る血液中に尿素の存否を調べた。この方法により，アンモニアから尿素の合成は肝臓においてのみ行われることがわかった。さらに肝臓の全摘出を受けたイヌでは認められる程の尿素の合成がないこと，肝臓の損傷の場合にも尿素の合成が減って，アンモニアの排出が増すことが示された。以上の結果によって，尿素の高等動物体内における合成は肝臓においてなされることが認められた。

　1930年頃までは，高等動物体内における尿素の合成について確実にはこの位のことが知られていたにすぎない。それ以来，尿素合成の化学機構が如何に複雑であるかが次々と示されていった。その発展の基礎を作ったのは1930年代の H. A. Krebs の研究である。

　まず肝臓組織の保生切片をアンモニア，炭酸を含んだ適当な塩類溶液に入れると，アンモニアが消失して尿素が形成することが見出された。適当な条件を選べば，尿素の合成は一時間に肝臓組織乾燥量4％に及ぶ。その値は肝臓の大きさを考えて計算すれば，動物の尿素排出全量を説明するに十分な値である。それゆえ，これが尿素形成の最も重要な道を示しているとみなされる。

D.		
神経節	shinkei-setsu	ganglion
中軸	chūjiku	axis
傾向	keikō	tendency
幹	miki	trunk
反応器官	hannō kikan	reacting organ
枝	eda	branches

末梢	masshō	peripheral
脊髄	sekizui	notochord
脳神経	nō-shinkei	cranial nerve
脊髄神経	sekizui-shinkei	spinal nerve

神経系　(S 149)

　高等動物では神経節がからだの中軸に集まる傾向が見られる。その結果，からだの前端から後端へのびた神経の幹ができる。この神経の幹を中枢神経系といい，からだ全体の統一をはかっている。

　これに対し，刺激を感覚器官から中枢に伝え，また，中枢から反応器官に伝える，いわば枝のような神経を末梢神経系という。高等動物では，中枢神経系として脳・脊髄などがあり，末梢神経系として脳神経・脊随神経などがある。

E. 甲状腺	kōjō-sen	thyroid gland
除去する	jokyo suru	to remove
すりつぶす	suri-tsubusu	pulverize
前葉	zenyō	anterior lobe
退化する	taika suru	to degenerate
回復する	kaifuku suru	to recover
やがて	yagate	in a short time
あらかじめ	arakajime	beforehand

ホルモンの相互作用　(S 162–163)

　甲状腺を除去すると，一般に異化作用が低下し，酸素の消費量や二酸化炭素の排出量が減少する。しかし，除去した甲状腺を，からだの他の部分に植えつけたり，別の個体の甲状腺を植えつけたりすると，この変化は見られなくなる。この場合，甲状腺をすりつぶした液を注射しても結果は同じである。

　脳下垂体前葉を除去すると，甲状腺は退化し，そのホルモンの分泌量が減少して，動物の発育が遅れる。また，甲状腺の大部分を除去したとき，脳下垂体前葉があると，やがてその甲状腺は回復してもとの大きさになるが，あらかじめ脳下垂体前葉をとり除いておくと，そのような甲状腺の回復が見られない。このように，脳下垂体前葉の甲状腺刺激ホルモンは，甲状腺のはたらきを調節する。

FINAL TRANSLATION TEST

　最近の電気生理学の発達にはめざましいものがある。これは直径 0.5 μ 以下の微小ガラス電極を種々の神経や筋肉の繊維に横からさしこんで，膜電位を測定したり，電気刺激を

与えることが出来るようになったからである。ここに膜電位というのは，生体細胞をつつんでいる半透過性の原形質膜を境界とする溶液の間に発生する電位差のことであって，その絶対値が測定できるようになったのである。例えば，食物が腸に送られて来ると，肝臓などから消化液が分泌されてこれを消化する。そのためには食物と消化液をよく混合し，いわゆる消化運動が行なわれなければならない。これを行なうのは平滑筋である。平滑筋の収縮によって消化運動が行なわれる。従って平滑筋の収縮運動を測定すれば消化運動がわかり，内臓の複雑な作用を解明する手がかりが得られる。平滑筋の運動は，これに直接ガラス電極をさしこんで，活動電位のスパイクを観察することによって解明される。このようにして得られた筋電図から，消化運動の異常を知ることもできるし，薬物を与えた場合の効果を知ることもできるのである。

　神経のはたらきがよくわかって来たのも電気生理学の成果である。例えば，ある物体を手でつかむ場合を考えてみよう。われわれはまず目で物体の位置を定め，適当に関節を曲げて，その位置まで手を動かさなければならない。この動作に必要な制御作用を行なっているのは脳であって，目や手の感覚を脳に伝達しているのは神経である。神経単位内の電位変化が伝達されるのであって，この場合も，電位変化の原因は，神経細胞の原形質膜が刺激によって透過性を変えることにある。走るというようなかんたんな動作でも，足と頭との神経による連結がなければ実行できないのである。

　このような電気生理学の研究とともに最近発達して来たのは生物医学工学で，理工学において発達して来た方法を生物体に対して適用するのが目的となっている。例えば，血液の流れを，拡散を伴なう粘性流体の流れとして解析したり，尿が腎臓から出て輸尿管を通り，ぼうこうにたまった後，尿道を通って体外に排出される過程を流体力学的に論じたり，骨について，通常の機械材料について行なうような引っ張り，衝撃，つかれ試験などを行なって，その機械的強度を解明するというような研究が行なわれている。このような研究は，人工臓器を設計する際のデータとなり，また自動車の衝突時における傷害を減少するための考え方などの基礎になっている。

LESSON 25
第二十五課

KANJI

脈	517	MYAKU
	3764	
厚	606	KŌ
	824	atsu(i)
薄	272a	HAKU
	4075	usu(i)
布	706	FU
	1468	
養	731	YŌ
	3671	
切	99	SETSU
	667	ki(ru)
主	237	SHU
	285	
髄	277b	ZUI
	5242	
新	256	SHIN
	2080	atara(shii)
口	27	KŌ
	868	kuchi

土	17	DO / TO
	1050	tsuchi
根	216	KON
	2261	ne
還	273a	KAN
	4750	
先	33	SEN
	571	saki
母	137	BO
	2466	
花	43	KA
	3909	hana
階	361	KAI
	5011	
能	691	NŌ
	853	
群	594	GUN
	3667	mu(re)
規	577	KI
	4285	

READING SELECTIONS

血管	kekkan	blood vessel
血液	ketsueki	blood
動脈	dōmyaku	artery
静脈	jōmyaku	vein
毛細血管	mōsai-kekkan	capillary
区別する	kubetsu suru	to distinguish
心臓	shinzō	heart
押し出す	oshi-dasu	to push out, force out
からだ（体）	karada	body
弾力	danryoku	resilience

はく動	hakudō	pulsation
末端	mattan	end
脈(はく)	myaku(haku)	pulse
手くび	tekubi	wrist
送りこむ	okuri-komu	to send into
薄い	usui	thin
ゆるい	yurui	slow
脈を打たない	myaku o utanai	does not produce a pulse
ポケット状の	poketto-jō no	pocket-like
弁	ben	valve
防ぐ	fusegu	to prevent
網目状に	amime-jō ni	in mesh-like fashion
分布する	bunpu suru	to be distributed
総(表面積)	sō(hyō-menseki)	entire (surface area)
養分	yōbun	nourishment, nutrient,
老廃物	rōhai-butsu	waste matter
…を通して	…o tōshite	via…, through…
占める	shimeru	to occupy, take up
有形成分	yūkei-seibun	the components having shape, the visible components
赤血球	sekkekkyū	red corpuscles
白血球	hakkekkyū	white corpuscles
血小板	kesshōban	blood platelets
血しょう	kesshō	blood plasma
中央	chūō	center
くぼむ	kubomu	to become hollow, form a hollow
男・女	otoko; onna	male; female
万	man	10, 000
ヘモグロビン	hemogurobin	hemoglobin
運搬	unpan	transport
大切な	taisetsu na	important
役割をはたす	yakuwari o hatasu	to play a role, perform a task
主として	shu to shite	mainly, primarily
骨髄	kotsuzui	bone marrow
新しく	atarashiku	anew, afresh
古い	furui	old
ひ臓	hizō	spleen

消化する	shōka suru	to digest
食作用（＝食細胞活動)	shoku-sayō	phagocytosis
食細胞	shoku-saihō	phagocyte
病原性の	byōgen-sei no	pathogenic
防御	bōgyo	defense, protection
リンパ腺	rinpa-sen	lymphatic gland, lymph node
固まる	katamaru	to harden
切る	kiru	to cut
傷	kizu	cut, wound
出血する	shukketsu suru	to bleed
切(り)口	kirikuchi	opening
凝固する	gyōko suru	to coagulate
かたまり	katamari	lump, clod
薄黄色	usu-kiiro	pale yellow
血餅	keppei	blood clot
血清	kessei	blood serum
からみあう	karami-au	to intertwine

血管と血液　(S 124–125)

血管。血管は動脈・静脈[1]・毛細血管に区別される。動脈は，心臓から押し出される血液をからだの各部分に運ぶ血管である。血管壁は厚くて弾力がある。心臓のはく動によって生ずる血液の圧力の変化は，周期的な波動として太い動脈からしだいに末端へと[2]伝わっていく。この周期的な波動を脈（脈はく）といい，手くび[3]などに触れて感じることができる。

　静脈は，からだの各部から心臓に血液を送りこむ血管である。その壁は薄くて弾力が小さい。血液は静脈内をゆるく流れ，動脈のように脈を打たない。静脈内にはポケット状の弁があって，血液の逆流を防いでいる。

　毛細血管は，動脈と静脈とをつなぐ壁の薄い細い管[4]で，からだの各組織に，網目状に分かれて密に分布している。したがって，毛細血管の内部の総表面積はかなり広い。血液は毛細血管内をゆっくり流れながら，薄い血管壁を通して，組織との間に養分・酸素・二酸化炭素・老廃物などの交換を行なう。

血液。血液の重量は，ヒトでは体重の約1/13を占める。その有形成分として赤血球・白血球・血小板があり，液体成分としては血しょうがある。

　ヒトの赤血球は直径8μ，厚さ2.4μぐらいの円板状の細胞で，核がなく，中央が少しくぼんでいる。血液1mm^{3}中に含まれる数は，男約500万個，女約450万個である。血液の

色は，赤血球中のヘモグロビンによるものである。ヘモグロビンは鉄を含む色素を成分とする複雑なたんぱく質で，酸素の運搬に大切な役割をはたしている。赤血球は，主として太く長い骨の骨髄中で新しくつくられ，その寿命はおよそ120日で，古くなったものはおもに肝臓やひ臓でこわされる。

　白血球には，いろいろな種類があるが，一般に赤血球より大きい細胞で，直径およそ10〜15μ，2個以上の核をもつものが多い。ヒトでは，血液1mm³中に約6,000〜8,000個ある。アメーバのような運動を行ない，薄い毛細血管の壁を通って組織内に出はいりする。細菌などをその細胞内に取り入れて消化する食作用という性質があるので，食細胞ともいわれ，病原性の細菌に対する防御のはたらきをする。白血球は，骨髄・ひ臓およびリンパ腺で新しくつくられる。血液は体外に出ると固まる性質がある。からだに傷を受けて出血しても，切り口が小さければ，しばらくするとそのままで自然に固まってしまう。これを血液の凝固という。血液を試験管の中で凝固させると，下部の赤黒いかたまりと上部の透明な薄黄色の液とに分かれる。かたまりを血餅，透明な液を血清という。血餅は繊維状のフィブリンが血球とからみあって固まっているものである。

窒素同化	chisso-dōka	nitrogen assimilation
核酸	kakusan	nucleic acid
りん脂質	rinshi-shitsu	phosphatide
クロロフィル	kurorofiru	chlorophyll
土	tsuchi	earth, ground
おもに（主に）	omo ni	chiefly, mainly
特殊な	tokushu na	special, distinct, unique
根	ne	root
まず（先ず）	mazu	first of all
還元する	kangen suru	to reduce (opposite of oxidize)
葉緑体	yōryoku-tai	chloroplast, chlorophyll granule
窒素の固定	chisso no kotei	nitrogen fixation
マメ（豆）	mame	beans
…につく	…ni tsuku	to be attached to…
根粒(細菌)	konryū(saikin)	root nodule (bacteria)
エンドウ	endō	peas
ダイズ（大豆）	daizu	soy beans
こぶ	kobu	lump, protuberance
供給する	kyōkyū suru	to supply, furnish
乏しい	toboshii	scarce, limited
土地	tochi	ground

生育する	sei-iku suru	to grow
宿主	shukushu	host
共生	kyōsei	symbiosis

窒素同化　(S 79–81)

　窒素は，たんぱく質・核酸・りん脂質およびクロロフィルなどの成分として，きわめて大切な元素である。

　植物は，土の中から窒素を，おもに無機窒素化合物として取り入れる。硝酸塩とアンモニウム塩とがそのおもなものである。植物体では，これらの無機窒素化合物や，特殊な場合には空気中の窒素から有機窒素化合物を合成するはたらきをもっている。これを窒素同化という。

<u>有機窒素化合物の生成</u>。根から吸収される無機窒素化合物のうちで，硝酸塩は根や葉の中で還元されて，まずアンモニウム塩に変わる。アンモニウム塩はさらに糖などから生じた有機酸と結合してアミノ酸となる。このようにしてつくられたアミノ酸の大部分は，互いに多数結合してたんぱく質となるが，その一部は核酸やクロロフィルなどをつくるのにも使われる。これらの化学変化には光が直接必要でないから，葉緑体を含まない細胞でも行なわれる。

<u>空中窒素の固定</u>。ふつうの高等植物は，空気中の窒素 N_2 を直接利用することはできないが，細菌のうちには，これを同化することのできるものがある。その一つは，マメ類の根についている根粒細菌である。エンドウ・ダイズなどの根には，小さなこぶのようなものがいくつも [5] 見られる。これを根粒といい，その細胞の中には根粒細菌がたくさんはいっていて，その中で空気中の窒素が原料となって窒素化合物がつくられる。この窒素化合物が植物体に供給されるので，マメ類は，窒素養分に乏しい土地にもよく生育することができる。

　根粒細菌は，宿主 [6] になるマメ類の種類によっていくつかの種類が [5] ある。そして，植物の体外でも生活することができるが，マメ類と共生していなければ，空気中の窒素の固定は行なわれない。

生殖	seishoku	reproduction
被子植物	hishi-shokubutsu	angiosperm
めしべ（雌ずい）	meshibe (shizui)	pistil
おしべ（雄ずい）	oshibe (yūzui)	stamen
子房	shibō	ovary
室	shitsu	loculus
胚珠	haishu	ovule
先端	sentan	tip

やく（葯）	yaku	anther
胚のう（母細胞）	hainō (bo-saihō)	embryo sac (mother cell)
減数分裂	gensū-bunretsu	reduction division, meiosis
消失する	shōshitsu suru	to disappear, vanish
卵細胞	ran-saihō	egg cell, ovum
助（胎）細胞	jo(tai)-saihō	synergid
反足細胞	hansoku-saihō	antipodal cell
極核	kyokukaku	pole nucleus
できあがる	deki-agaru	to be completed
花粉母細胞	kafun-bo-saihō	pollen mother cell
成熟する	seijuku suru	to be(come) ripe
柱頭	chūtō	stigma
先	saki	tip
粘液	nen'eki	viscous liquid

植物の生殖細胞　S 221–222

　被子植物の生殖器官のうち，生殖に直接関係するのはめしべとおしべとである。めしべの下部を子房といい，内部はいくつかの⁽⁵⁾室に分かれていることが多く，中に胚珠という球状の組織がある。また，おしべの先端にはやくがある。

　胚珠の中には1個の胚嚢母細胞がある。これは減数分裂をして4個の細胞となるが，そのうちの3個は消失し，残った1個（胚嚢細胞）はさらに3回の分裂によって，8個の細胞になる。つまり，卵細胞1，助胎細胞2，反足細胞3，極核2となって胚嚢ができあがる。

　おしべのやくには，多数の花粉母細胞を生じ，これが減数分裂によって4個ずつの花粉細胞に分かれ，その一つ一つが成熟して花粉になる。花粉の形にはいろいろあるが，大きさは20〜100μぐらいで，球形またはだ円体形をしているものが多い。めしべの柱頭の先には突起があったり，粘液を出したりして，花粉がつきやすいようになっていることが多い。

分類	bunrui	classification
基礎	kiso	basis, foundation
類縁関係	ruien-kankei	relationship
段階	dankai	grade, step, level
整理する	seiri suru	to arrange, put in order
編成する	hensei suru	to organize
相違点	sōi-ten	point of difference
着目する	chakumoku suru	to notice, pay attention to
幾通りもの	ikutōri mo no	many kinds of, various
（不）可能	(fu)kanō	(im)possibility

科学的に	kagaku-teki ni	scientifically
いったい（一体）何を	ittai nani o	what (on earth)
かぎ	kagi	key
種々雑多な	shuju-zatta na	all kinds of
容易に	yōi ni	easily
役だてる	yaku-dateru	to serve
系統的に	keitō-teki ni	systematically
個々の	koko no	each, individual
形態	keitai	form, shape
生理	seiri	physiology
発生	hassei	development
形質	keishitsu	character
場合場合に応じて	baai-baai ni ōjite	depending on each individual case
本質的と	honshitsu-teki to	as essential
系統分類	keitō-bunrui	phylogenetic system
決め手	kimete	deciding factor
意見	iken	opinion
種	shu	species
子を生ずる	ko o shōzuru	to produce offspring
お互い（＝互い）	otagai	
能力	nōryoku	ability
群	mure, gun	herd, group
定義	teigi	definition
交配	kōhai	cross mating
相同器官	sōdō-kikan	homologous organs
類縁	rui-en	affinity
順に	jun ni	in order
属	zoku	genus
科	ka	family
目	moku	order
綱	kō	class
門	mon	phylum
界	kai	kingdom
設ける	mōkeru	to establish, institute
亜の字（＝亜という字）	a no ji	the symbol 亜
亜属	azoku	subgenus
亜種	ashu	subspecies
変種	henshu	variety
品種	hinshu	form

規約	kiyaku	agreement, rule
万国共通の	bankoku-kyōtsū no	universal, common to all countries
学名	gakumei	scientific name
ヒト	hito	man (i.e., *Homo sapiens*)
ノイバラ（＝ノバラ）	noibara	wild rose
日本語	Nihon-go	Japanese (language)
名称	meishō	name, designation
和名	wamei	Japanese name
ラテン語	Raten-go	Latin
確立する	kakuritsu suru	to establish
二名法	nimei-hō	binomial nomenclature
国際命名規約	kokusai-meimei kiyaku	international agreement on nomenclature
禁じる	kinjiru	to prohibit

分類の基礎　(S 302–304)

　地球上には，現在いろいろの生物がすんでいる。それらの生物のなかで，互いに類縁関係のあるものをその程度によっていくつか[5]の段階に整理し，編成することを分類という[7]。その場合，どの相違点に着目するかによって幾通りも[5]の分類が可能であるが，科学的にはいったい何を「鍵」として，どのように分類しているのであろうか。

　生物を分類する目的は，たんに種々雑多な生物を機械的に整理し，その結果を容易に利用できるようにするというだけでなく，自然界に存在する生物すべて[8]の類縁関係を明らかにし，これを系統的に配列することである。したがって，個々の生物のもつ形態・生理・生殖・発生，その他いろいろの形質をすべて[9]考慮し，場合場合に応じて，最も本質的と考えられるものを見いだして「鍵」とし，おのおのの生物の系統中における自然の位置関係が明らかになるようにする必要がある。このような分類法は系統分類または自然分類といわれる。しかし，どのような形質が本質的なものであるかについて，絶対的な決め手はなく，分類学者の間で意見の違っていることも少なくない。

　生物を分類する基本の単位を種という。これは高等動物の場合，「お互いの間に子を生ずる能力のある自然の群で，他の同様な群との間に生殖能力をもたないもの」と定義されている。この定義は下等な生物にはあてはまらないが，実際に交配実験を行なうことが不可能と近い[10]生物群もかなり多い。そこで，ふつうには「相同器官の類縁の程度」に基づき，種から始まり，順に属・科・目・綱・門・界の段階が設けられている。さらに細かく分ける必要のある場合には，それぞれの段階の間に，亜の字をつけた段階を設ける。たとえば，亜属は種よりも高いが属よりは低い段階である。種をさらに細かく分けたものに亜

種・変種・品種がある。

　Homo Sapiens, Rosa Polyantha などの名は，一定の規約によって決定された万国共通の名であって，学名とよばれる。これに対しヒト・ノイバラといった日本語の名称を和名[11]という。

　学名にはラテン語が用いられる。上の例で Homo, Rosa というのは属名であり，また Sapiens, Polyantha は種名で，この二つを並べたものが学名である。このようにして生物名を構成する方法はリンネ C.V. Linné (1707〜1778) により確立されたもので二名法という。もちろん，同一の生物に対し異なった種名を与えたり，異なった生物に同一名を用いることは国際命名規約により禁じられている。

KEKKAN TO KETSUEKI

Kekkan: Kekkan wa dōmyaku, jōmyaku, [1] mōsai-kekkan ni kubetsu sareru. Dō-myaku wa, shinzō kara oshi-dasareru ketsueki o, karada no kaku-bubun ni hakobu kekkan de aru. Kekkan-heki wa, atsukute danryoku ga aru.

　Shinzō no hakudō ni yotte shōzuru ketsueki no atsuryoku no henka wa, shūki-teki na hadō to shite futoi dōmyaku kara shidai ni mattan e to [2] tsutawatte iku. Kono shūki-teki na hadō o myaku (myakuhaku) to ii, tekubi [3] nado ni furete kanjiru koto ga dekiru.

　Jōmyaku wa, karada no kakubu kara shinzō ni ketsueki o okuri-komu kekkan de aru. Sono kabe wa usukute danryoku ga chiisai. Ketsueki wa jōmyaku-nai o yuruku nagare, dōmyaku no yō ni myaku o utanai. jōmyaku-nai ni wa poketto-jō no ben ga atte, ketsueki no gyakuryū o fuseide iru. Mōsai-kekkan wa, dōmyaku to jōmyaku to o tsunagu kabe no usui hosoi kan [4] de, karada no kaku-soshiki ni, amime-jō ni wakarete mitsu ni bunpu shite iru. Shitagatte, mōsai-kan no nai-bu no sōhyō-menseki wa kanari hiroi. Ketsu-eki wa mōsai-kekkan-nai o yukkuri nagare-nagara, usui kekkan-heki o tōshite, soshiki to no aida ni yōbun, sanso, ni-sanka-tanso, rōhai-butsu nado no kōkan o okonau.

Ketsueki: Ketsueki no jūryō wa, hito de wa taijū no yaku jūsan-bun-no-ichi o shimeru. Sono yūkei-seibun to shite sekkekkyū, hakkekkyū, kesshōban ga ari, ekitai-seibun to shite wa kesshō ga aru.

　Hito no sekkekkyū wa chokkei hachi-mikuron, atsusa ni-ten-yon-mikuron gurai no enban-jō no saihō de, kaku ga naku, chūō ga sukoshi kubonde iru. Ketsueki ichi-rippō-mirimētoru-chū ni fukumareru kazu wa, otoko yaku go-hyakuman-ko, onna yaku yonhyaku-gojū-man-ko de aru.

　Ketsueki no iro wa, sekkekkyū-chū no hemogurobin ni yoru mono de aru. Hemogurobin wa tetsu o fukumu shikiso o seibun to suru fukuzatsu na tanpaku-shitsu de, sanso no unpan ni taisetsu na yakuwari o hatashite iru.

　Sekkekkyū wa, shu to shite futoku nagai hone no kotsuzui-chū de atarashiku

tsukurare, sono jumyō wa oyoso hyaku-nijū-nichi de, furuku natta mono wa omo ni kanzō ya hizō de kowasareru.

Hakkekkyū ni wa, iroiro na shurui ga aru ga, ippan ni sekkekkyū yori ōkii saihō de, chokkei oyoso jū-naishi-jūgo mikuron, niko-ijō no kaku o motsu mono ga ōi. Hito de wa, ketsueki ichi-rippō-mirimētoru-chū ni yaku rokusen-naishi-hassen-ko aru. Amēba no yō na undō o okonai, usui mōsai-kekkan no kabe o tōtte soshiki-nai ni de-hairi suru. Saikin nado o sono saihō-nai ni tori-irete shōka suru shoku-sayō to iu seishitsu ga aru no de, shoku-saihō to mo iware, byōgen-sei no saikin ni taisuru bōgyo no hataraki o suru. Hakkekkyū wa, kotsuzui, hizō, oyobi rinpa-sen de atarashiku tsukurareru.

Ketsueki wa taigai ni deru to katamaru seishitsu ga aru. Karada ni kizu o ukete shukketsu shite mo, kiriguchi ga chiisakereba, shibaraku suru to sono mama de shizen ni katamatte shimau. Kore o ketsueki no gyōko to iu.

Ketsueki o shiken-kan no naka de gyōko saseru to, kabu no aka-guroi katamari to jōbu no tōmei na usu-kiiro no eki to ni wakareru. Katamari o keppei, tōmei na eki o kessei to iu. Keppei wa sen'i-jō no fiburin ga kekkyū to karami-atte katamatte iru mono de aru.

CHISSO-DŌKA

Chisso wa, tanpaku-shitsu, kakusan, rinshi-shitsu oyobi kurorofiru nado no sei-bun to shite, kiwamete taisetsu na genso de aru.

Shokubutsu wa, tsuchi no naka kara chisso o, omo ni muki-chisso-kagōbutsu to shite tori-ireru. Shōsan-en to anmoniumu-en to ga sono omo na mono de aru.

Shokubutsu-tai de wa, korera no muki-chisso-kagōbutsu ya, tokushu na baai ni wa kūki-chū no chisso kara yūki-chisso-kagōbutsu o gōsei suru hataraki o motte iru. Kore o chisso-dōka to iu.

Yūki-chisso-kagō-butsu no Seisei: Ne kara kyūshū sareru muki-chisso-kagō-butsu no uchi de, shōsan-en wa ne ya ha no naka de kangen sarete, mazu, anmoniumu-en ni kawaru. Anmoniumu-en wa sara ni tō nado kara shōjita yūki-san to ketsugō shite amino-san to naru. Kono yō ni shite tsukurareta amino-san no dai-bubun wa, tagai ni tasū-ketsugō shite tanpaku-shitsu to naru ga, sono ichibu wa kakusan ya kurorofiru nado o tsukuru no ni mo tsukawareru. Korera no kagaku henka ni wa hikari ga chokusetsu hitsuyō de nai kara, yōryoku-tai o fukumanai saihō de mo okonawareru.

Kūchū-chisso no Kotei: Futsū no kōtō-shokubutsu wa, kūki-chū no chisso N_2 o cho-kusetsu riyō suru koto wa dekinai ga, saikin no uchi ni wa, kore o dōka suru koto no dekiru mono ga aru. Sono hitotsu wa, mame-rui no ne ni tsuite iru kon-ryū-saikin de aru. Endō, daizu nado no ne ni wa, chiisa na kobu no yō na mono ga ikutsu mo [5] mirareru. Kore o konryū to ii, sono saihō no naka ni wa konryū-saikin ga takusan haitte ite, sono naka de kūki-chū no chisso ga genryō

to natte chisso-kagōbutsu ga tsukurareru. Kono chisso-kagōbutsu ga shokubutsu-tai ni kyōkyū sareru no de, mame-rui wa, chisso-yōbun ni toboshii tochi ni mo yoku sei-iku suru koto ga dekiru.

Konryū-saikin wa, shukushu[6] ni naru mame-rui no shurui ni yotte ikutsu ka[5] no shurui ga aru. Soshite, shokubutsu no taigai de mo seikatsu suru koto ga de-kiru ga, mame-rui to kyōsei shite inakereba, kūki-chū no chisso no kotei wa okonawarenai.

SHOKUBUTSU NO SEISHOKU-SAIHŌ

Hishi-shokubutsu no seishoku-kikan no uchi, seishoku ni chokusetsu kankei suru no wa meshibe to oshibe to de aru.

Meshibe no kabu o shibō to ii, naibu wa ikutsu ka[5] no shitsu ni wakarete iru koto ga ōku, naka ni haishu to iu kyūjō no soshiki ga aru. Mata, oshibe no sen-tan ni wa yaku ga aru.

Haishu no naka ni wa ikko no hainō-bo-saihō ga aru. Kore wa gensū-bunretsu o shite yonko no saihō to naru ga, sono uchi no sanko wa shōshitsu shi, nokotta ikko (hainō-saihō) wa sara ni sankai no bunretsu ni yotte, hakko no saihō ni naru. Tsumari ran-saihō ichi, jotai-saihō ni, hansoku-saihō san, kyokukaku ni to natte hainō ga deki-agaru.

Oshibe no yaku ni wa, tasū no kafun-bo-saihō o shōji, kore ga, gensū-bunretsu ni yotte yonko-zutsu no kafun-saihō ni wakare, sono hitotsu-hitotsu ga seijuku shite kafun ni naru.

Kafun no katachi ni wa iroiro aru ga, ōkisa wa nijū naishi hyaku mikuron gurai de, kyūkei mata wa daentai-kei o shite iru mono ga ōi. Meshibe no chūtō no saki ni wa, tokki ga attari, nen'eki o dashitari shite, kafun ga tsuki-yasui yō ni natte iru koto ga ōi.

BUNRUI NO KISO

Chikyū-jō ni wa, genzai iroiro no seibutsu ga sunde iru. Sorera no seibutsu no naka de, tagai ni ruien-kankei no aru mono o sono teido ni yotte ikutsu ka no dankai ni seiri shi, hensei suru koto o bunrui to iu.[7] Sono baai, dono sōi-ten ni chakumoku suru ka ni yotte iku-tōri mo no bunrui ga kanō de aru ga, kagaku-teki ni wa ittai nani o "kagi" to shite, dono yō ni bunrui shite iru no de arō ka?

Seibutsu o bunrui suru mokuteki wa, tan ni, shuju-zatta na seibutsu o kikai-teki ni seiri shi, sono kekka o yōi ni riyō dekiru yō ni suru to iu dake de naku, shizen-kai ni sonzai suru seibutsu subete[8] no ruien-kankei o akiraka ni shi, kore o keitō-teki ni hairetsu suru koto de aru. Shitagatte koko no seibutsu no motsu keitai, seiri, seishoku, hassei, sono ta iroiro no keishitsu o subete[9] kōryo shi, baai-baai ni ōjite, mottomo honshitsu-teki to kangaerareru mono o mi-idashite "kagi" to shi, ono-ono no seibutsu no keitō-chū ni okeru shizen no ichi-kankei ga akiraka

ni naru yō ni suru hitsuyō ga aru. Kono yō na bunrui-hō wa keitō-bunrui mata wa shizen-bunrui to iwareru. Shikashi, dono yō na keishitsu ga honshitsu-teki na mono de aru ka ni tsuite, zettai-teki na kimete wa naku, bunrui-gakusha no aida de iken no chigatte iru koto mo sukunaku nai.

Seibutsu o bunrui suru kihon no tan'i o "shu" to iu. Kore wa kōtō-dōbutsu no baai, "o-tagai no aida ni ko o shōjiru nōryoku no aru shizen no mure de, ta no dōyō na mure to no aida ni seishoku-nōryoku o motanai mono" to teigi sarete iru. Kono teigi wa katō na seibutsu ni wa atehamaranai ga, jissai ni, kōhai-jikken o okonau koto ga fu-kanō ni chikai[9] seibutsu-gun mo kanari ōi. Soko de, futsū ni wa "sōdō-kikan no ruien no teido" ni motozuki, "shu" kara hajimari, jun ni "zoku," "ka," "moku," "ko," "mon", "kai" no dankai ga mōkerarete iru. Sara ni komakaku wakeru hitsuyō no aru baai ni wa, sorezore no dankai no aida ni, "a" no ji o tsuketa dankai o mōkeru. Tatoeba, "azoku" wa shu yori mo takai ga, zoku yori wa hikui dankai de aru. Shu o sara ni komakaku waketa mono ni "ashu", "henshu", "hinshu" ga aru.

Homo sapiens, Rosa polyantha nado no na wa, ittei no kiyaku ni yotte kettei sareta bankoku-kyōtsū no na de atte, gakumei to yobareru. Kore ni taishi hito, noibara to itta Nihongo no meishō o wamei[10] to iu.

Gakumei ni wa Raten-go mochi-irareru. Ue no rei de *Homo, Rosa* to iu no wa zokumei de ari, mata *sapiens, polyantha* wa shumei de, kono futatsu o narabeta mono ga gakumei de aru. Kono yō ni shite seibutsu-mei o kōsei suru hōhō wa Rinne (C.v Linné (1707-1778)) ni yori kakuritsu sareta mono de, nimei-hō to iu.

Mochiron, dōitsu no seibutsu ni taishi kotonatta shumei o ataetari, kotonatta seibutsu ni dōitsu-mei o mochi-iru koto wa kokusai-meimei-kiyaku ni yori kinji-rarete iru.

BLOOD VESSELS AND BLOOD

Blood Vessels: Blood vessels are classified as arteries, veins, and capillaries. Arteries are blood vessels which carry the blood forced out from the heart to all parts of the body. The walls of these blood vessels are thick and resilient.

The changes in blood-pressure resulting from the pulsations of the heart are propagated from the large arteries gradually on out to the extremities as a periodic wave motion. This periodic wave motion is called "the pulse," and it can be felt by touching the wrist or other locations.

Veins are blood vessels which channel the blood back into the heart from all parts of the body. Its walls are thin and low in resilience. The blood flows slowly in the veins, and there is no pulsing as in the arteries. There are pocket-like valves in the veins which prevent back-flow. Capillaries are tiny, thin-walled vessels connecting the veins and the arteries; they are divided in a mesh-like fashion and densely distributed throughout the body tissue. Therefore, the total internal

surface area of the capillaries is quite extensive. The blood, as it flows slowly through the capillaries, engages in exchanges of nutrients, oxygen, carbon dioxide, and waste matter with the tissues via the thin blood-vessel walls.

Blood: In man blood accounts for about 1/13th of the body weight. It contains red corpuscles, white corpuscles, and platelets as visible components and plasma as a liquid component. Human red blood corpuscles are circular disc-shaped cells 8μ in diameter and 2.4μ in thickness, have no nucleus, and are slightly concave at the center. The number of red blood corpuscles in 1 cubic millimeter of blood is about 5×10^6 for the male and about 4.5×10^6 for the female.

The color of blood is due to the hemoglobin in the red blood corpuscles. Hemoglobin, a complex protein which has a pigment component containing iron, plays an important role in oxygen transport.

The red corpuscles are produced chiefly in the marrow of large, long bones; their lifetime is about 120 days, the aging ones being destroyed mainly in the liver and spleen.

There are various kinds of white corpuscles; they are generally larger than red corpuscle cells, about $10–15\mu$ in diameter, and frequently have 2 or more nuclei.

One cubic millimeter of human blood contains about 6000–8000 of them. They execute movements like an amoeba and can go in and out of the tissue by passing through the thin walls of the capillaries. They have the property of phagocytosis in which they ingest such things as bacteria into their cells and digest them. They are therefore called phagocytes and perform the function of protecting (the body) against pathogenic bacteria. New white corpuscles are produced in the bone marrow, spleen, and lymph glands.

Blood has the property of clotting when it emerges from the body. Even though the body suffers a wound and bleeds, if the opening is small, the blood will harden naturally in a short while. This process is called coagulation.

If we have blood coagulate in a test tube, it separates into reddish-black lumps below and a transparent, pale yellow liquid above. The lumps are called blood clots and the transparent liquid is called blood serum. The blood clots are a hardened mass of red corpuscles intertwined with thread-like fibrin.

NITROGEN ASSIMILATION

Nitrogen is an extremely important element, as it is a component of proteins, nucleic acids, phosphatides, and chlorophyll.

Plants take in nitrogen from the soil chiefly as inorganic nitrogen compounds, the main ones being nitrates and ammonium salts. A plant has the capability of synthesizing organic nitrogen compounds from these inorganic nitrogen compounds and, in certain cases, from atmospheric nitrogen. This is called nitrogen assimilation.

The Formation of Organic Nitrogen Compounds: Nitrates, which are among the inorganic nitrogen compounds absorbed by the roots, are reduced in the roots or leaves, being first converted into ammonium salts. These in turn combine with organic acids arising from sugars and other substances to form amino acids. Most of the amino acids thus produced bond together in multiples to form proteins, but some are also used in making nucleic acids, chlorophyll, and other compounds. Since light is not directly necessary for these reactions, they occur even in cells which do not contain chloroplasts.

The Fixation of Atmospheric Nitrogen: Most higher plants cannot make direct use of atmospheric nitrogen, but there are bacteria which can assimilate it. One type is the root nodule bacteria which are attached to the roots of beans. A great number of small protuberances called root nodules are seen on the roots of peas, soy beans, and other legumes. Many root nodule bacteria are present in their cells, and nitrogen compounds are produced there using atmospheric nitrogen as the starting material. Beans therefore can grow even in soil which is poor in nitrogenous nutrients as the nitrogen compounds are supplied by the plant itself.

There are several kinds of root nodule bacteria depending on the variety of bean acting as host. These bacteria can live outside the body of the plant but if they do not have a symbiotic relation with the bean plant, they cannot fix atmospheric nitrogen.

THE REPRODUCTIVE CELLS OF PLANTS

Among the reproductive organs of angiosperms, those having the most direct connection with reproduction are the pistil and the stamen.

The lower part of the pistil is called the ovary and its interior is often divided into several loculi, in which there are globular tissues called ovules. Furthermore, at the tip of the stamen there is the anther.

Inside the ovule there is a single embryo sac mother cell. The latter undergoes meiosis and becomes four cells, of which three vanish and the remaining one (the embryo sac cell) subsequently divides three times giving eight cells. The embryo sac is finally completed with 1 egg cell, 2 synergids, 3 antipodal cells, and 2 pole nuclei.

The pollen mother cells are produced in the anther of the stamen; these each undergo meiosis dividing into 4 pollen cells, each one of which ripens into pollen.

Pollen comes in a variety of forms; they range in size from about 20 to 100μ and are frequently spherical or ellipsoidal in shape. There are projections on the tip of the pistil stigma which, along with the secretion of a viscous liquid and many other features, provide for the ready attachment of pollen particles.

THE FUNDAMENTALS OF CLASSIFICATION

Various living things inhabit the earth at present. Ordering and organizing those living things into several levels according to the extent of their mutual relationships is called classification. In doing this, however, there are many possible ways of making classfications according to which differences (among the various living things) are given attention, and so we ask what exactly is the key and how does one really classify scientifically.

The purpose of classifying living things is not simply to provide a readily usable mechanical ordering of their variety but rather to clarify the relationships between all living things in the natural world and to arrange them systematically. It is necessary, therefore, to consider all of the various characters which each animal possesses—its formation, development, propagation, physiology—and then to discover in each individual case the essential feature which, taken as the key, will serve to clarify the natural position and relationships of each living thing within the system. This method of classifying is called a phylogenetic or natural system. There is, however, no absolutely decisive factor regarding which characters are the essential ones, and there exist more than a few differences of opinion among taxonomists.

The fundamental unit in classifying living things is the species. For higher animals this is defined as those animals which are able tQ produce offspring with members of their own natural group but which have no reproductive ability with those in other similar groups. This definition does not apply to lower organisms though in actual fact there are quite a few forms of life for which cross-breeding experiments are close to impossible. Accordingly, it is customary to take the degree of affinity between homologous organs as a basis and to establish an order of levels beginning with species and proceeding to genus, family, order, class, phylum, and kingdom. When it is necessary to subdivide further, levels denoted with the prefix sub- are introduced between the respective levels. For example, sub-genus ranks above species but below genus. In the further subdivision of species there are sub-species, varieties, and forms.

Names such as *Homo sapiens* and *Rosa polyantha* are called scientific names and are universal terms established according to fixed conventions. In contrast *hito* and *noibara* are Japanese names.

Latin is used in scientific names. In the two examples above, *Homo* and *Rosa* are the genus names, *sapiens* and *polyantha* the species names, and the two together are the scientific name. This method of constructing the names for living things was established by Linné (1707—1778) and is called binomial nomenclature.

There are, of course, international nomenclature conventions which prevent the

assignment of different names to the same living thing or the use of the same name for different living things.

EXPLANATORY NOTES

(1) jōmyaku · · · · · · · · · · · · · · · The character 静 is almost always given the reading *SEI*. The reading *JŌ*, occuring in the combination 静脈 is unusual.

(2) ...to tsutawatte iku · · · · · · This is short for...*to iu yō ni tsutawatte iku.*

(3) tekubi · · · · · · · · · · · · · · · · · 首　*kubi*　　　neck
　　　　　　　　　　　　　　手首　*tekubi*　　wrist
　　　　　　　　　　　　　　足首　*ashikubi*　ankle

(4) kabe no usui hosoi kan · · · "A slender tube with thin walls." Here *kabe no usui* (=*kabe ga usui*) and *hosoi* both modify *kan*. When two adjectives modify the same noun, the usual construction is: *futoku*(*te*) *nagai hone* "a long thick bone." But *kabe no usukute tsuyoi kan* would mean "a tube with thin, strong walls."

(5) ikutsu mo (no) · · · · · · · · · "A great many"; compare with *ikutsu ka* (*no*) "a few," "some", "several".

(6) shukushu · · · · · · · · · · · · · · "Host" (in the biological sense). The same characters would be read *yadonushti*, the *kun*-reading, if the reference were to the manager of an inn.

(7) sorera no...to iu · · · · · · · · *Sorera...mono o* is the object of *seiri shi.*

(8) seibutsu subete · · · · · · · · · "All the living things." Note that *subete* may follow the noun, as is the case here, or precede it; in the latter case the particle *no* is needed: *subete no seibutsu.* Here we know that *subete no ruienkankei* is not intended, because *seibutsu* would then have no particle to indicate its function in the sentence.

(9) keishitsu o subete · · · · · · · Here *subete* goes with *keishitsu;*
　　　　　　　　　　　　　　one could also write *keishitsu no subete o.*

(10) kōhai-jikken...chikai · · · · This clause modifies *seibutsu-gun.*

(11) wamei · · · · · · · · · · · · · · · · The symbol 和 wa is an abbreviation for 大和 *Yamato* meaning "Japan".
　　　　　　　　　　　　　　The opposite of 和 is 洋 *yō* indicating "foreign." Hence:
　　　　　　　　　　　　　　和食　　*washoku*　　Japanese food
　　　　　　　　　　　　　　洋食　　*yōshoku*　　foreign food
　　　　　　　　　　　　　　和洋書　*wayō-sho*　Japanese and foreign books

SUPPLEMENTARY READINGS

A. 随腔   zuikō   pith cavity
    みたす   mitasu   to fill
    柔らかい   yawarakai   soft
    あずかる   azukaru   to take a part in, play a
                                           role in

    海綿様   kaimen-yō   spongy
    基質   kishitsu   substrate, matrix
    網状繊維   mōjō-sen'i   reticulin fibres
    洞様血管   dōyō-kekkan   sinusoid
    幼胚期   yōhai-ki   beginning embryonic stage
    原基   genki   rudiment
    骨化   kokka   ossification
    原始   genshi   original
    侵入する   shinnyū suru   to invade
    造血   zōketsu   blood production
    遅れる   okureru   to be late
    開始する   kaishi suru   to begin
    機能   kinō   process, function
    休止する   kyūshi suru   to stop, discontinue
    継続する   keizoku suru   to continue
    主要な（＝おもな）   shuyō na   chief, main, principal

骨　髄　(SJ 341)

　骨の髄腔をみたす柔らかい組織で，赤血球・白血球・血小板の形成にあずかる各種の細胞，あるいは脂肪細胞などが，海綿様構造の基質の間に存在する。基質には銀によく染まる網状繊維があり，また洞様血管とよばれる太い血管が多く分布している。幼胚期に骨原基に骨化が起るとともに原始骨髄が形成され，この髄腔に血管が侵入すると骨髄造血がはじまる。

　骨髄造血は，他の臓器の造血作用より遅れて開始されるが，他の臓器の造血機能が休止した後にも継続され，主要な造血器管の役割を果す。

B. 還元滴定   kangen-tekitei   reductimetry
    標準容液   hyōjun-yōeki   standard solutions
    第一鉄塩   daiichi-tetsu-en   ferrous salt
    亜ヒ酸   ahi-san   arsenous acid
    チオ硫酸ナトリウム   chio-ryūsan-natoriumu   sodium thiosulphate

ヨードメトリー	yōdo-metorii	iodometry

還元滴定　(3RJ 274)

標^{ひょう}準^{じゅん}溶液として還元剤を滴定。第一鉄塩滴定，亜ヒ酸滴定などがある。ヨー素滴定のうち，チオ硫酸ナトリウムを使うヨードメトリーもこれに属する。

C.	基準	kijun	standard, basis
	種小名	shushō-mei	specific epithet, trivial name
	採用する	saiyō suru	to adopt, accept
	形式	keishiki	form
	終りに	owari ni	at the end
	新組み合わせ	shin-kumi-awase	new combination
	添える	soeru	to attach, append
	付記する	fuki suru	to add, append
	慣例	kanrei	usual practice

二　名　法　(SJ 759)

生物学で生物の群の基準を種とし，この種をラテン語^ごで属名と種小名との2語^ごの組み合わせとして表現する方法。動物・植物ともに現行命名規約が採用^{さい}している学名の形式である。終^{おわ}りに命名者の名をつけることもあるが，なくてもよい。動物分類学では新組み合わせの際にも最初の命名者の名を添^そえるが，植物分類学では逆に新組み合わせ者の名を付記^きする慣^{かん}例がある。

D.	藻類	sōrui	algae
	栄養器管	eiyō-kikan	vegetative organ
	茎	kuki	stem

植物の器管　(S 29)

植物のうちでも下等なものは藻類^{そう}などのように，からだ全体が葉状で，いろいろの器管のはっきりした区^く別がない。しかし，高等植物では器管の分化が進み，栄養^{えい}器管としての根・茎・葉，生殖器管としての花がある。

FINAL TRANSLATION TEST
光　合　成　(3RJ 1073)

植物は土中に根を張って，茎^{くき}，葉，花などをささえると同時に，土中の水分とこれに溶存している養分とを吸い上げる。根の先端の近くにある一群の根毛によって吸収された水液が高い所まで上がって行くための原動力となるのは，主として太陽の熱エネルギーであ

る。すなわち，水分は太陽熱のため水蒸気となって，葉面にある気孔から蒸散する。また，葉の縁を見ると気孔に似た裂け目が不規則に並んでいるが，これは葉脈の先端で水孔と呼ばれ，そこからも水液が押し出される。これらが根の吸水力発生の原因となるのである。このように植物では養分の希薄溶液を吸い上げる作用があるが，水を押し出す力，すなわち，根圧もあることは，ヘチマの茎を切ると，切り口から水液が多量に出て来ることからもわかる。

　植物体の細胞を構成する物質の主なものは有機物質であり，母細胞が分裂してその数を増し成長を続けるためには，有機物質が必要である。植物は動物のように動きまわって食物をとることが出来ないが，どうして必要な有機物質を取り入れるのであろうか。緑色植物やある種の細菌は，光のエネルギーにより，主として空気中から得た炭酸を同化して有機物を合成する能力があるのである。この光合成は独立栄養の一形式であって，炭酸の還元に伴ない，高等植物やクロレラのように酸素分子を発生するもの，紅色細菌のように硫化水素その他の物質の酸化を行なうものがある。多くの場合デンプンが主要生成物で，前者の場合は $CO_2 + H_2O \longrightarrow (CH_2O) + O_2$ によって行なわれ，生成したデンプンは主として種子，根，地下茎にたくわえられるが，茎では髄などにたくわえられる。地表上の物質変化過程としては水の蒸発についで大きく，光合成による炭酸固定は1年間 2×10^{10}t であって，地球上に分布する有機物の大部分，また大気中の酸素分子は光合成により生じたものである。光合成の機構は複雑でまだ完全には明らかでないが，最も新しい考え方は次の通りである。

1)　光エネルギーの化学エネルギーへの転化，光リン酸化。

2)　光によるニコチンアミドアデニンジヌクレオチドリン酸（NADP）の還元

3)　それに伴なう O_2 の発生

4)　1)によって生じたアデノシン三リン酸（ATP）と2)によって生じた還元型 NADP を用いて炭酸を有機物に変化させる反応。

この内，1),2),3)の段階では光を必要とするので明反応と呼び，4)を暗反応という。クロロフィル（葉緑素）およびカロチノイドに吸収された光は増感作用によって1個のクロロフィル分子の励起に用いられ，それから放出された電子はフェレドキシンに与えられ，ついには NADP を還元する。電子を失ったクロロフィル分子は，第2のクロロフィル系の供給する電子により，キノンやチトクロムの媒介によって還元されて，元の状態にもどる。第2のクロロフィル系は第1よりも短波長の光線で作用して水の光分解にあずかり，水酸イオンから電子をうばうのであって，その結果酸素ガスが発生する。この過程の電子伝達によってNADPの還元とともに酸化的リン酸化が起こって，ADP と無機リン酸から ATP が生ずる。これを光リン酸化というが，第1のクロロフィル系の照射によって生じ

たフェレドキシンの還元型からチトクロム系に電子がわたされてリン酸化が起こることもある。光合成細菌の場合は第2のクロロフィル系がはたらいているという事実はみとめられず，外からの物質（たとえば硫化水素）からキノン，チトクロムを通じてクロロフィルへ電子伝達が行なわれると考えられている。炭酸の固定は，最初グリセリン酸—3—リン酸のカルボキシル基炭素に行なわれることが明らかにされ，Calvin らによって糖生成の回路が明らかにされた。その過程で ATP と還元型 NADP が用いられるのである。

APPENDIX A
KANJI FREQUENCY LISTS

In order to have a basis for selecting the *kanji* to be emphasized in this reader, frequency studies were made for physics, chemistry, and biology. For each field a list of the 400 most important characters was prepared. There was of course considerable overlap among the lists, 627 different *kanji* being included in the three lists. The texts used for the frequency counts are as follows:

Subject	Textbook Used for Frequency Study	Study Made by
Physics	*Butsuri-B*, S. Kaya (ed); Kōgakusha	R.B. Bird
Chemistry	*Kagaku-B*, by U. Subata, S. Tsuda, and O. Shimaura; Dai-Nihon-Tosho	N. Inoue and students
Biology	*Seibutsu*, by T. Miwa and H. Oka; Sanseidō	N. Inoue and students

High level high-school textbooks wese chosen for the frequency studies, because it was felt that the *kanji* encountered there would represent a wide spectrum of subjects and that they would emphasize the rudimentary vocabulary which a foreign student would have to begin with.

Below we tabulate the top 524 characters resulting from combining the above-described frequency lists. This list includes all characters which appeared in the top 300 of any one list as well as those which appeared in the top 400 of two or more lists. This tabulation then gives an approximate ranking of the *kanji* in decreasing order of importance as well as separate rankings for physics, chemistry, and biology. In addition we show the lesson in which each *kanji* is introduced. In the right-hand column an asterisk(*) indicates those characters which are *kyōiku-kanji* (the 881 characters required in elementary school), and a small circle (o) indicates those which are not included in the *tōyō-kanji* (the 1850 basic characters).

This textbook emphasizes through the 20 *kanji* introduced in each lesson 500 characters, of which

490 appear on the list of 524 below

  5 were on the list below 524

  5 were not on any list

376 are *kyōiku kanji*

123 are *tōyō kanji* but not *kyōiku kanji*

  1 is not *tōyō kanji*

The beginning student can feel confident that the reading selections in this book *do* emphasize the most important characters for technical reading. Mastery of our recommended 500 *kanji* will enable him to read technical Japanese with considerable facility.

No.	Kanji	Phys	Chem	Biol	Lesson		No.	Kanji	Phys	Chem	Biol	Lesson	
1	体	3	13	4	1	*	35	表	61	69	72	1	*
2	子	5	6	11	7	*	36	部	72	122	21	8	*
3	物	11	11	1	1	*	37	的	115	68	35	5	*
4	分	19	10	3	7	*	38	電	1	20	201	14	*
5	水	17	2	20	6	*	39	結	144	25	63	2	*
6	質	31	12	7	2	*	40	色	183	34	19	13	*
7	中	24	17	18	9	*	41	温	40	57	140	7	*
8	化	48	3	9	3	*	42	入	73	65	107	8	*
9	合	36	8	17	5	*	43	動	8	232	5	1	*
10	原	37	19	31	4	*	44	点	33	67	152	4	*
11	性	51	15	25	7	*	45	学	157	28	68	4	*
12	一	23	42	30	1	*	46	験	53	21	183	2	*
13	管	47	23	29	9	*	47	二	52	37	171	3	*
14	変	25	43	48	3	*	48	重	34	50	182	4	*
15	液	90	7	23	9	*	49	圧	14	80	174	6	*
16	気	10	16	97	6	*	50	場	68	141	67	6	*
17	量	29	22	74	2	*	51	酸	264	1	12	15	*
18	用	27	39	62	3	*	52	作	75	36	173	3	*
19	素	108	4	16	7	*	53	光	12	249	36	13	*
20	度	7	26	101	1	*	54	力	2	108	188	2	*
21	上	26	61	50	3	*	55	種	189	86	24	10	*
22	図	6	78	60	5	*	56	応	212	33	56	10	*
23	成	107	29	13	7	*	57	高	63	102	137	9	*
24	反	65	40	45	2	*	58	器	71	177	55	11	*
25	数	43	49	61	2	*	59	小	59	157	89	2	*
26	大	22	94	39	2	*	60	下	84	114	110	4	*
27	出	45	77	33	10	*	61	考	89	95	124	8	*
28	生	109	46	2	4	*	62	熱	44	30	239	10	*
29	実	39	79	44	2	*	63	加	54	18	241	2	*
30	発	100	45	22	12	*	64	形	76	223	14	6	*
31	定	32	51	85	1	*	65	多	176	116	28	12	*
32	同	46	60	75	1	*	66	示	82	58	195	4	*
33	間	28	125	40	1	*	67	面	35	204	98	8	*
34	方	16	93	87	6	*	68	要	194	73	80	5	*

No.	Kanji	Phys	Chem	Biol	Lesson		No.	Kanji	Phys	Chem	Biol	Lesson	
69	解	192	41	121	15	*	103	明	162	97	221	7	*
70	行	106	212	38	5	*	104	向	20	195	267	1	*
71	状	171	123	66	7	*	105	有	252	98	134	7	*
72	個	193	115	54	8	*	106	平	62	169	255	6	*
73	強	83	106	181	13	*	107	時	87	298	108	1	*
74	石	58	64	251	5	*	108	調	135	209	150	8	*
75	機	126	121	126	12	*	109	起	67	119	313	6	*
76	通	94	139	141	13	*	110	他	185	154	162	12	*
77	関	88	190	96	2	*	111	組	277	184	42	5	*
78	見	104	200	71	13	*	112	正	113	181	212	6	*
79	単	86	167	127	2	*	113	基	302	47	159	14	*
80	内	91	264	27	8	*	114	離	102	224	189	1	
81	対	69	229	86	3	*	115	違	181	162	176	4	
82	長	49	297	57	5	*	116	目	177	124	220	10	*
83	法	105	66	237	3	*	117	交	117	346	59	15	*
84	係	101	203	105	2	*	118	必	263	148	144	10	*
85	炭	316	14	79	16	*	119	全	204	170	155	7	*
86	外	130	218	69	11	*	120	自	199	163	185	4	*
87	期	191	138	95	5	*	121	吸	331	171	46	17	
88	置	55	83	301	4	*	122	球	110	322	116	4	*
89	類	319	111	10	16	*	123	後	122	217	215	3	*
90	流	4	193	254	9	*	124	本	282	131	143	14	*
91	構	272	91	91	8	*	125	核	154	339	70	16	
92	少	178	120	157	4	*	126	例	111	166	292	1	*
93	比	57	90	309	1	*	127	金	81	38	...	14	*
94	造	289	74	94	17	*	128	属	127	48	398	14	*
95	位	30	235	194	2	*	129	速	13	354	207	1	*
96	等	78	178	208	1	*	130	回	42	342	193	5	*
97	現	131	234	100	10	*	131	塩	...	9	120	16	*
98	式	79	35	353	3	*	132	粒	146	165	275	16	
99	地	139	236	93	4	*	133	理	160	149	278	7	*
100	前	179	176	113	3	*	134	溶	...	5	139	15	
101	次	56	27	395	2	*	135	使	132	132	334	11	*
102	態	187	179	112	7	*	136	直	38	289	271	1	*

No.	Kanji	Phys	Chem	Biol	Lesson		No.	Kanji	Phys	Chem	Biol	Lesson	
137	空	74	75	...	6	*	171	界	60	...	175	8	*
138	研	268	135	197	9	*	172	各	234	219	233	6	*
139	蒸	165	82	354	12		173	異	286	320	81	12	*
140	立	155	172	279	7	*	174	不	318	137	236	17	*
141	赤	266	152	187	13	*	175	脂	...	72	169	19	
142	無	383	85	138	21	*	176	別	309	192	191	22	*
143	過	255	118	235	6	*	177	特	257	258	178	7	*
144	極	50	109	...	8	*	178	料	359	71	264	19	*
145	受	215	326	73	10	*	179	注	...	186	58	18	*
146	糖	...	84	82	18		180	間	141	107	...	14	*
147	運	41	...	129	1	*	181	鉄	196	54	...	12	*
148	究	267	134	222	9	*	182	放	119	239	344	12	*
149	元	231	32	364	16	*	183	題	114	143	...	14	*
150	含	...	70	106	16		184	計	70	189	...	7	*
151	最	156	291	179	6	*	185	銅	218	44	...	15	
152	射	80	357	196	13		186	増	137	348	228	5	*
153	線	9	174	...	1	*	187	利	197	226	291	11	*
154	当	147	142	347	11	*	188	抗	64	...	200	9	
155	常	175	293	168	7	*	189	細	259	...	6	9	*
156	果	217	253	167	2	*	190	振	21	246	...	5	
157	則	116	145	382	3	*	191	移	260	294	164	10	*
158	積	118	202	324	3	*	192	消	299	308	115	17	*
159	第	...	59	135	22	*	193	伝	240	...	32	10	*
160	進	123	370	155	6	*	194	接	190	331	202	10	*
161	相	151	366	132	6	*	195	配	358	247	119	19	*
162	両	145	309	199	12	*	196	周	136	140	...	5	*
163	般	219	238	211	10		197	銀	203	76	...	11	*
164	集	346	136	186	16	*	198	事	99	185	...	11	*
165	板	96	230	347	10	*	199	人	230	364	147	17	*
166	鉛	163	63	...	15		200	知	253	228	263	9	*
167	近	159	313	205	8	*	201	象	198	307	238	10	*
168	観	227	53	...	2	*	202	陽	186	112	...	15	*
169	心	138	395	153	13	*	203	白	...	103	198	19	*
170	以	244	216	225	11	*	204	黄	...	158	145	20	*

No.	Kanji	Phys	Chem	Biol	Lesson		No.	Kanji	Phys	Chem	Biol	Lesson	
205	互	303	207	245	14		239	系	390	379	88	17	*
206	倍	174	265	323	16	*	240	酢	···	100	312	22	
207	在	341	245	177	16	*	241	棒	143	270	···	12	
208	活	···	266	51	22	*	242	紙	310	105	···	19	*
209	約	290	104	377	14	*	243	粉	388	191	287	21	*
210	説	363	127	281	23	*	244	突	164	···	253	3	
211	存	247	267	258	3	*	245	列	173	310	389	14	*
212	何	221	101	···	15	*	246	池	168	256	···	15	*
213	試	···	31	293	18	*	247	所	134	396	346	6	*
214	収	327	316	131	17	*	248	沸	328	99	···	18	
215	和	232	96	···	3	*	249	型	326	···	103	17	*
216	晶	242	89	···	12		250	食	···	327	104	20	*
217	側	180	···	154	9	*	251	膜	···	384	47	18	
218	固	205	130	···	8	*	252	半	172	391	320	5	*
219	濃	···	55	282	21		253	裂	344	···	90	23	
220	察	262	126	399	9	*	254	三	182	254	···	9	*
221	植	···	330	15	21	*	255	続	237	206	···	15	*
222	測	66	287	···	2	*	256	環	···	321	125	19	
223	油	300	56	···	11	*	257	値	128	319	···	4	
224	得	223	211	381	2	*	258	角	23	353	···	5	*
225	精	···	317	49	22	*	259	縮	313	345	243	12	
226	日	322	259	240	17	*	260	開	312	324	268	23	*
227	酵	···	288	83	21		261	窒	···	147	308	16	
228	割	353	222	247	17		262	然	380	260	265	16	*
229	者	395	244	184	17	*	263	胞	···	···	8	21	
230	端	150	···	224	11		264	静	170	···	290	14	*
231	達	306	356	166	24	*	265	年	314	349	251	17	*
232	代	381	371	84	22	*	266	磁	13	···	···	15	
233	口	···	227	161	25	*	267	波	15	···	···	6	*
234	求	120	268	···	17	*	268	号	315	153	···	16	*
235	陰	249	146	···	15		269	意	311	161	···	18	*
236	導	92	303	···	7	*	270	硫	···	24	···	15	
237	触	329	183	338	19		271	血	···	···	26	24	*
238	装	229	173	···	11		272	様	279	373	277	12	*

No.	Kanji	Phys	Chem	Biol	Lesson		No.	Kanji	Phys	Chem	Biol	Lesson	
273	乳	···	299	180	20		307	規	362	155	···	25	*
274	程	273	389	269	8	*	308	転	152	···	368	11	*
275	燃	364	117	···	19	*	309	微	295	···	226	10	
276	透	384	263	286	18		310	工	337	188	···	17	*
277	葉	···	···	34	23	*	311	緑	···	374	151	21	*
278	卵	···	···	37	23		312	殖	···	···	76	22	
279	低	285	388	266	7	*	313	由	317	210	···	4	*
280	肪	···	255	234	22		314	皮	···	···	77	21	*
281	遺	···	···	41	23	*	315	抵	77	···	···	9	
282	引	133	360	···	4	*	316	菌	···	···	78	21	
283	経	···	···	43	23	*	317	逆	271	314	396	12	*
284	左	323	363	261	13	*	318	決	283	378	321	11	*
285	率	103	393	···	10	*	319	硝	···	81	···	21	
286	神	···	···	52	23	*	320	飽	333	198	···	19	
287	節	379	···	123	24	*	321	融	334	199	···	18	
288	操	···	52	···	18		322	差	200	···	335	10	*
289	織	···	···	53	20	*	323	秒	85	···	···	4	*
290	媒	354	150	···	18		324	価	···	87	···	19	*
291	像	149	355	···	13	*	325	希	···	88	···	15	*
292	右	296	392	270	13	*	326	路	208	···	331	14	*
293	取	236	273	···	8	*	327	道	243	···	298	17	*
294	維	···	279	230	20		328	毛	···	···	92	18	*
295	曲	207	···	304	8	*	329	亜	···	92	···	15	
296	密	228	350	383	8		330	非	301	243	···	10	*
297	落	216	···	295	4	*	331	折	95	···	···	13	*
298	切	307	375	280	25	*	332	繊	···	284	262	20	
299	減	261	325	376	8	*	333	層	···	381	165	17	*
300	混	···	62	···	16	*	334	音	97	···	···	6	*
301	鏡	298	···	214	13	*	335	壁	274	···	274	8	
302	糸	226	···	288	5	*	336	針	98	···	···	15	
303	官	···	···	64	23	*	337	照	···	···	99	23	*
304	参	···	398	117	23	*	338	土	···	292	259	25	*
305	胚	···	···	65	23	°	339	根	···	···	102	25	*
306	激	386	···	130	21		340	新	···	323	229	25	*

No.	Kanji	Phys	Chem	Biol	Lesson		No.	Kanji	Phys	Chem	Biol	Lesson	
341	着	…	250	307	22	*	375	腸	…	…	146	24	*
342	筋	…	…	109	24		376	覚	…	…	148	24	*
343	沈	…	110	…	18		377	浸	…	213	387	18	
344	呼	…	…	111	21		378	腺	…	…	149	…	ο
345	仕	112	…	…	11	*	379	記	…	151	…	16	*
346	弱	361	201	…	18	*	380	屈	153	…	…	13	
347	製	…	113	…	19	*	381	品	…	215	390	20	*
348	虫	…	…	114	20	*	382	限	245	…	360	7	*
349	適	360	372	285	22	*	383	較	…	274	332	20	
350	養	…	…	118	25	*	384	灰	…	156	…	21	
351	張	121	…	…	12	*	385	帯	284	332	…	14	*
352	感	…	…	122	24	*	386	脳	…	…	157	24	
353	述	391	182	…	16	*	387	軸	158	…	…	4	
354	真	124	…	…	14	*	388	習	…	159	…	…	*
355	算	278	296	…	14	*	389	剤	…	160	…	21	
356	円	125	…	…	5	*	390	衝	161	…	…	3	
357	断	248	…	328	9	*	391	室	…	164	…	20	*
358	刺	…	…	128	21		392	残	375	240	…	21	*
359	留	…	128	…	19	*	393	主	…	334	283	25	*
360	黒	…	192	388	20	*	394	摩	166	…	…	9	
361	距	129	…	…	1		395	偶	385	…	232	23	
362	還	…	129	…	25		396	擦	167	…	…	9	
363	失	396	278	357	22	*	397	乾	370	248	…	20	
364	垂	225	…	356	10		398	樹	…	168	…	19	
365	族	…	133	…	19	*	399	止	169	…	…	11	*
366	臓	…	…	133	24		400	嚢	…	…	170	…	ο
367	脊	…	…	136	…	ο	401	境	…	…	172	24	*
368	確	288	300	…	9	*	402	盛	258	365	…	11	
369	容	140	…	…	8	*	403	保	241	383	…	3	*
370	骨	…	…	142	24		404	炎	…	175	…	22	
371	絶	142	…	…	5	*	405	薬	…	180	…	20	*
372	似	…	280	314	17	*	406	換	…	261	372	22	
373	荷	143	…	…	14	*	407	負	184	…	…	14	*
374	滴	…	144	…	19		408	木	336	…	300	…	*

No.	Kanji	Phys	Chem	Biol	Lesson		No.	Kanji	Phys	Chem	Biol	Lesson	
409	伸	188	...	...	12		443	布	382	...	284	25	*
410	髄	...	...	190	25		444	名	...	276	391	21	*
411	天	357	285	...	16	*	445	脈	...	...	216	25	*
412	先	...	347	296	25	*	446	門	...	...	217	...	*
413	芽	...	...	192	21	*	447	海	...	...	218	22	*
414	析	...	194	...	16		448	再	...	...	219	23	*
415	与	195	...	...	5		449	香	...	220	...	19	
416	業	...	196	...	20	*	450	焦	220	...	...	13	
417	洗	...	197	...	20		451	硬	...	221	...	22	
418	初	201	...	...	4	*	452	遠	222	...	...	13	*
419	花	393	...	159	25	*	453	雄	...	...	223	23	
420	際	256	...	397	8	*	454	及	224	...	...	3	
421	膨	202	...	...	12		455	紫	294	380	...	13	
422	雌	...	...	203	23		456	復	...	225	...	...	*
423	幼	...	...	204	23		457	共	374	302	...	...	*
424	連	340	...	315	...	*	458	味	...	277	400	22	*
425	冷	...	205	...	...	*	459	椎	...	...	227	...	°
426	泌	...	...	206	24		460	臭	...	231	...	21	
427	巻	287	...	370	11	*	461	頭	...	...	231	24	*
428	送	324	397	386	24	*	462	書	...	233	...	16	*
429	散	292	...	365	11	*	463	燈	233	...	...	15	*
430	源	206	...	...	12		464	弾	235	...	...	10	
431	団	...	318	340	...	*	465	芳	...	237	...	19	
432	青	...	208	...	20	*	466	弦	238	...	...	6	
433	径	209	...	...	5		467	写	239	...	...	13	*
434	藻	...	...	209	...	°	468	完	389	301	...	...	*
435	排	...	...	210	24		469	焼	...	...	241	18	*
436	誘	210	...	...	14		470	末	...	312	380	...	*
437	柱	211	...	...	...	*	471	炉	...	242	...	19	
438	顕	335	...	327	23		472	腎	...	...	242	...	°
439	育	...	...	213	23	*	473	母	...	...	244	25	*
440	検	213	...	...	17	*	474	効	246	...	...	12	*
441	幅	214	...	...	6		475	複	...	...	246	24	*
442	衡	...	214	...	21		476	影	345	...	352	...	

No.	Kanji	Phys	Chem	Biol	Lesson		No.	Kanji	Phys	Chem	Biol	Lesson	
477	能	...	...	248	25	*	511	昇	351	386	...	...	
478	産	...	...	249	...	*	512	準	397	340	...	...	*
479	雑	...	...	250	24	*	513	階	...	...	289	25	*
480	縁	250	...	...	14		514	印	387	352	...	...	*
481	飛	251	...	...	11	*	515	純	290	...	...	18	*
482	項	...	251	...	...		516	星	291	...	...	17	*
483	染	...	252	...	20		517	干	293	...	...	13	
484	返	367	336	...	...	*	518	林	...	...	294	...	*
485	太	254	...	...	9	*	519	暗	378	...	366	15	*
486	尿	...	...	256	24		520	科	...	295	...	...	*
487	肉	...	...	257	24	*	521	命	...	...	297	17	*
488	除	...	328	379	...	*	522	急	297	...	...	12	*
489	殿	...	257	...	18		523	区	...	...	299	...	*
490	走	...	...	260	24	*	524	占	...	...	376	376	
491	指	...	262	...	19	*				....			
492	群	...	...	262	25	*	531	渉	305	...	...	13	
493	偏	265	...	...	15		532	鉱	...	305	...	22	*
494	投	269	...	...	...	*	537	毒	...	311	...	22	*
495	凝	...	269	...	18		580	論	...	351	...	20	*
496	短	270	...	...	3	*	585	材	...	...	359	20	*
497	因	...	...	272	23	*				....			
498	軽	...	271	...	18	*	...	想	...	...	...	7	*
499	安	...	272	...	22	*	...	粘	...	...	...	9	
500	腔	...	...	273	...	○	...	械	...	...	...	20	*
501	手	275	...	358	15	*	...	厚	...	...	...	25	*
502	付	...	275	...	19	*	...	薄	...	...	...	25	
503	車	276	...	...	11	*							
504	標	369	359	...	...	*							
505	並	280	...	...	14								
506	山	281	...	...	...	*							
507	煮	...	281	...	22								
508	火	...	282	...	18	*							
509	充	283	...	...	...								
510	番	...	286	...	16	*							

APPENDIX B
THE 500 KANJI TABULATED ACCORDING TO "ON" READING

(with lesson number)

ア

ア	亜	15
アツ	圧	6
アン	安	22
	暗	15

イ

イ	以	11
	位	2
	異	12
	移	10
	意	18
	違	4
	維	20
	遺	23
イク	育	23
イチ	一	1
イン	引	4
	因	23
	陰	15

ウ

ウ	右	13
ウン	運	1

エ

エキ	液	9
エン	円	5
	炎	22
	塩	16
	鉛	15
	遠	13
	縁	14

オ

オウ	応	10
オン	音	6
	温	7

カ

カ	下	4
	火	18
	化	3
	加	2
	何	15
	花	25
	果	2
	価	19
	荷	14
	過	6
ガ	芽	21
カイ	回	5
	灰	21
	界	8
	海	22
	械	20
	開	23
	階	25
	解	15
ガイ	外	11
カク	各	6
	角	5
	核	16
	覚	24
	較	20
	確	9
ガク	学	4
カツ	活	22
	割	17
カン	干	13
	官	23
	巻	11
	乾	20
	間	1
	換	22
	感	24
	関	2
	管	9
	還	25
	環	19
	観	2
ガン	含	16

キ

キ	気	6
	希	15
	記	16
	起	6
	基	14
	規	25
	期	5
	器	11
	機	12
ギャク	逆	12
キュウ	及	3
	吸	17
	求	17
	究	9
	急	12
	球	4
キョ	距	1
キョウ	強	13
	境	24
	鏡	13
ギョウ	業	20
	凝	18
キョク	曲	8
	極	8
キン	近	8
	金	14
	菌	21
	筋	24
ギン	銀	11

ク

クウ	空	6
グウ	偶	23
クツ	屈	13
グン	群	25

ケ

ケイ	形	6
	系	17
	径	5
	係	2
	型	17
	計	7
	経	23
	軽	18
ゲキ	激	21
ケツ	血	24
	決	11
	結	2
ケン	見	13
	研	9
	検	17
	顕	23
	験	2
ゲン	元	16
	弦	6
	限	7
	原	4
	現	10
	減	8
	源	12

コ

コ	固	8
	呼	21
	個	8
ゴ	互	14
コウ	口	25
	工	20
	向	1
	交	15
	行	5
	考	8
	光	13

Reading	Kanji	No.
タ		
タ	他	12
	多	12
タイ	太	9
	体	1
	対	3
	帯	14
	態	7
ダイ	大	2
	代	22
	第	22
	題	14
タツ	達	24
タン	単	2
	炭	16
	短	3
	端	11
ダン	断	9
	弾	10
チ		
チ	地	4
	池	15
	知	9
	値	4
	置	4
チツ	窒	16
チャク	着	22
チュウ	中	9
	虫	20
	注	18
チョウ	長	5
	張	12
	腸	24
	調	8
チョク	直	1
チン	沈	18
ツ		
ヅ	図	5
ツウ	通	13
テ		
テイ	低	7
	抵	9
	定	1
	程	8
テキ	的	5
	滴	19
	適	22
テツ	鉄	12
テン	天	16
	点	4
	転	11
デン	伝	10
	電	14
	殿	18
ト		
ド	土	25
	度	1
トウ	当	11
	透	18
	等	1
	燈	15
	糖	18
ドウ	同	1
	動	1
	道	17
	銅	15
	導	7
トク	特	7
	得	2
ドク	毒	22
トツ	突	3
ナ		
ナイ	内	8
ニ		
ニ	二	3
ニク	肉	24
ニチ	日	17
ニュウ	入	8
	乳	20
ニョウ	尿	24
ニン	人	17
ネ		
ネツ	熱	10
ネン	年	17
	粘	9
	燃	19
ノ		
ノウ	能	25
	脳	24
	濃	21
ハ		
ハ	波	6
ハイ	胚	23
	配	19
	排	24
バイ	倍	16
	媒	18
ハク	白	19
	薄	25
ハツ	発	12
ハン	反	2
	半	5
	板	10
	般	10
バン	番	16
ヒ		
ヒ	比	1
	皮	21
	非	10
	飛	11
ビ	微	10
ヒツ	必	10
	泌	24
ヒョウ	表	1
ビョウ	秒	4
ヒン	品	20
フ		
フ	不	17
	布	25
	付	19
	負	14
ブ	部	8
フク	幅	6
	複	24
フツ	沸	18
ブツ	物	1
フン	分	7
	粉	21
ヘ		
ヘイ	平	6
	並	14
ヘキ	壁	8
ベツ	別	22
ヘン	変	3
	偏	15
ホ		
ホ	保	3
ボ	母	25
ホウ	方	6
	芳	19
	放	12
	法	3
	胞	21
	飽	19
ボウ	肪	22
	棒	12
	膨	12
ホン	本	14
マ		
マ	摩	9
マク	膜	18
ミ		
ミ	味	22
ミツ	密	8
ミャク	脈	25
ム		
ム	無	21
メ		
メイ	名	21
	命	17
	明	7
メン	面	8
モ		
モウ	毛	18
モク	目	10

APPENDIX C
THE 500 KANJI TABULATED ACCORDING TO STROKE COUNT

(with ON readings and lesson number)

1

一 ICHI ITSU 1

2

力 RIKI RYOKU 2
二 NI 3
入 NYŪ 8
人 JIN 17

3

大 TAI, DAI 2
小 SHŌ 2
上 JŌ 3
及 KYŪ 3
下 KA, GE 4
与 YO 5
子 SHI, SU 7
三 SAN 9
干 KAN 13
工 KŌ, KU 17
口 KŌ 25
土 DO, TO 25

4

比 HI 1
反 HAN 2
化 KA 3
引 IN 4
少 SHŌ 4
円 EN 5
方 HŌ 6
水 SUI 6
分 FUN, BUN 7
内 NAI 8
中 CHŪ 9
太 TAI 9
止 SHI 11
心 SHIN 13
互 GO 14

手 SHU 15
元 GEN, GAN 16
天 TEN 16
日 NICHI JITSU 17
収 SHŪ 17
不 FU 17
火 KA 18
毛 MŌ 18
切 SETSU 25

5

加 KA 2
用 YŌ 3
示 SHI, JI 4
生 SEI, SHŌ 4
由 YŪ, YU 4
半 HAN 5
石 SEKI SHAKU 5
圧 ATSU 6
平 HEI 6
正 SEI 6
立 RITSU 7
出 SHUTSU 10
目 MOKU 10
必 HITSU 10
仕 SHI 11
外 GAI 11
以 I 11
他 TA 12
右 U, YŪ 13
左 SA 13
写 SHA 13
本 HON 14
号 GŌ 16
白 HAKU 19
付 FU 19
皮 HI 21
代 DAI 22
失 SHITSU 22
幼 YŌ 23

主 SHU 25
母 BO 25
布 FU 25

6

向 KŌ 1
同 DŌ 1
次 JI 2
式 SHIKI 3
存 ZON, SON 3
地 CHI, JI 4
自 SHI, JI 4
糸 SHI 5
合 GŌ 5
回 KAI 5
行 KŌ, GYŌ 5
気 KI 6
各 KAKU 6
成 SEI 7
全 ZEN 7
有 YŪ 7
考 KŌ 8
曲 KYOKU 8
伝 DEN 10
当 TŌ 11
両 RYŌ 12
多 TA 12
光 KŌ 13
色 SHOKU SHIKI 13
列 RETSU 14
池 CHI 15
交 KŌ 15
在 ZAI 16
年 NEN 17
吸 KYŪ 17
虫 CHŪ 20
灰 KAI 21
名 MEI 21
安 AN 22
再 SAI 23

因 IN 23
血 KETSU 24
肉 NIKU 24
先 SEN 25

7

体 TAI 1
位 I 2
対 TAI, TSUI 3
作 SA, SAKU 3
初 SHO 4
角 KAKU 5
図 ZU, TO 5
形 KEI 6
状 JŌ 7
低 TEI 7
近 KIN 8
抗 KŌ 9
究 KYŪ 9
応 Ō 10
利 RI 11
車 SHA 11
決 KETSU 11
伸 SHIN 12
折 SETSU 13
見 KEN 13
赤 SEKI 13
何 KA 15
希 KI 15
亜 A 15
含 GAN 16
求 KYŪ 17
系 KEI 17
似 JI 17
沈 CHIN 18
芳 HŌ 19
材 ZAI 20
芽 GA 21
別 BETSU 22
卵 RAN 23

尿	NYŌ	24	沸	FUTSU	18	型	KEI	17	浸	SHIN	18
走	SŌ	24	注	CHŪ	18	香	KŌ	19	純	JUN	18
花	KA	25	価	KA	19	指	SHI	19	脂	SHI	19

8

物	BUTSU MOTSU	1	炉	RO	19	食	SHOKU	20	留	RYŪ	19
定	TEI	1	青	SHŌ, SEI	20	室	SHITSU	20	紙	SHI	19
直	CHOKU	1	乳	NYŪ	20	洗	SEN	20	配	HAI	19
表	HYŌ	1	呼	KO	21	品	HIN	20	料	RYŌ	19
例	REI	1	刺	SHI	21	染	SEN	20	残	ZAN	21
実	JITSU	2	肪	BŌ	22	臭	SHŪ	21	剤	ZAI	21
果	KA	2	味	MI	22	胞	HŌ	21	粉	FUN	21
法	HŌ	3	毒	DOKU	22	活	KATSU	22	骨	KOTSU	24
突	TOTSU	3	炎	EN	22	海	KAI	22	根	KON	25
和	WA	3	参	SAN	23	神	SHIN	23	脈	MYAKU	25
学	GAKU	4	官	KAN	23	胚	HAI	23	能	NŌ	25
長	CHŌ	5	育	IKU	23	送	SŌ	24			
的	TEKI	5	泌	HITSU	24	厚	KŌ	25			

周	SHŪ	5		**9**			**10**			**11**	
径	KEI	5	度	DO	1	速	SOKU	1	動	DŌ	1
波	HA	6	単	TAN	2	時	JI	1	得	TOKU	2
空	KŪ	6	係	KEI	2	原	GEN	4	球	KYŪ	4
所	SHO	6	変	HEN	3	値	CHI	4	組	SO	5
弦	GEN	6	則	SOKU	3	振	SHIN	5	進	SHIN	6
性	SEI, SHŌ	7	後	GO, KŌ	3	起	KI	6	理	RI	7
明	MEI	7	前	ZEN	3	素	SO, SU	7	常	JŌ	7
固	KO	8	保	HO	3	特	TOKU	7	部	BU	8
取	SHU	8	点	TEN	4	容	YŌ	8	密	MITSU	8
知	CHI	9	重	JŪ	4	個	KO	8	液	EKI	9
抵	TEI	9	秒	BYŌ	4	高	KŌ	9	側	SOKU	9
垂	SUI	10	要	YŌ	5	流	RYŪ	9	断	DAN	9
受	JU	10	音	ON	6	差	SA	10	細	SAI	9
板	HAN	10	相	SŌ	6	般	HAN	10	粘	NEN	9
非	HI	10	計	KEI	7	射	SHA	13	率	RITSU	10
事	JI	11	限	GEN	7	通	TSŪ	13	現	GEN	10
使	SHI	11	面	MEN	8	真	SHIN	14	接	SETSU	10
油	YU	11	界	KAI	8	荷	KA	14	移	I	10
放	HŌ	12	研	KEN	9	帯	TAI	14	転	TEN	11
効	KŌ	12	飛	HI	11	針	SHIN	15	盛	SEI	11
屈	KUTSU	13	巻	KAN	11	核	KAKU	16	張	CHŌ	12
金	KIN	14	発	HATSU	12	倍	BAI	16	異	I	12
並	HEI	14	急	KYŪ	12	記	KI	16	強	KYŌ	13
述	JUTSU	16	逆	GYAKU	12	書	SHO	16	渉	SHŌ	13
析	SEKI	16	負	FU	14	造	ZŌ	17	問	MON	14
者	SHA	17	約	YAKU	14	消	SHŌ	17	基	KI	14
命	MEI, MYŌ	17	炭	TAN	16	弱	JAKU	18	陰	IN	15
			星	SEI	17	透	TŌ	18	偏	HEN	15
									粒	RYŪ	16
									混	KON	16

窒	CHITSU	16	集	SHŪ	16	試	SHI	18	雑	ZATSU	24
族	ZOKU	19	然	ZEN, NEN	16	殿	DEN	18			
乾	KAN	20	番	BAN	16	触	SHOKU	19	**15**		
黄	Ō, KŌ	20	検	KEN	17	飽	HŌ	19	線	SEN	1
黒	KOKU	20	道	DŌ	17	業	GYŌ	20	質	SHITSU	2
械	KAI	20	割	KATSU	17	較	KAKU	20	衝	SHŌ	3
菌	KIN	21	媒	BAI	18	鉱	KŌ	22	導	DŌ	7
第	DAI	22	焼	SHŌ	18	照	SHŌ	23	調	CHŌ	8
偶	GŪ	23	軽	KEI	18	雌	SHI	23	摩	MA	9
経	KEI	23	無	MU	21	感	KAN	24	確	KAKU	9
脳	NŌ	24	硝	SHŌ	21	節	SETSU	24	熱	NETSU	10
排	HAI	24	植	SHOKU	21	腸	CHŌ	24	器	KI	11
規	KI	25	硬	KŌ	22	新	SHIN	25	縁	EN	14
			着	CHAKU	22	群	GUN	25	論	RON	20
12			換	KAN	22				遺	I	23
間	KAN	1	殖	SHOKU	22	**14**			養	YŌ	25
運	UN	1	煮	SHA	22	関	KAN	2			
等	TŌ	1	酢	SAKU	22	増	ZŌ	5	**16**		
距	KYO	1	開	KAI	23	態	TAI	7	積	SEKI	3
量	RYŌ	2	裂	RETSU	23	際	SAI	8	壁	HEKI	8
測	SOKU	2	葉	YŌ	23	構	KŌ	8	機	KI	12
結	KETSU	2	雄	YŪ	23	管	KAN	9	膨	BŌ	12
短	TAN	3	達	TATSU	24	察	SATSU	9	燈	TŌ	15
軸	JIKU	4	筋	KIN	24	種	SHU	10	融	YŪ	18
落	RAKU	4	覚	KAKU	24	端	TAN	11	操	SŌ	18
絶	ZETSU	5	階	KAI	25	銀	GIN	11	糖	TŌ	18
期	KI	5				様	YŌ	12	凝	GYŌ	18
場	JŌ	6	**13**			像	ZŌ	13	燃	NEN	19
最	SAI	6	数	SŪ	2	静	SEI, JŌ	14	樹	JU	19
幅	FUKU	6	置	CHI	4	誘	YŪ	14	薬	YAKU	20
過	KA	6	違	I	4	算	SAN	14	激	GEKI	21
温	ON	7	想	SŌ	7	酸	SAN	15	衡	KŌ	21
極	KYOKU	8	微	BI	10	銅	DŌ	15	濃	NŌ	21
減	GEN	8	蒸	JŌ	12	磁	JI	15	頭	TŌ ZU	24
程	TEI	8	鉄	TETSU	12	層	SŌ	17			
象	SHŌ	10	源	GEN	12	膜	MAKU	18	還	KAN	25
弾	DAN	10	遠	EN	13	製	SEI	19	薄	HAKU	25
装	SŌ	11	電	DEN	14	滴	TEKI	19			
散	SAN	11	路	RO	14	維	I	20	**17**		
棒	BŌ	12	鉛	EN	15	酵	KŌ	21	擦	SATSU	9
晶	SHŌ	12	解	KAI	15	緑	RYOKU	21	縮	SHUKU	12
焦	SHŌ	13	続	ZOKU	15	適	TEKI	22	環	KAN	19
紫	SHI	13	暗	AN	15	精	SEI	22	繊	SEN	20
属	ZOKU	14	溶	YŌ	15	説	SETSU	23			
陽	YŌ	15	塩	EN	16	境	KYŌ	24	**18**		
硫	RYŪ	15	意	I	18	複	FUKU	24	離	RI	1
									験	KEN	2

観	KAN	2	織	SHIKI SHOKU	20			臓	ZŌ	24
題	DAI	14	顕	KEN	23	**19**		髄	ZUI	25
類	RUI	16				鏡	KYŌ	13		

APPENDIX D
THE 500 KANJI TABULATED ACCORDING
TO NELSON'S RADICALS

(with ON readings and lesson number)

1 一
一 ICHI / ITSU 1
三 SAN 8
与 YO 5
下 KA, GE 4
互 GO 14
天 TEN 16
不 FU 17
平 HEI 6
正 SEI 6
両 RYŌ 12
再 SAI 23
亜 A 15

1 丨
中 CHŪ 9
内 NAI 8
由 YŪ, YU 4
本 HON 14
出 SHUTSU 10
向 KŌ 1
曲 KYOKU 8
果 KA 2
表 HYŌ 1

1 丶
必 HITSU 10
半 HAN 5
求 KYŪ 17
単 TAN 2
業 GYŌ 20

1 ノ
及 KYŪ 3
少 SHŌ 4
失 SHITSU 22
年 NEN 17
系 KEI 17
卵 RAN 23

垂 SUI 10
重 JŪ 4
殿 DEN 18

1 乚
乳 NYŪ 20

1 亅
事 JI 11

2 二
二 NI 3
元 GEN, GAN 16

2 亠
主 SHU 25
交 KŌ 15
育 IKU 23
変 HEN 3
率 RITSU 10

2 人
人 JIN 17
以 I 11

2 亻
化 KA 3
他 TA 12
仕 SHI 11
付 FU 19
代 DAI 22
似 JI 17
伝 DEN 10
位 I 2
伸 SHIN 12
体 TAI 1
低 TEI 7
作 SA, SAKU 3
何 KA 15
価 KA 19

例 REI 1
使 SHI 11
係 KEI 2
保 HO 3
倍 BAI 16
値 CHI 4
個 KO 8
偶 GŪ 23
側 SOKU 9
偏 HEN 15
像 ZŌ 13

2 へ
合 GŌ 5
全 ZEN 7
含 GAN 16
命 MEI, MYŌ 17

2 儿
先 SEN 25

2 入
入 NYŪ 8

2 八
分 FUN, BUN 7

2 ⺌
並 HEI 14
前 ZEN 3

2 冂
円 EN 5
同 DŌ 1
周 SHŪ 5

2 冖
写 SHA 13

2 冫

次 JI 2
弱 JAKU 18
凝 GYŌ 18

2 刀
切 SETSU 25

2 刂
別 BETSU 22
刺 SHI 21
割 KATSU 17

2 力
力 RIKI / RYOKU 2
加 KA 2
効 KŌ 12
動 DŌ 1

2 十
直 CHOKU 1
真 SHIN 14
乾 KAN 20

2 卜
上 JŌ 3
点 TEN 4

2 厂
反 HAN 2
圧 ATSU 6
灰 KAI 21
厚 KŌ 25
原 GEN 4

2 ム
参 SAN 23
能 NŌ 25

2 又
収 SHŪ 17

3		口
口	KŌ	25
右	U, YŪ	13
号	GŌ	16
吸	KYŪ	17
味	MI	22
呼	KO	21
品	HIN	20
器	KI	11
3		囗
因	IN	23
回	KAI	5
図	ZU, TO	5
固	KO	8
3		土
土	DO, TO	25
在	ZAI	16
地	CHI, JI	4
型	KEI	17
基	KI	14
場	JŌ	6
塩	EN	16
境	KYŌ	24
増	ZŌ	5
壁	HEKI	8
3		夊
各	KAKU	6
3		夕
外	GAI	11
多	TA	12
名	MEI	21
3		大
大	TAI, DAI	2
太	TAI	9
3		女
安	AN	22
媒	BAI	18
3		子
子	SHI, SU	7
存	ZON, SON	3
学	GAKU	4
3		宀
官	KAN	23
定	TEI	1
実	JITSU	2
室	SHITSU	20
容	YŌ	8
密	MITSU	8
察	SATSU	9
3		寸
導	DŌ	7
3		小
小	SHŌ	2
3		⺌
光	KŌ	13
当	TŌ	11
常	JŌ	7
3		尸
尿	NYŌ	24
屈	KUTSU	13
属	ZOKU	14
層	SŌ	17
3		山
炭	TAN	16
3		工
工	KŌ, KU	17
左	SA	13
3		己
巻	KAN	11
3		巾
布	FU	25
希	KI	15
帯	TAI	14
幅	FUKU	6
3		干
干	KAN	13
3		幺
幼	YŌ	23
3		广
応	Ō	10
度	DO	1
3		弋
式	SHIKI	3
3		弓
引	IN	4
弦	GEN	6
張	CHŌ	12
強	KYŌ	13
弾	DAN	10
3		彡
形	KEI	6
3		彳
径	KEI	5
後	GO	3
得	TOKU	2
微	BI	10
衝	SHŌ	3
衡	KŌ	21
4		心
心	SHIN	13
急	KYŪ	12
想	SŌ	7
感	KAN	24
態	TAI	7
4		忄
性	SEI, SHŌ	7
4		戈
成	SEI	7
4		戸
所	SHO	6
4		手
手	SHU	15
4		扌
抗	KŌ	9
折	SETSU	13
抵	TEI	9
指	SHI	19
振	SHIN	5
排	HAI	24
接	SETSU	10
換	KAN	22
操	SŌ	18
擦	SATSU	9
4		攵
散	SAN	11
数	SŪ	2
4		文
対	TAI	3
4		斤
断	DAN	9
新	SHIN	25
4		方
方	HŌ	6
放	HŌ	12
族	ZOKU	19
4		日
日	NICHI	17
明	MEI	7
時	JI	1
暗	AN	15
4		曰
星	SEI	17
晶	SHŌ	12
量	RYŌ	2
最	SAI	6
題	DAI	14

4		木	沈	CHIN	18	**4**		牛	硬	KŌ	22

糸 SHI 5
約 YAKU 14
純 JUN 18
紙 SHI 19
素 SO, SU 7
組 SO 5
細 SAI 9
経 KEI 23
紫 SHI 13
絶 ZETSU 5
結 KETSU 2
続 ZOKU 15
維 I 20
緑 RYOKU 21
線 SEN 1
縁 EN 14
繊 SEN 20
縮 SHUKU 12
織 SHIKI 20

6   罒
置 CHI 4

6   羊
差 SA 10
着 CHAKU 22
群 GUN 25
養 YŌ 25

6   耂
考 KŌ 8
者 SHA 17

6   耳
取 SHU 8

6   聿
書 SHO 16

6   肉
肉 NIKU 24

6   月
有 YŪ 7
肪 BŌ 22
胚 HAI 23

胞 HŌ 21
脈 MYAKU 25
脂 SHI 19
脳 NŌ 24
期 KI 5
腸 CHŌ 24
膜 MAKU 18
膨 BŌ 12
臓 ZŌ 24

6   自
自 SHI, JI 4
臭 SHŪ 21

6   舟
般 HAN 10

6   色
色 SHIKI / SHOKU 13

6   艹
芳 HŌ 19
花 KA 25
芽 GA 21
荷 KA 14
菌 KIN 21
葉 YŌ 23
蒸 JŌ 12
落 RAKU 4
薬 YAKU 20
薄 HAKU 25

6   虫
虫 CHŪ 20

6   血
血 KETSU 24

6   行
行 KŌ, GYŌ 5

6   衣
裂 RETSU 23
装 SŌ 11
製 SEI 19

6   衤
初 SHO 4
複 FUKU 24

6   西
要 YŌ 5

7   見
見 KEN 13
規 KI 25
覚 KAKU 24
観 KAN 2

7   角
角 KAKU 5
触 SHOKU 19
解 KAI 15

7   言
計 KEI 7
記 KI 16
試 SHI 18
誘 YŪ 14
説 SETSU 23
論 RON 20
調 CHŌ 8

7   豆
頭 TŌ 24

7   豸
象 SHŌ 10

7   貝
則 SOKU 3
負 FU 14
質 SHITSU 2

7   赤
赤 SEKI 13

7   走
走 SŌ 24
起 KI 6

7   足
距 KYO 1
路 RO 14

7   身
射 SHA 13

7   車
車 SHA 11
転 TEN 11
軸 JIKU 4
軽 KEI 18
較 KAKU 20

7   辶
近 KIN 8
述 JUTSU 16
送 SŌ 24
逆 GYAKU 12
透 TŌ 18
速 SOKU 1
造 ZŌ 17
通 TSŪ 13
進 SHIN 6
違 I 4
達 TATSU 24
過 KA 6
道 DŌ 17
運 UN 1
遠 EN 13
適 TEKI 22
遺 I 23
還 KAN 25

7   阝
部 BU 8

7   酉
配 HAI 19
酢 SAKU 22
酵 KŌ 21
酸 SAN 15

7   釆
番 BAN 16

8   金

APPENDIX E

READINGS OF MATHEMATICAL EXPRESSIONS

Since the reading of mathematical expressions in Japanese, as in English, varies widely with the degree of formality and the academic level, no exhaustive list can be persented here. The readings given below represent the most common usage but many small variations may be encountered. Note that letters such as x and y should be pronounced as in English, with one exception: z is read *zetto*. Many words are actually English words pronounced in the Japanese way, such as rūto (root), ōbā (over), purasu (plus), ikōru (equal) mainasu (minus), roggu (log), bekutoru (vector), gurajiento (gradient), daibājensu (divergence), and rotēshon (rotation).

EXPRESSION	JAPANESE READING	PRONUNCIATION
x^2	x の二乗	x no nijō; x no jijō
	x の平方	x no heihō
x^3	x の三乗	x no sanjō
	x の立方	x no rippō
x^4	x の四乗	x no yonjō
$\sqrt{x}$	x の平方根	x no heihō-kon
	ルート x	rūto x
	x の二乗根	x no nijō-kon
$\sqrt{x^3}$	ルート x 三乗	rūto, x sanjō
$\sqrt[3]{x}$	x の立方根	x no rippō-kon
	x の三乗根	x no sanjō-kon
$\sqrt[4]{x}$	x の四乗根	x no yonjō-kon
$x^{5/3}$	x の三分の五乗	x no sanbun no gojō
xy	x,y	x,y
	x かける y	x kakeru y
x/y	y 分の x	y-bun no x
	x オーバー y	x ōbā y
$x+y=z$	x たす y は z	x tasu y wa z (zetto)
	x プラス y イコール z	x purasu y ikōru z (zetto)
$x-y \neq z$	x マイナス y は z に等しくない	x mainasu y wa z ni hitoshiku nai
	x ひく y は z でない	x hiku y wa z de nai
$x!$	x の階乗	x no kaijō
$x(x-1)$	x かける x マイナスいち	x kakeru x mainasu ichi
	x かっこ x マイナスいちかっことじる.	x kakko x mainasu ichi kakko tojiru
$\log_{10}x$	x の常用対数	x no jōyō-taisū
$\log_{e}x$	x の自然対数	x no shizen-taisu
$\log_{a}x$	a を底にした x の対数	a o tei ni shita x no taisū

	a を底とする x の対数	a o tei to suru x no taisū
$x - \log_a x$	x マイナスロッグ x てい a	x mainasu roggu x tei a
a^x	a の x 乗	a no x-jō
dy/dx	dy, dx	dy, dx
	dy オーバー dx	dy ōbā dx
	y の x についての微分	y no x ni tsuite no bibun
	y の x に関する微分	y no x ni kansuru bibun
	y の x に関する一次の導関数	y no x ni kansuru ichiji no dō-kansū
d^2y/dx^2	y の x についての二階微分	y no x ni tsuite no nikai-bibun
	y の x に関する二次の導関数	y no x ni kansuru niji no dō-kansū
$(\partial y/\partial x)_t$	y の x についての偏微分	y no x ni tsuite no hen-bibun
	y の x に関する偏微分, t 一定	y no x ni kansuru hen-bibun, t ittei
$\int f(x)\,dx$	f,x の不定積分	f,x no futei-sekibun
	f,x の x に関する (不定) 積分	f, x no x ni kansuru (futei) sekibun
	f,x の x についての積分	f, x no x ni tsuite no sekibun
$\int_a^b f(x)\,dx$	f,x の a から b までの積分	f,x no a kara b made no sekibun
	f,x の a,b 間の定積分	f,x no a,b kan no teisekibun
	下限 a, 上限 b とした f,x の定積分	kagen a, jōgen b to shita f, x no tei-sekibun
$(A \cdot B)$	A と B のスカラー積	A to B no sukarā-seki
	A と B の内積	A to B no naiseki
$[A \times B]$	A と B のベクトル積	A to B no bekutoru-seki
	A と B の外積	A to B no gaiseki
∇T	グラジェント T	gurajiento T
	デル T	deru T
	T の勾配	T no kōbai
$(\nabla \cdot v)$	ダイバージェンス v	daibājensu v
	v の発散	v no hassan
$[\nabla \times v]$	カール v	kāru v
	ロテーション v	rotēshon v
	v の回転	v no kaiten

APPENDIX F
INDEX TO CONSTRUCTION EXAMPLES

(Numbers indicate lessons in which examples are found)

APPENDIX G

INDEX TO EXPLANATORY NOTES

APPENDIX H

DICTIONARIES AND REFERENCE WORKS

As a minimum reference library, we recommend the appropriate volumes in the series on Japanese scientific terms compiled by the Ministry of Education in Japan plus one or more of the scientific dictionaries which are published by Iwanami Shoten.

Each of the volumes in the Ministry of Education series listed below has Japanese-English and English-Japanese sections. The Japanese-English section is arranged in the ABC order of the *romaji* readings, but it uses a *romaji* system which is not phonetic. The phonemes *hu, si, sya, sye, syo, syu, ti, tya, tye, tyo, tyu, zi, zya, zye, zyo, zyu* are read *fu, shi, sha, she, sho, shu, chi, cha, che, cho, chu, ji, ja, je, jo,* and *ju,* respectively. In both sections all technical terms are also given in *kanji* or *katakana.*

文部省編　　学術用語集

Mathematics	数　学　編	大日本図書株式会社発行
Astronomy	天　文　学　編	日本学術振興会発行
Physics	物　理　学　編	大日本図書株式会社発行
Seismology	地　震　学　編	日本学術振興会発行
Spectroscopy	分　光　学　編	日本学術振興会発行
Chemistry	化　学　編	南　江　堂　発　行
Chemistry (enlarged ed.)	化学編(増訂版)	日本化学会発行
Zoology	動　物　学　編	大日本図書株式会社発行
Botany	植　物　学　編	大日本図書株式会社発行
Genetics	遺　伝　学　編	日本学術振興会発行
Mechanical Engineering	機　械　工　学　編	日本機械学会発行
Electrical Engineering	電　気　工　学　編	電　気　学　会　発　行
Architecture	建　築　学　編	日本建築学会発行
Shipbuilding	船　舶　工　学　編	日本造船学会発行
Metrology	計　測　工　学　編	計測自動制御学会発行
Civil Engineering	土　木　工　学　編 (絶版)	土　木　学　会　発　行 (Out of print)
Mining and Metallurgy	採鉱ヤ金学編 (絶版)	日　本　鉱　業　会　発　行 (Out of print)

The dictionaries published by Iwanami Shoten are in the fields of mathematics, physical sciences, and biological sciences, and they are standard Japanese scientific reference encyclopedias. Entries are ordered in the traditional phonetic pattern of *a, i, u, e, o, ka, ga, ki, gi, kya, gya....* After each entry, the English, French, German, and Russian equivalents are given in parentheses, and each volume has

an index of English, French, German, and Russian scientific terms.

岩波書店の辞典

Physics and Chemistry	玉虫文一等編，岩波理化学辞典．1971. 3rd ed.
Biology	山田常雄等編，岩波生物学辞典．1969. 6th ptg.
Mathematics	日本数学会編，岩波数学辞典．1970. 2nd ed.

There are authoritative encyclopedias in every scientific and technical field which provide more thorough coverage of the special vocabulary in each area. The following are excellent for the indicated subjects.

Physics	日本物理学会編，現代物理用語，培風館，1973. 1st ed.
Chemistry	橋本吉郎著，英日日英最新化学辞典，三共出版，1971. 1st ed.
Analytical Chemistry	日本分析化学会編，分析化学化学用語辞典，広川書店，1971. 1st ed.
Biology	永野為武編，生物学用語辞典，三共出版，1972. 2nd ed.
Botany	下郡山正己等編，最新植物用語辞典，広川書店．
Medicine	宮野成二著，系統的にみた医学，生物学領域の英語述語辞典，広川書店，1973. 3rd ed.
Pharmacy	日本薬学会薬学用語委員会編，薬学用語辞典，広川書店，1971. 1st ed.
Hydraulic Engineering	大塚啓司編，上下水道用語辞典，水道産業新聞社，1971. 1st ed.
Air Conditioning and Sanitary Engineering.	空気調和，衛生工学会用語委員会編，空気調和，衛生用語集，空気調和，衛生工学会，1972. 1st ed.
Electrical Engineering	武田謙二著，新電気用語辞典，啓文社，1971. 15th ed.
Mechanical Engineering	機械工学用語辞典編集委員会編，機械工学用語辞典，抜報堂，1967. 8th ed.
	機械術語大辞典編纂委員会編，和・英・独機械術語大辞典，オーム社，1974, 1st ed.
Automatic Control	大島康次郎編，自動制御用語事典，オーム社，1969. 1st ed.
Automotive Engineering	大須賀和助編，自動車用語辞典，精文館，1972. revised ed.
Metals	長崎誠三編，金属用語集，日本金属学会，1973. 1st ed.
Metallurgy	金属術語辞典編集委員会編，アグネ金属術語辞典，アグネ 1970, revised ed., 6th printing
Petroleum Technology	石油学会編，改訂新版石油用語集，朝倉，1971. 1st ed.
Polymers	ポリマー辞典編集委員会編，ポリマー辞典，1973. 1st ed. 2nd printing
Environmental Sciences	石橋弘毅編，環境用語集，共立出版，1971. 1st ed.
Industrial Pollution	日本工業立地センター編，産業公害用語集，北越文化興業，1965. 1st ed.

The following handbook is very valuable for the appropriate translation of the names of government agencies, research institutes, industrial corporations, and other official institutions.

村田聖明編，和英，翻訳ハンドブック。Japan Times. 1971. 1st ed.